Penguin Education

Matthew Arnold on Education

Edited with an Introduction by Gillian Sutherland

Matthew Arnold on Education

Edited with an Introduction by
Gillian Sutherland

Penguin Education

Penguin Education
A Division of Penguin Books Ltd,
Harmondsworth, Middlesex, England
Penguin Books Inc, 7110 Ambassador Road,
Baltimore, Md 21207, USA
Penguin Books Australia Ltd,
Ringwood, Victoria, Australia

First published 1973

Made and printed in Great Britain by
Cox and Wyman Ltd, London, Reading and Fakenham
Set in Monotype Times

Contents

Preface

Selections of snippets from a writer's work always appear unsatisfactory. This would be particularly so in the case of Matthew Arnold's prose, since the power of his argument frequently depends upon the cumulative effect of a succession of amply illustrated points. I have tried, therefore, to give the items I have chosen in full. The only exceptions to this are the omission of a few points of purely local or highly specialist interest from his reports as a school inspector, the detailed account of French schools from *The Popular Education of France*, and the Preface to *Culture and Anarchy*.

Everyone working on Arnold is deeply indebted to Professor R. H. Super's magisterial edition of *The Collected Prose Works of Matthew Arnold* (1960), of which seven volumes have now appeared. Professor Super has taken as his basic text in each case the last one over which Arnold is known to have exercised any supervision, and where possible I have followed him. Professor Super's edition has, however, only reached 1878, and he has not included any of Arnold's regular reports as an inspector of schools. The text of *Ecce, Convertimur ad Gentes*, therefore, is that given in volume 11 of the posthumous edition of Arnold's *Collected Works* (1903); and the texts of the reports for 1852, 1869 and 1880 are those given in the edition of Arnold's reports prepared for the Education Department by F. S. Marvin, HMI, and published in 1908. This is fuller than the edition prepared by Sir Francis Sandford in 1889.

The reports and essays selected are not arranged in chronological order but in the order of their mention in the Introduction. In the case of the essays the date of first appearance in print is given in brackets after the title.

Notes at the foot of the page are Arnold's own. The notes following the texts are the editor's. These have been kept to a minimum and I have only translated quotations on the occasions when Arnold does not do this in the preceding or succeeding sentences. In making decisions of this kind there is always the risk of getting the balance wrong and providing too much information about some aspects and too little about others. Anyone wanting more information should turn, in the first instance, to Super and Marvin; and the notes indicate some of the secondary material available.

Finally, I owe a great deal to my colleague Jean Gooder, whose knowledge of Arnold's literary work is far more extensive than mine. Our discussions helped me considerably in formulating the Introduction, although I alone, of course, must take responsibility for the final version.

Introduction

Matthew Arnold was born in 1822, the third son of Dr Thomas Arnold, who from 1828 until a year before his early death in 1842 was headmaster of Rugby. After reading Classical 'Greats' at Oxford, and a very brief spell teaching at Rugby, Matthew became in 1848 private secretary to Lord Lansdowne, Lord President of the Council in the Whig government. In 1849, thinly veiled in anonymity, he published a first book of poems. By 1851, however, he was looking for an appointment which was more secure, if more strenuous and less glamorous, in order to be able to get married. As Lord President of the Council Lord Lansdowne was the minister responsible for education, and he obligingly nominated Matthew Arnold one of Her Majesty's Inspectors of Schools, an appointment Arnold was to hold for the next thirty-five years.

His experience as an HMI has been cited by many critics of differing standpoints as giving a special weight to Matthew Arnold's social and educational writings.[1] But this is misleading and not an argument that Arnold himself would have wanted to use. Paradoxically, the most important aspect of his work as an inspector was that it engendered a preoccupation with the schools he was not allowed to inspect; and the paternal example and poetry were at least as important as his professional experience in helping him formulate his ideas on education. The interest of Arnold's writing on education lies in his development of a powerful elitist argument from an essentially class-structured view of English society; and all three factors must be taken into account in any attempt to examine this.

The only schools directly aided by the state in nineteenth-century England, and therefore the only schools inspected by the government, were 'elementary' schools, those schools providing a training in the rudiments for the children of the labouring poor, who were likely to begin work at the age of ten, or at the latest, twelve.[2] Schools for the middle and upper classes – 'secondary' schools as they were beginning to be called – were entirely without state aid or regulation and ranged all the way from the ancient foundations such as Eton and Rugby, through endowed grammar schools like Leeds, new proprietary foundations such as Marlborough, to the private ventures whose horrors gave rise to Dotheboys Hall.[3]

This situation may well have been a consequence of the fact that England had industrialized first from a relatively low educational base. That is to say, neither the formal scientific training available, nor the level of literacy among the mass of the population, seem to have been critical or crucial factors in assisting take-off.[4] Successful capitalists and entrepreneurs were thus unlikely to value education as a means to economic achievement. Instead, the traditional narrowly classical education of a gentleman tended to become a symbol of a rise already accomplished. Successful capitalists and entrepreneurs marked their achievement by sending their sons to the old public schools or to the host of proprietary schools which soon sprang up, claiming to provide a similar training, but at reduced rates. Middle-class demands for education thus appeared to be concerned chiefly with its social and decorative functions; and the regulation and satisfaction of these demands could safely be left to the mechanism of the free market.

By contrast working-class demands for education had a political dimension from a very early stage. For many of the poor and propertyless, knowledge appeared the one immediate source of power within their grasp. From the beginning of the nineteenth century there was an energetic debate in government circles as to whether these demands should be suppressed, regulated, or even aided by the state. In 1833 the Whig government decided to make an annual grant to elementary education, channelling its distribution through two national voluntary societies, the National Society for the Promotion of the Education of the Poor according to the Principles of the Established Church, and the Dissenter-supported British and Foreign School Society, to which most of the existing schools were affiliated. In 1839 a Committee of the Privy Council, headed by the Lord President, was created to oversee work in education, the grant was increased, and the first inspectors were appointed. Although individual schools were now entitled to apply for grant, whether or not they were affiliated to one of the societies, the two societies continued to dominate the scene. After a series of rows they forced the Privy Council Office to agree to consult them in making appointments to the inspectorate and to arrange the inspection of schools on a denominational rather than a geographical basis. In 1851, therefore, Matthew Arnold found himself compelled to inspect nothing but nonconformist schools, scattered over a third of the country.

The system of aiding existing schools was not the most effective way of bringing education to those areas of the country where there was none – it tended rather to resemble 'giving to them that hath'. Legislation in 1870 – Forster's Education Act – at last supplemented the network of voluntary schools with new 'board' schools. In areas where there were not enough schools, or no schools at all, it was made possible to elect a school board with power to draw on the rates for money to build and run new schools. This somewhat reduced the importance of the two societies, although they were to remain powerful pressure groups for the rest of the century; and it did make it possible to reorganize inspection arrangements and put them on a geographical basis. In 1871 Matthew Arnold was assigned to inspect all the elementary schools in what he called 'a *perfect* district: *Westminster* and a small rural district round Harrow [his home]'.[5]

The district may have been perfect; but this was still not enough to reconcile him wholly to the work. In 1851 he had written to his wife: 'I think I shall get interested in the schools after a little time'[6] and his *Report for 1852* (reprinted below) shows his conscientiousness. But in 1886, at the grand banquet given by the Westminster teachers on the occasion of his retirement, he confessed frankly:

> though I am a schoolmaster's son . . . school teaching or school inspecting is not the line of life I should naturally have chosen. I adopted it in order to marry a lady who is here tonight and who feels the kindness as warmly and as gratefully as I do. (Cheers.) My wife and I had a wandering life of it at first. There were but three inspectors for all England. My district went right across from Pembroke Dock to Great Yarmouth. We had no home; one of our children was born in lodgings at Derby with a workhouse, if I recollect right, behind and a penitentiary in front. (Laughter.) But the irksomeness of my new duties was what I felt most, and during the first year or so this was sometimes almost insupportable. But I met daily in the schools with men and women discharging duties akin to mine, duties as irksome as mine, duties less well paid than mine, and I asked myself, Are they on roses? Would they not by nature prefer, many of them, to go where they liked and do what they liked instead of being shut up in school? I saw them making the best of it; I saw the cheerfulness and efficiency with which they did their work, and I asked myself again, How do they do it? Gradually it grew into a habit with me to put myself into their places, to try to enter into their feelings, to represent to myself their life, and I assure you I got many lessons from them.[7]

It seems significant and even a little sad that in this speech he made no mention of the one period when he did engage in a passionate crusade about the nature of elementary education. Between 1858 and 1861 a Royal Commission under the Duke of Newcastle reviewed the provision and grant structure of elementary education. Its members reported that teachers were tending to neglect the average and not-so-bright children, concentrating instead on the few bright children and pushing them on to something approaching secondary education. They proposed a scheme which was intended both to remedy this and to extend the provision of schools: county education boards should be established with power to aid schools out of the rates. These payments should be dependent upon the performance of each child, each year, in examinations in the '3Rs' conducted by a county inspector. This would leave the central government free to provide additional financial help on a different basis and HMI free, as before, to consider more general aspects of the tone and conduct of the school.

Inter-denominational conflicts about the religious instruction to be given in rate-aided schools ensured that the county board scheme did not get off the ground. But a system of 'payment by results' seemed attractive to those in the Education Department, notably the Vice-President of the Committee of Council, Robert Lowe,[8] and the Permanent Secretary, Ralph Lingen, who were concerned about the increasing spiral of education expenditure. In 1861 Lowe and Lord Granville, the Lord President, issued a new Code of regulations governing grants, reorganizing the system of *government* grant on the lines proposed by the Newcastle Commission for a *county* grant. All the existing block grants to schools, except the building grant, were replaced by a capitation grant of 12s. per child per year: 4s. of this depended upon the child's regular attendance, the rest upon his performance each year in examinations in the '3Rs' conducted by HMI. The examinations were arranged in a series of 'standards' and the child was expected to move up one every year.

There were immediate protests. Sir James Kay-Shuttleworth, Lingen's predecessor as Permanent Secretary, published a long pamphlet with a detailed attack on both the Code and the Newcastle Commission's conclusions. But this was very much meat for the specialist and Matthew Arnold undertook to produce something for the general reader. This was *The Twice-Revised Code*, first published anonymously in *Fraser's Magazine* in 1862 and reprinted immediately as a pamphlet. The essay (reprinted below) was a devastating attack, in which Arnold, the brilliant polemicist, and Arnold, the conscientious inspector of elementary schools, combined to assault a scheme which treated the process of education as comparable to a factory assembly line, with the teachers paid at piece rates. Large numbers were sold and it did much to improve the quality of the Commons debates on the Code. Eventually some of the Code's more extreme features were modified.

But the principle of payment by results remained to dominate the grant structure in elementary education until 1890. Yet Arnold gradually withdrew from the attack. He remained critical of a number of aspects of the system; but by 1869 he was writing: 'no-one questions the advantage of an individual grant-rewarded examination ...' (see his *Report for 1869*, reprinted below). In his evidence to the Royal Commission on Elementary Schools, which sat from 1886 to 1888 under the Chairmanship of Lord Cross, he suggested that the best solution would have been to organize the grant for children between seven and ten only on a basis of payment by results.[9] It sounds all very lame beside the splendid thunder of *The Twice-*

Revised Code; and as the *Reports* for 1869 and 1880 (reprinted below) suggest, this essay stands out as a single high peak in Arnold's writing about elementary schools.

The reasons for this withdrawal are complex and intertwined. At the simplest level, of course, it was not easy to attack the government department which was actually employing you; and as the sales of the pamphlet rose, Arnold began to contemplate the possibility of his dismissal.[10] From the mid-1860s onwards he made repeated but invariably unsuccessful attempts to obtain other appointments.[11] More generally, his withdrawal echoes the detachment felt by many members of the Education Department from the life and work of elementary schools. These schools provided simply a limited training for the children of the labouring poor. The inspectors and the higher officials of the Department were all of them 'gentlemen' and graduates, some very distinguished. They had neither attended elementary schools nor taught in them, nor were they likely to send their children to them. It was thus all too easy to regard the work of elementary schools as distinct and separate from the process they themselves knew as education and thus approach it with a different set of criteria and expectations. Sir George Kekewich, Permanent Secretary from 1890 to 1902, put it crudely but not altogether unfairly when he wrote:

> the staff of distinguished and aristocratic scholars from the universities treated elementary education and elementary teachers with contempt. Their cherished creed was that no education mattered or was of any real value except Classics and Mathematics. ... They had no use for village Hampdens, nor any idea that a child from the 'lower classes' might, after all, possess a modicum of brains. A ploughman's son was destined to be a ploughman as his father was.[12]

Matthew Arnold never attained these lofty heights of disdain. But he was well aware of the gap, as his comments about the rawness of pupil teachers in his *Report for 1852* and the recurrent contrasts he draws between middle- and working-class children in his *Report for 1880* show; and the extraordinary essay *Ecce, Convertimur ad Gentes*, first delivered as an address to the Ipswich Working Men's Association (and reprinted below), suggests that the element of patronage was not totally absent from his approach. Telling his audience of working men firmly, 'we at present do tend to have our higher class in general materialized, our middle class vulgarized, and our lower class brutalized', he then goes on to appeal for their support in establishing a state system of schools for the middle class, to provide a proper leadership in society and, after a generation or so, models which the brute working class might begin to emulate. The whole essay is almost a dramatization of Arnold's class-structured view of society.[13]

But the near-effrontery with which Arnold asserts the priority of middle-class education to a working-class audience points to a much more serious and substantial reason for his failure to sustain the passion of his attack on payment by results. He was utterly convinced that the problems of middle-class education were greater and far more intractable than those of working-class education. His most powerful writing on education was his writing on middle-class or secondary education. Thus he was paying his Ipswich audience the compliment of being totally honest with them.

The first full emergence of Matthew Arnold's preoccupation with secondary education in fact only just preceded the Revised Code controversy At the beginning of 1859 he was invited to go to France, Switzerland and Holland to report on their popular education for the Newcastle Commission. He accepted with alacrity. Since his undergraduate days he had had a deep affection for and interest in French life and culture; and, as he wrote to his mother:

> You know that I have no special interest in the subject of public education, but a mission like this appeals even to the general interest which every educated man cannot help feeling in such a subject. I shall for five months get free from the routine work of it, of which I sometimes get very sick, and be dealing with its history and principles.[14]

His report for the Commission shows that the investigation provided just such a stimulus as he had hoped. In the final chapter of his report on France (reprinted below) he made an overt comparison between French and English popular education and their implications for the social structure and hierarchy of each country. After long consideration he added to the whole report an introductory chapter entitled 'Democracy'. He also secured permission to publish the report as a separate book, under his own name. As soon as this was accomplished, he sought an opportunity to develop his position further, publishing *A French Eton or Middle-Class Education and the State* in *Macmillan's Magazine* in 1863–4. In this and in 'Democracy' (both reprinted below) he set the whole discussion of popular education in a political as well as a social context. He addressed himself for the first time to the question of leadership in a democracy, drawing not only on his knowledge of France and England but also on what he had read about America, in particular de Tocqueville's *Démocratie en Amérique*. He argued that a democratic system of government, like any other, needed a ruling elite to function properly:

> Nations are not truly great solely because the individuals composing them are numerous, free and active; but they are great when these numbers, this freedom and this activity are employed in the service of an ideal higher than that of an ordinary

man, taken by himself. Our society is probably destined to become more democratic; who or what will give a high tone to the nation then? That is the grave question (see below, p. 106).

He saw the decay of the old aristocratic leadership as an inevitable concomitant of democracy; the filling of the vacuum, the creation of a middle class fit to lead, not only in a political sense but in a cultural and moral sense also, was thus the central problem for a would-be democratic society. The French, Arnold maintained, had begun to face the problem through the construction of an educational *system*. Their elementary schools were but the lowest tier in a state-supported and state-regulated system, which reached through secondary schools to the Normal Schools for the training of teachers and the Universities. The French state aided and set standards for the education of the children of the bourgeoisie as well as those of the labouring poor. In England, by contrast, the elementary schools were a phenomenon in isolation, part of no system, with no examples to follow. The secondary schools represented a bewildering and in some cases depressing variety of experiments. The coherence, the shared cultural standards, the carefully structured mobility that a fully articulated state education system could bring, were all lacking.

His investigation of schools abroad was thus in a very obvious way a catalyst in Matthew Arnold's thinking about educational problems. But two other formative influences also seem worth mention: the example of his father and the pattern of his development as poet and literary critic. Any suggestions about the direct influence of Dr Arnold's work at Rugby must remain tentative in the extreme. It was not an influence that Matthew Arnold ever chose fully to discuss; and it is plain that it took him a considerable time to come to terms with the extraordinarily powerful image and memory of his father, crystallized so soon after Dr Arnold's death in 1842 by Arthur Stanley's biography.[15] Matthew Arnold's poem 'Rugby Chapel', commemorating his father, was written only in 1857 and then not published until 1867;[16] and in it he lamented the inability of his own generation to match the certainty and strength of men like his father:

Souls tempered with fire,
Fervent, heroic and good,
Helpers and friends of mankind.

At the same time, he celebrated the inspiration of the example; and it seems worthwhile at least juxtaposing Matthew Arnold's preoccupation with the education of the new leaders of English society against his father's work as a teacher. The contrast that Matthew himself drew in 'Rugby Chapel' is there: Dr Arnold wrote and lectured with a total seriousness and a strongly marked sense of moral absolutes. Much of Matthew Arnold's most powerful writing depends for its force upon an accumulation of irony. The pursuit of perfection is his only certainty. Nevertheless both were concerned with the moral objectives of society and the nature and education of its leaders. In his Inaugural Lecture as Regius Professor of Modern History at Oxford a year before his death, Dr Arnold claimed that:

What is a nation's main object, is therefore a question which must be asked, before we can answer whether its inner life, and consequently its outward life also, which depends upon the inner life, is to be called good or evil. Now it does not seem easy to conceive that a nation can have any other object than that which is the highest object of every individual in it: if it can, then the attribute of sovereignty which is inseparable from nationality becomes the dominion of an evil principle. For suppose for instance that a nation as such is not cognizant of the notions of justice and humanity, but that its highest object is wealth, or dominion or security. It then follows that the sovereign power in human life, which can influence the minds and compel the action of us all, is a power altogether unmoral; and if unmoral, and yet commanding the actions of moral beings, then evil. Again, if being cognizant of the notions of justice and humanity it deliberately prefers other objects to them, then here is the dominion of an evil principle still more clearly. But if it be cognizant of them and appreciates them rightly, then it must see that they are more to be followed than any objects of outward advantage; then it acknowledges moral ends as a higher good than physical ends, and thus, as we said, agrees with every good individual man in its estimate of the highest object of national no less than of individual life.[17]

In English society he saw the public schools as having a special place. 'There is', he said, 'or there ought to be, something very ennobling in being connected with an establishment at once ancient and magnificent, where all about us, and all the associations belonging to the objects around us should be great, splendid and elevating.'[18] Within his own school kingdom of Rugby he laid immense stress on the power and responsibilities of the leaders of the school community, the Sixth Form. Stanley wrote that:

Nothing, accordingly, so shook his hopes of doing good as weakness or misconduct in the Sixth. 'You should feel', he said, 'like officers in the army or navy, whose want of moral courage would, indeed, be thought cowardice.' 'When I have confidence in the Sixth', was the end of one of his farewell addresses, 'there is no post in England which I would exchange for this; but if they do not support me, I must go.'[19]

The further factor or importance in understanding the development of Matthew Arnold's thinking on education is his development as a poet and literary critic. This is simultaneously both obvious and impossible to discuss in any proper sense in an essay of this size. One can hope only to establish a large signpost, as it were, to the direction any fuller discussion should take. The decade 1857–67, in which Matthew Arnold's concern for middle-class education was fully articulated, was also the decade in which he held the Chair of Poetry at Oxford. His lectures gave him the opportunity to explore a range of aspects of literary culture; and towards the end he began to examine the notion of culture itself. His last lecture at Oxford in 1867 was called 'Culture and its enemies'; it was published and followed up by several more essays in the *Cornhill Magazine*, and all these were then collected, revised, with some gestures towards the vigorous debate they had already generated, and published as one essay under the title *Culture and Anarchy*. In this essay (reprinted below) his preoccupations with the nature of culture and the problems of the middle class were knit together; and he explored at length what he saw as the cultural and political crises already generated by the deficiencies of the English middle class. *Culture and Anarchy* is at once the fullest development of the themes of 'Democracy' and *A French Eton* and of his Oxford lectures and his *Essays in Criticism*.[20]

The totality of his vision is thus one of the most important aspects of Matthew Arnold's writing about middle-class education. But the fact that he was a poet should not be treated as the sole justification for examining his social criticism. As I have tried to show, his analysis of the existing situation in England was a sophisticated one; and the peculiar interest and importance of his social criticism lies in the interplay between his vision and this analysis. He wrote little about the direct consequences of industrialization, yet he was fully aware of the dynamism released by the process and the peculiarities of the English situation in relation to this. He was convinced that a society which treated secondary education as having primarily social and decorative functions would develop a vacuum of leadership – in fact, was already beginning to do so. It is the combination of this analysis with the absolute nature of his vision of culture that makes his plea for the creation of a national *system* of education, to form and direct the new elite, so powerful.

Report for 1852

I have the honour of presenting to your Lordships my general report upon the schools which have come under my inspection during the past year.

It will be obvious that an account of 104 schools scattered over this wide extent of country can have no pretensions to be considered an adequate account of the state of education within its limits; besides omitting altogether all schools connected with the Church of England, such an account fails also to embrace many Wesleyan and still more British schools situated within the limits of the district to which it relates, but not receiving aid under the Minutes of 1846. With the general state of education in my district, therefore, I cannot profess myself from personal observation familiar; and even with respect to the 104 institutions which I have seen, and my observations on which supply the materials for this report, I feel that I am far from possessing that intimate acquaintance with them which I could desire; the great majority of them I have as yet visited but once: and I therefore wish to be understood in this report as calling the attention of managers and teachers to those facts connected with their schools which have principally struck me, and which I shall chiefly notice on my future visits, rather than as confidently criticizing what I have seen in their schools.

By a circular letter dated 14 October 1851, the attention of Her Majesty's Inspectors of Schools was particularly called to several subjects, among which that of school fees occupied the first place. With this subject I will begin, for the treatment of it will involve the mention of other matters on which I am anxious to make some remarks.

Of the institutions which I have visited during the past year, forty-seven come under the general designation of British schools, though not all of them immediately connected with the British and Foreign School Society; thirty-five are Wesleyan schools; twenty-two are quite independent.

The total income of 112 schools, representing little more than the total income of the institutions inspected, is stated by the managers at £12,774 1s. Of this sum £6192 17s. is stated to have proceeded from the school pence, that is, in round numbers, one half of the total costs of these schools has been collected from the scholars themselves. This is a large proportion; and it would be still larger if the number of Wesleyan schools, among the 112 whose aggregate income is stated, were greater. The Wesleyan schools have established, generally speaking, a rate of payment on the part of their scholars higher than that which is made in the other elementary schools that I have seen. This rate of payment varies from 2d. to 8d. per week for each scholar; in some schools a majority of the scholars pay 3d., in others 4d.; but in none less than 2d. It is obvious that these rates of payment must generally exclude the children of the very poor; and although these are not altogether excluded (for arrangements are sometimes made in Wesleyan schools by which poor children are admitted at a reduced rate of payment, either by subscribers' tickets, or on the recommendation of members of the school committee) yet on the whole, the Wesleyan schools which I have seen must be considered as existing for the sake of the children of tradesmen, of farmers, and of mechanics of the higher class, rather than for the sake of the children of the poor. In fact, these schools are sometimes nothing else than private schools, in which the salaries of the teachers, the school furniture, and the books are provided out of the school pence, the managers supplying little more than the building in which the school is held. It is evident that schools of this kind have not the first claim to assistance from public funds, which are designed to promote the education of the poor. And I think it may well be a question for the managers of Wesleyan schools to consider whether it is not desirable for them to extend the basis of their educational operations, and to confer on a wide circle the benefits of their excellent schools. A lower rate of payments would in my opinion greatly extend their sphere of usefulness, while their present high character for respectability need in no degree be impaired.

But apart from this question of the exclusion of the poorest class of scholars, and taking the Wesleyan schools as they now stand, I wish to notice the conveniences and the inconveniences which I conceive to result from the present system of high payments.

The conveniences are – the better and more instructed class of children frequenting these schools as compared with that frequenting cheaper ones; the greater intelligence of their parents, and greater sense of the advantage of having their children educated, with consequently greater disposition, as well as greater means, to keep them longer at school.

The inconveniences are the inconveniences of private schools in general – the disposition of parents to interfere, and the diminished independence of the teacher. Parents who pay 6d. a week for the instruction of their children are apt to criticize nicely, though not always judiciously, the institution where that instruction is given. They desire this and that for their child, and they object to this and that and, being often not very reasonable persons, they greatly embarrass a teacher. They are exceedingly apt, for instance, to object to the employment of their children as monitors, on the ground that teaching takes them away from learning; yet, so long as the allowance of pupil-teachers to a school is not greater than at present,[1] the employment of a certain number of monitors is almost indispensable; and, in my opinion, to be employed as a monitor during a part of his time is most useful to the advanced scholar himself as well as to the school. To the less advanced scholar it is no doubt injurious; but it is in the case of the advanced scholar, where the payment is high, that the complaint arises.

The teacher's independence is diminished, because, when his salary is principally or entirely derived from the school pence, the favour of the parents becomes of the greatest importance to him; hence it arises that the children of these schools, though disciplinable, are often not well disciplined, owing to the master's fear of offending parents by a strictness which may appear to them excessive. This is a most important matter. I am convinced there is no class of children so indulged, so generally brought up (at home at least) without discipline, that is, without habits of respect, exact obedience, and self-control, as the children of the lower middle class in this country. The children of very poor parents receive a kind of rude discipline from circumstances, if not from their parents; the children of the upper classes are generally brought up in habits of regular obedience, because these classes are sufficiently enlightened to know of what benefit such a training is to the children themselves; but children of the class I am alluding to receive no discipline from circumstances, for they are brought up amidst comparative abundance; they receive none from their parents, who are only half educated themselves, and can understand no kindness except complete indulgence; and, in consequence, nowhere have I seen such insubordination, such wilfulness, and such a total want of respect for their parents and teachers as among these children. The teacher's hands cannot be too much strengthened in the schools which this class frequents; for, if they are not disciplined at school, they will, while young, be disciplined nowhere; and a scale of fees is peculiarly undesirable, which makes the teacher dependent on the favour of their parents, and unwilling to risk that favour by introducing strict habits of discipline.

There is another inconvenience arising out of the system of payments in these schools; that is – the instruction is disordered by it. This happens in the following way. Some children are admitted at a lower rate of payment than others; those who pay least are to be taught least; consequently scholars perfectly capable of taking their place with the highest class, but unable to make the highest payment, are thrown back into the lower classes, and comparatively neglected. Again, those who pay most are to learn most; accordingly, those children who make the highest payments are put into the highest class, whether fit for it or no. They are often new-comers, very ill-taught, and wholly incapable of profiting by lessons such as those given in the highest class ought to be. A plan more calculated to derange and dislocate the instruction of a school it would be difficult to imagine; and the teacher who is responsible for that instruction ought, in my opinion, always to decline to adopt it.

I shall not mention by name the particular Wesleyan schools in which I have found the highest rates of payment existing. I do not think it necessary to do so, for I hope at my next visit to find the rates lowered; nor do I mean to deny that the Wesleyan schools in general are, even at present, very useful. I am most glad to see them in the receipt of Government aid. There are many cases, indeed, in which the burden thrown on the local promoters of these schools is as heavy as that thrown on the local promoters of British or national schools; but, at any rate, the advantages obtained from the employment, through Government aid, of apprentices and certificated teachers, are such as the Wesleyan schools could hardly hope to obtain through any private pecuniary outlay; and it is no doubt desirable that the funds at your Lordships' disposal should, if possible, after assisting to provide the means of education for the really poor, be used to improve the quality of education for a class in somewhat better circumstances.

What I have said above applies equally, of course, to those British schools in which the fees are on the same high scale as they are in most Wesleyan schools. Generally, however, they are on a lower scale in British schools, and these schools do certainly bear a large part in the elementary education of the poor strictly so called. Still it may be doubted whether even these thoroughly reach the lowest strata of society. In country places it is no doubt true that the resources of Dissenting as compared with those of Church schools are so inferior as almost to compel a higher rate of payment in the former; but in large towns this is by no means invariably the case; here the British schools often have a large and wealthy body of contributors, and here it is that the unsectarian and neutral character of these schools peculiarly fits them to be common centres, in which the children of a population divided into innumerable sects may be harmoniously educated together. Since, however, this unsectarian character of the British schools often practically operates to their disadvantage in point of support, one is the more anxious that schools based on an admirable principle should at least do nothing to render themselves difficult of access by the establishment of rates of payment higher than those in competing schools in the same locality.

Before quitting the subject of school fees, I wish to mention a plan pursued in one of the schools under my inspection, and which, though not available for elementary schools in general, I should be glad to see adopted in more schools of its own class. It is a school established for the children of the workpeople employed by an iron company in a very remote part of the country. This school is not maintained by the company, nor by the payments of the children who frequent it; but a weekly deduction is made from the wages of every person employed in the works, whether married or single, to form a fund to defray the expenses of the school, of a library, and of medical attendance. Those who have families pay no more than those who have none, and any number of his children may be sent to the school by the head of a family without his having to pay any additional subscription. The school is regarded as existing for the common benefit of all, directly or indirectly, now or at a future time. The deduction, I was assured, is submitted to without reluctance. In other places, masters and agents have informed me that they should be afraid to attempt such a plan, dreading the discontent it would produce; but as it was an experience of its advantages, and not any superior enlightenment on the part of the workpeople, which made it succeed in the case I have mentioned, I am inclined to think it might be made to succeed elsewhere also, with a little management and patience at first introducing it. By such a plan, in localities where masters and companies cannot support schools at their sole expense, and where a rude population have little sense of the advantages of education to their children, and little disposition to make sacrifices for it, ample funds are raised for the support of a school, and it becomes the direct interest of the population to avail themselves of an institution to which they are in any case forced to contribute.

The Welsh schools that I have seen are generally on the British system. Those connected with mining and manufacturing establishments stand on a peculiar footing of their own; those not so connected generally charge low fees, are well attended, and may be considered as really receiving the children of the poor. Indeed, the poor population of Wales is so entirely a Dissenting population, that the British schools acquire a peculiar importance there, and they are filled with the same class of children that one sees in the National schools in England. The children in them are generally docile and quick in apprehension, to a greater degree than English children; their drawback, of course, is that they have to acquire the medium of information, as well as the information itself, while the English children possess the medium at the outset. There can, I think, be no question but that the acquirement of the English language should be more and more insisted upon by your Lordships in your relations with these schools as the one main object for which your aid is granted. Whatever encouragement individuals may think it desirable to give to the preservation of the Welsh language on grounds of philological or antiquarian interest, it must always be the desire of a Government to render its dominions, as far as possible, homogeneous, and to break down barriers to the freest intercourse between the different parts of them. Sooner or later, the difference of language between Wales and England will probably be effaced, as has happened with the difference of language between Cornwall and the rest of England; as is now happening with the difference of language between Brittany and the rest of France; and they are not the true friends of the Welsh people who, from a romantic interest in their manners and traditions, would impede an event which is socially and politically so desirable for them.

With a view to enable pupil-teachers in Welsh schools the better to acquire a knowledge of English, the late Mr Fletcher[2] proposed that they should be sent for six months in the middle or latter part of their apprenticeship to perform their duties in English schools. The great objection to such an arrangement is that English schools might not be very willing to accept teachers imperfectly acquainted with the language in which they would have to teach. Difficulty, I think, would also often arise on the part of the parents of the pupil-teachers and the managers of the schools employing them, when arrangements came to be made for meeting the expense of their six months' residence in England. I myself cannot but think that it is from the masters of Welsh schools that the promotion of the use of English in their schools must come, and that at present the masters themselves of these schools, not knowing English thoroughly well, do not employ it in their intercourse with their apprentices and scholars by any means so much as they should. If it were possible for Welsh students to be sent invariably to English training schools, and on leaving the training schools to be employed for two or three years in English schools, before returning into Wales, that I think would be the plan most likely to bring about an increased use of English in the Welsh schools. Such students, possessing, it may be presumed, at least a fair acquaintance with English at the end of their apprenticeship, would increase it to a complete familiarity while residing at an English training school, and associating with English students; they would thus be perfectly serviceable in English schools; and a year or two's habit of teaching in English in these schools would give them that thorough mastery of the language which alone will induce them to speak it without reluctance and of their own accord.

With respect to the organization both of British and of Wesleyan schools, I regard it as being at present in a state of transition. It tends, I think, to become eventually very much alike in both, as the original masses in Wesleyan schools are broken up, and the original fractions in British schools are massed together. The vice of the strict Glasgow system[3] is that numbers of children do not really come under teaching at all; of the strict British system,[4] that numbers of children came under teaching so inadequate as to be hardly better than none. The problem is to discover an organization which shall maintain a just proportion between the teaching power in a school and the numbers taught in it.

When this problem has been solved – when the children are finally arranged in divisions, neither too large nor too small – I hope that the plan of retaining them in the same divisions for all parts of their work will be more extensively tried than it has been hitherto. At present there are few schools in which a child is not put into one division for reading, into another for writing, into another for arithmetic; and masters seem to have no notion of the increased regularity and steadiness of attention that a child gains by going through his whole day's work with the same associates, and under the same teacher. I am convinced that the benefit to the children themselves and to the discipline of the school, which would result from retaining them in the same divisions, would more than compensate any additional trouble which the necessity of varying the instruction in particular subjects, such as arithmetic, to children equal in most subjects, and therefore classed together, might impose upon the teacher.

In the institutions which I have visited during the past year, I have continually felt the want of infant schools. It seems to me that more good schools are clogged and impeded in their operations by a mass of children under eight years of age, at the bottom of them, than from any other cause. Yet the parents will not send the older children without sending these also. The only remedy for the inconvenience, where the expense of two but not of three schools in the same institution can be supported, is to adopt the plan of having mixed schools. The older children of both sexes are then in one school, the infants of both sexes in another. The Wesleyan schools which follow this plan appear to me to gain thereby a great advantage, and one which the British schools often lose by their anxiety to separate the boys from the girls. I must say that I have never yet seen any inconvenience arise from bringing together boys and girls in the same schools, if their playgrounds are kept distinct. Indeed, the education of girls, when they learn with boys and from a master, appears to me to gain that very correctness and stringency which female education generally wants; while a female teacher is no doubt the person best qualified to instruct infants of both sexes.

The circular of 1851, before alluded to, called attention to the subject of industrial schools besides that of school fees, and also to the state and prospects of female pupil-teachers. A subsequent circular directed attention to the subject of elementary drawing. Industrial schools and drawing I hope to speak of in my next report.

With respect to female pupil-teachers, I think it right to remark on the serious amount of ill-health, especially in the later years of their apprenticeship, which I have found amongst them. Managers of schools cannot be too strongly reminded that the physical qualifications of girls presented as candidates for apprenticeship require to be most carefully observed, and that the duties of pupil-teachers are such that delicacy of constitution alone, without any positive infirmity, unfits a girl for discharging them without great risk. I am sure your Lordships cannot be too strict in guarding against the admission to apprenticeship of sickly children, boys as well as girls; intelligent as they often are, they always want many qualities which a teacher should never be without. It may be a question, perhaps, whether an affliction like lameness or the loss of a limb, where the general health is good, need always be considered as a disqualification for the office of pupil-teachers; but where the general health is decidedly feeble (and the managers ought always to ascertain this) a child should never be presented as a candidate.

On one other topic, in connection with the subject of pupil-teachers, I am anxious to touch in conclusion. In the general opinion of the advantages which have resulted from the employment of them, I most fully concur; and of the acquirements and general behaviour of the greater number of those of them whom I have examined I wish to speak favourably. But I have been much struck in examining them towards the close of their apprenticeship, when they are generally at least eighteen years old, with the utter disproportion between the great amount of positive information and the low degree of mental culture and intelligence which they exhibit. Young men, whose knowledge of grammar, of the minutest details of geographical and historical facts, and above all of mathematics, is surprising, often cannot paraphrase a plain passage of prose or poetry without totally misapprehending it, or write half a page of composition on any subject without falling into gross blunders of taste and expression. I cannot but think that, with a body of young men so highly instructed, too little attention has hitherto been paid to this side of education; the side through which it chiefly forms the character; the side which has perhaps been too exclusively attended to in schools for the higher classes, and to the development of which it is the boast of what is called classical education to be mainly directed. I attach little importance to the study of languages, ancient or modern, by pupil-teachers, for they can seldom have the time to study them to much purpose without neglecting other branches of instruction which it is necessary that they should follow; but I am sure that the study of portions of the best English authors, and composition, might with advantage be made a part of their regular course of instruction to a much greater degree than it is at present. Such a training would tend to elevate and humanize a number of young men, who at present, notwithstanding the vast amount of raw information which they have amassed, are wholly uncultivated; and it would have the great social advantage of tending to bring them into intellectual sympathy with the educated of the upper classes.

The Twice-Revised Code (1862)[1]

The Archbishop of Canterbury said a few months ago at Maidstone, that the Revised Code, lately promulgated by the Committee of Council on Education, must at last stand or fall according to the verdict pronounced upon it by the *common sense of the country*. His Grace could not have said a truer thing. But the common sense of the country finds itself at some loss for clear data to guide it in coming to a verdict. The system of our Education Department bristles with details so numerous, so minute, and so intricate, that any one not practically conversant with this system has great difficulty in mastering them, and, by failing to master them, may easily be led into error.* With a certain amount of trouble, however, even the details of our Council Office system may of course be mastered. But such an amount of trouble the general public will not take. From this cause the pamphlet of a master of the subject – of the founder of our public elementary education, Sir James Shuttleworth – fails, it seems to us, perfectly to meet the occasion with which it has to deal. For readers already familiar with the subject, for school-managers, school-teachers, school-inspectors, it is admirable: for the general reader it is somewhat too copious. For this last, it goes too much into detail; it presupposes more acquaintance with the subject than he is likely to possess. Every member of Parliament, every one who has to *discuss* the new Code, should read Sir James Shuttleworth's pamphlet. Every one who is disposed to go deeply into the subject should read it. For those who are not disposed to do this, who desire only to know the essential facts of the case, so as to be able to form an opinion upon it, a simpler statement is required – a statement dealing less with the details of the subject and more with its *rationale*.

Such a statement we here propose to attempt. We propose, at this last moment before the Parliamentary discussion comes, to show the general reader (1) what it is that the Revised Code will actually do, (2) why its authors are trying to do this, (3) what is the merit of their design in itself,

*For want of this practical acquaintance, a writer so able and so exact as Dr Vaughan bases an argument upon the assertion that a low certificate from the Committee of Council does not at present entitle its holder to any grant of money. The assertion and the argument from it are alike erroneous.[2]

and what, moreover, is the prospect of its accomplishing what it intends. And we shall notice, in conclusion, the changes in his original scheme which have just been propounded by Mr Lowe, and examine the value and importance of these.

1. What the Revised Code will actually *do*, is to reduce considerably the grants at present contributed by the State towards the support of schools for the poor. This is what it will certainly and indisputably do. It may do other things besides, but about its doing these other things there is much dispute; about its effecting a reduction of existing grants there is no dispute. The reduction may be more or less great; Sir James Shuttleworth, the best of authorities on such a matter, estimates it at two-fifths, or £175,000 a year, of the money now annually paid; Archdeacon Sinclair, representing the National Society, estimates it at 40 per cent (the same thing). Even Mr Lowe admits that there will be a loss, although he declares such an estimate of it as the above to be exaggerated. It is possible that this estimate may not be exactly correct; but that the reduction will be considerable, no one who has any real acquaintance with the subject denies. It is probably safe to reckon it at nearly two-fifths of the present annual grant.

The heads of a public department are not, in general, the persons most forward in proposing to contract the operations of their own department, and to reduce its expenditure. Of any such want of self-denying disinterestedness the heads of our Education Department cannot be accused. They have propounded a scheme which – while it dismays and discourages the supporters of that system of State-aid to public education, which the infinite zeal and adroitness of Sir James Shuttleworth, the infinite moderation and sagacity of Lord Lansdowne, founded in this country with so much difficulty – delights and animates all the bitterest adversaries of that system. It is from these adversaries, almost as much surprised as rejoiced, that the framers of the Revised Code have received the warmest approval. A clergyman, well known in the North Midland Counties for his uncompromising opposition to all State interference in national education, procured from a Yorkshire meeting, filled with ardent Voluntaries who shared his own opinions, a vote of entire adhesion to the new Code. Mr Crossley, member for the West Riding, an Independent and a Voluntary, declared at an Education Conference lately held, that 'the new Minute of the Privy Council had given fresh heart and life to the opponents of the system'. Those members of the late Education Commission who, though not refusing to sign their names to the recommendations of their fellow Commissioners, signed them with the reservation that to the principle of State intervention in this matter they were still opposed, confess that while the action of the majority of their own body was at variance with their wishes, the present action of the Committee of Council is quite in conformity with them. 'It is a step in the right direction,' says Mr Miall. 'The penny will become a halfpenny, the halfpenny will become a farthing, and the farthing nothing at all.'[3]

We will not stop here to ask how it is that the Education Department should itself have promulgated a Code such as those most hostile to the very existence of that department would have been glad to promulgate had they possessed the power. The secretary who drew up the new Code should have been Mr Miall; the vice-president who defended it should have been Mr Baines. But this is a mere question of persons. What we are here concerned to ask, what the general reader will care to know, is on what grounds the reduction to be effected by the new Code is proposed; why its authors have been, as they profess, induced to make it.

2. These grounds are the following. 'The duty of a State in public education is,' it is said, 'when clearly defined, to obtain the greatest possible quantity of reading, writing and arithmetic for the greatest number.' These are, so far as the State is concerned, 'the education of the people'. To obtain the greatest possible quantity of these is 'the requirement of a State'; and to attempt to give this greatest possible quantity is 'to attempt to give as much as the State can be expected to give'. To give this is 'the one thing which the elementary schools of the State are bound to do, just as the one thing a brewer is bound to do is to make good beer'. But the State has hitherto given more than this. It has paid for a machinery of instruction extending itself to many other things besides this. It has thus been paying for discipline, for civilization, for religious and moral training, for a superior instruction to clever and forward children – all of them matters quite out of its province to pay for: it has not exclusively kept its grants for the matters exclusively meriting them, the reading, writing and arithmetic.

In thus acting, the State has of course been extravagant. But not only has it been extravagant, inasmuch as it has been paying for what it had no business to pay for: by attending to this it has relaxed its attention to those elementary matters which alone concerned it. These have suffered in consequence. While inspectors were reporting on the tone and general influence of a school, on the discipline and behaviour of the children, on the geography and history of the first class, the indispensable elements, the reading, writing and arithmetic, were neglected.

The Education Commission reported 'that the children attend long enough to afford an opportunity of teaching them to read, write and cipher; but that a large proportion of them, in some districts, do not even learn to read; that they do not write well; and that they learn their arithmetic in such a way as to be of little practical use in after life.' They declared their opinion that, 'even under the present conditions of school age and attendance, it would be possible for at least *three-fifths* of the children on the books of the schools to learn to read and write without conscious difficulty, and to perform such arithmetical operations as occur in the ordinary business of life.' They came to the conclusion that 'the existing system has hitherto educated successfully only one-fourth of its pupils'. Seven-twentieths of the present body of scholars in our State-aided schools ought to read, write and cipher well, who do not.

At the same time, the Commissioners bore the strongest testimony to the superiority of these schools in discipline, in method, in general instruction, to all elementary schools not aided by the State.

Well then, it was said, here has the State been creating a system which 'suits admirably in all points but one, but that one unfortunately is *the education of the people*.' It was proposed to cure the error by paying solely for the reading, writing and arithmetic actually taught, and by lowering the standard of instruction. The 'principles involved in the Code which are really worth contending for, are', it was declared, '*payment by results*; requiring all managers to make their own terms with teachers, and *the lowering the standard of popular education*.'

But we must remark here that another 'principle' also was said to be 'involved' in the new Code, along with these principles of payment by results and lowering the standard of popular education. This other principle is no less than (what do our readers think?) 'the *extending more widely the area and benefit* of popular education'. This, they will naturally say, is a most important addition. This 'principle' is undoubtedly, if it be involved in the new Code, one well 'worth contending for'. And it therefore urgently behoves us to be well assured whether it is really involved in the new Code or no; for we may be very sure that the two points on which, in the House of Commons, the framers of the Code will chiefly rely for winning to it the support of the country gentlemen, and indeed of that large body of members, with fair intentions but without special acquaintance with the subject, whose votes must decide the fate of the new scheme, will be these:

(a) that the Code will repress the exorbitant pretensions of schoolmasters, and reduce the over-ambitious instruction of their highest classes.

(b) *that it will carry instruction into the 'waste places' of the country*, and, in Dr Vaughan's words, 'extend the advantages of education, to a certain though limited amount, to a larger number than heretofore'.

Now the plain truth is, that to hold out this expectation that the new Code will extend the advantages of education to the waste places of the country, to places too poor or too neglected to obtain these advantages under the present system, is to hold out an expectation utterly and entirely delusive. Its framers should be challenged to prove *how* the new Code will do this. We hope they will be pressed very closely on this point. The present system, they will keep saying – Mr Lowe said it the other day – leaves untouched many of the most necessitous places in the country; it helps most those who can best help themselves. True, let them be answered, this is a just reproach to bring against the old system; *only show us how your new system will in this respect do better*. 'Somebody or other must gain', it is said, 'by a redistribution in which so many are said to lose.' But this is not a case of *redistribution*, but of reduction. Two-fifths of the sum at present contributed by the State to the support of schools for the poor are to be suddenly taken away. Why *must* 'somebody or other', among the maintainers of such schools, gain by this? On the contrary, Archdeacon Sinclair declares, '*everybody* loses'. And so far are the 'waste places' of the country from gaining, that they will be among the heaviest losers. We assert this deliberately; let the framers of the Revised Code disprove it if they can. Take the very type of a 'waste place': some remote rural village in Wiltshire or Nottinghamshire, with a school of about forty children; the school of this place would obtain from the Committee of Council under the Revised Code annual assistance to the amount of £10; at the present moment it can obtain from them, without having to fulfil one condition which it would not have to fulfil under the Revised Code, and the attendance of the scholars being reckoned as precisely the same in both cases – it can obtain £30. Let the country gentleman who complains that the present system leaves poor and remote districts untouched, while it lavishes its aid on wealthy centres of population, and who hopes for some amendment in this respect from the new Code, behold the amendment which he will actually obtain!

The principles really involved in the new Code remain, therefore, those stated above – *payment by results*, those results being understood to be good reading, good writing and good arithmetic, the proper 'requirement of a State' from the schools which it aids; and the lopping off of all payments hitherto made for anything else. In other words, *reduction* and a *prize-scheme*.

The proposal of the Royal Commissioners had been very different. They had proposed two grants; one of them to be paid, as at present, for the general maintenance of the school and its machinery if these were such as to deserve maintaining at all; in other words, 'in consideration of the discipline, efficiency, and general character of the school' – of all those matters not touched by an individual examination of the scholars in reading, writing and arithmetic – duly attested by the inspector; the other, like the new sole grant established by the Revised Code, to be paid in direct reward of proficiency, proved by examination, of individual scholars in the three branches of instruction, supposed to be suffering – 'in consideration of the attainment of a certain degree of knowledge in reading, writing and arithmetic'. Thus the Royal Commissioners proposed two grants: a *maintenance-grant* and a *prize-grant*. But the money for one of these grants they proposed to raise by a rate. An education-rate is, or is supposed to be, impossible at present to introduce in this country; so one of the two grants proposed by the Commissioners the Privy Council authorities resolved to abandon. They selected for sacrifice that one which from all their own previous practice and traditions they might have been expected to retain, the *maintenance-grant*; a contribution, not in the nature of prizes for the proficiency, in certain subjects, of individual scholars, but in the nature of assistance towards the payment of teachers, towards the general support of the school. They adopted, as henceforth their sole grant, that one which was new and foreign to their traditions and practice, the *prize-grant*. No aid was henceforth to be given towards the maintenance of teachers, the support of the school, in consideration of the school's 'discipline, efficiency, and general character'; but in consideration of each examination successfully passed before the inspector, by scholars fulfilling certain conditions of age and attendance, in reading, writing and arithmetic, a certain reward was to be paid. This was called payment by results; and the reduction of two-fifths on the total contribution of the State will arise from limiting the State's contribution to a payment for reading, writing and arithmetic only, and only for proved proficiency in these.

It is sometimes alleged, indeed, that the aid of the State will still, under the Revised Code, be partly given in consideration of the 'discipline, efficiency, and general character' of the school, inasmuch as on the inspector's unfavourable report of these, one-half of the grant which we have called the prize-grant may be stopped. But this allegation is really, when closely looked into, quite illusory; as illusory as the allegation that the new Code will carry instruction into the waste places of the country, now neglected. It amounts to this; that the elementary schools of England, already mulcted by the new Code of two-fifths of the sum which they formerly received for maintaining their discipline, efficiency, and good general character, may be mulcted one and a half-fifth more, if, with their reduced rate of aid, they fail still to maintain these. This is not the old payment for maintaining these matters; it is a new penalty for not maintaining them. The sole objects judged worthy of the grants of the State are the reading, writing and arithmetic; but of these grants part is forfeited if the objects no longer deemed worthy of State grants are not provided for all the same. Singular encouragement for these latter! Religion, according to Mr Lowe's latest revision of his plan, is to be *encouraged* in a similar manner; that is, some more of the grant is to be forfeited if the religious instruction is found to have been neglected. These forfeitures, however, will seldom be pronounced. Inspectors are, after all, human; and where so much aid has been stopped already, an inspector will probably try very hard not to see anything which might force him to stop more.

State aid to popular education diminished in amount, and was administered under the conditions of a prize-scheme for proved proficiency in reading, writing and arithmetic, on the plea that the State has hitherto been paying for matters with which it has no concern, that 'the greatest quantity of reading, writing and arithmetic for the greatest number' is 'the requirement of the State', is, so far as the State is concerned, 'the education of the people'; on the plea that this State requirement has hitherto been ill satisfied because attention was not exclusively enough given to it that it will be satisfied better when attention is concentrated upon it and withdrawn from supererogatory matters – this is in fact, stripped of all official details and plainly expressed, the meaning of the original Revised Code. We have now to examine the merit of these pleas.

3. We will take the last plea first. It is founded on the declaration of the Royal Commissioners that a very large proportion of the scholars, even in inspected schools, carry very little instruction away with them; that even under the present conditions of school-age and attendance a much greater number of children might 'learn to read and write without conscious difficulty, and to perform such arithmetical operations as occur in the ordinary business of life'; that, in fact, 'so many as seven twentieths of the children ought to learn as much as this, even under the present conditions, who do not'. Now, is this true? About the fact, that a very large proporiton of the scholars, even in inspected schools, carry very little instruction away with them when they leave school, there can be no doubt: the inspectors themselves declare it; the Royal Commissioners are careful to assure us that they assert this on the authority of the inspectors themselves, and not on that of their own Assistant-Commissioners. But what are we to say to the next assertion of the Royal Commissioners, that, this fact being granted, it is, even under the present conditions of school-age and attendance, remediable; that even now seven-twentieths of the scholars ought to learn to read, write and cipher much better than they do? As to the truth of this second assertion, there is by no means the same agreement. School-teachers deny it, school-managers deny it, Sir James Shuttleworth denies it, the most experienced of the inspectors deny it. They declare the fact of the ignorance in which so many poor children, after passing through our elementary

schools, still remain; but they give an explanation of this fact which is not that of the Royal Commissioners. 'We know this,' says Mr Watkins, '*and we know also the cause*. It is the shortness of school-life. You cannot cram into the space of two or three years the instruction which ought to occupy five or six. Yet this is what is being done now, and must be done so long as the present inexorable demands of labour continue.' The Royal Commissioners, however, will not admit such an explanation as this; they attribute the ignorance complained of to other causes; to the neglect of the lower classes of his school by the master, to his over-ambitious teaching of the higher classes, to his imperfect teaching of the elementary parts of instruction, reading, writing and arithmetic, to all. They say that reading, writing and arithmetic might be much better taught than they are now, and to a much greater number. Who is in the right, and where lies the real truth in this matter?

Everything depends here upon a rigid exactitude in the use of terms. And there has been, on the contrary, much laxity. Sir James Shuttleworth and others have shown with triumph, from the reports of the inspectors, that a vastly greater proportion of scholars than that given by the Commissioners are returned as reading, writing and ciphering fairly or well. It has been retorted with equal triumph that this only proves how fallacious these reports of the inspectors are; for this proportion, calculated from their reports, is quite inconsistent with the state of imperfect instruction known to exist, and indeed admitted elsewhere by the inspectors themselves. The truth is, the terms *fair* and *good*, when applied to the reading, writing and arithmetic of our elementary schools, are not always used in precisely the same sense, and do not carry, to the minds of all who hear them used, precisely the same impression.

We wish to avoid all unnecessary detail, so we will illustrate this from the case of reading only. If, when we speak of a scholar reading fairly or well, we merely mean that reading in his accustomed lesson-book, his provincial tone and accent being allowed for, his want of home-culture and refinement being allowed for, some inevitable interruptions in his school attendance being allowed for, he gets through his task fairly or well, then a much larger proportion of scholars in our inspected schools than the one-fourth assigned by the Royal Commissioners may be said to read fairly or well. And this is what the inspectors mean when they return scholars as reading fairly or well. Such reading as this might honestly be said to meet sufficiently the requirement of the Commissioners that a scholar shall 'read without conscious difficulty'. Holding the Commissioners fast to this expression of theirs, we may safely assert that – whatever may be the value of their assertion that as many of the scholars as three-fifths *may be* taught, even under the present conditions of school age and attendance, to 'read without conscious difficulty' – the assertion that as few of the scholars as one-fourth *are actually* at present taught so to read is completely erroneous.

But the truth is, the Commissioners presently shift their terms a little. In order to read *fairly* or *well*, it is no longer enough to read *without conscious difficulty*; it is necessary to read *in an intelligent manner*.

It is necessary, to use Dr Vaughan's words, that the scholar shall be able to *read the Bible with intelligence*; it is necessary, to use the words of one of the ablest and most ardent of the Assistant-Commissioners – Mr Fraser – that he shall be able to *read the newspaper with sufficient ease to be a pleasure to himself and to convey information to listeners*. The Commissioners, in adopting these words, no longer confine themselves to the requirement that the scholar shall *read without conscious difficulty*; they understand by fair or good reading something more than this. They abandon what may be called the scholastic and professional acceptation of these terms; they adopt the acceptation of them current in the world and among the educated classes.

Now if it is understood by the assertion that a child in an elementary school reads fairly or well, that he reads in an intelligent manner, that he can read the Bible with intelligence, that he can read the newspaper sufficiently well to be a pleasure to himself and his hearers, then no doubt the inspectors, in reporting so large a proportion of children in inspected schools as reading fairly or well, have asserted what is most untrue. If this is what is understood by reading fairly or well, the Commissioners, in declaring that not more than one-fourth of the children in inspected schools now read fairly or well, have asserted what is most true. Whether they are equally right in asserting that at least three-fifths of them *ought*, even under present conditions, to learn to read fairly or well in this sense, is quite another question.

But the inspectors have themselves given the clearest proof that they at least do not use the terms *fairly* or *well* in this absolute sense. Mr Norris, who has been much quoted on this point, expressly tells us that the newspaper-test is one which he has applied only in his good schools, and that even these good schools failed to stand it. 'Where I found a school *much above par in reading*,' he says, 'I tested the *first class* by giving them a newspaper and telling them to read aloud some paragraph; but in not more than twenty out of 169 schools did I find a first class able to read a newspaper at sight.' He, at any rate, does not mean when he says that a poor child goes through his reading-lesson well or fairly, can read without conscious difficulty, that he is an *intelligent* reader, can *read the newspaper so as to give pleasure to himself and others*. He knows very well, as all persons know who are familiar with the poor and their life, and who do not take their standards from the life of the educated classes, that the goodness of a poor child's reading is something relative, that absolute standards are here out of place.

The Commissioners are certainly mistaken if they imagine that three-fifths of the children in our elementary schools can, under the present conditions, be brought to read *fairly* or *well* in the absolute sense, which, by slightly shifting their terms, they have come to attach to these words. What renders impossible the attainment by so many of a power so considerable – a power which is a real lasting acquirement for the whole life – is the utter want of care for books and knowledge in the homes from which the great majority of them come forth, to which the great majority of them return; in a word, the general want of civilization in themselves and in those among whom they pass their lives. It is the advance of them and their class in civilization which will bring them nearer to this power, not the confining them to reading-lessons, not the striking out lessons on geography or history from the course of our elementary schools. Intelligent reading – reading such as to give pleasure to the reader himself and to his hearers – is a very considerable acquirement; it is not very common even among the children of the rich and educated class. When children in this class possess it, they owe it not to the assiduity with which they have been taught reading and nothing but reading, but partly to natural aptitude, far more to the civilizing and refining influences, the current of older and educated people's ideas and knowledge, in the midst of which they have been brought up. It may safely be said the the religious teaching and the general information given in schools for the poor supply – most imperfectly indeed, but still in some sort or other supply – a kind of substitute for this current, the loss of which would do harm to those mechanical parts of instruction on which it is now proposed to lay exclusive stress. Some remarks in the *Guardian* newspaper bring this out very well. 'Reading', it is there said, 'is not a merely mechanical art; good reading requires many of the qualities of good oratory; nor will the most elaborate drill enable dullness and ignorance to wear the appearance of intelligent skill. The *general intellectual cultivation* which in late years we have all been promoting in schools is the best preparation for such reading as will please and interest reader and hearer alike.' And the Commissioners themselves quote the case of a school at Greenwich, in which backward readers, kept to reading-lessons only, were found to make less progress even in reading than others equally backward whose lessons were of a more varied cast. The most experienced inspectors, too, declare that the schools in which the general instruction is best are precisely the schools in which the elementary instruction is best also.

The Commissioners, therefore, probably overestimated both the actual neglect of elementary instruction in schools for the poor, and the possible improvement in it which the creating a prize-grant exclusively for proficiency in this instruction might bring about. But after all, the Commissioners proposed still to keep what we have called the *maintenance-grant* – the grant by which aid is given to a school not as a mere machine for teaching reading, writing and arithmetic, but as a living whole with complex functions, religious, moral, and intellectual. So far as a school by its full and efficient discharge of all these functions acts beneficially on the elementary instruction, the Commissioners helped it still so to act; for they proposed still to assist the school in the full and efficient discharge of all of them. But the same cannot be said of the framers of the Revised Code, who withdraw the subsidy altogether, and leave only a system of prizes for three particular subjects. Yet an advocate of this Code – the Assistant-Commissioner whom we have already quoted, Mr Fraser – has published a pamphlet, of which the whole scope is this – that the new Code really tends to promote the acquirement of general information in schools, certainly will not tend to discourage it, because (as we have already shown) good reading is impossible without general information and intelligence. Was there ever such reasoning heard of? If for the very object you have in view, good reading, cultivation in other subjects is necessary, why cut off all grants for these subjects in the hope of thereby getting better reading? How are you thus brought one step nearer to the end you have in view? How are you not rather pushed several steps farther back from it? The schools even with these auxiliary subjects encouraged by your grants have failed to produce reading good enough to satisfy you, and you hope, by discouraging these, to make them produce better. Thus it turns out that by persisting to teach just what you rebuke them for teaching, the schools are to produce the result which you desire! And when, in spite of your rebuke, in spite of the withdrawal of your grants, they have persisted in giving some general cultivation, as that without which good reading is impossible, you turn round and assure them that after all the best friends of this general cultivation are yourselves!

This plea, then, for the change introduced by the Revised Code – that elementary instruction has suffered from the undue attention given to higher instruction, that it will be amended by concentrating upon it the exclusive encouragement of the State – cannot stand. We pass to the other plea, that the State has hitherto been paying for matters with which it has no concern; that the requirement of the State from the schools which it aids is the greatest possible quantity of reading, writing and arithmetic for the greatest number, and this alone.

Mr Cumin, perhaps the cleverest of the Assistant-Commissioners, declares that the parents of our poor scholars care solely for good elementary instruction for their children, that they care nothing about the higher instruction generally superadded to this, that the higher instruction is due to the ambitiousness of the teacher or to the requirements of the Privy Council Office. A little more experience would have convinced Mr Cumin that this is often by no means so. A little more experience would have shown him teachers and managers struggling with difficulty against the demand for ornamental accomplishments for their children by parents who imagine that these tend to make ladies and gentlemen of them; it would have shown him teachers excusing themselves for teaching geography in their lower classes by the plea that if they did not teach something of this kind the parents would remove their children to private schools which professed to teach more subjects; it would have shown him the scholars of the highest class themselves putting a pressure upon the master to teach them mathematics or French or even Latin. He would have found that one of the most successful baits by which private schools, more expensive and less efficient, draw scholars away from public schools, is the lure of a more ambitious programme. There is a great deal of folly in all this; but the source of it lies in something natural and respectable – the strong desire of the lower classes to raise themselves. The faults of the teachers themselves, so visible, so pardonable, and so little pardoned, proceed from this desire. It is by no means clear to us that this effort of the humbler classes towards a higher stage of civilization deserves no assistance from the State. It certainly requires direction, and the only way of obtaining the right to give it direction is to give it some assistance. The present, however, is an unpropitious time for dwelling on this topic. That tide of reactionary sentiment against everything supposed to be in the least akin to democracy which, in presence of the spectacle offered by America, is now sweeping over Europe, it is useless at this moment to try to stem. *Now is your hour and the power of darkness.* Democracy, by its faults and extravagances, has almost deserved even so undiscriminating a reaction. But while forbearing at this inauspicious time to press the claims of the higher instruction of the lower classes upon State encouragement,* let the friends of these claims steadily refuse to ignore them. When a writer in *Blackwood's Magazine* contemptuously tells the parish schoomaster that 'if he thinks that the men whom the State wants for "cutting and polishing" the little boys and girls of the labouring classes are those who claim a social equality with surgeons and lawyers, he very much mistakes the feeling of the country', let us remind him that Coleridge, certainly no levelling Radical, desired 'a schoolmaster in every parish who

* 'The poor man's child,' says the excellent President of the Wesleyan Education Committee, Mr Scott, in his letter to Lord Granville, '*deserves a better education than this new regulation will give.*'

in due time, and under condition of a faithful performance of his arduous duties, *should succeed to the pastorate*, so that both he and the pastor should be labourers in different compartments of the same field, *with such difference of rank as might be suggested in the names pastor and sub-pastor, or as now exists between rector and curate*'. Let us repeat the wise admonition of M. de Rémusat to the upper classes, uttered only the other day: 'Attaquez avec courage tous les problèmes de l'avenir de la société où le sort vous a placés, *en pénétrant avec intelligence et avec sympathie dans les sentiments qui l'animent et dans les pensées qui la guident, en formant avec elle ces liens de solidarité morale sans lesquels tous les avantages de l'éducation ou de la fortune excitent l'envie et ne donnent pas l'influence*.'[4]

But, whatever may be the case as to the higher instruction, it is surely beyond a doubt that the 'discipline, efficiency, and general character' of its elementary schools are 'requirements of a State', as well as the successful teaching of reading, writing and arithmetic. Yet for these, to which the Royal Commissioners expressly devoted a grant from the State, the Revised Code gives nothing. Two-fifths of the money which now goes to maintain these, it takes away, on the plea that even with this reduction, good reading, writing and arithmetic may be sufficiently encouraged; and that, when these have been sufficiently encouraged, the State has nothing more to do. Limit the State's duty, in the schools of the nation, to offering a capitation grant for every good reader, writer and cipherer? You might as well limit the State's duty, in the prisons of the nation, to the offering a capitation grant for every reformed criminal! But in prisons, it will be said, the State has another interest besides the reformation of the criminal – the protection of society. We answer: and so, too, in schools the State has another interest besides the encouragement of reading, writing and arithmetic – *the protection of society*. It has an interest in them so far as they keep children out of the streets, so far as they teach them – the dull as well as the clever – an orderly, decent and human behaviour; so far as they civilize the neighbourhood where they are placed. It owes to its schools for the poor something more than *prizes*, it owes them *help for maintenance*. It owes them that very *subsidy* which Mr Lowe is so indignant at now giving, and so impatient to withdraw. Whether this help is bestowed in the form of a contribution towards the payment of the teachers, or in that of a contribution towards the general expenses of the school, matters little. But for every school-machinery which is thrown out of gear, for every glimmer of civilization which is quenched, for every poor scholar who is no longer humanized, owing to a reduction, on the plea that reading, writing and arithmetic are all the State ought to pay for in our present State expenditure for elementary schools, the State will be directly responsible. It will be as responsible as it would be for the harm to society of any deterioration which should be brought about in our prison-system by a reduction, on the plea that reformed criminals are all the State ought to pay for in the present expenditure for prisons.

Lord Stanley said the other day at Leeds that he should be satisfied 'if three-fourths of all those who attend day-schools could be sent out into the world knowing thoroughly how to read, write and cipher; having acquired, in addition, those habits of order, discipline and neatness, which a well-managed school gives, and having been taught the elementary truths of religion'. Well, the State, if the Revised Code is adopted, will do something towards giving Lord Stanley satisfaction. It will give prizes for the production of good reading, writing and ciphering. But for the formation of 'those habits of order, discipline and neatness, which a well-managed school gives', it will give nothing. For the inculcation of the elementary truths of religion, it will give nothing. But these, say the advocates of the Revised Code, it is the clergyman's duty to see cared for. True, it is his duty; but what a course for the State, to put a clergyman's duty at variance with his interests! Instead of strengthening his hands, it creates a temptation for him to stimulate in his parish school the secular rather than the religious instruction, and then tells him that it is his duty to overcome this temptation! Why, this is as if a highwayman, who puts his pistol to your head and demands your money or your life, were to tell you at the same time that you would be a very cowardly fellow if you did not resist him. 'I should like nothing better,' you might answer, 'than to show a proper spirit, and to do my duty as a man; but I should like also not to have my brains blown out for doing it.'

But even supposing that, alarmed at discovering what grave evils will follow the withdrawal of a large amount of the aid now given to elementary schools, the framers of the Revised Code were to consent to increase their capitation grant, so that the amount of this aid should still remain the same, the Revised Code would yet remain open to the most serious objections. The partisans of the Code at first laid great stress on its economy. But it was soon evident that they must not base its excellence on its economy alone; for a Minute abolishing all grants whatever to education would have been more economical still, and therefore more excellent. Of late, therefore, they have changed their ground a little, and all the stress is now laid on the Code's *efficiency*. The concessions just announced somewhat diminish the reduction at first threatened. 'Lord Granville and Mr Lowe do not', we are now told, 'propose to diminish the grant, or to exclude one child from a share in it. But it will henceforth be *no work, no pay*.' 'I cannot promise', says Mr Lowe, 'that the new scheme will be economical, but if it is not economical, it will be *efficient*.' 'I am not aware', says Dr Vaughan, 'that a positive diminution of expenditure is a prominent object of the changes proposed.' But 'who shall complain', he asks, 'if henceforth the State should say. "What I give, I choose to give as the reward of success; of success in teaching the rudiments"?' The State, we have said, owes to its elementary schools more than 'prizes for success in teaching the rudiments'; it is a social and political blunder to confine its duty towards such schools to the duty of offering these. If, however, under the name of 'prizes for success in teaching the rudiments', it gives as much as it formerly gave under the name of 'grants in consideration of the discipline, efficiency, and general character' of schools, the bad consequences of this social and political blunder are no doubt lessened. They are not by any means removed; for it is idle to say that when the State proclaims 'success in teaching the rudiments' to be the sole object of its rewards, other matters, really of vital importance to the State – the humanizing of that multitude of children whose home-training is defective, who are very rude, ignorant, or dull, very unlikely to obtain prizes, and whom, therefore, under the operation of such a prize-scheme as that proposed, '*it will not pay to teach*'* – it is idle to say that this, that the forming those 'habits of order, discipline, and neatness', the inculcating those 'elementary truths of religion', which Lord Stanley wishes to be formed and inculcated, will not be made in some degree secondary, will not, therefore, to some extent suffer. But even if this were not so, even should the social and political blunder entirely disappear, a great administrative blunder would remain. The State would be forced to appropriate to the *supervision* of public education much too large a proportion of its whole grant for public education; a great deal of money would have to be spent in maintaining inspectors, which would be better spent in maintaining schools. This is the inconvenience of losing sight of the State's proper business. The State's proper business in popular education is to help in the creation and maintenance of the schools necessary; to cause fit local bodies to be appointed with the function of watching over these schools; and, finally, itself to exercise over these bodies, and their performance of their functions, a general supervision. When it goes far beyond this, when it makes its aid a system of prizes requiring the most minute and detailed examinations; when it tries to test the acquirements of every individual child to whose instruction it contributes, it goes beyond its province; it invests itself with municipal, not imperial, functions, it creates an administrative expenditure which is excessive. It is as if (to revert to our old comparison of prisons) the State, proposing to support prisons by a capitation

*The words of the Memorial read by a deputation from the Educational Societies to Lord Granville.

grant on reformed criminals, had to ascertain for what criminals the grant was due. The staff of officers to conduct this minute inquisition would absorb funds which might have provided prison-discipline enough to reform scores of criminals. Even at present the cost of inspection forms a very large item in the expenditure of the Committee of Council. Under the operation of the prize-scheme proposed by the new Code, this cost would be doubled. 'The first piece of statesmanship we have had on this subject' would be guilty of this grave administrative blunder! The last remaining friends of 'voluntary energy and spontaneity' would create a mass of State mechanism only to be paralleled in China! Examination, we are told, is now the rule of our public service. Yes; but where, except in China, is examination the rule not only for every public servant, but for all those to whom the public servant's, action extends? Yet this is the rule which Mr Lowe institutes, by examining – not his own inspectors before appointment – but every child in the schools which these inspectors visit. This is as if the State undertook, not only to send the exciseman before the Civil Service Commissioners, but to send before them also all the people who drink beer!

Such are the merits of the Revised Code. It will not do what it proposes to do; it will not 'extend the advantages of education to a larger number than heretofore' and it will not remove 'the unsatisfactory state of elementary instruction in inspected schools'. It will not make the distribution of the Parliamentary grant for education 'more general and more effective'. And, even were it to do what it proposes, the means by which it proposes to do this would still be objectionable; namely, the confining the State's part in popular education to the offering 'prizes for success in teaching the rudiments', and the compelling the State to institute, in order to test this success, an immense system of individual examination.

Concocted in the recesses of the Privy Council Office, with no advice asked from those practically conversant with schools, no notice given to those who largely support schools, this new scheme of the Council Office authorities – by which they abruptly revolutionize the system which they were appointed to administer, stab in the back the ward committed to their guardianship – has taken alike their friends and enemies by surprise. Their own inspectors, education-societies, school-managers, are astounded. Their enemies, while enjoying their triumph, can hardly believe that they have obtained it so easily. They cannot refrain from scornfully complimenting the Committee of Council on the facility with which it has yielded. 'We learnt with *equal surprise and satisfaction*', say the Edinburgh Reviewers, 'the prompt and radical remedy which the Lords of the Education Committee were already prepared (as it now appears) to apply to the evils and shortcomings we had endeavoured to point out. The justification of our strictures is therefore complete, since the heads of the department are so conscious of these defects that they have since promulgated a Minute which rescinds the whole of their former code of regulations, and substitutes an entirely new system for that of 1846. All that we take to be proved at present is, that *the old system is irrevocably condemned by the very persons who have administered it*.' And the reviewers applaud the new plan proposed, because it will give 'greater liberty of action to managers, more self-reliance to teachers'; not caring to add that in their opinion it is a great pity managers should not be made yet more free, and teachers yet more self-reliant, by the abolition of all State aid to them whatever.

But they accept the Revised Code as an instalment, as the 'commencement of the end' of a system of State aid to national education, that palpable 'defiance of the laws of supply and demand'. The enemies of such a system are relieved to discover that their own maxims are now predominant in the Council Office; that the authorities there are indeed still encumbered with 'this system of which Sir James Shuttleworth was the author', but that they are convinced that 'it is time to halt', to 'arrest the growth for the future of this vested interest', which, by making State payments to schoolmasters, he created. They find Mr Lingen, the Secretary, himself deprecating any further extension of the system; apprehending that it must become unmanageable, enlarging on its administrative difficulties. Sir James Shuttleworth, who knows the details of this business at least as well as Mr Lingen, makes very short work of these administrative difficulties. A more honourable and indefatigable public servant than Mr Lingen does not exist; but the most indefatigable man sees difficulties in a course for which he has no love. Mr Lingen's difficulties show the presence, in the heart of the Education Department, of this want of love for the very course which such a department is created to follow.

The present heads of this department would certainly never have instituted it. They cannot well abolish it outright, but they reduce its action as much as possible. They share in their hearts the feelings of those who think the existence of such a department opposed to English habits, and undesirable. Indeed, this existence is opposed to so great a body of English habits and English prejudices, that one wonders how it ever found means to establish itself. It found them, almost entirely, in the zeal and perseverance of one man, Sir James Shuttleworth. He has been taunted with not possessing the graces of style, the skill of the literary artist; but he possesses that which is perhaps almost as useful as these, and which those who taunt him do not always exhibit – a thorough knowledge of this subject of popular education. And how comes he to know it so well? Alas! there is no royal road to knowledge in these matters; he knows it in the only way by which this subject ever can be well known – he knows it because he loves it. Statesmen – and among them Lord Lansdowne deserves to be named the first – who perhaps did not share his zeal, were yet wise and open-minded enough to see the benefits which might be wrought by it. So, in the face of immense prejudice, of angry outcry, of vehement opposition, the Education Department was established. The good which it did reconciled to it gradually even that body, which by its nature shares most strongly the popular prejudices on this matter, which had been warmest in its opposition, loudest in its outcry – the clergy. Because they have thus outgrown a vain prejudice, the clergy are now reproached with inconsistency, with being debauched by Government grants, with 'relying too little upon personal exertion', with 'importunately petitioning for public alms'. The old cry, so hollow, yet to the heedless so plausible, is again raised: 'it is time that our schools should be thrown back upon that mode of maintenance which is the most independent.' Independent for whom? For those for whose sake these schools exist – the poor and their children? Is a poor man more independent by receiving help from his squire or his rector towards his child's education, than by receiving it from the State? Are his reasonable wishes as to the kind of that education more likely to be respected by his local, or by his imperial benefactor? To state a commonplace like this fully, is to refute it. Experience, the best of teachers, has convinced the clergy of the hollowness of this and other like commonplaces which once deluded them. Their schools have been dearer to them than their prejudices. As they saw the change gradually worked in the country by the Education Grant – as they began to perceive the benefits for the present and future of a steady current of communication opened, for help, sympathy, and guidance, between the Government of this country and the schools of the lower classes – their prejudices were dispersed or forgotten, and the system which it is now proposed to 'simplify' until it becomes, in Mr Miall's words, 'nothing at all', grew precious to them. Their attachment will probably even now save it from destruction. Their experience has been a truer guide to the clergy than has their enlightenment to organs of public opinion, such as the *Guardian* or the *Spectator*, most friendly to the improvement and gradual elevation of the lower classes, but so sensitive to the faults of the present system that they are disposed to welcome the Revised Code for attacking it. To such friends of the lower classes we may well say: *you know not what you do*. It is because there is something *vital* in the connexion established between the State and the lower classes by the old system, that this system – with all its complication, all its expensiveness, all its mistakes, with all the false taste of many of its schoolmasters and students, all their pretentiousness, all their sciolism, all their nonsense – was yet precious; it is because the Revised Code, by destroying – under the specious pleas of simplifying, of giving greater liberty of action to managers – this vital connexion, takes the heart out of the old system, that it is so condemnable.

For it withdraws from popular education, so far as it can, all serious guidance, all initiatory direction by the State; it makes the action of the State upon this as mechanical, as little dynamical, as possible. It turns the inspectors into a set of registering clerks, with a mass of minute details to tabulate, such a mass as must, in Sir James Shuttleworth's words, 'necessarily withdraw their attention from the religious and general instruction, and from the moral features of the school.' In fact the inspector will just hastily glance round the school, and then he must fall to work at the 'log-books'. And this to ascertain the precise state of each individual scholar's reading, writing and arithmetic. As if there might not be in a school most grave matters needing inspection and correction; as if the whole school might not be going wrong, at the same time that a number of individual scholars might carry off prizes for reading, writing and arithmetic! It is as if the generals of an army – for the inspectors have been the veritable generals of the educational army – were to have their duties limited to inspecting the men's cartouch-boxes. The organization of the army is faulty – inspect the cartouch-boxes! The camp is ill-drained, the men are ill-hutted, there is danger of fever and sickness. Never mind; inspect the cartouch-boxes! But the whole discipline is out of order, and needs instant reformation – no matter; inspect the cartouch-boxes! But the army is beginning a general movement, and that movement is a false one; it is moving to the left when it should be moving to the right: it is going to a disaster! That is not your business; inspect, inspect the cartouch-boxes!

'But what was to be done?' cry Mr Lowe and his friends. 'It was impossible for us,' says Mr Lowe, 'to remain quiet under the actual imputations cast upon the system'. 'Not being able to avail itself of the suggestion of a county rate, nor yet, *in the face of a recent exposure, to ask Parliament for a large increase of the grant*, all the Committee of Council could do', say Mr Lowe's friends, 'was to do as it has done, to *economize*; and it is in its economies that the Minute differs from the report of the Royal Commissioners.' Not quite so; it differs from it, radically, in the principle on which it makes its grants, in that it makes its grants for reading, writing and arithmetic only, while the Royal Commissioners proposed to make theirs partly for these, but partly also for the 'discipline, efficiency, and general character' of the school. But the Committee of Council was not reduced to one of the three alternatives, of either proposing a county rate, or else asking Parliament, *in the face of a recent exposure*, for a large increase of the grant; or else, those two courses being impossible, economizing. It might surely have made itself quite certain, whether an *exposure* had actually befallen its system, and to what this *exposure* amounted. It might have made some inquiry on this matter of its own officers, whose credit was greatly concerned. It made none. If it had satisfied itself, as we are persuaded it might have satisfied itself, that the Royal Commissioners had not clearly seen the real truth of this matter of the elementary instruction; that *well* and *ill*, in this matter, are relative terms; that of the children in our inspected schools much more than the Commissioners' one-fourth read well, considering their condition and opportunities – very much less than the Commissioners' three-fifths could be brought, with their present condition and opportunities, to read well absolutely – if it had explained this, if it had declared, as it might have declared with perfect truth, that it had itself emphatically insisted on the importance of the elementary instruction; that it had struggled for its advancement, that it was prepared to struggle for it still – such an explanation, we are convinced, would have been willingly accepted. The Committee might have proved its sincerity by very simple administrative changes. It had already directed its inspectors to pay special attention to the elementary instruction, but it had retained (and still retains) its crowded programme of subjects for examination. By striking out the great majority of these, by reducing the subjects entered on the official programme from twenty-three to five – religious knowledge, reading, writing, arithmetic, and *general information* – and by directing the inspector to refuse to examine in the last if he be dissatisfied with the results of his examination in the four others; by permitting him to recommend *partial* stoppage of grants when thus dissatisfied (at present he can recommend entire stoppage only) – the Committee of Council, at the same time that it would have somewhat diminished its consumption of stationery (no light merit), would, we feel certain, have done far more to promote elementary instruction than the Revised Code will ever effect.

But we must not forget that we write for the general reader, and that we have promised him to avoid official details as much as possible. We will not trouble him with the very simple expedients by which, as Sir James Shuttleworth shows, the minor administrative knots which fill Mr Lingen with such dismay – the multiplication of Post Office orders and of petty separate payments in the same school – might have been untied without the sword of the Revised Code. Nor will we discuss even more important changes which it was time to bring about, but which, like the consolidation of small payments just mentioned, might have been brought about without a revolution. The details of the Privy Council Office system have grown up gradually; some of them must have been the result of accident; all of them are fit matter for revision. It can hardly have been by the deliberate judgement of men of sagacity that that meritorious work, *Morell's Analysis of Sentences*, was made the intellectual food of girls of sixteen. It can hardly have been by the deliberate judgement of men of taste that another meritorious work, *Warren's Extracts from Blackstone's Commentaries*, was selected, for the astonishment of Quintilians yet unborn, to be the authorized textbook for readers, the chosen field in which the student of elocution should exhibit his powers. It must have been by an accident that those two odious words, *male* and *female* (for *man* and *woman*, *boy* and *girl*), established themselves so firmly in the vocabulary of a department charged with the propagation of humane letters and refinement, from whence they are invading the common language of the whole country, carrying into the relations of social human life the terminology of the Zoological Gardens. The Revised Code contains, we see, regulations for changing certain matters in the training of pupil-teachers and students. It must have been by an accident that these were omitted. But we will not discuss these things here. We will not discuss the organization of inspection; inspection with its sixty inspectors, all performing the independent functions and receiving something like the salary of inspectors-general, but not chosen (they are far too numerous) with the care with which inspectors-general should be chosen; not possessing (they are far too numerous) that access to their chief by which inspectors-general enlighten him as to what is really going on outside the walls of the central office – inspection which the Revised Code reorganizes not at all, but proposes to make, by introducing a plan of immense examinations, more vast, more expensive, and more unwieldy. We will only say in passing, that we are convinced the right course to follow is not to increase the number of Privy Council Office inspectors, but rather to reduce it; that the State – instead of attempting itself to carry out a vast system of minute local examinations by means of its own inspectors in chief, highly paid and sent from a distance – should avail itself for such purposes of a local and cheaper machinery, supervising the operations of this by their own inspectors greatly reduced in number. This is what is done in Holland with signal success, and we are sure it might be done here. Our denominational system affords, indeed, peculiar facilities for it. We feel certain that in the case of National schools (which form the vast majority of those aided by the Committee of Council), the ordinary inspection of these would be perfectly well performed by the diocesan inspectors – appointed as at present, but receiving a small allowance from the Committee of Council for their travelling expenses – acting under the supervision of the Committee of Council's inspector in chief, and removeable from the Committee of Council's service (but from that only) by the Lord President. The diocesan inspectors are in general men of precisely the same age, standing, and experience as the majority of the young clerical inspectors. They could hardly be asked to act under the supervision of these; but under the supervision of an inspector in chief much their superior in standing and experience they would willingly act. These inspectors in chief would have large districts, would be few in number (ten or fifteen would probably suffice for all England), might therefore be selected with great care and discrimination, and would be, like the provincial inspectors in Holland, the only salaried inspectors of the State. As in Holland, they would yearly re-inspect a certain number of the schools inspected by their local inspectors, and would maintain among these uniformity of practice and standard. At the same time, they would form a body of men not too numerous to have concert among themselves, and to communicate with the central office. Similar means might be found to provide for the inspection of British, Wesleyan, or Roman Catholic schools, which lie chiefly in or about the large towns. The inspectors at present are at once very expensive, and a mob. Under the Revised Code they will be still more expensive, and still more a mob.

Finally, we will not even discuss the much vexed question of the teachers' augmentation grants, by its handling of which the Revised Code has raised such a storm. We will not attack this handling. We will even say that the teachers have not, in our opinion, either a vested interest or a legal claim. They have only what is called, in common life, *a very hard case*. We think a payment in consideration of a teacher's place in an examination for honours a bad form of help for the State's help towards school-maintenance to take. We do not think it the State's business itself to hold examinations for honours, any more than we think it its business itself to examine all the little readers in the country. We should be sorry to see less mental life and activity among the young schoolmasters, but we should be glad if this could find its vent and look for its honours (as it is beginning to look for them) in the examinations of bodies such as the London University and its affiliated institutions, rather than in the examinations of a Government Department. The examinations of the Committee of Council should address themselves to ascertain a teacher's *competence* only; there we agree with the framers of the Revised Code. But we think they might have managed to establish this principle for their future operations, without wholly disregarding the hopes, the legitimate confidence, engendered by their own past operations; without throwing twenty thousand persons into despair. So, again, with the aid to training colleges. We do not blame the framers of the Revised Code for wishing to set some limits to this. The State has aided the creation of too many of these institutions, often in the wrong places, and at needless expense. Limitation was necessary. But we could wish some better means had been originally devised for accomplishing this limitation, by processes which the training colleges might have accepted, and which would not have abruptly deranged all their operations; by processes which their inventors might not have been, after all, forced to abandon.

These are matters, however, in which the Council Office authorities might perfectly well have proposed any needful changes, although it behoved them to plan such changes prudently. Everyone admits that the old system, *in its details*, was, as Mr Lowe called it, 'a tentative, provisional, and preliminary one'. But recognizing that the mind of the country was not yet ripe for the final settlement of this question of popular education, not able to adopt the county rate of the Royal Commissioners, but explaining what had been the real success of the system they administered, explaining what there was erroneous in the complaints against it, proposing certain salutary administrative changes, the Council Office authorities might, we are convinced, with the cheerful acquiescence of the country, have asked Parliament, not 'for a large increase of their grant', but for a continuation of their former grant, for the means of carrying on their old system for the present; thus saving intact for the future the vital principle of that system – the principle, that the State owes to schools for the poor support 'in consideration of their discipline, efficiency, and general character', and a supervision which addresses itself, above all, to these. *Their strength was to sit still.*

Instead of this, they have accepted with alacrity the first summons of their adversaries, and are cheerfully preparing to abandon all their positions. If these are ever to be reoccupied they will all have to be fought for over again. Instead of reserving this question for the future, they settle it now; by proposing a change which abandons the essential part of their old system, severs all vital connexion between the State and popular education, substitutes for the idea of a *debt* and a *duty* on the State's part towards this, the idea of a *free gift*, a gratuitous boon of *prizes*; for a supervision of the whole movement of popular education – its method, its spirit, and its tendency – a mechanical examination of certain scholars in three branches of instruction. For to this must State inspection inevitably dwindle, when to these the grants of the State are confined. Where the State's treasure is bestowed, there will its heart be also.

But Lord Granville and Mr Lowe have just announced certain concessions. Some of these are slight, others are more important. They none of them remove the worst faults of the Code, although two of them partially correct its greatest absurdities. The framers of the Code have actually discovered that they 'pushed their principle too far when they proposed to examine infants under six years of age!' They have positively found out that to discourage the retention in school of all children over eleven years of age is not a good way of promoting popular education! From such quickness of apprehension what might not be expected? But then throughout the whole speech of the real author of this Code – Mr Lowe – shines clearly forth the spirit which still animates him, and which makes even his concessions valueless. That spirit is a spirit of hostility to the system which he administers, and to its fundamental principles. It is in vain that he declares – to conjure the alarm which he has excited – that 'he has no wish to disturb any of the fundamental principles of the present system'. With his next breath he avows that 'his only plan is to sweep away the existing system'. Reproached with inconsistency, he explains that he only means to sweep away the *annual grants* of the present system. That is, he means to sweep away just what is essential in the present system – its *maintenance-grants*, its recognition of the State's duty to aid schools for the poor 'in consideration of their discipline, efficiency, and general character'. And this he calls 'not disturbing any fundamental principle of the present system!' We suppose he must imagine that the 'fundamental principle of the present system' is its vice-president, and that so long as that functionary subsists, the system is whole. So, again, he consents to spare the training colleges a little longer, but he consents to this unwillingly and with menaces. So, too, forced to give up his examination of infants – forced to mar in this particular the beautiful simplicity of his scheme, forced to admit into it, in some small measure, the accursed thing, the maintenance-grant, the *subsidy* – he relieves his mind by lamenting over the decay of that voluntary spirit which once regarded all State grants with such jealousy, by intimating that, 'were he at liberty to choose abstractedly what he thought best for the education of the country', he would have no such grants at all. He has the air of apologizing to the Voluntaries for not being able to give them perfect satisfaction. We are convinced they will receive his apologies most indulgently. His momentary bowing in the house of Rimmon will be forgiven him. It is so evident that his heart is in the right place! It is so manifest that his desires are in the heaven of Voluntaryism with Mr Baines, even though his practice be condemned to grope a little longer in the earthly gloom of State connexion!

But of his enmity to the present system, Mr Lowe gave a yet more striking proof than these apologies. It is understood that the inspectors are, as a body, favourable to that system, and averse to the Revised Code: their reports are quoted in contradiction of the assumptions on which the Code is based. Mr Lowe determined to punish them. The habits of English public life, the high tone of English public men, in general prescribe to a Minister the most punctilious consideration for those who serve under him. He spares and screens these, though it be to his own hindrance. His generosity in this respect is one of Lord Palmerston's most popular qualities; rather than resist its impulse, he has incurred on more than one occasion serious embarrassment. From no such embarrassment will Mr Lowe suffer. With the unscrupulousness of passion – growing desperate as the dangers of his 'little subject' thickened round him – he, in his late speech, flung to the winds every restraint of official delicacy. In his Code he had sacrificed the principles of his department; in his speech he sacrificed its persons. The best part of that performance was an elaborate attack upon his own inspectors. Of this Lord Granville is incapable. But Lord Granville is not the real leader in this struggle.

What will be the issue of the discussion now impending? We have good hopes. The disposition hitherto shown by the House of Commons has been excellent; the attachment of the country at large to a system from which vast practical benefit has been derived is strong. But we are not confident. The friends of the Revised Code are numerous, resolute, and powerful. There is Mr Lowe, a political economist of such force, that had he been by when the Lord of the harvest was besought 'to send labourers into his harvest', he would certainly have remarked of that petition that it was 'a defiance of the laws of supply and demand', and that the labourers should be left to come of themselves. There is *The Times*, which naturally upholds Mr Lowe. There is the *Daily News*, unable on this subject to shake off what it has shaken off on so many others, a superstitious reverence for old watchwords of those extreme Dissenters, who for the last ten years have seemed bent on proving how little the future of the country is to owe to their intelligence. There are the friends of economy at any price, always ready to check the hundreds of the national expenditure, while they let the millions go. There are the selfish vulgar of the upper classes, saying in their hearts that this educational philanthropy is all rubbish, and that the less a poor man learns except his handicraft the better. There are the clever and fastidious, too far off from its working to see the substantial benefits which a system, at all national, of popular education confers on the lower classes, but offended by its superficial faults. All these will be gratified by the triumph of the Revised Code, and they are many. And there will be only one sufferer – *the education of the people.*

Report for 1869

During the school year more than 25,000 children passed under my inspection; of these about 13,000 were presented for examination grants.

The total rate of failure, which in 1866–7 was 13 per cent, rose in 1867–8 to 14·56 per cent, but declined in 1868–9 to 11·3 per cent. Of last year's failures, 20 per cent were in arithmetic, 7·7 per cent in writing, and 6 per cent in reading.

This gradation not ill represents the degrees of difficulty in teaching by rote the three matters of arithmetic, writing and reading. I have repeatedly said that it seems to me the great fault of the Revised Code, and of the famous plan of *payment by results,* that it fosters teaching by rote; I am of that opinion still. I think the great task for friends of education is, not to praise *payment by results,* which is just the sort of notion to catch of itself popular favour, but to devise remedies for the evils which are found to follow the applications of this popular notion. The school examinations in view of *payment by results* are, as I have said, a game of mechanical contrivance in which the teachers will and must more and more learn how to beat us. It is found possible, by ingenious preparation, to get children through the Revised Code examination in reading, writing and ciphering, without their really knowing how to read, write and cipher.

To take the commonest instance: a book is selected at the beginning of the year for the children of a certain standard; all the year the children read this book over and over again, and no other. When the Inspector comes they are presented to read in this book; they can read their sentence or two fluently enough, but they cannot read any other book fluently. Yet the letter of the law is satisfied, and the more we undertake to lay down to the very letter the requirements which shall be satisfied in order to earn grants, the more do managers and teachers conceive themselves to have the right to hold us to this letter. Suppose the inspector were to produce another book out of his pocket, and to refuse grants for all the children who could not read fluently from it. The managers and teacher would appeal to the Code, which says that the scholar shall be required to read 'a paragraph from a reading book used in the school', and would the Department sustain an Inspector in enforcing such an additional test as that which has been mentioned?

The circle of the children's reading has thus been narrowed and impoverished all the year for the sake of a *result* at the end of it, and the *result* is an illusion.

The reading test affords the greatest facilities for baffling those who imposed it, and therefore in reading we find fewest failures, but the writing test is managed almost as easily. Let us take the middle of a school, generally the weakest part, and the part which requires most careful teaching – the scholars in the Third Standard. There are books of the Third Standard which, what with verse, pages of words for spelling, exercises for dictation, and sums, contain for the prose reading-lesson less than fifty pages of good-sized print. The writing test for scholars of the Third Standard is to write from dictation a sentence from that same lesson of their reading book in which they have just previously been set to read. Verse is not commonly used for the reading of the Third Standard; an examiner would hardly choose to set the very dictation exercises given in the lesson book; there remain the fifty prose pages which the scholar has been reading and re-reading all the year. His eye and memory have become familiar with them; he has just refreshed his acquaintance with one of them by reading it; from this page he is now set to write a sentence slowly dictated to him by a few words at a time. Can it be said that because a child can spell this sentence tolerably and thus produce the required result, he may therefore be set down as able to write easy sentences from dictation? And must we not own that this *result* also is in great measure an illusion? We see accordingly, that though the rate of failure in writing does exceed that in reading, yet it exceeds it very slightly, and both are quite inconsiderable.

In arithmetic, the rate of failure is much more considerable. To teach children to bring right two sums out of three without really knowing arithmetic seems hard. Yet even here, what can be done to effect this (and it is not so very little) is done, and our examination in view of *payment by results* cannot but encourage its being done. The object being to ensure that on a given day a child shall be able to turn out, worked right, two out of three sums of a certain sort, he is taught the mechanical rule by which sums of this sort are worked, and sedulously practised all the year round in working them; arithmetical principles he is not taught, or introduced into the science of arithmetic. The rate of failure in this branch also will thus, in all probability, be gradually reduced, but, meanwhile, the most notable result attained will be that which has been happily described by my colleague, Mr Alderson, when he says: 'Unless a vigorous effort is made to infuse more intelligence into its teaching, *government arithmetic* will soon be known as a modification of the science peculiar to inspected schools, and remarkable chiefly for its meagreness and sterility'.

Those who know the German schools know the extreme care taken there to teach elementary matters in such a way as to develop as much as possible the intelligence of the children and to give them some real mental power. M. Baudouin's report to the French Government on the primary and secondary schools of Germany, Switzerland, and Belgium, a work which is, I believe, in the library of the Department, exhibits in full detail illustrations of this prominent feature in German teaching. In my opinion, the want of it in English schools is, and long has been, at least as real a shortcoming in them as their imputed neglect of the lower and more backward children. Not less than this neglect it needs, and has long needed, on the part of the Education Department, some action to correct it.

The Minute of 20 February 1867 was meant to correct that impoverishment of the instruction, which was due to the mechanical routine brought in by the Revised Code examination.[1]

But it proceeds just in the same course as that examination proceeds. It attempts to lay down, to the very letter, the requirements which shall be satisfied in order to earn grants. The teacher, in consequence, is led to think, not about teaching his subject, but about managing to hit these requirements. He limits his subject as much as he can, and within these limits tries to cram his pupils with details enough to enable him to say, when they produce them, that they have fulfilled the Departmental requirements, and fairly earned their grant. The ridiculous results obtained by teaching geography, for instance, under these conditions, may be imagined. A child who has never heard of Paris or Edinburgh, will tell you measurements of England in length and breadth, and square mileages, till his tongue is tired. I have known a class, presented in English history, to take the period for Caesar's landing to the Norman Conquest, and to be acquainted in much detail with the Roman invasion of Anglesey; but Carnarvon, on the coast opposite Anglesey, being mentioned, they neither knew what Prince of Wales was born there, nor to whom the title of Prince of Wales belonged. Another class took the period from Caesar's landing to the reign of Egbert, and knew the history of this period, or what passes for its history, minutely, but only one of them had heard of the Battle of Waterloo. It is true, for this sort of unsound performance Inspectors pluck candidates for the supplementary grants much more freely than they pluck candidates for the main grants. But this is only because these supplementary grants are so insignificant that managers and teacher care comparatively little whether they are obtained or not, and meanwhile, the object of the Department, to counteract the narrow, unintelligent mode of instruction encouraged by the Revised Code, is not attained.

Great stress has been laid on the declaration of the Duke of Newcastle's Commission, that 'the object is to find some constant and stringent motive to induce teachers to do that part of their duty which is at once most unpleasant and most important'. This unpleasant and important part of their duty, according to the same Commission, is 'to see that all the children under their charge really learn to read, write and cipher thoroughly well'. And some of my colleagues speak as if this undoubtedly important and desirable object were certainly attained by giving to our examinations their present character, and as if whoever wished to modify that present character, contested the importance and desirability of that object. 'If children are not well taught and trained in the lower classes,' says Mr Duport, 'they will never be taught at all.' And again, 'First, let a school be thoroughly in working order from top to bottom as regards accuracy of elementary grounding.' Undoubtedly; but is a child's elementary grounding in thorough working order, because he can read fluently a sentence in a short book which he has been reading and re-reading all the year? But perhaps it is only meant that the elementary grounding is in thorough working order comparatively with what it was formerly, before the legislation of 1862. This is a hard comparison to make with accuracy, so as to be sure that the improvement in question has actually taken place. To say with confidence *yes*, one ought to have known well a district of schools, and the same district, for at least five or six years before the legislation of 1862 as well as after it; whereas some of those who say *yes* with most confidence, seem but, before 1862, to have been well acquainted with one school. However, no one questions the advantage of an individual grant-rewarded examination, or that the Newcastle Commissioners did well in suggesting it, or that the Education Department did well in giving effect to this suggestion; the real question is, and it is eminently a question for educationists, since the general public has neither care nor skill for it, and is sure to be perfectly satisfied as soon as it hears of *paying by results* – the real question is, whether we have not somewhat overdone this sort of examination by attaching to it so overwhelming a share of our grants, and consequently so overwhelming an importance; and whether some improved mode of combining it with the old inspection might not be hit on.

It is urged, indeed, that the remedy is in the inspector's hands, because 'it can only be by the express recommendation of an inspector that any school obtains its full grant while it produces nothing better than mechanical results, and if, after due warning, any school continues to do so, the reason must lie in the inspector's acting on only half of his instructions'. So it is the inspector's neglect of duty which appears to be in fault. But I ask again – suppose the Inspector were to produce a book out of his pocket, and to pluck all the children who could not read fluently from it, would the Department sustain him? The managers would appeal to the Code, which says that the scholar shall be required to read 'a paragraph from a reading book used in the school'. It is just the weakness of a system which attempts to prescribe exactly the *minimum* which shall be done, and which makes it highly penal to fall short of this *minimum*, that when the *minimum* is somehow produced, there seems a good deal of hardship in still exacting a penalty. If the Inspector inflicted deductions to any such extent as really to grapple with the evil of mechanical teaching, I cannot but think that he would find himself in collision with that very necessary official notification concerning the power of inflicting deductions, which he received at the outset – *My Lords do not wish this power to be exercised in any but serious cases.*

Again, it is urged that an Inspector is not forbidden by the Revised Code to retain 'a liberal and intelligent inspection' along with the new examination, and that an inspector who has an assistant has ample time for such inspection. But the question is, not whether an Inspector can make such an inspection, but whether the school will care much for it when it is the new examination which brings the grant, and whether it will do as much good as it formerly did when it is no longer much cared for.

All test examinations, it is said again, may be said to narrow reading upon a certain given point, and to make it mechanical. If a man wants a certificate or diploma of you, you say you will give it him if he learns this and that, which you prescribe; and you may be said to cramp his studies by thus limiting them. Certainly, if a man wants a certificate, or a diploma, or honours, of you, you must fix just what he shall get them for, which is by no means of the same extent as a liberal education. But this is a reason against making an excessive use of such test examinations, of turning too much of a man's reading into reading for certificates, diplomas, or honours. That is why our University system of examinations, competitions, and honours is so little favoured in Germany.* But, at any rate, to make a narrowing system of test examinations govern the whole inspection of our primary schools, when we have before us, not individuals wanting a diploma from us, but organizations wanting to be guided by us into the best ways of learning and teaching, seems like saddling ourselves with a confessed cause of imperfection unnecessarily.

Admitting the stimulus of the test examination to be salutary, we may therefore yet say that when it is over-employed it has two faults: it tends to make the instruction mechanical, and to set a bar to duly extending it. School grants earned in the way fixed by the Revised Code – by the scholar performing a certain *minimum* expressly laid down beforehand – must inevitably concentrate the teacher's attention on the means for producing this *minimum*, and not simply on the good instruction of his school. The danger to be guarded against is the mistake of treating these two – the producing this *minimum* successfully and the good instruction of a school – as if they were identical. The safeguard seems to be in reducing the overwhelming preponderance of this examination and its results, at the same time that we retain all its useful stimulus.

In my report two years ago I said: '*More free play for the Inspector, and, in consequence, more free play for the teacher.*' As long as the whole grant-earning examination turns on results precisely and literally specified by the

* The least studious of German countries, Austria, is the one most abounding in university examinations like our own. 'Le pays à examens, l'Autriche, est précisément celui dans lequel on ne travaille pas,' says M. Laboulaye.

Department beforehand, so long the inspection will be mechanical and unintelligent, and it will inevitably draw the teaching after it.

It will be remembered that the Duke of Newcastle's Commission attached great importance to leaving *inspection* just as it was, the new capitation-grant examination being, therefore, kept subordinate to it, and committed to a subordinate functionary; for when, practically, the substantive result of the Inspector's proceedings in a school is the grant for this examination, it will, whatever the Department may say, efface everything else.

The Newcastle Commission proposed 15s. per head as the *maximum* grant to be earned per scholar. Our actual *maximum* is 12s. per head, the grant under the Minute of February being so insignificant (about £13,000, I think, last year for the whole of England), that it is not worth taking into account. Of this 12s. 4d. is maintenance grant, paid on average attendance; 8s. is capitation grant on examination in reading, writing and ciphering.

Some such plan as the following seems to be calculated to temper what is excessive and retain what is useful in the system now in force: suppose, the 4s. grant on attendance being left as it is, the examination grant were reduced from 8s. to 6s.; 2s. on reading, 2s. on writing, 2s. on arithmetic, instead of 2s. 8d. on each of these branches as at present. To the 2s. thus saved let there be added a third shilling, making a 3s. grant on average attendance, to be paid if the Inspector finds the school taught with *intelligence*, if he finds *proper extent* given to the instruction, if he finds the work done *in good form and style*, and if, finally, the staff of pupil-teachers is not less than one for every forty scholars after the first twenty-five. The Inspector to have the power to recommend the reduction of this higher instruction grant by thirds for failure in any one of the three first points specified. The fourth point to be a condition of the grant being paid at all.

The stipulation in point the third (that as to *form and style* of work) would give the Department an opportunity of checking the Inspector's recommendations and verifying their accuracy, because the paper work of the Fourth, Fifth, and Sixth Standards, in which this merit of *form and style* would chiefly appear, is sent up to the Department. But some confidence must be reposed in the Inspector if the inspection is to have any life at all.

Thus there would be three grants, an *attendance grant* of 4s., an *elementary examination grant* of 6s., a *higher instruction grant* of 3s.; total grant to be earned, 13s. The need for grants under the Minute of February, and for that Minute itself, would cease. The reduced grant for elementary examination might, perhaps, be made earnable by schools not under certificated teachers, if they were reported healthy, properly fitted, and conducted with due order.

The Department might with advantage recommend managers to pay out of the higher instruction grant a sum to the principal teacher not less than the sum he would formerly have received as gratuity for instructing his pupil-teachers. The recommendation would be sufficient in general without an absolute appropriation of the grant or a part of it; but the Department might also reserve the power of withholding the grant altogether in cases where it appeared from the Inspector's report that the recommendation was disregarded without fully sufficient cause. Some encouragement of this kind to make teachers seek diligently for pupil-teachers, and cordially instruct them, I look upon as almost indispensable if our pupil-teacher system is again to become what it once was, and what our coming wants require. The institution also of a system of superannuation grants for teachers cannot be much longer delayed.

Several of my colleagues have said how acceptable and useful the yearly volume of minutes and reports issued by the Committee of Council would be to the teachers of schools under inspection. Blue-books are often reproached with being costly to produce and unread when produced; it seems a pity not to convey the Education Blue Book to quarters where it would be read with keen interest and turned to practical use.

The questions of compulsory schooling, gratuitous schooling, secular schooling, are rapidly passing out of the sphere of abstract discussion, and entering into the sphere of practical politics. In that sphere, however they may be settled, it will not and cannot be on their merits; and it seems vain to repeat the considerations proper to one sphere when the matter is about to be settled in another. As to compulsory schooling, I will only say that in no country is the text '*The bread of the needy is their life; he that depriveth them therof is a man of blood*', felt with so much force as here; that a law of direct compulsion on the parent and child would therefore, probably, be every day violated in practice; and that, so long as this is the case, to a law levelled at the parent and child, a law levelled at the employer is preferable. As to gratuitous schooling, which is supposed to follow necessarily upon compulsory schooling, I will only remark that in Prussia, where schooling is compulsory, and really compulsory, there is no primary school which does not levy a school fee, though a low one.

There remains the question of secular schooling, and this is a question of which the solution is above all likely to be governed by politics, lay or religious, and, by being so governed, may do serious harm to education. I address myself on this point to the managers of British schools, with many of whom I have an acquaintance of now nearly twenty years. One of the main objects for which their schools were instituted was to promote the knowledge of the Bible. That this or any other branch of instruction will be really provided for by the Sunday school no serious educationist believes; but neither is it really provided for if it is withdrawn from inspection. My own observation, my inquiries, and the entries of the teachers in their log-books, all convince me that the knowledge of the Bible in British schools is not what their managers would wish it to be. The other day, in a school where the managers were so solicitous for this instruction that they begged me to hear and take part in an examination in it, the question was asked in the boys' school, 'Of whom was it said, '*Behold an Israelite indeed in whom is no guile*', and who said it?' Not a boy could tell. The same question was asked in the girls' school in the afternoon with the same result. This does not surprise me, for it follows naturally from the Bible knowledge of the children being wholly excluded from the matters which appear in the school's inspection. Let the managers of British schools set an example which other managers also, if they are wise, may follow. Let them make the main outlines of Bible history, and the getting by heart a selection of the finest Psalms, the most interesting passages from the historical and prophetical books of the Old Testament, and the chief parables, discourses, and exhortations of the New, a part of the regular school work, to be submitted to inspection and to be seen in its strength or weakness like any other. This could raise no jealousies; or, if it still raises some, let a sacrifice be made of them for the sake of the end in view. Some will say that what we propose is but a small use to put the Bible to; yet it is that on which all higher use of the Bible is to be built, and its adoption is the only chance for saving the one elevating and inspiring element in the scanty instruction of our primary schools from being sacrificed to a politico-religious difficulty. There was no Greek school in which Homer was not read; cannot our popular schools, with their narrow range and their jejune alimentation in secular literature, do as much for the Bible as the Greek schools did for Homer?

Report for 1880

I find that of the specific subjects English literature, as it is too ambitiously called – in plain truth the learning by heart and reciting of a hundred lines or two of standard English poetry – continues to be by far the most popular. I rejoice to find it so; there is no fact coming under my observation in the working of our elementary schools which gives me so much satisfaction. The acquisition of good poetry is a discipline which works deeper than any other discipline in the range of work of our schools; more than any other, too, it works of itself, is independent of the school teacher, and cannot be spoiled by pedantry and injudiciousness on his part. Some people regard this my high estimate of the value of poetry in education with suspicion and displeasure. Perhaps they may accept the testimony of Wordsworth with less suspicion than mine. Wordsworth says, 'To be incapable of a feeling of poetry, in my sense of the word, is to be without love of human nature and reverence for God'. And it is only through acquaintance with poetry and with good poetry, that this 'feeling of poetry' can be given.

Good poetry does undoubtedly tend to form the soul and character; it tends to beget a love of beauty and of truth in alliance together, it suggests, however indirectly, high and noble principles of action, and it inspires the emotion so helpful in making principles operative. Hence its extreme importance to all of us; but in our elementary schools its importance seems to me to be at present quite extraordinary. I hope that, instead of its being confined to children in the Fifth and Sixth Standards, this excellent discipline of poetry will be retained for the children of the Fourth Standard, and brought into use universally for at least these three standards.

Happily, the poetry exercise has, as I have said already, become popular in schools, and it will, I am confident, become more and more so. Sir John Lubbock says that in some board schools in Lambeth he asked the children which they preferred of four of their subjects of instruction – grammar, history, geography, and elementary science – and that a very large majority were in favour of elementary science. I do not quite understand how he took his comparison; he does not mention whether the children whose votes he took were all of them learning all these four subjects or not. But, at any rate, if he will come into Westminster and will ask the children in the schools there who are taking two class subjects and two specific subjects, poetry being one of these latter, which of the four they prefer, I think I can assure him that he will find a most decisive majority for poetry.[1]

The choice of passages to be learnt is of the utmost importance, and requires close and intelligent observing of the children. Some years ago it was the fashion to make them learn Goldsmith's *Deserted Village*, at the recommendation, I believe, of the late Lord Lyndhurst; or rather, he had given high praise to this poem, and recommended it as a poem to be got by heart, and so it was supposed that the children in our elementary schools might with advantage learn it. Nothing could be more completely unsuitable for them, and this being soon proved by the event, the use of the poem for the purpose in question has happily almost ceased. That the poetry chosen should have real beauties of expression and feeling, that these beauties should be such as the children's hearts and minds can lay hold of, and that a distinct point or centre of beauty and interest should occur within the limits of the passage learnt, all these are conditions to be insisted upon.

Some of the short pieces by Mrs Hemans, such as *The Graves of a Household, The Homes of England, The Better Land*, are to be recommended, because they fulfil all three conditions; they have real merits of expression and sentiment, the merits are such as the children can feel, and the centre of interest, these pieces being so short, necessarily occurs within the limits of what is learnt. On the other hand, in extracts taken from Scott and Shakespeare, the point of interest is often not reached within the hundred lines which is all that children in the Fourth Standard learn. The judgement scene in *The Merchant of Venice* affords me a good example of what I mean. Taken as a whole, this famous scene has, I need not say, great power; it is dramatic poetry of the first order, it is also well within our school children's comprehension, and very interesting to them. Teachers are fond of selecting it to be learnt by heart, and they are quite right. But what happens is this. The children in the Fourth Standard begin at the beginning, and stop at the end of 100 lines; now, the children in the Fourth Standard are often a majority of the children learning poetry, and this is all their poetry for the year. But within these hundred lines the real interest of the situation is not reached, neither do they contain any poetry of signal beauty and effectiveness. How little, therefore, has the poetry exercise been made to do for these children, many of whom will leave school at once, and learn no more poetry! The conclusion I wish to draw is, that the teacher should always take care that the year's poetry of a class shall contain the best poetry in the piece chosen for them, and the central point of interest in it; not be mere prelude and introduction to this centre of interest. To secure this, the teacher may without scruple plunge into the middle of a scene of a passage, and make his children take their 100 lines there explaining to them, of course, the situation at the point where they begin. If they remain another year, they can take a new passage or scene under the same conditions. This is a far better course than to throw a year away, as is frequently done now, upon comparatively ineffective poetry, with the intention that the child, if he remains at school, may next year continue the same passage and reach the point of interest.

I insist at such length upon this poetry exercise, because of the increasing use of it, and because of its extreme importance. Stress is laid upon the necessity of the children knowing thoroughly the meaning of what they recite, and it is assumed that to secure their knowing this is the simplest matter in the world, and that not to secure it proves inexcusable negligence in the teacher. I am more and more refusing to pass children who do not know the meaning of words which occur in what they recite, but I proceed gradually and with caution. If I had begun by rigidly rejecting every child ignorant of the meaning of every word in what he recited, I should never have got the poetry exercise established in my schools at all. The scanty vocabulary of our school children, and their correspondent narrow range of ideas, must be known and allowed for if one is to guide their instruction usefully. I have found in London schools children of twelve years old, able to pass well in reading, writing and arithmetic, who yet did not know what 'a steed' was. I found in a good school the other day a head class of some thirty, only one of whom knew what 'a ford' was. 'Steed' is a literary word, 'ford' is a word of country life, not of town life; still they are words, one is apt to think, universally understood by every one above five years old. But even common words of this kind are not universally understood by the children with whom we deal. Very many words are in their reading lessons passed over as certainly known to them, to which they attach no meaning at all, or a wrong one. The poetry exercise is invaluable by causing words to be dwelt upon and canvassed, by leading the children to grasp the meaning of new words, and by thus extending the range of their ideas. But the slowness and difficulty of the process, which are as incontestable as its high value, must be borne in mind, and we must have patience with that slowness and difficulty.

I should like, above all, to see this poetry exercise made no longer an extra subject, but a part of the regular work of the school, which would then consist of the three elementary matters, of the class subjects, and of this. And I repeat what I said in my last report, that I see no good reason at all for keeping the fourth schedule, or schedule of extra subjects, on its present footing. Provision is now made in the Code for teaching elementary science as a class subject; grammar, geography, physical geography, history and domestic economy are also class subjects. Others may be added at pleasure; and the fourth schedule is really, therefore, superfluous in respect of many of its subjects, since why should physical geography, domestic economy and certain branches of natural science do double duty, both as class subjects and as extra subjects? Extra subjects ought properly, as the name implies, to be subjects not for whole classes and sections of a school, but for certain forward scholars who may with advantage go on to a higher school, and need some previous preparation for it. I think the Manchester Grammar School requires, from boys admitted to it from elementary schools, besides the matters of elementary school instruction, some knowledge also of geometry, French, and Latin. And this, in my opinion, suggests just what our fourth schedule should be; it should be designed to meet the case of the few picked scholars who win a passage up into higher schools, and it should include only these matters of geometry, French, and Latin, without which the higher schools will not admit them. Algebra, mechanics, mensuration, and German are not required for a boy's admission to a higher school. But they are not class subjects, it will be answered, and unless you put them into the fourth schedule, there will be no provision for teaching them at all. I answer that for the children in our elementary schools, children under thirteen, there is no need or use of a provision for teaching them at all.

But Sir John Lubbock says that we wish our own children to study a variety of subjects, and why not the children in elementary schools? And an earnest and widely lamented friend of popular education said once, I remember, that he should like to have Greek and Sanscrit taught to the children in board schools, if it were possible. Aspirations safeguarded by an *if it were possible* cannot, it may be thought, do much harm; nevertheless such aspirations do tend to make us lose sight of the actual present conditions of our problem in popular education, and so far they do harm. Sir John Lubbock talks of the variety of subjects which we make our own children study, and I am not at all sure that we do not make them study too great a variety. But at any rate, there is this difference: take thirty of our own children between the ages of ten and thirteen, and you will not find one of them who does not know what *a steed* is or what *a ford* is. You have, therefore, a totally different material to work upon. And even to talk of lessons in Greek and Sanscrit for such scholars as those whom in our elementary schools we have to deal with, is dangerous trifling, because it tends to make us forget the pressing reality.

Not that the ideal which we should propose to ourselves for the school-course in these schools is not a high or a large one. It is the ideal admirably fixed long ago by Comenius, an early and wise school reformer, who is now too much forgotten. 'The aim is', says Comenius, 'to train generally all who are born men to all which is human.' Without pedantry and without platitudes, we should all seek to reach this aim in the most practical manner.

It may be said that there are at present but three obligatory subjects in our schools, fewer, by much, than in the schools anywhere else. Our only obligatory matters of instruction are reading, writing and arithmetic. An aided school is not required to teach anything besides these. But additional grants are offered for teaching as class subjects any two of the following: geography, natural history, physical geography, natural philosophy, history, social economy, grammar, and, in the case of girls, needlework. To this list additions may be made. Grants are further offered for teaching as extra, or specific, subjects any two of the following: English literature, mathematics, Latin, French, German, mechanics, animal physiology, physical geography, botany, and, in the case of girls, domestic economy. Finally, a grant is offered for teaching music. Evidently there is here a very complicated arrangement; but I will not touch upon that now. The point for notice is that we have three matters of instruction which are obligatory, and nineteen or more which are optional, or, as our French neighbours say, facultative, but encouraged by grants. However, for only five of these facultative matters can grants be claimed in one and the same year by a school: for two class subjects, two extra or specific subjects, and music. Apparently, it is thought by many people that, except religious instruction no instruction whatever will be given for which a grant cannot be claimed. And Sir John Lubbock is afraid that if the fourth schedule is swept away, a child will get no secular instruction except in the three obligatory matters, in two of the facultative matters assigned as class subjects, and in music. And this is plainly insufficient. A girl of twelve ought not to be learning too many things, but she ought to be learning more than reading, writing and arithmetic, a little English grammar, needlework, and singing. A boy of twelve ought to be learning more than the matters here enumerated, even though geography or elementary natural science be in his case added in lieu of needlework.

It is not my province to discuss our present mode of making grants, which leads to such difficulties in forming a proper programme of school instruction. I will only remark, in passing, that of our forms of payment for results by far the best form is the grant for class subjects, which turns upon the performance not of each individual child, but of the class. Only there should be provision for withholding this grant in respect of a class which decidedly fails to earn it, while paying it to the classes which do earn it. At present there is no such provision; the grant has to be paid for the whole body of classes claiming it, or refused for the whole body. But what I wish now to do is to suggest to teachers the sort of programme they should strive to establish for the instruction in their schools, leaving the Government grants to adjust themselves to that programme as they may.

Besides the obligatory matters laid down in the Code, and leaving out of view religious instruction, needlework for girls, domestic economy, cookery, technical instruction of whatever kind, and drill and gymnastics, a teacher should in general endeavour to teach to all children of the Second and Third Standards something of poetry or poetic literature, grammar, geography, *Natur-kunde* or elementary natural science, and music. For the standards above he should add to these history. So that, in general, our school children, of from eight years of age to ten, should all be receiving instruction in these eight matters, reading, writing, arithmetic, poetry, or poetic literature, grammar, geography, *Natur-kunde*, and music. Our school children of from ten years of age to thirteen should all be receiving more advanced instruction in these eight matters, with history as a ninth matter, added. And a picked few of these older children should be taught, further, the rudiments of French and Latin, and elementary geometry.

Religious instruction stands by itself, and will be regulated in each school according to circumstances. The other matters which I have left out of view – needlework, domestic economy, cookery, technical instruction, gymnastics and drill – have all of them their importance as things to be taught, some of them their necessity. But parts of mental training they none of them directly are; and however the Code may mix them up with such, they should resolutely, in the teacher's view, be kept separate from them.

A school earns the bulk of its grant on passes in the three obligatory matters, and on the attendance. The attraction of the smaller grants for class subjects and extra subjects should not be allowed to waste the teaching of a school, and to make it intricate and confused. A rational programme, simply carried out, should be the great object: five or six matters added, as a part of the regular school course to the three elementary matters, and taught to the children in their classes. A teacher may say: 'Oh, but the Code tells me to prepare a class of children to pass, say, in physical geography as a class subject, and then to prepare, again, the same children to pass individually in physical geography as a specific subject. I must find time for both, and the kind of preparation required for earning the two grants is not the same.' Or a teacher may say: 'You advise me to make a part of the regular school course, but the Code will not let a girl bring us a grant for poetry unless she first gets up a handbook of domestic economy, a subject not in your programme, and for which I have not time.' I answer: 'The Code does not *compel* you to do as you say; it offers you a few shillings for doing so. If in this respect the intricate arrangements of the Code conflict with the due following out of a good programme, disregard them, and sacrifice the few shillings of grant.' School boards, which have other public resources than the parliamentary grant, should certainly adopt this course as regards the grants for class subjects and specific subjects. Their first object should be a sound programme of instruction simply followed out; if our over-complicated machinery for grants on class subjects and on specific subjects is found to interfere with the due following out of a sound programme, that machinery is likely in process of time to be amended, and meantime, the programme should not be sacrificed to it. The remarks on school studies which come from the Inspectors of the London School Board seem to me to be in general full of good sense. These Inspectors should do their utmost to get good programmes established, not dependent on the Code's regulation of its minor grants; and the board should assist their action. In some directions I cannot but think the board's outlay excessive, but I should welcome some outlay for a purpose like this.

I see it urged by the National Union of Elementary Teachers that to require parsing from children of the Fourth Standard, who are examined in grammar, is too much, and that it is enough if these children learn the parts of speech. I watch with great interest the representations with regard to school instruction which come from teachers, and on several important points in which the teachers desire a change, I am, as I have often declared, in agreement with them. As to this particular point of the grammar to be required in the Fourth Standard, I notice it because I attach such great importance to grammar as leading the children to reflect and reason, as a very simple sort of logic, more effective than arithmetic as a logical training, because it operates with concretes, or words, instead of with abstract or figures. In general, I am not at all averse to a proposal that we should require less from the learner and that what he learns should be learned better; and I think that some of what we now require in grammar is over-subtle and unprofitable.

But parsing is the very best of the discipline of grammar, and it is not too hard for Fourth Standard children, if it is taught judiciously. The analytic character of our language enables a teacher to bring its grammar more easily within a child's reach; an advantage should be taken of this analytic character, instead of teaching English grammar as was the old plan, with a machinery borrowed from the grammar of synthetic languages. I am glad to observe that in the instruction of pupil-teachers the analytic method of parsing is coming into use more and more. The metaphysics of mood and tense are what puzzle children; now, the real characters of mood and tense are remarkably absent from our language, and of what remains of them an important part, the subjunctive mood, is more and more passing out of actual use. In the expressions, 'If he live', 'If he be dead', *live* and *be* are real subjunctives; but we are more and more ceasing to use them, and we say, 'If he lives', 'If he is dead'. To call 'He may love', or 'He might love' subjunctives or potentials because 'amet' or 'amaret' are subjunctives or potentials in Latin, is as absurd as it would be to call μέλλετε ἀποθνήσκειν in the relaxed Greek of the New Testament (if ye live after the flesh, ye shall die), a future tense because the future would have been used in classical Greek. Teachers will find that by following the analytic method in English grammar they save the children's minds from much puzzle, enable them to understand more readily the employment of case, mood, and tense, where they do occur, and beget in them an interest in what is one of the most naturally interesting of things – language. And at the same time they are teaching English grammar in the true philosophical way.

The teachers object, again, to the rule that class subjects shall be taught through reading lessons and according to schemes previously approved by the Inspectors. They would prefer to have a scheme laid down in the Code for graduated examination in them. Sir John Lubbock, who speaks with great authority upon such a matter, observes that, at any rate, 'to teach scientific subjects through reading lessons is the worst way in which they could be taught.' He says that on these subjects 'it is much better that the instruction should be given orally and with the aid of the blackboard.' I have myself the greatest respect for oral teaching with the aid of the blackboard, and am inclined to limit its freedom neither by reading lessons to serve as texts, nor by schemes of my own devising, nor even by any schemes laid down in the Code. I shall show the utmost readiness in accepting practical endeavours to teach class subjects according to the wants and capacities of the classes to be taught. But as elementary science is new as a class subject, I should be glad if the teachers of my district would bear in mind, in making their plans for teaching it, that here is a line where our proceedings must at first be tentative, and where we have great need to keep our eyes and minds open.

Tentative, indeed, should very much more of our school proceedings be considered than the lessons in elementary science only. It is impossible to see an institution like the district school at Norwood, which I had lately the pleasure of visiting with Mr Chadwick, without feeling that the case of the advocates for short-time schooling, balanced by an equal or nearly equal time of industrial training and of well-planned bodily exercise, deserves, at any rate, serious attention. Industrial training, domestic economy and cookery should not be mixed up with the school work proper, but they have a very high value when well arranged as a whole by themselves, to alternate with it and balance it. Bodily exercise, also, and recreation, deserve far more care in our schools than they receive. We take too little thought for the bodies of our school children, we are too intent on forcing more and still more into their minds, unregardful how easily the attention, at their age, may be over-tired. True, the children in our elementary schools are not like the boys whom I saw exercising to the sound of music at Norwood – boys, very many of whom have to be weaned by judicious physical training from a native preference for sitting still in corners telling one another Jack Sheppard stories. But neither are they like the boys in the schools where we ourselves were brought up, boys living under such favourable conditions that their physical development may in general be trusted to take care of itself. In London at all events, and in our great towns generally, the children frequenting elementary schools are by no means living under such favourable conditions. Short-time schooling, organized as in large towns it is easy to organize it, and balanced by industrial training and bodily exercises, is actually more effective, so its advocates maintain, than our present long-time schooling, besides its evident advantages in giving health and hardiness, and besides its great saving of expense. A large urban school with two sides to it, a school side and an industrial and gymnastical side, built for a thousand children, becomes available for twice that number if one-half of the children use each side for one-half of the day, and the other half for the other.

The question of expense, as I said in my last report, is a very serious one and becomes more and more serious. The cost on each child in average attendance in the London board schools is now very nearly £3 for London in general, and above £3 for my own district, Westminster. But on the grave topic of the board's expenditure I shall not now enlarge. Meanwhile the teachers must not take an old friend for their enemy, because he says that the impossible cannot last, and that in attempting to put the immense, ever-extending service of popular education on such a footing of expense as the board does, it attempts the impossible. I hope for and I foresee a good future for our teachers, but not by those means.

Ecce, Convertimur ad Gentes (1879)[1]

I cannot help asking myself how I come to be standing here tonight. It not unfrequently happens to me, indeed, to be invited to make addresses and to take part in public meetings – above all in meetings where the matter of interest is education; probably because I was sent, in former days, to acquaint myself with the schools and education of the Continent, and have published reports and books about them. But I make it a general rule to decline the invitation. I am a school-inspector under the Committee of Council on Education, and the Department which I serve would object, and very properly object, to have its inspectors starring it about the country, making speeches on education. An inspector must naturally be prone to speak of that education of which he has particular cognizance, the education which is administered by his own Department, and he might be supposed to let out the views and policy of his Department. Whether the inspectors really knew and gave the Department's views or not, their speeches might equally be a cause of embarrassment to their official superiors.

However, I have no intention of compromising my official superiors by talking to you about that branch of education which they are concerned in administering – elementary education. And if I express a desire that they should come to occupy themselves with other branches of education too, branches with which they have at present no concern, you may be quite sure that this is a private wish of my own, not at all prompted by my Department.

You may rely upon it, that the very last thing desired by that Department itself, is to invade the provinces of education which are now independent of it. Nobody will ever be able to accuse the Committee of Council of carrying an Afghanistan war into those provinces, when it might have remained quietly within its own borders. There is a Latin law-maxim which tells us that it is the business of a good judge to seek to extend his jurisdiction – *boni judicis est ampliare jurisdictionem.* That may be characteristic of a good judge, but it is not characteristic of a British Government in domestic affairs generally, certainly not in the concerns of education.

And for this reason: because the British Government is an aristocratic government. Such a government is entirely free from the faults of what is commonly called a bureaucracy. It is not meddlesome, not fussy, not prone to seek importance for itself by meddling with everybody and everything; it is by nature disposed to leave individuals and localities to settle their own affairs for themselves as much as possible. The action of individuals and localities, left to themselves, proves insufficient in this point and in that; then the State is forced to intervene. But what I say is, that in all those domestic matters, such as the regulation of workhouses, or of factories, or of schools, where the State has, with us, been forced to intervene, it is not our aristocratic executive which has sought the right of intervention, it is public opinion which has imposed the duty of intervention upon our aristocratic executive. Our aristocratic system may have its faults, but the mania for State interference everywhere is not one of them. Above all, in regard to education this has been conspicuously the case. Government did not move in the matter while it could avoid moving.

Of course, even when it was at last obliged to move, there were some people to be found who cried out against it for moving. In the early days of the Committee of Council, one clergyman wrote that he was not going to suffer Lord John Russell, 'or any other Turkish Bashaw', to send an inspector into his schools; and Archdeacon Denison threatened, as is well known, to have the poor inspector drowned in a horsepond. But these were eccentric men, living in a fantastic world of their own. To men who inhabit the real world, it was abundantly apparent that our Government moved in the matter of public education as late as it could, that it moved as slowly as it could, as inoffensively as it could; and that throughout, instead of stimulating public opinion to give it additional powers, it has confined itself to cautiously accepting and discharging the functions which public opinion has insisted on laying upon it.

You may be sure that this will continue to be the case; that if more part in public education comes to be assigned to the Government in this country, it is not that the Government seeks it, it is that the growth of opinion will compel the Government to undertake it. So that if I speak of the desirableness of extending to a further class of schools the action of the State, it is well understood that I am not, as in bureaucratic Prussia I might be, revealing the secret aims and ambitions of the Education Department. All the aims of that Department have been clearly manifested to be the other way.

Well, but why am I here? I am here, in the first place, because I heard that your Working Men's College, which holds its annual meeting tonight, and which I was asked to address, is the largest body of the kind in England. Bodies of this kind, with their classes, their lectures, their libraries, their aspirations, are a testimony, however poor and imperfect may be the use often made of them, they are, as it seems to me, a testimony, they are a profession of faith, which is both affecting and valuable. They are a profession of belief in the saving power of light and intelligence, a profession of belief in the use and in the practicability of trying to know *oneself* and the world, *to follow*, as Dante says, *virtue and knowledge*.

No one can accuse us English, as a nation, of being too forward with such professions of faith in the things of the mind. No one can accuse us of not showing ourselves enough aware, how little good may in many cases come from professions of this sort, how much they may disappoint us, what a contrast their performance often is to their promise, how much they often bring with them which is hollow and nonsensical. We are very shy, as every one knows, of all public homage to the power of science and letters. We have no National Institute. In a short time there will be held in Paris a reception, and it is called, of one of the most famous men of letters in France, or indeed in all Europe – M. Renan – at the French Academy. That reception, and the discourse of the new member, will be for our neighbours over in France one of the very foremost events of the year. Hardly any parliamentary field-day will call forth greater interest and excitement. Every one will want to be present, every one will be eager to know what is said, every one will discuss what is said. We English keenly feel the unreality, as we call it, which attends displays of this kind. We prefer that our own celebrations should be for incidents of a more practical character; should be such as the dinner and speechifying, for instance, at the opening of the annual season for the Buckhounds.

But above all, we are on our guard against expecting too much from institutions like this Working Men's College. We are reminded what grand expectations Lord Brougham and the other friends of knowledge cheap and popular, the founders of the Mechanics' Institutes, held out; what tall talk they indulged in; and we are told to look and see how little has come of it all. Nature herself fights against them and their designs, we are told. At the end of his day, tired with his labour, the working man in general cannot well have the power, even if he have the will, to make any very serious and fruitful efforts in the pursuit of knowledge. Whatever high professions these institutions may start with, inevitably their members will come, it is said, to decline upon a lower range of claim and endeavour. They will come to content themselves with seeking mere amusement and relaxation from their Institute. They will visit its reading-rooms merely to read the newspapers, to read novels; and they are not to be blamed for it.

No, perhaps they are not to be blamed for it, even if this does happen. And yet the original, lofty aspiration, the aspiration after the satisfactions, solace, and power which are only to be got from true knowledge, may have been right after all. In spite of the frequent disappointment, the constant difficulty, it may have been right. For to arrive at a full and right conception of things, to know one's self and the world – which is knowledge; then to act firmly and manfully on that knowledge – which is virtue; this is the native, the indestructible impulse of the spirit of man. All the high-flown commonplaces about the power of knowledge, and about the mind's instinctive desire of it, have their great use, whenever we can so put them as to feel them animating and inspiring to us. For they are true in themselves; only they are discredited by being so often used insincerely. The profession of faith of institutes like your College, that knowledge is power, that there is an intelligible law of things, that the human mind seeks to arrive at it, and that our welfare depends on our arriving at it and obeying it, this profession of faith, I say, is sound in itself, it is precious, and we do well to insist upon it. It puts in due prominence a quality which does not always get enough regard in this country – intelligence.

Goethe, the great poet of Germany, and the greatest critic, perhaps, that has ever lived, went so far as to say boldly of our nation (which, notwithstanding, he highly esteemed and admired): *der Engländer ist eigentlich ohne Intelligenz* – 'the Englishman is, properly speaking, without intelligence'. Goethe by no means meant to say that the Englishman was stupid. All he meant was, that the Englishman is singularly without a keen sense of there being an intelligible law of things, and of its being our urgent business to ascertain it and to make our doings conform to it. He meant that the Englishman is particularly apt to take as the rule of things what is customary, or what falls in with his prepossessions and prejudices, and to act upon this stoutly and without any misgiving, as if it were the real natural rule of things. He meant that the Englishman does not much like to be told that there is a real natural rule of things, presenting itself to the intelligence; to be told that our action, however energetic, is not safe unless it complies with this real and intelligible rule. And I think Goethe was right here, and that the Englishman, from his insularity, and from his strength, and from some want of suppleness in his mind, does often answer to the description which Goethe gives of him.

Now it is a grave thing, this indifference to the real natural and rational rule of things, because it renders us very liable to be found fighting against nature, and that is always calamitous. And so I come at last to the entire reason for my being here tonight. There is a point, in which our action, as a community, seems to me quite at variance with what the rational rule of things would prescribe, and where we all suffer by its being thus at variance. I have tried in vain for twenty years to make the parties most directly concerned see the mischief of the present state of things. I want to interest you in the matter. I speak to you as a Working Men's College, the largest in England, representing the profession of faith that what we need is intelligence, the power to see things as they really are, and to shape our action accordingly. I look upon you, I say, as representing that profession of faith, and representing it as entertained by the class of working men. You, too, are concerned in the failure which I want to remedy, though not directly concerned in it. But you *are* concerned in it, and that gravely; we are all gravely concerned in it.

You will, I am sure, suffer me to speak to you with perfect frankness, even though what I say should offend some of those who hear me. My address is to the class of working men; but there are present before me tonight, I know, hearers from other classes too. However, the only possible use of my coming here would be lost if I did not speak to you with perfect frankness. I am no politician. I have no designs upon your borough, or upon any borough, or upon parliamentary honours at all. Indeed, I have no very ardent interest – if you will allow me to speak for a moment of myself and of what interests me – in politics in their present state in this country. What interests me is English civilization; and our politics in their present state do not seem to me to have much bearing upon that.

English civilization – the humanizing, the bringing into one harmonious and truly humane life, of the whole body of English society – that is what interests me. I try to be a disinterested observer of all which really helps and hinders that. Certain hindrances seem to me to be present with us, and certain helps to be wanting to us. An isolated observer may easily be mistaken, and his observations greatly require the test which other minds can exert upon them. If I fail to carry you with me in what seems to me to be perfectly clear, that is against the soundness of my observations and conclusions. But that I may have the chance of carrying you with me, it is necessary that I should speak to you with entire frankness. Then it will appear whether your aid, or the aid of any among you, is to be had for removing what seems to me one great hindrance, and for providing what seems to me one great help, to our civilization.

For twenty years, then – ever since I had to go about the Continent to learn what the schools were like there, and observed at the same time the people for whom the schools existed and the conditions of their life, and compared it with what was to be found at home – ever since that time, I have felt convinced that for the progress of our civilization, here in England, three things were above all necessary: a reduction of those immense inequalities of condition and property amongst us, of which our land-system is the base; a genuine municipal system; and public schools for the middle classes. I do not add popular education. Even so long as twenty years ago, popular education was already launched. I was myself continually a witness of the progress it was making; I could see that the cause of popular education was safe. The three points, then, were reduction of our immense inequalities of condition and property, a municipal system extended all through the country, and public schools for the middle classes. These points are hardly dreamed of in our present politics, any one of them.

Take the first of the three. Mr Gladstone, who ought to know, ridicules the very notion of a cry for equality in this country; he says that the idea of equality has never had the slightest influence upon English politics; nay, that, on the contrary, we have the religion of inequality. There is, indeed, a little bill brought forward in Parliament year after year – the Real Estates Intestacy Bill – which proposes that there should be equality in the division of a man's land amongst his children after his death, in case he happens to die without a will. It is answered, that if a man wants his land to go thus equally amongst his children, he has only just to take the trouble of making a will to that effect; and that, in the absence of a will, his land had better follow the rule of the present general system of landed inheritance in this country, a system which works well. And nothing more is said, except, perhaps, that one hears a few timid words of complaint about the hardship inflicted upon younger children by this system.

But, for my part, I am not so much concerned about the younger children. My objection to the present system is not on their account; but because I think that, putting their supposed natural rights quite out of the question, the present system does not work well now at all, but works altogether badly. I think that now, however it may have worked formerly, the system tends to materialize our upper class, vulgarize our middle class, brutalize our lower class. If it does not do that, I have no other objection to make to it. I do not believe in *any* natural rights; I do not believe in a natural right, in each of a man's children, to his or her equal share of the father's property. I have no objection to the eldest son taking all the land, or the youngest son, or the middle daughter, on one condition: that this state of things shall really work well, that it shall be for the public advantage.

Once our present system of landed inheritance had its real reason and justification – it worked well. When the modern nations of Europe were slowly building themselves up out of the chaos left by the dissolution of the Roman empire, a number of local centres were needed for the process, with a strong hereditary headman over each; and this natural need the feudal land-system met. It seems to me, it has long seemed to me, that, the circumstances being now quite changed, our system of immense inequalities of condition and property works not well but badly, has the natural reason of things not for it but against it. It seems to me that the natural function is gone for which an aristocratic class with great landed estates was required; and that when the function is gone, and the great estates with an infinitely multiplied power of ministering to mere pleasure and indulgence remain, the class owning them inevitably comes to be materialized, and the more so the more the development of industry and ingenuity augments the means of luxury.

The action of such a class materializes all the class of newly enriched people as they rise. The middle class, having above them this materialized upper class, with a wealth and luxury utterly out of their reach, with a standard of social life and manners, the offspring of that wealth and luxury, seeming utterly out of their reach also, are inevitably thrown back too much upon themselves, and upon a defective type of civilization. The lower class, with the upper class and its standard of life still farther out of their reach, and finding nothing to attract them or to elevate them in the standard of life of the middle classes, are inevitably, in their turn, thrown back upon themselves, and upon a defective type of civilization. I speak of classes. In all classes, there are individuals with a happy nature and an instinct for the humanities of life, who stand out from their class, and who form exceptions.

Now, the word *vulgarized* as applied to the middle class, and *brutalized* as applied to the lower class, may seem to you very hard words. And yet some of you, at any rate, will feel that there is a foundation for them. And whether you feel it or not, the most competent, the most dispassionate observers feel it, and use words about it much more contemptuous and harsher than mine. The question is not, whether you or I may feel the truth of a thing of this kind; the question is, whether the thing is really so. I believe that it is so; that with splendid qualities in this nation at large, that with admirable exceptions to be found in all classes, we at present do tend to have our higher class in general materialized, our middle class vulgarized, and our lower class brutalized; and that this tendency we owe to what Mr Gladstone calls our religion of inequality.

True, no one here in England combines the fact of the defects in our civilization with the fact of our enormous inequality. People may admit the facts separately; the inequality, indeed, they cannot well deny; but they are not accustomed to combine them. But I saw, when I began to think about these matters, that elsewhere the best judges combined this fact of great social imperfection with the fact of great inequality. I saw that Turgot, the best and wisest statesman whom France has ever had, himself one of the governing and fortunate class, made inequality answerable for much of the misery of the modern nations of Europe. 'Everywhere', says Turgot, 'the laws have favoured that inequality of fortunes which corrupts a certain number, to doom the rest to degradation and misery.' Vehement as this language sounds, I saw that the spectacle France is described as presenting, under the old system, was enough to account for it. I saw that the French peasants, under that system, were described by a sober and grave authority as presenting the appearance of a number of puny, dingy, miserable creatures, half clad and half articulate, creeping about on the surface of the ground and feebly scratching it. I saw that Tocqueville, coming after the French Revolution, and a severe judge of its faults and of the faults of democracy, spoke of inequality much as Turgot spoke of it. 'The common people is more uncivilized in aristocratic countries', says Tocqueville, 'than in others, because there, where persons so powerful and so rich are met with, the weak and the poor feel themselves overwhelmed, as it were, with the weight of their own inferiority; not finding any point by which they may recover equality, they despair of themselves altogether, and suffer themselves to fall into degradation'.

And then I saw the French peasant of the present day, who has been made by equality. There is a chorus of voices from all sides in praise of his condition. First, let us take, as in duty bound, your principal, Mr Barham Zincke, who has been staying in a French peasant's home this last summer, and has published in the *Fortnightly Review*, in two delightful articles which ought to be reprinted in a cheap form, an account of what he beheld.* Your principal says that 'the dense peasant population of the Limagne' – the region where he was staying, in the heart of France – 'are, speaking of them as a body, honest, contented, hard-working, hardy, self-respecting, thrifty, and self-supporting.' He gives a charming account of their manners and courtesy, as well as of their prosperity; and he pronounces such a population to be a State's greatest wealth. Prince Bismarck appears to agree with your principal, for he declares that the social condition of France seems to have greater elements of soundness – this well-being of the French peasant counting foremost among them all – than the social condition of

* See *Fortnightly Review* for November and December 1878.

any other nation of Europe. A learned Belgian economist, M. de Laveleye, chimes in with Prince Bismarck and with your principal, and declares that France, being the country of Europe where the soil is more divided than anywhere else except in Switzerland and Norway, is, at the same time, the country where material wellbeing is most widely spread, where wealth has of late years increased most, and where population is least outrunning those limits which, for the comfort and progress of the working classes themselves, seem necessary. Finally, I come back again to another countryman of our own, Mr Hamerton, who lives in France. He speaks of the French peasant just as your principal speaks of him, and he ends by saying: 'The interval between him and a Kentish labourer is enormous.' What, that black little half-human creature of the times before the Revolution, feebly scratching the earth's surface, and sunk far below the point which any English peasantry ever sank to, has now risen to this, that the interval between him and a Kentish labourer – no such bad specimen of our labourers either – is enormous! And this has been brought about by equality.

Therefore, both the natural reason of the thing and also the proof from practical experience seem to me to show the same thing: that for modern civilization some approach to equality is necessary, and that an enormous inequality like ours is a hindrance to our civilization. This to me appears so certain, that twenty years since, in a preface to a book about schools, I said that I thought so. I said the same thing more at length quite lately, in a lecture* at the Royal Institution, an institution which has been stigmatized by a working man as being 'the most aristocratic place in England'. I repeat it here because it is a thing to be thought over and examined in all its bearings, not pushed away out of sight. If our inequality is really unfavourable to our civilization, sooner or later this will be perceived generally, and our inequality will be abated. It will be abated by some measure far beyond the scope of our present politics, whether by the adoption of the French law of bequest, which now prevails so widely upon the Continent, or, as Mr Mill thought preferable, by fixing the maximum of property which any one individual may take by bequest or inheritance, or in some other manner. But this is not likely to come in our time, nor is it to be desired that such a change should come while we are yet ill prepared for it. It is a matter to which I greatly wish to direct your thoughts, and to direct the thoughts of all who think seriously. I enlarge upon it tonight, because it renders so very necessary a reform in another line, to which I shall come finally. But it is not itself a matter where I want to enlist your help for a positive present measure to reform.

Neither is the matter which I am next going to mention a matter of this

*Published in the *Fortnightly Review* for March 1878.

kind. My second point, you remember, was the extension of municipal organization throughout the whole country. No one in England seems to imagine that municipal government is applicable except in towns. All the country districts are supposed to require nothing more than the parish vestry, answering to that sort of mass-meeting of the parishioners in the churchyard, under the presidency of the parson, after service on Sundays, which Turgot describes in the country districts of France before the Revolution. Nothing, as I have frequently said, struck me more, both in France and elsewhere on the Continent, than the working of the municipality and municipal council as established everywhere, and to observe how it was the basis of all local affairs, and the right basis. For elementary schools, for instance, the municipal basis is undoubtedly the natural and right one; and we are embarrassed, and must be embarrassed, so long as we have not the municipal basis to use for them in the rural districts of this country. For the peasant, moreover, for the agricultural labourer, municipal life is a first and invaluable stage in political education; more helpful by far, because so much more constant, than the exercise of the parliamentary franchise. So this is my second point to which I should like members of institutions like yours to turn their thoughts, as a thing very conducive to that general civilization which it is the object of all cultivating of our intelligence to bring about. But this, too – the establishment of a genuine municipal system for the whole country – will hardly, perhaps, come in our time; men's minds have not yet been sufficiently turned to it for that. I am content to leave this also as a matter for thought with you.

Not so with my third point, where I hope we may actually get something done in our time. I am sure, at all events, we *need* to get something actually done towards it in our time. I want to enlist your interest and help towards this object – towards the actual establishment of public schools for the middle classes.

The topics which suggest themselves to me in recommendation of this object are so numerous that I hardly know which of them to begin with; and yet I have occupied your attention a good while already, and I must before long come to an end of my discourse. As I am speaking to a Working Men's College, I will begin with what is supposed to have most weight with people; I will begin with the direct interests in this matter of yourselves and your class. By the establishment of public schools for the middle classes, I mean an establishment of the same kind as we now have for popular education. I mean the provision by law, throughout the country, of a supply of properly guaranteed schools, in due proportion to the estimated number of the population requiring them; schools giving secondary instruction, as it is called – that fuller and higher instruction which comes after elementary instruction – and giving it at a cost not exceeding a certain rate.

Now for your direct interest in the matter. You have a direct interest in having facilities to rise given to what M. Gambetta, that famous popular leader in France, calls the new social strata. This rise is chiefly to be effected by education. Promising subjects come to the front in their own class, and they pass then, by a second and higher stage of education, into the class above them, to the great advantage of society. It is hardly too much to say that you and your class have in England no schools by which you can accomplish this rise if you are worthy of it.

In France they exist everywhere. Your principal tells us, that he found in the village where he was staying in the Limagne, six village lads, peasants' children, who were attending the secondary schools in Clermont. After all their losses, after all the milliards they have had to pay to Germany, the French have been laying out more and more in the last few years on their public secondary schools; and they do not seem so much worse off in their pecuniary condition at this moment than practical nations which make no such expenditure. At this very time a commission is sitting in France, to consider whether secondary instruction may not be brought into closer connection with elementary instruction than it is at present, by establishing schools more perfectly fitted than the present secondary schools to meet the wants of the best subjects who rise from the schools below.

Now, you often see the School Boards, here in this country, doing what is in my opinion an unwise thing, making the programme of their elementary schools too ambitious. The programme of the elementary school should be strictly limited. Those who are capable and desirous of going higher should do it either by means of evening classes such as you have here, or by means of secondary schools. But why do the School Boards make this mistake – for a mistake I think it is, and it gives occasion to the enemies of popular education to represent it as an unpractical and pretentious thing. But why do they make the mistake? They make it because, in the total absence in this country of public secondary schools, and in the inconvenience arising from this state of things, they are driven to make some attempt to supply the deficiency. Discourage, then, the School Boards in their attempt to make the elementary school what it cannot well be; but make them join with you in calling for public secondary schools, which will accomplish properly what they are aiming at.

But all this is socialism, we are told. An excellent man, Professor Fawcett,[2] tells us that the most marked characteristic of modern socialism is belief in the State. He tells us that socialism and recourse to the action of the State go always together. The argument is an unfortunate one just at this moment, when the most judicious of French newspapers, the *Journal des Débats*, informs us that in France, which we all consider a hotbed of State-action and of centralization, socialism has quite disappeared. However, this may perhaps turn out not to be true. At any rate, Professor Fawcett says that the working men of this country cannot be too much cautioned against resort to the State, centralization, bureaucracy, and the loss of individual liberty; that the working class cannot be too much exhorted to self-reliance and self-help.

Well, I should have thought that there had been no lack of cautions and exhortations in this sense to us English, whether we are working men or whatever we may be. Why, we have heard nothing else ever since I can remember! And ever since I was capable of reflection I have thought that such cautions and exhortations might be wanted elsewhere, but that giving them perpetually in England was indeed carrying coals to Newcastle. The inutility, the profound inutility, of too many of our Liberal politicans, comes from their habit of for ever repeating like parrots, phrases of this kind. In some countries the action of the State is insufficient, in others it is excessive. In France it is excessive. But hear a real Liberal leader, M. Gambetta, in reply to the invectives of *doctrinaires* against the State and its action. 'I am not for the abuses of centralization,' said M. Gambetta at Romans, 'but these attacks on *the State*, which is France, often make me impatient. I am a defender of *the State*. I will not use the word centralization; but I am a defender of the national *centrality*, which has made the French nation what it now is, and which is essential to our progress.' Englishmen are not likely, you may be sure, to let the State encroach too much; they are not likely to be not lovers enough of individual liberty and of individual self-assertion. Our dangers are all the other way. Our dangers are in exaggerating the blessing of self-will and self-assertion, in not being ready enough to sink our imperfectly informed self-will in view of a large general result.

Do not suffer yourselves, then, to be misled by declamations against the State, against bureaucracy, centralization, socialism, and all the rest of it. The State is just what Burke very well called it, long before M. Gambetta: *the nation in its collective and corporate character*. To use the State is simply to use cooperation of a superior kind. All you have to ask yourselves is whether the object for which it is proposed to use this cooperation is a rational and useful one, and one likely to be best reached in this manner. Professor Fawcett says that socialism's first lesson is, that the working man can acquire capital without saving, through having capital supplied to him by the State, which is to serve as a fountain of wealth perennially flowing without human effort. Well, to desire to use the State for that object is irrational, vain, and mischievous. Why? Because the object itself is irrational and impossible. But to use the State in order to get, through that high form of cooperation, better schools and better guaranteed schools than you could get without it, is rational, because the object is rational. The schools may be self-supporting if you like. The point is, whether by their being public schools, State schools, they are or are not likely to be better schools, and better guaranteed, than you could get in any other way. Indisputably they are likely to be better, and to give better guarantees. Well, then, this use of the State is a use of cooperation of a very powerful kind for a good and practicable purpose; and cooperation in itself is peculiarly of advantage, as I need not tell you, to the middling and ill off. Rely upon it that we English can use the State without danger; and that for you to be deceived by the cry against State interference is to play the game of your adversaries, and to prolong for yourselves a condition of certain inferiority.

But I will ask you to do more than to consider your own direct interest in the establishment of public schools for the middle classes. I will ask you to consider the general interest of the community. The friends and flatterers of the middle classes – and they have many friends and flatterers – have been in the habit of assuring us, that the predominance of the middle classes was all that we required for our well-doing. Mr Bright, a man of genius, and who has been a great power in this country, has always seemed to think that to insure the rule of the middle classes in this country would be to bring about the millennium.[3] Perhaps the working class has not been without its flatterers too, who have assured it that it ought to rule because it was so admirable. But you will observe, that my great objection to our enormous inequality, and to our aristocratic system, is not that it keeps out from power worthier claimants of it, but that it so grievously mars and stunts both our middle class and our lower class, so keeps them in imperfection. It is not the faults and imperfections of our present ruling class itself which strike me so much. Its members have plenty of faults and imperfections, but as a whole they are the best, the most energetic, the most capable, the honestest upper class which the world has ever seen. What strikes me is the bad effect of their rule upon others.

The middle classes cannot assume rule as they are at present – it is impossible. And yet in the rule of this immense class, this class with so many correspondences, communications, and openings into the lower class, lies our future. There I agree with Mr Bright. But our middle class, as it is at present, *cannot* take the lead which belongs to it. It has not the qualifications. Seriousness it has, the better part of it; it may even be said to have sacrificed everything to seriousness. And of the seriousness and of the sense for conduct in this nation, which are an invaluable treasure to it, and a treasure most dangerously wanting elsewhere, the middle classes are the stronghold. But they have lived in a narrow world of their own, without openness and flexibility of mind, without any notion of the variety of powers and possibilities in human life. They know neither man nor the world; and on all the arduous questions presenting themselves to our age – political questions, social questions, the labour question, the religious question – they have at present no light, and can give none. I say, then, they *cannot* fill their right place as they are now; but you, and I, and every man in this country, are interested in their being able to fill it.

How are they to be made able? Well, schools are something. Schools are not everything; and even public schools, when you get them, may be far from perfect. Our public elementary schools are far from perfect. But they throw into circulation year by year among the working classes – and here is the great merit of Mr Forster's Act – a number of young minds trained and intelligent, such as you never got previously; and this must tell in the long run. Our public secondary schools, when we get them, may be far from perfect. But they will throw into circulation year by year, among the middle classes, a number of young people with minds instructed and enlarged as they never are now, when their schools are, both socially and intellectually, the most inadequate that fall to the lot of any middle class among the civilized nations of Europe. And the improvement so wrought must tell in the end, and will gradually fit the middle classes to understand better themselves and the world, and to take their proper place, and to grasp and treat real politics – politics far other than their politics of dissent, which seem to me quite played out. This will be a work of time. Do not suppose that a great change of this kind is to be effected off-hand. But we may make a beginning for it at once, and a good beginning, by public schools for the middle classes.

For twenty years I have been vainly urging this upon the middle classes themselves. Now I urge it upon you. Comprehend, that middle-class education is a great democratic reform, of the truest, surest, safest kind. Christianity itself was such a reform. The kingdom of God, the grand object of Jesus Christ, the grand object of Christianity, is mankind raised, as a whole, into harmony with the true and abiding law of man's being, living as we were meant to live. Those of old who had to forward this work found the Jewish community – to whom they went first – narrow, rigid, sectarian, unintelligent, of impracticable temper, their heads full of some impossible politics of their own. Then they looked around, and they saw an immense world outside the Jewish community, a world with a thousand faults, no doubt, but with openness and flexibility of mind, new and elastic, full of possibilities – and they said: *we turn to the Gentiles!* Do not be affronted at being compared to the Gentiles; the Gentiles were the human race, the Gentiles were the future. Mankind are called in one body to the peace of God; that is the Christian phrase for civilization. We have by no means reached that consummation yet; but that, for eighteen centuries, we have been making way towards it, we owe to the Gentiles and to those who turned to them. The work, I say, is not nearly done yet; and our Judaic and unelastic middle class in this country is of no present service, it seems, for carrying it forward. Do you, then, carry it forward yourselves, and insist on taking the middle class with you. You will be amply repaid for the effort, in your own fuller powers of life and joy, in any event. We may get in our time none of the great reforms which we have been talking about; we may not even get public schools for the middle classes. But we are always the better, all of us, for having aimed high, for having striven to see and know things as they really are, for having set ourselves to walk in the light of that knowledge, to help forward great designs, and to do good. 'Consider whereunto ye are born! ye were not made to live like brutes, but to follow virtue and knowledge'.

The Popular Education of France, Chapter 14

The Popular Education of France and England Compared. Results on the People (1861)

In what numbers has the population yet, in France, actually arrived in the public schools? What proportion of it remains wholly untaught? What sort of education do those who are taught carry away with them? These are questions which, as I have already said, cannot all of them at present be satisfactorily answered. I believe, however, that the great mass of the population now passes, at some time or other, through the schools. It is an indisputable fact that the attendance in the schools for adults has been for some time falling off, because the actual adult population has grown up in possession of the elementary knowledge which these schools offer. It is a great thing that the primary schools do actually exist almost everywhere in France; they are there, they are always at the population's service, without long journeys, without high fees, without unjust conditions. It is something that the demand for children's labour is as yet considerably less in agricultural France than in manufacturing England. But I should be deceiving the reader if I led him to suppose that the French people exhibits any real ardour in seeking education for its children, or that the bait of the gain to be drawn from his child's labour is, when offered, one whit better resisted by a French than by an English parent. Nay, in the great manufacturing region of France, in the Department of the North*, public opinion and positive law prove far less powerful than in England to contend with the cupidity of the employer, the necessities of the employed. The French law prescribes that the child's day, in a manufactory, shall be of ten hours; the law is not observed; the child works habitually for twelve. Of these ten hours the law commands that two at least shall be given to schooling; when these two hours are given at all, the master habitually makes the child's day, already of twelve hours in defiance of the law, of fourteen hours, in order not to lose the time taken for schooling, In hardly any of the manufactories is there a school for the children employed.† In the towns without great manufactures, and in the agricultural districts, more children do, I believe, attend school than in similar places in England. But even these attend very irregularly, and are very easily withdrawn; there are just the same complaints from the French inspectors as from the English, of the desertion of schools in summer and autumn. I have looked through the returns, for a number of departments, of the declarations made by conscripts when drawn for the army, as to their own ability to read and write; the number of those declaring themselves unable to do either is remarkable‡, and contrasts strangely

*Even from the well-educated Alsace the inspectors report that the mill-schools are far too few in number, and that the manufacturers *exploitent les enfants*, in defiance of the law. But in the Gard I found that the companies carrying on works had very generally established schools for their workmen's children. There are very good schools of this kind at Alais. They are private schools (*écoles libres*), and the schooling is free; none of the children are half-timers, as they do not go to work till they are fourteen. The teachers are well-paid, receiving £70 or £80 a year; and the best teachers quit the public schools to take charge of these schools of private companies.

†I have great pleasure in saying that M. Magin mentioned to me, as a signal exception, a manufactory at Coudekerke-Branche, near Dunkirk, belonging to an Englishman, in which there is an excellent school for both the girls and the boys employed on the establishment.

‡Even here, however, there is progress. In the Drôme (academy of Grenoble) 42 per cent of the conscripts drawn in 1842 declared themselves unable to read and write; of those drawn in 1855, only 26 per cent. In the Aube (academy of Dijon) the conscripts declaring themselves unable to read and write were 21 per cent in 1845, 13 per cent in 1854. In the Haute Marne (in the same academy-district) they were 27 per cent in 1828, only 7 per cent in 1855. In the Doubs (academy of Besançon) they were, even in 1837, but 6 per cent; in 1855 they were 3 per cent. In the Haute Saône, 21 per cent in 1835, 9 per cent in 1855. In the district of the Academy of Paris, there were drawn in 1835, for the department of the Eure and Loir, 738 conscripts unable to read and write; in 1858, 522. For the Seine and Marne, 727 in 1835, 380 in 1855.

Even in the most backward part of the Paris district, the department of the Cher, the number of schools has more than doubled in the last twenty years, the number of scholars more than tripled; the number of girl-scholars has sextupled. In the most backward department of all France, the Nièvre, the number of inhabitants able to read and write is declared to have nearly tripled in the twenty years from 1835 to 1855.

with the alleged attendance of the primary schools. It is true that conscripts show almost always an impulse, upon these occasions, to cheapen themselves as much as possible, and to acknowledge nothing which may make them more eligible objects for a service which they try to escape. Officers have assured me that men often turned out to be able to read and write perfectly well, who when drawn had declared themselves incapable of doing either. But it is true, also, that many a peasant boy does actually lose all his school-learning between the day when he leaves school, and the day when he is drawn for army; he is not the least studious by nature, and his class are not the least studious; they have an incorrigible preference for the knowledge to be acquired at the cabaret, at the village-ball, in the great world, over that to be acquired in solitude and from books. Even when fully retained, the instruction carried away from a French primary school is also, undoubtedly, most elementary; although, as I have before said, not quite so elementary as one who merely reads the programme in the law would think*, and although not, in my opinion, more elementary than, at present, the instruction offered by a state like France or like England to all its people, ought to be and must be. Still, unquestionably, as regards the actual school-learning of the French peasant, the merit of the French system is more in its probable future than in its actual past or present – the schools are there.

Yet – and I now come to the last of the topics which I undertook to treat – I am convinced that, small as may be the result yet produced in actual school learning by the school legislation of France, the result which it has produced upon the temper and intelligence of the population has not been unimportant. But I shall have need of all the reader's indulgence while I attempt to exhibit this important but somewhat impalpable result.

The intelligence of the French people is well known; in spite of their serious faults, in spite of their almost incredible ignorance, it places them among the very foremost of ancient or modern nations. It is the source of their highest virtue (for the bravery of this people is rather a physical than a moral virtue), of a certain natural equity of spirit in matters where most other nations are intolerant and fanatical. I suppose that this intelligence is a thing not altogether peculiar and innate in the people of France; if it were, the upper classes, adding high culture to this exclusive natural gift, would

*Taking at hazard forty-two communal schools in the department of the Haute Garonne, I found that, of the *facultative matters* of primary instruction, history and geography were taught in thirty-seven of them, geometry in twenty-eight, drawing in twenty-three, singing in nineteen, physical science in one, agriculture in none. Much is said in France about agricultural instruction for the elementary and normal schools; but up to the present time next to nothing has been done.

exhibit over the upper classes of other nations a superiority of which they certainly have not given proof. If it is culture which develops this intelligence in the higher ranks of all nations, then of some culture or other the French masses, in spite of their want of book-learning, must be feeling the beneficent operation, if they show an intelligence which the masses of other nations do not possess. This culture they do actually receive; many influences are at work in France which tend to impart it to them; amongst these influences I number their school-legislation.

This works partly by its form, partly by its spirit. By its form it educates the national intelligence, no otherwise than as all French legislation tends thus to educate it; but even this is worth noticing. It is not a light thing that the law, which speaks to all men, should speak an intelligible human language, and speak it well. Reason delights in rigorous order, lucid clearness and simple statement. Reason abhors devious intricacy, confused obscurity, and prolix repetition. It is not unimportant to the reason of a nation, whether the form and text of its laws present the characters which reason delights in, or the characters which reason abhors. Certainly the text of an English Act of Parliament never carried to an uneducated English mind anything but bewilderment. I have myself heard a French peasant quote the Code Napoleon; it is in every one's hands; it is its rational form, hardly less than its rational spirit, that the Code has to thank for a popularity which makes half the nations of Europe desirous to adopt it. If English law breathed in its spirit the wisdom of angels, its form would make it to foreign nations inaccessible. The style and diction of all the modern legislation of France are the same as those of the Code. Let the English reader compare, in their style and diction alone, M. Guizot's education law with the well-known bill of a most sincere and intelligent friend of English education, Sir John Pakington.[1] Certainly neither was the French law drawn by M. Guizot himself, nor the English bill by Sir John Pakington; each speaks the current language of its national legislation. But the French law (with a little necessary formality, it is true) speaks the language of modern Europe; the English bill speaks the language of the Middle Ages, and speaks it ill. I assert that the rational intelligible speech of this great public voice of her laws has a directly favourable effect upon the general reason and intelligence of France.

From the form I pass to the spirit. With still more confidence I say – it is not a light thing for the reason and equity of a nation that her laws should boldly utter prescriptions which are reasonable and equitable. It is not a light thing for the spread, among the French masses, of a wise and moderate spirit on the vital and vexed questions of religion and education, that the law of 1833 should say firmly, *Le voeu des pères de famille sera toujours consulté et suivi en ce qui concerne la participation de leurs enfants à l'instruction religieuse.*[2] It is not a light thing that the whole body of modern French legislation on these critical questions should hold a language equally firm, equally liberal. To this it is owing that in a sphere where the popular cry, in other countries, either cannot be relied on or is sure to be wrong, there exists in France a genial current of sound public opinion, blowing steadily in the right quarter. To this it is owing that from dangers which perpetually thwart and threaten intellectual growth in other countries, intellectual growth in France is comparatively secure. To this, finally, it is owing that even on questions beyond this sphere – if they assume a sufficient generality and do not demand a large knowledge of particular facts, of which the mass of Frenchmen is deplorably ignorant – the habit of intelligence continues in the French people to be active and to enlighten. It is with truth that M. Guizot says in his latest work: 'C'est la grandeur de notre pays que *les esprits ont besoin d'être satisfaits en même temps que les intérêts.*'[3]

I wish to make perfectly clear to the reader what I mean. I am by no means praising the whole legislation of the French State. I am by no means praising the general principle of action by which the State, in France, has been guided. There are many points on which it has not informed its people at all; there are many points on which it has informed them ill. It is possible (this is a fair matter for discussion) that, even although on some points it has informed them well, it may have made them pay for that information too high a price. What I say is, that on certain capital points the State in France has by its legislation and administration exercised a directly educative influence upon the reason and equity of its people*, and that of this influence the mental temper of the French people does actually show the fruits.

It would be an interesting, but far too lengthy task, to inquire into the causes which have prevented the State, in England, from performing these educative functions for the intelligence of its people. The State in England

*To give a curious practical instance. In Corsica, the condition of the woman had for years been that of a mere beast of burden. In order to raise it, the French Government determined to put the elementary schools of the island in her hands. Under M. Fortoul's administration a normal school for young women was established at Ajaccio, and 18,000 francs a year granted for its support. Wherever it was possible, the charge of the primary school was given to a mistress. At first the men strenuously resisted for their children the degradation of being taught by that inferior creature, a woman; but the Government stood firm. Women are now established in charge of a great number of the schools of Corsica, and the consideration and respect paid to the sex has notably increased.

Again: Corsican vengeance is proverbial. In the hope of creating in the young generation a better sentiment, the Government has, in all the schools of the island, covered the walls with texts inculcating forgiveness of injuries, and against private revenge.

has shown neither taste nor aptitude for the practice of government as a profound and elaborate art; it has done what was absolutely indispensable, and has left its people to do the rest, if it could, for itself.

Its people has willingly acquiesced in a non-interference agreeable to its independent spirit, and in great measure imposed by its mistrust. Doubtless, the vigour of the national character has under this state of things greatly benefited. Yet it has its inconveniences. The State in England administers so little, so much dreads the suspicion of undue usurpation, that, when occasionally called upon to administer on a great scale, it finds its organism cramped by disuse and apprehension; it moves as a man, whose limbs had been bound for years, would move when first set free and told to walk. The people, with no help from a power greater than its own, with no suggestions from an intelligence higher than its own, fails in functions for which the intelligence and power of an ordinary individual are not sufficient. How often one is forced to say of it, when one sees it attempting these functions, that it seems, *propter libertatem libertatis perdere causes* – to have won the mechanism of free institutions through its energy, to lack the means of turning them to good account through its ignorance! How often may one observe, in any local community in England, that almost everything which individual energy has to do, is well done; almost everything which the collective reason of the community has to do, is ill done! Still, there are some remarkable instances in which, even in England, the national intelligence has been positively influenced by the action of Government. The legislation of free trade – at first established, not in virtue of an irresistible national conviction, but by the initiative of a great Minister and by the exertions of an active party which, though numerous and intelligent, was still a party – has ended by itself creating in its own favour that national sentiment which it did not find, and by educating public opinion on political economy in a sense which the best judges pronounce sound, and to a height to which the public opinion of no other nation has yet been educated. But matters of trade and commerce concern the direct material interests of a nation. With these every government must perforce deal; and here, besides, the English State is on a ground which it imagines solid and secure. With the moral and spiritual interests of a nation, governments find themselves less imperiously called to deal; and here, besides, the English State is on a ground which it imagines shifting and unsafe. It deals with them as little as it can; it sometimes deals with them as if it was the organ of the popular clamour which shouts one thing today and another tomorrow; it hardly ever deals with them as if it was *the organ of the national reason.*

It even appears unconscious or incredulous that on these matters a national reason exists. It treats all opinions as of an equal value, and seems to think that the irrational, if expressed as loudly as the rational, must weigh with it as much. It seems not to believe that an opinion has any inherent weakness by virtue of being absurd; or that, in confronting it, the strength of superior reason is really any strength at all. Its proceedings in this respect are in very remarkable contrast with those of the State in France. I will given an example of what I mean, and to find it I will not go beyond the subject of education.

In dealing with education, a government must often meet with questions on which there are two opposite opinions, and both rational. If it is wise, it will invariably treat such opinions with due respect, and will be guided, in deciding between them, by the character of the times, the state of the circumstances, the dispositions of its people. Shall public education be in the hands of the clergy or in the hands of the laity? Shall the instruction given in primary schools be exclusively secular, or shall it be also religious? Here are two questions, upon each of which opposite opinions, both having a ground of reason, may fairly be maintained. In inclining to either, in abandoning its own inclinations on the side of either, a government may be taking a course which reason sanctions; at any rate it is giving victory or defeat to arguments of which reason can take cognizance. The national intelligence can at least follow it in its operations. But a government, in dealing with education, will also sometimes meet with opinions which have no ground in reason, which are mere crotchets, or mere prejudices, or mere passions. Will it have the clearness of vision to discern whether they are such, or the courage, if they are, to treat them as such? That is the question. Will it encourage and illuminate the national intelligence by firmly treating what is unintelligent as unintelligent, what is fanatical as fanatical, in spite of the loudness with which it may be clamoured? Or will it wound and baffle and confuse the national intelligence by treating what is unintelligent as if it were intelligent, as if it were a real power, as respectfully to be parleyed with, as possible to be inclined to, as reason herself? The reader will be conscious that the State has sometimes followed, in England, the latter course.

It will be rejoined, I know, that in France the State is absolute and can crush alike unreason or reason as it pleases. But this is an error. Among the many remarkable words recorded of the first Napoleon, none are more remarkable than those in which, on more than one occasion, he pointed out the limits to the power of the State in France, the limits even to a power such as his own. Of representative institutions, he said, he might allow as little as he pleased; after the anarchy of the Revolution, the nation was demanding a strong government. With the spirit of revolution, with the spirit of reaction, with all party-spirit, he might, with firmness, deal as he pleased; priestly intolerance, Voltairian intolerance, he was strong enough to disregard; only one force even *he* was not strong enough to disregard, and that was a great force of rational and respectable sentiment in the mass of the French people. Happy for him had he always remembered his own words! Happy if he had not pursued an extravagant and personal policy till he made all the rational sentiment of France warmly hostile to him, or coldly indifferent! But what he said is true; it is impossible for the State, in modern France, to go counter to a great current of rational sentiment. It must, in its acts, have its stand upon some ground of reason, and it can afford to treat cheaply only unreason. When a priest demands to rebaptize dissenters admitted to a public school, when a dissenter demands to be exempted from school-taxation because it hurts his conscience to help to maintain schools in which may be taught a religion which he dislikes, such pretensions as these the French State treats as phantoms which it may confidently disdain – for they are *irrational.*

I say, then, that by its form and by its contents, by its letter and by its spirit, by its treatment of reason and by its treatment of prejudice, in what it respects and in what it does not respect, the school-legislation of modern France fosters, encourages, and educates the popular intelligence and the popular equity.

This is a great national advantage. But there are some national disadvantages which sometimes flow, or seem to flow, from national education; disadvantages which those who never inquire beyond the school itself are apt to overlook, but which all those to whom schools are interesting mainly as instruments of general civilization, will certainly desire to find noticed by me. Some alleged disadvantages there are, which, in France as in England, hardly merit discussion. Eminent personages complained to me that already popular education in France was carried so far that society began to be dislocated by it; that the labourer would no longer stay in his field, nor the artisan in his workshop; that every labourer would be an artisan, every artisan a clerk. This is the language which we have all heard so often, from those who think that the development of society can be arrested because a farmer's wife finds it hard to get a cookmaid. It is sufficient to say to those who hold it, that it is vain for them to expect that the lower classes will be kind enough to remain ignorant and unbettered merely for the sake of saving them inconvenience. But there are other disadvantages which are more serious. I say boldly, that an English or a French statesman might well hesitate to establish an elaborate system of national education, if it were proved to him that the necessary result of such a system must be to produce certain effects which have accompanied it elsewhere – to Prussianize his people or to Americanize it.

I speak with respect of an important nation, which has done great things with small means, and with which rests the future of Germany. To what I say of it, I cannot here give due development; I must leave it to the judgement of the best European observers. But I say that the Prussian people, under its elaborate system of education, has become a studious people, a docile people, a well-informed people, if you will – but also a somewhat pedantic, a somewhat sophisticated people. I say that this pedantry, this formalism, takes away something from a people's vital strength. I say that a people loses under them much of the genial natural character, much of the rude primitive vigour, which are the great elementary force of nations.

I speak with more than respect, with warm interest, of a great nation of English blood, and with which rests, in large measure, the future of the world. With a boundless energy of character, with a boundless field for adventure, the American people has unquestionably not been enervated by education; but under a universal system of comparatively advanced education, without certain correctives, the American people has become an energetic people, a powerful people, a highly-taught people, if you will – but also an overweening, a self-conceited people. I say that this self-conceit takes away much from a nation's vital worth. The two grand banes of humanity, says Spinoza, are indolence and self-conceit: self-conceit is so noxious because it arrests man in the career of self-improvement; because it vulgarizes his character and stops the growth of his intellect. The Greek oracle pronounced wisest of men him who was most convinced of his own ignorance: what, then, can be the wisdom of a nation profoundly convinced of its own attainment? After all that has been said, it remains immutably true that 'a little knowledge is a dangerous thing', unless he who possesses it knows that it *is* a little; and that he may know this, it is almost indispensable for him to have before his eyes objects which suggest heights of grandeur, or intellect, or feeling, or refinement, which he has never reached. This is the capital misfortune of the American people, that it is a people which has had to grow up without ideals.

The proud day of priesthoods and aristocracies is over, but in their day they have undoubtedly been, as the law was to the Jews, schoolmasters to the nations of Europe, schoolmasters to bring them to modern society; and so dull a learner is man, so rugged and hard to teach, that perhaps those nations which keep their schoolmasters longest are the most enviable. The great ecclesiastical institutions of Europe, with their stately cathedrals, their imposing ceremonial, their affecting services; the great aristocracies of Europe, with their lustre of descent, their splendour of wealth, their reputation for grace and refinement – have undoubtedly for centuries served as ideals to ennoble and elevate the sentiment of the European masses. Assuredly, churches and aristocracies often lacked the sanctity or the refinement ascribed to them; but their effect as distant ideals was still the same: they remained above the individual, a beacon to the imagination of thousands; they stood, vast and grand objects, ever present before the eyes of masses of men in whose daily avocations there was little which was vast, little which was grand; and they preserved these masses from any danger of overrating with vulgar self-satisfaction an inferior culture, however broadly sown, by the exhibition of a standard of dignity and refinement still far above them.

The masses of the great American people have grown up without this salutary standard. Neither in Church nor in State have they had the spectacle of any august institution before their eyes. The face of the land is covered with a swarm of sects, all of them without dignity, some of them without decency. They have no aristocracy. Accustomed to see nothing grander or more venerable than himself and his fellows, but accustomed to see everywhere a certain mediocre culture diffused with indisputable breadth, the common American, who possesses this, and who sees none higher, grows up with a sense of advantage, which is natural, but also with a sense of perfect self-satisfaction, which is deteriorating. The occasional contact with real superiority finds him half incredulous, half resentful. Thus widely cultured, but thus limited in its culture, and thus unconscious of its limitation, the American people offers a spectacle full of interest, indeed, but inspiring the most grave reflections – the spectacle of a people which threatens to lose its power of intellectual and moral growth.*

Is it to be apprehended (the question involuntarily arises) that diffused and improved education may possibly make the common people of France and England pedantic like the Prussians, or self-conceited like the Americans? England and France have many safeguards against either danger. Against the first they have ample security in the extraordinary fullness with which both retain, amidst all their civilization, the activity of what the poet calls 'the savage virtues of the race'. In both, though manifesting itself in very different forms, is stubbornly operant a constitutional preference for the animal over the intellectual life; excessive in one point of view, indeed, requiring greatly to be tempered by education; but, in another point of view, natural and reassuring. In the figured language of which he is a master, M. Michelet said to me of his own people, that it was a *nation de barbares, civilisée par la conscription.*[4] The civilizing influence of the conscription may be matter for question; but there can be no question that the masses, both of the French and of the English people, retain a superabundance of the native

*The above was written at the beginning of last year, when the important events now agitating the American States had not yet occurred.

and barbarous vigour of primitive man, which book-learning may wholesomely temper, but will never vanquish.

Against the second danger the preservatives which England possesses must be evident to every one. The most aristocratic people in the world, as one of the most eloquent of its admirers called it, has naturally the aristocratic virtue of not too easily admiring; it has seen so much which is grand and splendid that it it not likely to be unduly enchanted with a mediocre culture, even when that culture is its own. Democratic France, it might at first sight seem, can have no such safeguards. But it must not be forgotten through what an education of hierarchies and grandeurs the French people has passed. The Revolution is of yesterday; the imagination of the French people was fashioned long before. For more than a thousand years France had the most brilliant aristocracy in Europe; her common people were the countrymen of the Montmorencies, the Birons, the Rohans. She is the eldest child of the Roman Catholic Church, a church magnificent even in its decline. At the present hour, when her feudal magnates are gone, when her ecclesiastical magnates are shorn of their splendour, she has an aristocracy to meet the best demands of the modern spirit – an aristocracy the choicest of its class in the world: she has the Institute. The servility which has degraded the scientific and learned societies of some other nations has, in the French Institute, not been allowed to triumph. It is a true aristocracy of the intellect of France; and, in worthily commanding national respect, where great objects to awaken national respect are rare – in rigidly tempering, in the domain of intellect, science, arts, and letters, the natural self-confidence of a democratic society – in making impossible, for the intelligent French common people, a vulgar and provincial self-satisfaction with a low rate of culture, however general – the blessings which it confers on France are incalculable.

I confess that when I contemplate the probable common immunity of England and France from two of the worst dangers which threaten the future progress of other nations, and when I call to mind other points in which the two peoples have at least an important negative resemblance, the interest with which I regard, in France, the constitution and prospects of a great national agent like popular education, becomes unbounded. The two peoples are alike in this, that they are each greater than all others, each unlike to any other. It is in vain that we call the French Celts, and ourselves Teutons: when nations have attained to the greatness of France and England, their peoples can have no profound identity with any people beyond their own borders. Torrents of pedantry have been poured forth on the subject of our Germanic origin; in real truth, we are at the present day no more Germans than we are Frenchmen. By the mixture of our race, by the Latinization of our language, by the isolation of our country, by the independence of our history, we have long since severed all vital connection with that great German stem which sixteen centuries ago threw out a shoot in this island. France is equally dissociated, by her own eminence, from her once fellow Celtic or Latin races. It is the same with the greatness of the peoples; each is unique, and has no adequate counterpart but in that of the other. From Messina to Archangel, and from Calais to Moscow, there reigns a universal striving after Parisian civilization; the ideas which move the masses (I do not speak of aristocratic and learned coteries) are, when ideas reach them at all, French ideas. Cross the Straits and you are in another world: in a world where French ideas have not a breath of influence; in a country assuredly not less powerful than France, assuredly of not less weight among the nations than France, but which owes that power and that weight to a different cause – to its incomparable faculty of extending and of establishing *itself*. Each of the two peoples is alike in its immense national feeling; each is alike, too, in its genuine surprise at the shortcomings of the other. An Englishman is astonished that, in an empire boasting of its civilization, the newspapers should not be allowed to say, on political matters, what they like; that the private citizen should have no remedy by civil action against the public functionary who exceeds his powers; that he should be without the protection which in England the Habeas Corpus Act affords against arbitrary imprisonment. A Frenchman is astonished that, in an empire boasting of its civilization, out of funds levied upon the Irish people for the maintenance of religion, the church of the small minority should be endowed, the church of the vast majority receive nothing; that, instead of being equal with the rest of the community before the law, a nobleman who commits a crime is not tried by the same judge as another man; that in the English army an officer, in the nineteenth century, buys his office.

To all these resemblances, which I call negative, the two peoples add the important positive resemblance above mentioned: that of all civilized nations they are incomparably the most natural, while of all unsophisticated nations they are incomparably the most civilized.

Well, then, to two nations thus alike in greatness, and so constituted that education can only augment their power and worth, what system of education do their Governments offer? In France, a national system, which, though very unpretending, is all that a government can prudently attempt to make universal – a system fixing a low level, certainly, of popular instruction, but one which the mounting tide of national wealth and well-being will inevitably push up higher. And this system is so framed as not only not to favour popular unreason or popular intolerance, but positively to encourage and educate popular reason and popular equity. In England, a system not national, which has undoubtedly done much for superior primary instruction, but which for elementary primary instruction has done very little. That it may accomplish something important for the latter, some have conceived the project of making it national. Against this project there are, it seems to me, grave objections. It is a grave objection, that the system is over-centralized – that it is too negligent of local machinery – that it is inordinately expensive. It is a graver, that to make it national would be to make national a system not salutary to the national character in the very points where that character most needs a salutary corrective; a system which, to the loud blasts of unreason and intolerance, sends forth no certain counter-blast; which submissively accompanies the hatefullest and most barren of all kinds of dispute, religious dispute, into its smallest channels – stereotypes every crotchet, every prejudice, every division, by recognizing it; and suggest to its recipients no higher rationality than it finds in them.

The Popular Education of France, Introduction

Democracy (1861)

I know that, since the Revolution, along with many dangerous, many useful powers of Government have been weakened (Burke, 1770).

In giving an account of education in certain countries of the Continent, I have often spoken of the State and its action in such a way as to offend, I fear, some of my readers, and to surprise others. With many Englishmen, perhaps with the majority, it is a maxim that the State, the executive power, ought to be entrusted with no more means of action than those which it is impossible to withhold from it; that the State neither would nor could make a safe use of any more extended liberty; would not, because it has in itself a natural instinct of despotism, which, if not jealously checked, would become outrageous; could not, because it is, in truth, not at all more enlightened, or fit to assume a lead, than the mass of this enlightened community.

No sensible man will lightly go counter to an opinion firmly held by a great body of his countrymen. He will take for granted, that for any opinion which has struck deep root among a people so powerful, so successful, and so well worthy of respect as the people of this country, there certainly either are, or have been, good and sound reasons. He will venture to impugn such an opinion with real hesitation, and only when he thinks he perceives that the reasons which once supported it exist no longer, or at any rate seem about to disappear very soon. For undoubtedly there arrive periods when, the circumstances and conditions of government having changed, the guiding maxims of government ought to change also. '*J'ai dit souvent*,' says Mirabeau,* admonishing the Court of France in 1790, '*qu'on devait changer de manière de gouverner, lorqsue le gouvernement n'est plus le même*.' And these decisive changes in the political situation of a people happen gradually as well as violently. 'In the silent lapse of events', says Burke,† writing in England twenty years before the French Revolution, 'as material alterations have been insensibly brought about in the policy and character of governments and nations, as those which have been marked by the tumult of public revolutions.'

I propose to submit to those who have been accustomed to regard all State-action with jealousy, some reasons for thinking that the circumstances which once made that jealousy prudent and natural have undergone an essential change. I desire to lead them to consider with me, whether, in the present altered conjuncture, that State action, which was once dangerous, may not become, not only without danger in itself, but the means of helping us against dangers from another quarter. To combine and present the considerations upon which these two propositions are based, is a task of some difficulty and delicacy. My aim is to invite impartial reflection upon the subject, not to make a hostile attack against old opinions, still less to set on foot and fully equip a new theory. In offering, therefore, the thoughts which have suggested themselves to me, I shall studiously avoid all particular applications of them likely to give offence, and shall use no more illustration and development than may be indispensable to enable the reader to seize and appreciate them.

The dissolution of the old political parties which have governed this country since the Revolution of 1688 has long been remarked. It was repeatedly declared to be happening long before it actually took place, while the vital energy of these parties still subsisted in full vigour, and was threatened only by some temporary obstruction. It has been eagerly deprecated long after it had actually begun to take place, when it was in full progress, and inevitable. These parties, differing in so much else, were yet alike in this, that they were both, in a certain broad sense, *aristocratical* parties. They were combinations of persons considerable, either by great

* *Correspondance entre le Comte de Mirabeau et le Comte de la Marck* (1951, vol. ii. p. 143), M. [Adolphe] de Bacourt.

† Burke's *Works* (1852, vol. iii. p. 115).

family and estate, or by Court favour, or lastly, by eminent abilities and popularity; this last body, however, attaining participation in public affairs only through a conjunction with one or other of the former. These connections, though they contained men of very various degrees of birth and property, were still wholly leavened with the feelings and habits of the upper class of the nation. They had the bond of a common culture; and, however their political opinions and acts might differ, what they said and did had the stamp and style imparted by this culture, and by a common and elevated social condition.

Aristocratical bodies have no taste for a very imposing executive, or for a very active and penetrating domestic administration. They have a sense of equality among themselves, and of constituting in themselves what is greater and most dignified in the realm, which makes their pride revolt against the overshadowing greatness and dignity of a commanding executive. They have a temper of independence, and a habit of uncontrolled action, which makes them impatient of encountering, in the management of the interior concerns of the country, the machinery and regulations of a superior and peremptory power. The different parties amongst them, as they successively get possession of the government, respect this jealous disposition in their opponents, because they share it themselves. It is a disposition proper to them as great personages, not as ministers; and as they are great personages for their whole life, while they may probably be ministers but for a very short time, the instinct of their social condition avails more with them than the instinct of their official function. To administer as little as possible, to make its weight felt in foreign affairs rather than in domestic, to see in ministerial station rather the means of power and dignity than a means of searching and useful administrative activity, is the natural tendency of an aristocratic executive. It is a tendency which is creditable to the good sense of aristocracies, honourable to their moderation, and at the same time fortunate for their country, of whose internal development they are not fitted to have the full direction.

One strong and beneficial influence, however, the administration of a vigorous and high-minded aristocracy is calculated to exert upon a robust and sound people. I have had occasion, in speaking of Homer, to say very often, and with much emphasis, that he is *in the grand style*. It is the chief virtue of a healthy and uncorrupted aristocracy, that it is, in general, in this grand style. That elevation of character, that noble way of thinking and behaving, which is an eminent gift of nature to some individuals, is also often generated in whole classes of men (at least when these come of a strong and good race) by the possession of power, by the importance and responsibility of high station, by habitual dealing with great things, by being placed above the necessity of constantly struggling for little things. And it is the source of great virtues. It may go along with a not very quick or open intelligence; but it cannot well go along with a conduct vulgar and ignoble. A governing class imbued with it may not be capable of intelligently leading the masses of a people to the highest pitch of welfare for them; but it sets them an invaluable example of qualities without which no really high welfare can exist. This has been done for their nation by the best aristocracies. The Roman aristocracy did it; the English aristocracy has done it. They each fostered in the mass of the peoples they governed – peoples of sturdy moral constitution and apt to learn such lessons – a greatness of spirit, the natural growth of the condition of magnates and rulers, but not the natural growth of the condition of the common people. They made, the one of the Roman, the other of the English people, in spite of all the shortcomings of each, great peoples, peoples *in the grand style*. And this they did, while wielding the people according to their own notions, and in the direction which seemed good to them; not as servants and instruments of the people, but as its commanders and heads; solicitous for the good of their country, indeed, but taking for granted that of that good they themselves were the supreme judges, and were to fix the conditions.

The time has arrived, however, when it is becoming impossible for the aristocracy of England to conduct and wield the English nation any longer. It still, indeed, administers public affairs; and it is a great error to suppose, as many persons in England suppose, that it administers but does not govern. He who administers, governs,* because he infixes his own mark and stamps his own character on all public affairs as they pass through his hands; and, therefore, so long as the English aristocracy administers the commonwealth, it still governs it. But signs not to be mistaken show that its headship and leadership of the nation, by virtue of the substantial acquiescence of the body of the nation in its predominance and right to lead, is nearly over. That acquiescence was the tenure by which it held its power; and it is fast giving way. The superiority of the upper class over all others is no longer so great; the willingness of the others to recognize that superiority is no longer so ready.

This change has been brought about by natural and inevitable causes, and neither the great nor the multitude are to be blamed for it. The growing demands and audaciousness of the latter, the encroaching spirit of democracy, are, indeed, matters of loud complaint with some persons. But these persons are complaining of human nature itself, when they thus complain of a manifestation of its native and ineradicable impulse. Life itself consists,

* *Administrer, c'est gouverner,* says Mirabeau; *gouverner, c'est régner; tout se réduit là.*

say the philosophers, in the effort *to affirm one's own essence*; meaning by this, to develop one's own existence fully and freely, to have ample light and air, to be neither cramped nor overshadowed. Democracy is trying *to affirm its own essence*; to live, to enjoy, to possess the world, as aristocracy has tried, and successfully tried, before it. Ever since Europe emerged from barbarism, ever since the condition of the common people began a little to improve, ever since their minds began to stir, this effort of democracy has been gaining strength; and the more their condition improves, the more strength this effort gains. So potent is the charm of life and expansion upon the living; the moment men are aware of them, they begin to desire them, and the more they have of them, the more they crave.

This movement of democracy, like other operations of nature, merits properly neither blame nor praise. Its partisans are apt to give it credit which it does not deserve, while its enemies are apt to upbraid it unjustly. Its friends celebrate it as the author of all freedom. But political freedom may very well be established by aristocratic founders; and, certainly, the political freedom of England owes more to the grasping English barons than to democracy. Social freedom – equality – that is rather the field of the conquests of democracy. And here what I must call the injustice of its enemies comes in. For its seeking after equality, democracy is often, in this country above all, vehemently and scornfully blamed, its temper contrasted with that worthier temper which can magnanimously endure social distinctions; its operations all referred, as of course, to the stirrings of a base and malignant envy. No doubt there is a gross and vulgar spirit of envy, prompting the hearts of many of those who cry for equality. No doubt there are ignoble natures which prefer equality to liberty. But what we have to ask is, when the life of democracy is admitted as something natural and inevitable, whether this or that product of democracy is a necessary growth from its parent stock, or merely an excrescence upon it. If it be the latter, certainly it may be due to the meanest and most culpable passions. But if it be the former, then this product, however base and blameworthy the passions which it may sometimes be made to serve, can in itself be no more reprehensible than the vital impulse of democracy is in itself reprehensible; and this impulse is, as has been shown, identical with the ceaseless vital effort of human nature itself.

Now, can it be denied, that a certain approach to equality, at any rate a certain reduction of signal inequalities, is a natural, instinctive demand of that impulse which drives society as a whole – no longer individuals and limited classes only, but the mass of a community – to develop itself with the utmost possible fullness and freedom? Can it be denied, that to live in a society of equals tends in general to make a man's spirits expand, and his faculties work easily and actively; while, to live in a society of superiors, although it may occasionally be a very good discipline, yet in general tends to tame the spirits and to make the play of the faculties less secure and active? Can it be denied, that to be heavily overshadowed, to be profoundly insignificant, has, on the whole, a depressing and benumbing effect on the character? I know that some individuals react against the strongest impediments, and owe success and greatness to the efforts which they are thus forced to make. But the question is not about individuals. The question is about the common bulk of mankind, persons without extraordinary gifts or exceptional energy, and who will ever require, in order to make the best of themselves, encouragement and directly favouring circumstances. Can any one deny, that for these the spectacle, when they would rise, of a condition of splendour, grandeur, and culture, which they cannot possible reach, has the effect of making them flag in spirit, and of disposing them to sink despondingly back into their own condition? Can any one deny, that the knowledge how poor and insignificant the best condition of improvement and culture attainable by them must be esteemed by a class incomparably richer-endowed, tends to cheapen this modest possible amelioration in the account of those classes also for whom it would be relatively a real progress, and to disenchant their imaginations with it? It seems to me impossible to deny this. And therefore a philosophic observer,* with no love for democracy, but rather with a terror of it, has been constrained to remark, that 'the common people is more uncivilized in aristocratic countries than in any others'; because there 'the lowly and the poor feel themselves, as it were, overwhelmed with the weight of their own inferiority.' He has been constrained to remark,† that 'there is such a thing as a manly and legitimate passion for equality, prompting men to desire to be, *all* of them, in the enjoyment of power and consideration.' And, in France, that very equality, which is by us so impetuously decried, while it has by no means improved (it is said) the upper classes of French society, has undoubtedly given to the lower classes, to the body of the common people, a self-respect, an enlargement of spirit, a consciousness of counting for something in their country's action, which has raised them in the scale of humanity. The common people, in France, seems to me the soundest part of the French nation. They seem, to me more free from the two opposite degradations of multitudes, brutality and servility, to have a more developed human life, more of what distin-

*M. [Alexis] de Tocqueville. See his *Démocratie en Amérique* (1835, vol. 1. p.11). 'Le peuple est plus grossier dans les pays aristocratiques que partout ailleurs. Dans ces lieux, où se rencontrent des hommes si forts et si riches, les faibles et les pauvres se sentent comme accablés de leur bassesse; ne découvrant aucun point par lequel ils puissent regagner l'égalité, ils désespèrent entièrement d'eux-mêmes, et se laissent tomber au-dessous de la dignité humaine.'

†*Démocratie en Amérique* (1835, vol. 1. p. 60).

guishes elsewhere the cultured classes from the vulgar, than the common people in any other country with which I am acquainted.

I do not say that grandeur and prosperity may not be attained by a nation divided into the most widely distinct classes, and presenting the most signal inequalities of rank and fortune. I do not say that great national virtues may not be developed in it. I do not even say that a popular order, accepting this demarcation of classes as an eternal providential arrangement, not questioning the natural right of a superior order to lead it, content within its own sphere, admiring the grandeur and high-mindedness of its ruling class, and catching on its own spirit some reflex of what it thus admires, may not be a happier body, as to the eye of the imagination it is certainly a more beautiful body, than a popular order, pushing, excited, and presumptuous; a popular order, jealous of recognizing fixed superiorities, petulantly claiming to be as good as its betters, and tastelessly attiring itself with the fashions and designations which have become unalterably associated with a wealthy and refined class, and which, tricking out those who have neither wealth nor refinement, are ridiculous. But a popular order of that old-fashioned stamp exists now only for the imagination. It is not the force with which modern society has to reckon. Such a body may be a sturdy, honest, and sound-hearted lower class; but it is not a democratic people. It is not that power, which at the present day in all nations is to be found existing; in some, has obtained the mastery; in others, is yet in a state of expectation and preparation.

The power of France in Europe is at this day mainly owing to the completeness with which she has organized democratic institutions. The action of the French State is excessive; but it is too little understood in England that the French people has adopted this action for its own purposes, has in great measure attained those purposes by it, and owes to its having done so the chief part of its influence in Europe. The growing power in Europe is democracy; and France has organized democracy with a certain indisputable grandeur and success. The ideas of 1789 were working everywhere in the eighteenth century; but it was because in France the State adopted them that the French Revolution became an historic epoch for the world, and France the lodestar of Continental democracy. Her airs of superiority and her overweening pretensions come from her sense of the power which she derives from this cause. Every one knows how Frenchmen proclaim France to be at the head of civilization, the French army to be the soldier of God, Paris to be the brain of Europe, and so on. All this, is no doubt, in a vein of sufficient fatuity and bad taste; but it means, at bottom, that France believes she has so organized herself as to facilitate for all members of her society full and free expanison; that she believes herself to have remodelled her institutions with an eye to reason rather than custom, and to right rather than fact; it means, that she believes the other peoples of Europe to be preparing themselves, more or less rapidly, for a like achievement, and that she is conscious of her power and influence upon them as an initiatress and example. In this belief there is a part of truth and a part of delusion. I think it is more profitable for a Frenchman to consider the part of delusion contained in it; for an Englishman, the part of truth.

It is because aristocracies almost inevitably fail to appreciate justly, or even to take into their mind, the instinct pushing the masses towards expansion and fuller life, that they lose their hold over them. It is the old story of the incapacity of aristocracies for ideas – the secret of their want of success in modern epochs. The people treats them with flagrant injustice, when it denies all obligation to them. They can, and often do, impart a high spirit, a fine ideal of grandeur, to the people; thus they lay the foundations of a great nation. But they leave the people still the multitude, the crowd; they have small belief in the power of the ideas which are its life. Themselves a power reposing on all which is most solid, material, and visible, they are slow to attach any great importance to influences impalpable, spiritual, and viewless. Although, therefore, a disinterested looker-on might often be disposed, seeing what has actually been achieved by aristocracies, to wish to retain or replace them in their preponderance, rather than commit a nation to the hazards of a new and untried future; yet the masses instinctively feel that they can never consent to this without renouncing the inmost impulse of their being; and that they should make such a renunciation cannot seriously be expected of them. Except on conditions which make its expansion, in the sense understood by itself, fully possible, democracy will never frankly ally itself with aristocracy; and on these conditions perhaps no aristocracy will ever frankly ally itself with it. Even the English aristocracy, so politic, so capable of compromises, has shown no signs of being able so to transform itself as to render such an alliance possible. The reception given by the Peers to the bill for establishing life-peerages was, in this respect, of ill omen. The separation between aristocracy and democracy will probably, therefore, go on still widening.

And it must in fairness be added, that as in one most important part of general human culture – openness to ideas and ardour for them – aristocracy is less advanced than democracy, to replace or keep the latter under the tutelage of the former would in some respects be actually unfavourable to the progress of the world. At epochs when new ideas are powerfully fermenting in a society, and profoundly changing its spirit, aristocracies, as they are in general not long suffered to guide it without question, so are they by nature not well fitted to guide it intelligently.

In England, democracy has been slow in developing itself, having met with much to withstand it, not only in the worth of the aristocracy, but also in the fine qualities of the common people. The aristocracy has been more in sympathy with the common people than perhaps any other aristocracy. It has rarely given them great umbrage; it has neither been frivolous, so as to provoke their contempt, nor impertinent, so as to provoke their irritation. Above all, it has in general meant to act with justice, according to its own notions of justice. Therefore the feeling of admiring deference to such a class was more deep-rooted in the people of this country, more cordial, and more persistent, than in any people of the Continent. But, besides this, the vigour and high spirit of the English common people bred in them a self-reliance which disposed each man to act individually and independently; and so long as this disposition prevails through a nation divided into classes, the predominance of an aristocracy, of the class containing the greatest and strongest individuals of the nation, is secure. Democracy is a force in which the concert of a great number of men makes up for the weakness of each man taken by himself; democracy accepts a certain relative rise in their condition, obtainable by this concert for a great number, as something desirable in itself, because though this is undoubtedly far below grandeur, it is yet a good deal above insignificance. A very strong, self-reliant people neither easily learns to act in concert, nor easily brings itself to regard any middling good, any good short of the best, as an object ardently to be coveted and striven for. It keeps its eye on the grand prizes, and these are to be won only be distancing competitors, by getting before one's comrades, by succeeding all by one's self; and so long as a people works thus individually, it does not work democratically. The English people has all the qualities which dispose a people to work individually; may it never lose them! A people without the salt of these qualities, relying wholly on mutual cooperation, and proposing to itself second-rate ideals, would arrive at the pettiness and stationariness of China. But the English people is no longer so entirely ruled by them as not to show visible beginnings of democratic action; it becomes more and more sensible to the irresistible seduction of democratic ideas, promising to each individual of the multitude increased self-respect and expansion with the increased importance and authority of the multitude to which he belongs, with the diminished preponderance of the aristocratic class above him.

While the habit and disposition of deference are thus dying out among the lower classes of the English nation, it seems to me indisputable that the advantages which command deference, that eminent superiority in high feeling, dignity, and culture, tend to diminish among the highest class. I shall not be suspected of any inclination to underrate the aristocracy of this country. I regard it as the worthiest, as it certainly has been the most successful, aristocracy of which history makes record. If it has not been able to develop excellences which do not belong to the nature of an aristocracy, yet it has been able to avoid defects to which the nature of an aristocracy is peculiarly prone. But I cannot read the history of the flowering time of the English aristocracy, the eighteenth century, and then look at this aristocracy in our own century, without feeling that there has been a change. I am not now thinking of private and domestic virtues, of morality, of decorum. Perhaps with respect to these there has in this class, as in society at large, been a change for the better. I am thinking of those public and conspicuous virtues by which the multitude is captivated and led – lofty spirit, commanding character, exquisite culture. It is true that the advance of all classes in culture and refinement may make the culture of one class, which, isolated, appeared remarkable, appear so no longer; but exquisite culture and great dignity are always something rare and striking, and it is the distinction of the English aristocracy, in the eighteenth century, that not only was their culture something rare by comparison with the rawness of the masses, it was something rare and admirable in itself. It is rather that this rare culture of the highest class has actually somewhat declined,* that than it has come to look less by juxtaposition with the augmented culture of other classes.

Probably democracy has something to answer for in this falling off of her rival. To feel itself raised on high, venerated, followed, no doubt stimulates a fine nature to keep itself worthy to be followed, venerated, raised on high; hence that lofty maxim, *noblesse oblige*. To feel its culture something precious and singular, makes such a nature zealous to retain and extend it. The elation and energy thus fostered by the sense of its advantages, certainly enhances the worth, strengthens the behaviour, and quickens all the active powers of the class enjoying it. *Possunt quia posse videntur.*[1] The removal of the stimulus a little relaxes their energy. It is not so much that they sink to be somewhat less than themselves, as that they cease to be somewhat more than themselves. But, however this may be, whencesoever the change may proceed, I cannot doubt that in the aristocratic virtue, in the intrinsic commanding force of the English upper class, there is a diminution. Relics of a great generation are still, perhaps, to be seen amongst them, surviving exemplars of noble manners and consummate culture; but they

*This will appear doubtful to no one well acquainted with the literature and memoirs of the last century. To give but two illustrations out of a thousand. Let the reader refer to the anecdote told by Robert Wood in his *Essay on the Genius of Homer* (London, 1775, p. vii), and to Lord Chesterfield's *Letters* (1845, vol. 1, pp. 115, 143; vol. 2, p. 54); and then say, whether the culture there indicated as the culture of a *class* has maintained itself at that level.

disappear one after the other, and no one of their kind takes their place. At the very moment when democracy becomes less and less disposed to follow and to admire, aristocracy becomes less and less qualified to command and to captivate.

On the one hand, then, the masses of the people in this country are preparing to take a much more active part than formerly in controlling its destinies; on the other hand, the aristocracy (using this word in the widest sense, to include not only the nobility and landed gentry, but also those reinforcements from the classes bordering upon itself, which this class constantly attracts and assimilates), while it is threatened with losing its hold on the rudder of government, its power to give to public affairs its own bias and direction, is losing also that influence on the spirit and character of the people which it long exercised.

I know that this will be warmly denied by some persons. Those who have grown up amidst a certain state of things, those whose habits, and interests, and affections, are closely concerned with its continuance, are slow to believe that it is not a part of the order of nature, or that it can ever come to an end. But I think that what I have here laid down will not appear doubtful either to the most competent and friendly foreign observers of this country, or to those Englishmen who, clear of all influences of class or party, have applied themselves steadily to see the tendencies of their nation as they really are. Assuming it to be true, a great number of considerations are suggested by it; but it is my purpose here to insist upon one only.

That one consideration is: On what action may we rely to replace, for some time at any rate, that action of the aristocracy upon the people of this country, which we have seen exercise an influence in many respects elevating and beneficial, but which is rapidly, and from inevitable causes, ceasing? In other words, and to use a short and significant modern expression which every one understands, what influence may help us to prevent the English people from becoming, with the growth of democracy, *Americanized*? I confess I am disposed to answer: on the action of the State.

I know what a chorus of objectors will be ready. One will say: rather repair and restore the influence of aristocracy. Another will say: it is not a bad thing, but a good thing, that the English people should be Americanized. But the most formidable and the most widely entertained objection, by far, will be that which founds itself upon the present actual state of things in another country; which says: Look at France! there you have a signal example of the alliance of democracy with a powerful State action, and see how it works.

This last and principal objection I will notice at once. I have had occasion to touch upon the first already, and upon the second I shall touch presently.

It seems to me, then, that one may save one's self from much idle terror at names and shadows if one will be at the pains to remember what different conditions the different character of two nations must necessarily impose on the operation of any principle. That which operates noxiously in one, may operate wholesomely in the other; because the unsound part of the one's character may be yet further inflamed and enlarged by it, the unsound part of the other's may find in it a corrective and an abatement. This is the great use which two unlike characters may find in observing each other. Neither is likely to have the other's faults, so each may safely adopt as much as suits him of the other's qualities. If I were a Frenchman I should never be weary of admiring the independent, individual, local habits of action in England, of directing attention to the evils occasioned in France by the excessive action of the State; for I should be very sure that, say what I might, the part of the State would never be too small in France, nor that of the individual too large. Being an Englishman, I see nothing but good in freely recognizing the coherence, rationality, and efficaciousness which characterize the strong State-action of France, of acknowledging the want of method, reason, and result which attend the feeble State action of England; because I am very sure that, strengthen in England the action of the State as one may, it will always find itself sufficiently controlled. But when either the *Constitutionnel* sneers at the do-little talkativeness of parliamentary government, or when the *Morning Star* inveighs against the despotism of a centralized administration, it seems to me that they lose their labour, because they are hardening themselves against dangers to which they are neither of them liable. Both the one and the other, in plain truth,

Compound for sins they are inclined to,
By damning those they have no mind to.

They should rather exchange doctrines one with the other, and each might thus, perhaps, be profited.

So that the exaggeration of the action of the State, in France, furnishes no reason for absolutely refusing to enlarge the action of the State in England; because the genius and temper of the people of this country are such as to render impossible that exaggeration which the genius and temper of the French rendered easy. There is no danger at all that the native independence and individualism of the English character will ever belie itself, and become either weakly prone to lean on others, or blindly confiding in them.

English democracy runs no risk of being overmastered by the State; it is almost certain that it will throw off the tutelage of aristocracy. Its real danger is, that it will have far too much its own way, and be left far too much to itself. 'What harm will there be in that?' say some; 'are we not a self-governing people?' I answer: 'We have never yet been a *self-governing democracy*, or anything like it.' The difficulty for democracy is how to find and keep high ideals. The individuals who compose it are, the bulk of them, persons who need to follow an ideal, not to set one; and one ideal of greatness, high feeling, and fine culture, which an aristocracy once supplied to them, they lose by the very fact of ceasing to be a lower order and becoming a democracy. Nations are not truly great solely because the individuals composing them are numerous, free, and active; but they are great when these numbers, this freedom, and this activity are employed in the service of an ideal higher than that of an ordinary man, taken by himself. Our society is probably destined to become much more democratic; who or what will give a high tone to the nation then? That is the grave question.

The greatest men of America, her Washingtons, Hamiltons, Madisons, well understanding that aristocratical institutions are not in all times and places possible; well perceiving that in their Republic there was no place for these; comprehending, therefore, that from these that security for national dignity and greatness, an ideal commanding popular reverence, was not to be obtained, but knowing that this ideal was indispensable, would have been rejoiced to found a substitute for it in the dignity and authority of the State. They deplored the weakness and insignificance of the executive power as a calamity. When the inevitable course of events has made our self-government something really like that of America, when it has removed or weakened that security for national dignity, which we possessed in *aristocracy*, will the substitute of the *State* be equally wanting to us? If it is, then the dangers of America will really be ours; the dangers which come from the multitude being in power, with no adequate ideal to elevate or guide the multitude.

It would really be wasting time to contend at length, that to give more prominence to the idea of the State is now possible in this country, without endangering liberty. In other countries the habits and dispositions of the people may be such that the State, if once it acts, may be easily suffered to usurp exorbitantly; here they certainly are not. Here the people will always sufficiently keep in mind that any public authority is a trust delegated by themselves, for certain purposes, and with certain limits; and if that authority pretends to an absolute, independent character, they will soon enough (and very rightly) remind it of its error. Here there can be no question of a paternal government, of an irresponsible executive power, professing to act for the people's good, but without the people's consent, and, if necessary, against the people's wishes; here no one dreams of removing a single constitutional control, of abolishing a single safeguard for securing a correspondence between the acts of government and the will of the nation. The question is, whether, retaining all its power of control over a government which should abuse its trust, the nation may not now find advantage in voluntarily allowing to it purposes somewhat ampler, and limits somewhat wider within which to execute them, than formerly; whether the nation may not thus acquire in the State an ideal of high reason and right feeling, representing its best self, commanding general respect, and forming a rallying-point for the intelligence and for the worthiest instincts of the community, which will herein find a true bond of union.

I am convinced that if the worst mischiefs of democracy ever happen in England, it will be, not because a new condition of things has come upon us unforeseen, but because, though we all foresaw it, our efforts to deal with it were in the wrong direction. At the present time, almost every one believes in the growth of democracy, almost every one talks of it, almost every one laments it; but the last thing people can be brought to do is to make timely preparation for it. Many of those who, if they would, could do most to forward this work of preparation, are made slack and hesitating by the belief that, after all, in England, things may probably never go very far; that it will be possible to keep much more of the past than speculators say. Others, with a more robust faith, think that all democracy wants is vigorous putting-down; and that, with a good will and strong hand, it is perfectly possible to retain or restore the whole system of the Middle Ages. Others, free from the prejudices of class and position which warp the judgement of these, and who would, I believe, be the first and greatest gainers by strengthening the hands of the State, are averse from doing so by reason of suspicions and fears, once perfectly well-grounded, but, in this age and in the present circumstances, well-grounded no longer.

I speak of the middle classes. I have already shown how it is the natural disposition of an aristocratical class to view with jealousy the development of a considerable State-power. But this disposition has in England found extraordinary favour and support in regions not aristocratical – from the middle classes; and, above all, from the kernel of these classes, the Protestant Dissenters. And for a very good reason. In times when passions ran high, even an aristocratical executive was easily stimulated into using, for the gratification of its friends and the abasement of its enemies, those administrative engines which, the moment it chose to stretch its hand forth, stood ready for its grasp. Matters of domestic concern, matters of religious profession and religious exercise, offered a peculiar field for an intervention gainful and agreeable to friends, injurious and irritating to enemies. Such an intervention was attempted and practised. Government lent its machinery and authority to the aristocratical and ecclesiastical party, which it regarded as its best support. The party which suffered comprised the flower and strength of that middle class of society, always very flourishing and robust in this country. That powerful class, from this specimen of the administrative activity of government, conceived a strong antipathy against all intervention of the State in certain spheres. An active, stringent administration in those spheres, meant at that time a High Church and Prelatic administration in them, an administration galling to the Purity party and to the middle class; and this aggrieved class has naturally no proneness to draw nice philosophical distinctions between State action in these spheres, as a thing for abstract consideration, and State action in them as they practically felt it and supposed themselves likely long to feel it, guided by their adversaries. In the minds of the English middle class, therefore, State action in social and domestic concerns became inextricably associated with the idea of a Conventicle Act, a Five-Mile Act, an Act of Uniformity. Their abhorrence of such a State action as this they extended to State action in general; and, having never known a beneficent and just State power, they enlarged their hatred of a cruel and partial State power, the only one they had ever known, into a maxim that no State power was to be trusted, that the least action, in certain provinces, was rigorously to be denied to the State, whenever this denial was possible.

Thus that jealousy of an important, sedulous, energetic executive, natural to grandees unwilling to suffer their personal authority to be circumscribed, their individual grandeur to be eclipsed, by the authority and grandeur of the State, became reinforced in this country by a like sentiment among the middle classes, who had no such authority or grandeur to lose, but who, by a hasty reasoning, had theoretically condemned for ever an agency which they had practically found at times oppressive. *Leave us to ourselves!* magnates and middle classes alike cried to the State. Not only from those who were full and abounded went up this prayer, but also from those whose condition admitted of great amelioration. Not only did the whole repudiate the physician, but also those who were sick.

For it is evident that the action of a diligent, an impartial, and a national government, while it can do little to better the condition, already fortunate enough, of the highest and richest class of its people, can really do much, by institution and regulation, to better that of the middle and lower classes. The State can bestow certain broad collective benefits, which are indeed not much if compared with the advantages already possessed by individual grandeur, but which are rich and valuable if compared with the makeshifts of mediocrity and poverty. A good thing meant for the many cannot well be so exquisite as the good things of the few; but it can easily, if it comes from a donor of great resources and wide power, be incomparably better than what the many could, unaided, provide for themselves.

In all the remarks which I have been making, I have hitherto abstained from any attempt to suggest a positive application of them. I have limited myself to simply pointing out in how changed a world of ideas we are living; I have not sought to go further, and to discuss in what particular manner the world of facts is to adapt itself to this changed world of ideas. This has been my rule so far; but from this rule I shall here venture to depart, in order to dwell for a moment on a matter of practical institution, designed to meet new social exigencies: on the intervention of the State in public education.

The public secondary schools of France, decreed by the Revolution and established under the Consulate, are said by many good judges to be inferior to the old colleges. By means of the old colleges and of private tutors, the French aristocracy could procure for its children (so it is said, and very likely with truth) a better training than that which is now given in the lyceums.[2] Yes; but the boon conferred by the State, when it founded the lyceums, was not for the aristocracy; it was for the vast middle class of Frenchmen. This class, certainly, had not already the means of a better training for its children, before the State interfered. This class, certainly, would not have succeeded in procuring by its own efforts a better training for its children, if the State had not interfered. Through the intervention of the State this class enjoys better schools for its children, not than the great and rich enjoy (that is not the question), but than the same class enjoys in any country where the State has not interfered to found them. The lyceums may not be so good as Eton or Harrow; but they are a great deal better than a *Classical and Commercial Academy*.

The aristocratic classes in England may, perhaps, be well content to rest satisfied with their Eton and Harrow. The State is not likely to do better for them. Nay, the superior confidence, spirit, and style, engendered by a training in the great public schools, constitute for these classes a real privilege, a real engine of command, which they might, if they were selfish, be sorry to lose by the establishment of schools great enough to beget a like spirit in the classes below them. But the middle classes in England have every reason not to rest content with their private schools; the State can do a great deal better for them. By giving to schools for these classes a public character, it can bring the instruction in them under a criticism which the stock of knowledge and judgement in our middle classes is not of itself at present able to supply. By giving to them a national character, it can confer on them a greatness and a noble spirit, which the tone of these classes is not of itself at present adequate to impart. Such schools would soon prove notable competitors with the existing public schools; they would do these a great service by stimulating them, and making them look into their own weak points more closely. Economical, because with charges uniform and under severe revision, they would do a great service to that large body of persons who, at present, seeing that on the whole the best secondary instruction to be found is that of the existing public schools, obtain it for their children from a sense of duty, although they can ill afford it, and although its cost is certainly exorbitant. Thus the middle classes might, by the aid of the State, better their instruction, while still keeping its cost moderate. This in itself would be a gain; but this gain would be slight in comparison with that of acquiring the sense of belonging to great and honourable seats of learning, and of breathing in their youth the air of the best culture of their nation. This sense would be an educational influence for them of the highest value. It would really augment their self-respect and moral force; it would truly fuse them with the class above, and tend to bring about for them the equality which they are entitled to desire.

So it is not State action in itself which the middle and lower classes of a nation ought to deprecate; it is State action exercised by a hostile class, and for their oppression. From a State action reasonably, equitably, and nationally exercised, they may derive great benefit; greater, by the very nature and necessity of things, than can be derived from this source by the class above them. For the middle or lower classes to obstruct such a State action, to repel its benefits, is to play the game of their enemies, and to prolong for themselves a condition of real inferiority.

This, I know, is rather dangerous ground to tread upon. The great middle classes of this country are conscious of no weakness, no inferiority; they do not want any one to provide anything for them. Such as they are, they believe that the freedom and prosperity of England are their work, and that the future belongs to them. No one esteems them more than I do; but those who esteem them most, and who most believe in their capabilities, can render them no better service than by pointing out in what they underrate their deficiences, and how their deficiencies, if unremedied, may impair their future. They want culture and dignity; they want ideas. Aristocracy has culture and dignity; democracy has readiness for new ideas, and ardour for what ideas it possesses. Of these, our middle class has the last only: ardour for the ideas it already possesses. It believes ardently in liberty, it believes ardently in industry; and, by its zealous belief in these two ideas, it has accomplished great things. What it has accomplished by its belief in industry is patent to all the world. The liberties of England are less its exclusive work than it supposes; for these, aristocracy has achieved nearly as much. Still, of one inestimable part of liberty, liberty of thought, the middle class has been (without precisely intending it) the principal champion. The intellectual action of the Church of England upon the nation has been insignificant; its social action has been great. The social action of Protestant Dissent, that genuine product of the English middle class, has not been civilizing; its positive intellectual action has been insignificant; its negative intellectual action – in so far as by strenuously maintaining for itself, against persecution, liberty of conscience and the right of free opinion, it at the same time maintained and established this right as a universal principle – has been invaluable. But the actual results of this negative intellectual service rendered by Protestant Dissent – by the middle class – to the whole community, great as they undoubtedly are, must not be taken for something which they are not. It is a very great thing to be able to think as you like; but, after all, an important question remains: *what* you think. It is a fine thing to secure a free stage and no favour; but, after all, the part which you play on that stage will have to be criticized. Now, all the liberty and industry in the world will not ensure these two things: a high reason and a fine culture. They may favour them, but they will not of themselves produce them; they may exist without them. But it is by the appearance of these two things, in some shape or other, in the life of a nation, that it becomes something more than an independent, an energetic, a successful nation – that it becomes a *great* nation.

In modern epochs the part of a high reason, of ideas, acquires constantly increasing importance in the conduct of the world's affairs. A fine culture is the complement of a high reason, and it is in the conjunction of both with character, with energy, that the ideal for men and nations is to be placed. It is common to hear remarks on the frequent divorce between culture and character, and to infer from this that culture is a mere varnish, and that character only deserves any serious attention. No error can be more fatal. Culture without character is, no doubt, something frivolous, vain, and weak; but character without culture is, on the other hand, something raw, blind, and dangerous. The most interesting, the most truly glorious peoples, are those in which the alliance of the two has been affected most successfully, and its result spread most widely. This is why the spectacle of ancient Athens has such profound interest for a rational man; that it is the spectacle of the culture of a *people*. It is not an aristocracy, leavening with its own high spirit the multitude which it wields, but leaving it the unformed multitude still; it is not a democracy, acute and energetic, but tasteless, narrow-minded, and ignoble; it is the middle and lower classes in the highest development of their humanity that these classes have yet reached. It was the *many* who relished those arts, who were not satisfied with less than those monuments. In the conversations recorded by Plato, or even by the matter-of-fact Xenophon, which for the free yet refined discussion of ideas have set the tone for the whole cultivated world, shopkeepers and tradesmen of Athens mingle as speakers. For any one but a pedant, this is why a handful of Athenians of two thousand years ago are more interesting than the millions of most nations our contemporaries. Surely, if they knew this, those friends of progress, who have confidently pronounced the remains of the ancient world to be so much lumber, and a classical education an aristocratic impertinence, might be inclined to reconsider their sentence.

The course taken in the next fifty years by the middle classes of this nation will probably give a decisive turn to its history. If they will not seek the alliance of the State for their own elevation, if they go on exaggerating their spirit of individualism, if they persist in their jealousy of all governmental action, if they cannot learn that the antipathies and the shibboleths of a past age are now an anachronism for them – that will not prevent them, probably, from getting the rule of their country for a season, but they will certainly *Americanize* it. They will rule it by their energy, but they will deteriorate it by their low ideals and want of culture. In the decline of the aristocratical element, which in some sort supplied an ideal to ennoble the spirit of the nation and to keep it together, there will be no other element present to perform this service. It is of itself a serious calamity for a nation that its tone of feeling and grandeur of spirit should be lowered or dulled. But the calamity appears far more serious still when we consider that the middle classes, remaining as they are now, with their narrow, harsh, unintelligent, and unattractive spirit and culture, will almost certainly fail to mould or assimilate the masses below them, whose sympathies are at the present moment actually wider and more liberal than theirs. They arrive, these masses, eager to enter into possession of the world, to gain a more vivid sense of their own life and activity. In this their irrepressible development, their natural educators and initiators are those immediately above them, the middle classes. If these classes cannot win their sympathy or give them their direction, society is in danger of falling into anarchy.

Therefore, with all the force I can, I wish to urge upon the middle classes of this country, both that they might be very greatly profited by the action of the State, and also that they are continuing their opposition to such action out of an unfounded fear. But at the same time I say that the middle classes have the right, in admitting the action of government, to make the condition that this government shall be one of their own adoption, one that they can trust. To ensure this is now in their own power. If they do not as yet ensure this, they ought to do so, they have the means of doing so. Two centuries ago they had not; now they have. Having this security, let them now show themselves jealous to keep the action of the State equitable and rational, rather than to exclude the action of the State altogether. If the State acts amiss, let them check it, but let them no longer take it for granted that the State cannot possibly act usefully.

The State – but what *is* the State? cry many. Speculations on the idea of a State abound, but these do not satisfy them; of that which is to have practical effect and power they require a plain account. The full force of the term, *the State*, as the full force of any other important term, no one will master without going a little deeply, without resolutely entering the world of ideas, but it is possible to give in very plain language an account of it sufficient for all practical purposes. The State is properly just what Burke called it – *the nation in its collective and corporate character*. The State is the representative acting-power of the nation; the action of the State is the representative action of the nation. Nominally emanating fiom the Crown, as the ideal unity in which the nation concentrates itself, this action, by the constitution of our country, really emanates from the ministers of the Crown. It is common to hear the depreciators of State action run through a string of ministers' names, and then say: 'Here is really your *State*; would you accept the action of these men as your own representative action? In what respect is their judgement on national affairs likely to be any better than that of the rest of the world?' In the first place I answer: Even supposing them to be originally no better or wiser than the rest of the world, they have two great advantages from their position: access to almost boundless means of information, and the enlargement of mind which the habit of dealing with great affairs tends to produce. Their position itself, therefore, if they are men of only average honesty and capacity, tends to give them a fitness for acting on behalf of the nation superior to that of other men of equal honesty and capacity who are not in the same position. This fitness may be yet further increased by treating them as persons on whom, indeed, a very grave responsibility has fallen, and from whom very much will be expected; nothing less than the representing, each of them in his own department, under the control of Parliament, and aided by the suggestions of public opinion, the collective energy and intelligence of his nation. By treating them as men on whom all this devolves to do, to their honour if they do it well, to their shame if they do it ill, one probably augments their faculty of well-doing; as it is excellently said: 'To treat men as if they were better than they are, is the surest way to *make* them better than they are.' But to treat them as if they had been shuffled into their places by a lucky accident, were most likely soon to be shuffled out of them again, and meanwhile ought to magnify themselves and their office as little as possible; to treat them as if they and their functions could without much inconvenience be quite dispensed with, and they ought perpetually to be admiring their own inconceivable good fortune in being permitted to discharge them; this is the way to paralyse all high effort in the executive government, to extinguish all lofty sense of responsibility; to make its members either merely solicitous for the gross advantages, the emolument and self-importance, which they derive from their offices, or else timid, apologetic, and self-mistrustful in filling them; in either case, formal and inefficient.

But in the second place I answer: if the executive government is really in the hands of men no wiser than the bulk of mankind, of men whose action an intelligent man would be unwilling to accept as representative of his own action, whose fault is that? It is the fault of the nation itself, which, not being in the hands of a despot or an oligarchy, being free to control the choice of those who are to sum up and concentrate its action, controls it in such a manner that it allows to be chosen agents so little in its confidence, or so mediocre, or so incompetent, that it thinks the best thing to be done with them is to reduce their action as near as possible to a nullity. Hesitating, blundering, unintelligent, inefficacious, the action of the State may be; but, such as it is, it is the collective action of the nation itself, and the nation is responsible for it. It is our own action which we suffer to be thus unsatisfactory. Nothing can free us from this responsibility. The conduct of our affairs is in our own power. To carry on into its executive proceedings the indecision, conflict, and discordance of its parliamentary debates, may be a natural defect of a free nation, but it is certainly a defect; it is a dangerous error to call it, as some do, a perfection. The want of concert, reason, and organization in the State, is the want of concert, reason, and organization in the collective nation.

Inasmuch, therefore, as collective action is more efficacious than isolated individual efforts, a nation having great and complicated matters to deal with must greatly gain by employing the action of the State. Only, the State power which it employs should be a power which really represents its best self, and whose action its intelligence and justice can heartily avow and adopt; not a power which reflects its inferior self, and of whose action, as of its own second-rate action, it has perpetually to be ashamed. To offer a worthy initiative, and to set a standard of rational and equitable action – this is what the nation should expect of the State; and the more the State fulfils this expectation, the more will it be accepted in practice for what in idea it must always be. People will not then ask the State, what title it has to command or reward genius and merit, since commendation and reward imply an attitude of superiority, for it will then be felt that the State truly acts for the English nation; and the genius of the English nation is greater than the genius of any individual, greater even than Shakespeare's genius, for it includes the genius of Newton also.

I will not deny that to give a more prominent part to the State would be a considerable change in this country; that maxims once very sound, and habits once very salutary, may be appealed to against it. The sole question is, whether those maxims and habits are sound and salutary at this moment. A yet graver and more difficult change – to reduce the all-effacing prominence of the State, to give a more prominent part to the individual – is imperiously presenting itself to other countries. Both are the suggestions of one irresistible force, which is gradually making its way everywhere, removing old conditions and imposing new, altering long-fixed habits, undermining venerable institutions, even modifying national character: *the modern spirit.*

Undoubtedly we are drawing on towards great changes; and for every nation the thing most needful is to discern clearly its own condition, in order to know in what particular way it may best meet them. Openness and flexibility of mind are at such a time the first of virtues. *Be ye perfect*, said the Founder of Christianity; *I count not myself to have apprehended*, said its greatest Apostle. Perfection will never be reached; but to recognize a period of transformation when it comes, and to adapt themselves honestly and rationally to its laws, is perhaps the nearest approach to perfection of which men and nations are capable. No habits or attachments should prevent their trying to do this; nor indeed, in the long run, can they. Human thought, which made all institutions, inevitably saps them, resting only in that which is absolute and eternal.

A French Eton or Middle-Class Education and the State (1863–4)

Forgetting those things which are behind, and reaching forth unto those things which are before (St Paul).

A lively and acute writer, whom English society, indebted to his vigilance for the exposure of a thousand delinquents, salutes with admiration as its Grand Detective, some time ago called public attention to the state of the 'College of the Blessed Mary' at Eton. In that famous seat of learning, he said, a vast sum of money was expended on education, and a beggarly account of empty brains was the result. Rich endowments were wasted; parents were giving large sums to have their children taught, and were getting a most inadequate return for their outlay. Science, among those venerable towers in the vale of the Thames, still adored her Henry's holy shade; but she did very little else. These topics, handled with infinite skill and vivacity, produced a strong effect. Public attention, for a moment, fixed itself upon the state of secondary instruction in England. The great class, which is interested in the improvement of this, imagined that the moment was come for making the first step towards that improvement. The comparatively small class, whose children are educated in the existing public schools, thought that some inquiry into the state of these institutions might do good. A Royal Commission was appointed to report upon the endowments, studies, and management of the nine principal public schools of this country – Eton, Winchester, Westminster, Charterhouse, St Paul's, Merchant Taylors', Harrow, Rugby, and Shrewsbury.[1]

Eton was really the accused, although eight co-respondents were thus summoned to appear with Eton; and in Eton the investigation now completed will probably produce most reform. The reform of an institution which trains so many of the rulers of this country is, no doubt, a matter of considerable importance. That importance is certainly lessened if it is true, as *The Times* tells us, that the real ruler of our country is 'the people', although this potentate does not absolutely transact his own business, but delegates that function to the class which Eton educates. But even those who believe that Mirabeau, when he said, 'he who administers, governs', was a great deal nearer the truth than *The Times*, and to whom, therefore, changes at Eton seem indeed matter of great importance, will hardly be disposed to make those changes very sweeping. If Eton does not teach her pupils profound wisdom, we have Oxenstiern's word for it that the world is governed by very little wisdom. Eton, at any rate, teaches her aristocratic pupils virtues which are among the best virtues of an aristocracy – freedom from affectation, manliness, a high spirit, simplicity. It is to be hoped that she teaches something of these virtues to her other pupils also, who, not of the aristocratic class themselves, enjoy at Eton the benefit of contact with aristocracy. For these other pupils, perhaps, a little more learning as well, a somewhat stronger dose of ideas, might be desirable. Above all, it might be desirable to wean them from the easy habits and profuse notions of expense which Eton generates – habits and notions graceful enough in the lilies of the social field, but inconvenient for its future toilers and spinners. To convey to Eton the knowledge that the wine of Champagne does not water the whole earth, and that there are incomes which fall below £5000 a year, would be an act of kindness towards a large class of British parents, full of proper pride, but not opulent. Let us hope that the courageous social reformer who has taken Eton in hand may, at least, reap this reward from his labours. Let us hope he may succeed in somewhat reducing the standard of expense at Eton, and let us pronounce over his offspring the prayer of Ajax: 'O boys, may you be cheaper-educated than your father, but in other respects like him; may you have the same loving care for the improvement of the British officer, the same terrible eye upon bullies and jobbers, the same charming gaiety in your frolics with the "Old Dog Tray" – but may all these gifts be developed at a lesser price!'

But I hope that large class which wants the improvement of secondary instruction in this country – secondary instruction, the great first stage of a liberal education, coming between elementary instruction, the instruction in the mother tongue and in the simplest and indispensable branches of knowledge on the one hand, and superior instruction, the instruction given by universities, the second and finishing stage of a liberal education, on the other – will not imagine that the appointment of a Royal Commission to report on nine existing schools can seriously help it to that which it wants. I hope it will steadily say to the limited class whom the reform of these nine schools (if they need reform) truly concerns – *tua res agitur*.[2] These nine schools are by their constitution such that they profess to reach but select portions of the multitudes that are claiming secondary instruction; and, whatever they might profess, being nine, they *can* only reach select portions. The exhibition which the Royal Commissioners have given us of these schools is indeed very interesting; I hope it will prove very useful. But, for the champions of the true cause of secondary instruction, for those interested in the thorough improvement of this most important concern, the centre of interest is not there. Before the English mind, always prone to throw itself upon details, has by the interesting Report of the Public School Commissioners been led completely to throw itself upon what, after all, in this great concern of secondary instruction, is only a detail, I wish to show, with all the clearness and insistence I can, where the centre of interest really lies.

To see secondary instruction treated as a matter of national concern, to see any serious attempt to make it both commensurate with the numbers needing it and of good quality, we must cross the Channel. The Royal Commissioners have thought themselves precluded, by the limits of their instructions, from making a thorough inquiry into the system of secondary instruction on the Continent. I regret that they did not trust to the vast importance of the subject for procuring their pardon even if they somewhat extended their scope, and made their survey of foreign secondary instruction exact. This they could have done only by investing qualified persons with the commission to seek, in their name, access to the foreign schools. These institutions must be seen at work, and seen by experienced eyes, for their operation to be properly understood and described. But to see them at work the aid of the public authorities abroad is requisite; and foreign governments, most prompt in giving this aid to accredited emissaries, are by no means disposed to extend it to the chance inquirer.

In 1859 I visited France, authorized by the Royal Commissioners who were then inquiring into the state of popular education in England, to seek, in their name, information respecting the French primary schools. I shall never cease to be grateful for the cordial help afforded to me by the functionaries of the French Government for seeing thoroughly the objects which I came to study. The higher functionaries charged with the supervision of primary instruction have the supervision of secondary instruction also; and their kindness enabled me occasionally to see something of the secondary schools – institutions which strongly attracted my interest, but which the Royal Commissioners had not authorized me to study, and which the French Minister of Public Instruction had not directed his functionaries to show me. I thus saw the lyceum, or public secondary school, of Toulouse – a good specimen of its class. To make clear to the English reader what this class of institutions is, with a view of enabling him to see, afterwards, what is the problem respecting secondary instruction which we in this country really have to solve, I will describe the Toulouse Lyceum.

Toulouse, the chief city of the great plain of Languedoc, and a place of great antiquity, dignity, and importance, has one of the principal lyceums to be found out of Paris. But the chief town of every French department has its lyceum, and the considerable towns of every department have their communal colleges, as the chief town has its lyceum. These establishments of secondary instruction are attached to academies, local centres of the Department of Public Instruction at Paris, of which there are sixteen in France. The head of an academy is called its 'rector', and his chief ministers are called 'academy-inspectors'. The superintendence of all public instruction (under the general control of the Minister of Public Instruction at Paris) was given by M. Guizot's education law to the academies; that of primary instruction has been, in great measure, taken away from them and given to the prefects; that of secondary or superior instruction still remains to them. Toulouse is the seat of an academy of the first class, with a jurisdiction extending over eight departments; its rector, when I was there in 1859, was an ex-judge of the Paris Court of Cassation, M. Rocher, a man of about sixty, of great intelligence, courtesy, and knowledge of the world. Ill-health had compelled him to resign his judgeship, and the Minister of Public Instruction, his personal friend, had given him the rectorate of Toulouse, the second in France in point of rank, as a kind of dignified retreat. The position of rector in France much resembles that of one of our heads of houses at Oxford or Cambridge. M. Rocher placed me under the guidance of his academy-inspector, M. Peyrot; and M. Peyrot, after introducing me to the primary inspectors of Toulouse, and enabling me to make arrangements with them for visiting the primary schools of the city and neighbourhood, kindly took me over the lyceum, which is under his immediate supervision.

A French lyceum is an institution founded and maintained by the State, with aid from the department and commune. The communal colleges are founded and maintained by the commune, with aid from the State. The Lyceum of Toulouse is held in large and somewhat gloomy buildings, in the midst of the city; old ecclesiastical buildings have in a number of towns been converted by the Government into public-school premises. We were received by the *proviseur*, M. Seignette. The provisor is the chief functionary – the head master – of a French lyceum; he does not, however, himself teach, but manages the business concerns of the school, administers its finances, and is responsible for its general conduct and discipline; his place is one of the prizes of French secondary instruction, and the provisor, having himself served a long apprenticeship as a teacher, has all the knowledge requisite for superintending his professors. He, like the professors, has gone through the excellent normal school out of which the functionaries of secondary instruction are taken, and has fulfilled stringent conditions of training and examination. Three chaplains – Roman Catholic priests – have the charge of the religious instruction of the lyceum; a Protestant minister, however, is specially appointed to give this instruction to pupils whose parents are of the reformed faith, and these pupils attend, on Sundays, their own Protestant places of worship. The lyceum has from three to four hundred scholars; it receives both boarders and day-scholars. In every lyceum which receives boarders there are a certain number of *bourses*, or public scholarships, which relieve their holders from all cost for their education. The school has three great divisions, each with its separate schoolrooms and playground. The playgrounds are large courts, planted with trees. Attached to the institution, but in a separate building, is a school for little boys from six to twelve years of age, called the *Petit Collège*; here there is a garden as well as a playground, and the whole school-life is easier and softer than in the lyceum, and adapted to the tender years of the scholars. In the *Petit Collège*, too, there are both boarders and day-scholars.

The schoolrooms of the lyceum were much like our schoolrooms here; large bare rooms, looking as if they had seen much service, with their desks browned and battered, and inscribed with the various carvings of many generations of schoolboys. The cleanliness, order, and neatness of the passages, dormitories, and sick-rooms were exemplary. The dormitories are vast rooms, with a teacher's bed at each end; a light is kept burning in them all the night through. In no English school have I seen any arrangements for the sick to compare with those of the Toulouse Lyceum. The service of the *infirmary*, as it is called, is performed by Sisters of Charity. The aspect and manners of these nurses, the freshness and airiness of the rooms, the whiteness and fragrance of the great stores of linen which one saw ranged in them, made one almost envy the invalids who were being tended in such a place of repose.

In the playground the boys – dressed, all of them, in the well-known uniform of the French schoolboy – were running, shouting, and playing, with the animation of their age; but it is not by its playgrounds and means of recreation that a French lyceum, as compared with the half-dozen great English public schools, shines. The boys are taken out to walk, as the boys at Winchester used to be taken out to *hills*; but at the end of the French schoolboy's walk there are no *hills* on which he is turned loose. He learns and practises gymnastics more than our schoolboys do; and the court in which he takes his recreation is somewhat more spacious and agreeable than we English are apt to imagine a *court* to be; but it is a poor place indeed – poor in itself and poor in its resources – compared with the *playing-fields* of Eton, or the *meads* of Winchester, or the *close* of Rugby.

Of course I was very desirous to see the boys in their school-rooms, and to hear some of the lessons; but M. Peyrot and M. Seignette, with all the goodwill in the world, were not able to grant to an unofficial visitor permission to do this. It is something to know what the programme of studies in a French lyceum is, though it would be far more interesting to know how that programme is practically carried out. But the programme itself is worth examining: it is the same for every lyceum in France. It is fixed by the Council of Public Instruction in Paris, a body in which the State, the Church, the French Academy, and the scholastic profession are all represented, and of which the Minister of Public Instruction is president. The programme thus fixed is promulgated by the Minister's authority, and every lyceum is bound to follow it. I have before me that promulgated by M. Guizot in 1833; the variations from it, up to the present day, are but slight. In the sixth, or lowest class, the boys have to learn French, Latin, and Greek Grammar, and their reading is Cornelius Nepos and Phaedrus, and, along with the fables of Phaedrus, those of La Fontaine. For the next, or fifth class, the reading is Ovid in Latin, Lucian's Dialogues and Isocrates in Greek, and *Télémaque* in French. For the fourth, besides the authors read in the classes below, Virgil in Latin and Xenophon in Greek, and, in French, Voltaire's *Charles XII*. For the third, Sallust and Cicero are added in Latin, Homer and Plutarch's *Moralia* in Greek; in French, Voltaire's *Siècle de Louis XIV*, Massillon's *Petit Carême*, Boileau, and extracts from Buffon. For the second class (our fifth form), Horace, Livy, and Tacitus, in Latin; in Greek, Sophocles and Euripides, Plato and Demosthenes; in French, Bossuet's

Histoire Universelle, and Montesquieu's *Grandeur et Décadence des Romains*. The highest class (our sixth form) is divided into two, a rhetoric and a philosophy class; this division – which is important, and which is daily becoming, with the authorities of French Public Instruction, an object of greater importance – is meant to correspond to the direction, literary or scientific, which the studies of the now adult scholar are to take. In place of the Pindar, Thucydides, Lucan, and Molière, of the rhetoric class, the philosophy class has chemistry, physics, and the higher mathematics. Some instruction in natural science finds a place in the school-course of every class; in the lower classes, instruction in the elements of human physiology, zoology, botany, and geology; in the second class (fifth form), instruction in the elements of chemistry. To this instruction in natural science two or three hours a week are allotted. About the same time is allotted to arithmetic, to special instruction in history and geography, and to modern languages; these last, however, are said to be in general as imperfectly learnt in the French public schools as they are in our own. Two hours a week are devoted to the correction of composition. Finally, the New Testament, in Latin or Greek, forms a part of the daily reading of each class.

On this programme I will make two remarks, suggested by comparing it with that of any of our own public schools. It has the scientific instruction and the study of the mother-tongue which our school-course is without, and is often blamed for being without. I believe that the scientific instruction actually acquired by French schoolboys in the lower classes is very little, but still a boy with a taste for science finds in this instruction an element which keeps his taste alive; in the special class at the head of the school it is more considerable, but not, it is alleged, sufficient for the wants of this special class, and plans for making it more thorough and systematic are being canvassed. In the study of the mother-tongue the French school-boy has a more real advantage over ours; he does certainly learn something of the French language and literature, and of the English our schoolboy learns nothing. French grammar, however, is a better instrument of instruction for boys than English grammar, and the French literature possesses prose works, perhaps even poetical works, more fitted to be used as classics for schoolboys than any which English literature possesses. I need not say that the fitness of works for this purpose depends on other considerations than those of the genius alone, and of the creative force, which they exhibit.

The regular school-lessons of a lyceum occupy about twenty-two hours in the week, but among these regular school-lessons the lessons in modern languages are not counted. The lessons in modern languages are given out of school-hours; out of school-hours, too, all the boarders work with the masters at preparing their lessons; each boarder has thus what we call a private tutor, but the French schoolboy does not, like ours, pay extra for his private tutor: the general charge for board and instruction covers this special tuition.

Now I come to the important matter of school-fees. These are all regulated by authority; the scale of charges in every lyceum and communal college must be seen and sanctioned by the academy-inspector in order to have legality. A day-scholar in the Toulouse Lyceum pays, in the lowest of the three great divisions of the school, 110f. (£4 8s. 4d.) a year; in the second division he pays 135f. (£5 8s. 4d.); in the third and highest division, 180f. (£7 4s. 2d.). If he wishes to share in the special tuition of the boarders, he pays from £2 to £4 a year extra. Next, for the boarders. A boarder pays, for his whole board and instruction, in the lowest division, 800f. (£32) a year; in the second division, 850f. (£34); in the highest division, 900f. (£36). In the scientific class the charge is £2 extra. The payments are made quarterly, and always in advance. Every boarder brings with him an outfit (*trousseau*) valued at 500f. (£20): the sum paid for his board and instruction covers, besides, all expense for keeping good this outfit, and all charges for washing, medical attendance, books, and writing materials. The meals, though plain, are good, and they are set out with a propriety and a regard for appearances which, when I was a boy, graced no school-dinners that I ever saw; just as, I must say, even in the normal schools for elementary teachers, the dinner-table in France contrasted strongly, by its clean cloth, arranged napkins, glass, and general neatness of service, with the stained cloth, napkinless knives and forks, jacks and mugs, hacked joints of meat, and stumps of loaves, which I have seen on the dinner-table of normal schools in England. With us it is always the individual that is filled, and the public that is sent empty away.

Such may be the cheapness of public-school education, when that education is treated as a matter of public economy, to be administered upon a great scale, with rigid system and exact superintendence, in the interest of the pupil and not in the interest of the school-keeper.* But many people, it will be said, have no relish for such cast-iron schooling. Well, then, let us look at a French school not of the State pattern – a school without the guarantees of State management – but, also, without the uniformity and constraint which this management introduces.

**L'administration des lycées est complètement étrangère à toute idée de spéculation et de profit*, says the Toulouse prospectus which lies before me; 'A lyceum is managed not in the least as a matter of speculation or profit', and this is not a mere advertising puff, for the public is the real proprietor of the lyceums, which it has founded for the education of its youth, and for that object only; the directors of the lyceum are simple servants of the public, employed by the public at fixed salaries.

A day or two after I had seen the Toulouse Lyceum, I started for Sorèze. Sorèze is a village in the department of the Tarn, a department bordering upon that in which Toulouse stands; it contains one of the most successful private schools in France, and of this school, in 1859, the celebrated Father Lacordaire was director. I left Toulouse by railway in the middle of the day; in two hours I was at Castelnaudary, an old Visigoth place, on a hill rising out of the great plain of Languedoc, with immense views towards the Pyrenées on one side and the Cevennes on the other. After rambling about the town for an hour, I started for Sorèze in a vehicle exactly like an English coach; I was outside with the driver, and the other places, inside and outside, were occupied by old pupils of the Sorèze school, who were going there for the annual *fête*, the *Speeches*, to take place the next day. They were, most of them, young men from the universities of Toulouse and Montpellier; two or three were settled in Paris, but, happening to be just then at their homes, at Béziers or Narbonne, they had come over like the rest: they seemed a good set, all of them, and their attachment to their old school and master was more according to one's notions of English school-life than French. We had to cross the Montagne Noire, an outlier of the Cevennes; the elevation was not great, but the air, even on the 18 May in Languedoc, was sharp, the vast distance looked grey and chill, and the whole landscape was severe, lonely, and desolate. Sorèze is in the plain on the other side of the Montagne Noire, at the foot of gorges running up into the Cevennes; at the head of these gorges are the basins from which the Canal du Midi – the great canal uniting the Mediterranean with the Atlantic – is fed. It was seven o'clock when we drove up the street, shaded with large trees, of Sorèze; my fellow-travellers showed me the way to the school, as I was obliged to get away early the next morning, and wanted, therefore, to make my visit that evening. The school occupies the place of an old abbey, founded in 757 by Pepin the Little; for several hundred years the abbey had been in the possession of the Dominicans, when, in Louis XVI's reign, a school was attached to it. In this school the king took great interest, and himself designed the dress for the scholars. The establishment was saved at the Revolution by the tact of the Dominican who was then at its head; he resumed the lay dress and returned, in all outward appearance, to the secular life, and his school was allowed to subsist. Under the Restoration it was one of the most famous and most aristocratic schools in France, but it had much declined when Lacordaire, in 1854, took charge of it. I waited in the monastic-looking court (much of the old abbey remains as part of the present building) while my card, with a letter which the Papal Nuncio at Paris, to whom I had been introduced through Sir George Bowyers' kindness, had obtained for me from the Superior of the Dominicans, was taken up to Lacordaire; he sent down word directly that he would see me; I was shown across the court, up an old stone staircase, into a vast corridor; a door in this corridor was thrown open, and in a large bare room, with no carpet or furniture of any kind, except a small table, one or two chairs, a small book-case, a crucifix, and some religious pictures on the walls, Lacordaire, in the dress of his order, white-robed, hooded, and sandalled, sat before me.

The first public appearance of this remarkable man was in the cause of education. The Charter of 1830 had promised liberty of instruction; liberty, that is, for persons outside the official hierarchy of public instruction to open schools. This promise M. Guizot's celebrated school law of 1833 finally performed; but, in the meantime, the authorities of public instruction refused to give effect to it. Lacordaire and M. de Montalembert opened in Paris, on the 7 May 1831, an independent free school, of which they themselves were the teachers; it was closed in a day or two by the police, and its youthful conductors were tried before the Court of Peers and fined. This was Lacordaire's first public appearance; twenty-two years later his last sermon in Paris was preached in the same cause; it was a sermon on behalf of the schools of the Christian Brethren. During that space of twenty-two years he had run a conspicuous career, but on another field than that of education; he had become the most renowned preacher in Europe, and he had re-established in France, by his energy, conviction, and patience, the religious orders banished thence since the Revolution. Through this career I cannot now attempt to follow him; with the heart of friendship and the eloquence of genius, M. de Montalembert has recently written its history; but I must point out two characteristics which distinguished him in it, and which created in him the force by which, as an educator, he worked, the force by which he most impressed and commanded the young. One of these was his passion for firm order, for solid government. He called our age an age 'which does not know how to obey – *qui ne sait guère obéir*'. It is easy to see that this is not so absolutely a matter of reproach as Lacordaire made it; in an epoch of transition society may and must say to its governors, 'Govern me according to my spirit, if I am to obey you'. One cannot doubt that Lacordaire erred in making absolute devotion to the Church (*malheur à qui trouble l'Église!*) the watch-word of a gifted man in our century; one cannot doubt that he erred in affirming that 'the greatest service to be rendered to Christianity in our day was to do something for the revival of the medieval religious orders.' Still, he seized a great truth when he proclaimed the intrinsic weakness and danger of a state of anarchy; above all, when he applied this truth in the moral sphere he was incontrovertible, fruitful for his nation, especially fruitful for the young. He dealt vigorously with himself, and he told others that the first thing for them was to do the same; he placed character above everything else. 'One may have spirit, learning, even genuis,' he said, 'and not *character;* for want of character our age is the age of miscarriages. Let us form Christians in our schools, but, first of all, let us form Christians in our own hearts; the one great thing is *to have a life of one's own.*'

Allied to this characteristic was his other – his passion, in an age which seems to think that progress can be achieved only by our herding together and making a noise, for the antique discipline of retirement and silence. His plan of life for himself, when he first took orders, was to go and be a village curé in a remote province in France. M. de Quélen, the Archbishop of Paris, kept him in the capital as chaplain to the Convent of the Visitation; he had not then commenced the *conférences* which made his reputation; he lived perfectly isolated and obscure, and he was never so happy. 'It is with delight', he wrote at this time, 'that I find my solitude deepening round me; "one can do nothing without solitude", is my grand maxim. A man is formed from within, and not from without. To withdraw and be with oneself and with God, is the greatest strength there can be in the world.' It is impossible not to feel the serenity and sincerity of these words. Twice he refused to edit the *Univers*; he refused a chair in the University of Louvain. In 1836, when his fame filled France, he disappeared for five years, and these years he passed in silence and seclusion at Rome. He came back in 1841 a Dominican monk; again, at Notre Dame, that eloquence, that ineffable *accent*, led his countrymen and foreigners captive; he achieved his cherished purpose of re-establishing in France the religious orders. Then once more he disappeared, and after a short station at Toulouse consigned himself, for the rest of his life to the labour and obscurity of Sorèze. 'One of the great consolations of my present life', he writes from Sorèze, 'is, that I have now God and the young for my sole companions.' The young, with their fresh spirit, as they instinctively feel the presence of a great character, so, too, irresistibly receive an influence from souls which live habitually with God.

Lacordaire received me with great kindness. He was above the middle height, with an excellent countenance; great dignity in his look and bearing, but nothing ascetic; his manners animated, and every gesture and movement showing the orator. He asked me to dine with him the next day, and to see the school festival, the *fête des anciens élèves*; but I could not stop. Then he ordered lights, for it was growing dark, and insisted on showing me all over the place that evening. While we were waiting for lights he asked me much about Oxford; I had already heard from his old pupils that Oxford was a favourite topic with him, and that he held it up to them as a model of everything that was venerable. Lights came, and we went over the establishment; the school then contained nearly three hundred pupils – a great rise since Lacordaire first came in 1854, but not so many as the school has had in old days. It is said that Lacordaire at one time resorted so frequently to expulsion as rather to alarm people.

Sorèze, under his management, chiefly created interest by the sort of competition which it maintained with lyceums, or State schools. A private school, in France, cannot be opened without giving notice to the public authorities; the consent of these authorities is withheld if the premises of the proposed school are improper, or if its director fails to produce a certificate of probation and a certificate of competency – that is, if he has not served for five years in a secondary school, and passed the authorized public examination for secondary teachers. Finally, the school is always subject to State-inspection, to ascertain that the pupils are properly lodged and fed, and that the teaching contains nothing contrary to public morality and to the laws; and the school may be closed by the public authorities on an inspector's report, duly verified. Still, for an establishment like the Sorèze school, the actual State-interference comes to very little; the Minister has the power of dispensing with the certificate of probation, and holy orders are accepted in the place of the certificate of competency (the examination in the seminary being more difficult than the examination for this latter). In France the State (Machiavel as we English think it), in naming certain matters as the objects of its supervision in private schools, means what it says, and does not go beyond these matters; and, for these matters, the name of a man like Lacordaire serves as a guarantee, and is readily accepted as such.

All the boys at Sorèze are boarders, and a boarder's expenses here exceed by about £8 or £10 a year his expenses at a lyceum. The programme of studies differs little from that of the lyceums, but the military system of these State schools Lacordaire repudiated. Instead of the vast common dormitories of the lyceums, every boy had his little cell to himself; that was, after all, as it seemed to me, the great difference. But immense stress was laid, too, upon physical education, which the lyceums are said too much to neglect. Lacordaire showed me with great satisfaction the stable, with more than twenty horses, and assured me that all the boys were taught to ride. There was the *salle d'escrime*, where they fenced, the armoury full of guns and swords, the shooting gallery, and so on. All this is in our eyes a little fantastic, and does not replace the want of cricket and football in a good field, and of freedom to roam over the country out of school-hours; in France, however, it is a good deal; and then twice a week all the boys used to turn out with Lacordaire upon the mountains, to their great enjoyment as the Sorèze people said, the Father himself being more vigorous than any of them. And the old abbey school has a small park adjoining it, with the mountains rising close behind, and it has beautiful trees in its courts, and by no means the dismal barrack-look of a lyceum. Lacordaire had a staff of more than fifty teachers and helpers, about half of these being members of his own religious order – Dominicans; all cooperated in some way or other in conducting the school. Lacordaire used never to give school-lessons himself, but scarcely a Sunday passed without his preaching in the chapel. The highest and most distinguished boys formed a body called the Institute, with no governing powers like those of our sixth form, but with a sort of common-room to themselves, and with the privilege of having their meals with Lacordaire and his staff. I was shown, too, a *Salle d'Illustres*, or Hall of Worthies, into which the boys are introduced on high days and holidays; we should think this fanciful, but I found it impressive. The hall is decorated with busts of the chief of the former scholars, some of them very distinguished. Among these busts was that of Henri de Larochejaquelein (who was brought up here at Sorèze), with his noble, speaking countenance, his Vendean hat, and the heart and cross on his breast. There was, besides, a theatre for public recitations. We ended with the chapel, in which we found all the school assembled; a Dominican was reading to them from the pulpit an edifying life of a scapegrace converted to seriousness by a bad accident, much better worth listening to than most sermons. When it was over, Lacordaire whispered to me to ask if I would stay for the prayers or go at once. I stayed; they were very short and simple; and I saw the boys disperse afterwards. The gaiety of the little ones and their evident fondness for the *Père* was a pretty sight. As we went out of chapel, one of them, a little fellow of ten or eleven, ran from behind us, snatched, with a laughing face, Lacordaire's hand, and kissed it; Lacordaire smiled, and patted his head. When I read the other day in M. de Montalembert's book how Lacordaire had said, shortly before his death, 'I have always tried to serve God, the Church, and our Lord Jesus Christ; besides these, I have loved – oh, dearly loved! – children and young people', I thought of this incident.

Lacordaire knew absolutely nothing of our great English schools, their character, or recent history; but then no Frenchman, except a very few at Paris who know more than anybody in the world, knows anything about anything. However, I have seen few people more impressive; he was not a great modern thinker, but a great Christian orator of the fourth century, born in the nineteenth; playing his part in the nineteenth century not so successfully as he would have played it in the fourth, but still nobly. I would have given much to stay longer with him, as he kindly pressed me; I was tempted, too, by hearing that it was likely he would make a speech the next day. Never did any man so give one the sense of his being a natural orator, perfect in ease and simplicity; they told me that on Sunday, when he preached, he hardly ever went up into the pulpit, but spoke to them from his place '*sans façon*'. But I had an engagement to keep at Carcassonne at a certain hour, and I was obliged to go. At nine I took leave of Lacordaire and returned to the village inn, clean, because it is frequented by the relations of the pupils. There I supped with my fellow-travellers, the old scholars; charming companions they proved themselves. Late we sat, much *vin de Cahors* we drank, and great friends we became. Before we parted, one of them, the Béziers youth studying at Paris, with the amiability of his race assured me (God forgive him!) that he was well acquainted with my poems. By five the next morning I had started to return to Castelnaudary. Recrossing the Montagne Noire in the early morning was very cold work, but the view was inconceivably grand. I caught the train at Castelnaudary, and was at Carcassonne by eleven; there I saw a school, and I saw the old *city* of Carcassonne. I am not going to describe either the one or the other, but I cannot forbear saying, Let everybody see the *cité de Carcassonne*. It is, indeed, as the antiquarians call it, the Middle Age Herculaneum. When you first get sight of the old city, which is behind the modern town – when you have got clear of the modern town, and come out upon the bridge over the Aude, and see the walled *cité* upon its hill before you – you rub your eyes and think that you are looking at a vignette in *Ivanhoe*.

Thus I have enabled, as far as I could, the English reader to see what a French lyceum is like, and what a French private school, competing with a lyceum, is like. I have given him, as far as I could, the facts; now for the application of these facts. What is the problem respecting secondary instruction which we in this country have to solve? What light do these facts throw upon that problem?

For the serious thinker, for the real student of the question of secondary instruction, the problem respecting secondary instruction which we in England have to solve is this: why cannot we have throughout England – as the French have throughout France, as the Germans have throughout Germany, as the Swiss have throughout Switzerland, the as Dutch have throughout Holland – schools where the children of our middle and professional classes may obtain, at the rate of from £20 to £50 a year, if they are boarders, at the rate of from £5 to £15 a year if they are day-scholars, an education of as good quality, with as good guarantees, social character, and advantages for a future career in the world, as the education which French children of the corresponding class can obtain from institutions like that of Toulouse or Sorèze?

There is the really important question. It is vain to meet it by propositions which may, very likely, be true, but which are quite irrelevant. 'Your French Etons,' I am told, 'are no Etons at all; there is nothing like an Eton in France.' I know that. Very likely France is to be pitied for having no Etons, but I want to call attention to the substitute, to the compensation. The English public school produces the finest boys in the world; the Toulouse Lyceum boy, the Sorèze College boy, is not to be compared with them. Well, let me grant all that too. But then there are only some five or six schools in England to produce this specimen-boy; and they cannot produce him cheap. Rugby and Winchester produce him at about £120 a year; Eton and Harrow (and the Eton school-boy is perhaps justly taken as the most perfect type of this highly extolled class) cannot produce him for much less than £200 a year. *Tantae molis erat Romanam condere gentem* – such a business is it to produce an article so superior. But for the common wear and tear of middling life, and at rates tolerable for middling people, what do we produce? What do we produce at £30 a year? What is the character of the schools which undertake for us this humbler, but far more widely interesting production? Are they as good as the Toulouse Lyceum and the Sorèze College? That is the question.

Suppose that the recommendations of the Public School Commissioners bring about in the great public schools all the reforms which a judicious reformer could desire – suppose that they produce the best possible application of endowments, the best possible mode of election to masterships; that they lead to a wise revision of the books and subjects of study, to a reinforcing of the mathematics and of the modern languages, where these are found weak; to a perfecting, finally, of all boarding arrangements and discipline: nothing will yet have been done towards providing for the great want – the want of a secondary instruction at once reasonably cheap and reasonably good. Suppose that the recommendations of the Commissioners accomplish something even in this direction – suppose that the cost of educating a boy at Rugby is reduced to about £100 a year, and the cost of educating a boy at Eton to about £150 a year – no one acquainted with the subject will think it practicable, or even, under present circumstances, desirable, to effect in the cost of education in these two schools a greater reduction than this. And what will this reduction amount to? A boon – in some cases a very considerable boon – to those who now frequent these schools. But what will it do for the great class now in want of proper secondary instruction? Nothing: for in the first place these schools are but two, and are full, or at least sufficiently full, already; in the second place, if they were able to hold all the boys in England, the class I speak of would still be excluded from them – excluded by a cost of £100 or £150 just as much as by a cost of £120 or £200. A certain number of the professional class, with incomes quite inadequate to such a charge, will, for the sake of the future establishment of their children, make a brave effort and send them to Eton or Rugby at a cost of £150 or £100 a year. But they send them there already, even at the existing higher rate. The great mass of middling people, with middling incomes, not having for their children's future establishment in life plans which make a public-school training indispensable, will not make this effort, will not pay for their children's schooling a price quite disproportionate to their means. They demand a lower school-charge – a school-charge like that of Toulouse or Sorèze.

And they find it. They have only to open *The Times*. There they read advertisement upon advertisement, offering them, 'conscientiously offering' them, in almost any part of England which suits their convenience, 'Education, £20 per annum, no extras. Diet unlimited, and of the best description. The education comprises Greek, Latin, and German, French by a resident native, mathematics, algebra, mapping, globes, and all the essentials of a first-rate commercial education.' Physical, moral, mental, and spiritual – all the wants of their children will be sedulously cared for. They are invited to an 'Educational Home', where 'discipline is based upon moral influence and emulation, and every effort is made to combine home-comforts with school-training. Terms inclusive and moderate.' If they have a child with an awkward temper, and needing special management, even for this particular child the wonderful operation of the laws of supply and demand, in this great commercial country, will be found to have made perfect provision. 'Unmanageable boys or youths (up to twenty years) are made perfectly tractable and gentlemanly in one year by a clergyman near town, whose peculiarly persuasive high moral and religious training at once elevates.' And all this, as I have said, is provided by the simple, natural operation of the laws of supply and demand, without, as *The Times* beautifully says, 'the fetters of endowment and the interference of the executive'. Happy country! happy middle classes! Well may *The Times* congratulate them with such fervency; well may it produce dithyrambs, while the newspapers of less-favoured countries produce only leading articles; well may it declare that the fabled life of the Happy Islands is already beginning amongst us.

But I have no heart for satire, though the occasion invites it. No one, who knows anything of the subject, will venture to affirm that these 'educational homes' give, or can give, that which they 'conscientiously offer'. No one, who knows anything of the subject, will seriously affirm that they give, or can give, an education comparable to that given by the Toulouse and Sorèze schools. And why? Because they want the securities which, to make them produce even half of what they offer, are indispensable – the securities of supervision and publicity. By this time we know pretty well that to trust to the principle of supply and demand to do for us all that we want in providing education is to lean upon a broken reed. We trusted to it to give us fit elementary schools till its impotence became conspicuous; we have thrown it aside, and called upon State aid, with the securities accompanying this, to give us elementary schools more like what they should be; we have thus founded in elementary education a system still, indeed, far from perfect, but living and fruitful – a system which will probably survive the most strenuous efforts for its destruction. In secondary education the impotence of this principle of supply and demand is as signal as in elementary education. The mass of mankind know good butter from bad, and tainted meat from fresh, and the principle of supply and demand may, perhaps, be relied on to give us sound meat and butter. But the mass of mankind do not so well know what distinguishes good teaching and training from bad; they do not here know what they ought to demand, and, therefore, the demand cannot be relied on to give us the right supply. Even if they knew what they ought to demand, they have no sufficient means of testing whether or no this is really supplied to them. Securities, therefore, are needed. The great public schools of England offer securities by their very publicity; by their wealth, importance, and connexions, which attract general attention to them; by their old reputation, which they cannot forfeit without disgrace and danger. The appointment of the Public School Commission is a proof, that to these moral securities for the efficiency of the great public schools may be added the material security of occasional competent supervision. I will grant that the great schools of the Continent do not offer the same moral securities to the public as Eton or Harrow. They offer them in a certain measure, but certainly not in so large measure: they have not by any means so much importance, by any means so much reputation. Therefore they offer, in far larger measure, the other security – the security of competent supervision. With them this supervision is not occasional and extraordinary, but periodic and regular; it is not explorative only; it is also, to a considerable extent, authoritative.

It will be said that between the 'educational home' and Eton there is a long series of schools, with many gradations; and that in this series are to be found schools far less expensive than Eton, yet offering moral securities as Eton offers them, and as the 'educational home' does not. Cheltenham, Bradfield, Marlborough, are instances which will occur to every one. It is true that these schools offer securities; it is true that the mere presence, at the head of a school, of a distinguished master like Mr Bradley is, perhaps, the best moral security which can be offered. But, in the first place, these schools are thinly scattered over the country; we have no provision for planting such schools where they are most wanted, or for insuring a due supply of them. Cheltenham, Bradfield, and Marlborough are no more a due provision for the Northumberland boy than the Bordeaux Lyceum is a due provision for the little Alsatian. In the second place, are these schools cheap? Even if they were cheap once, does not their very excellence, in a country where schools at once good and cheap are rare, tend to deprive them of their cheapness? Marlborough was, I believe – perhaps it still is – the cheapest of them; Marlborough is probably just now the best-taught school in England; and Marlborough, therefore, has raised its school-charge. Marlborough was quite right in so doing, for Marlborough is an individual institution, bound to guard its own interests and to profit by its own successes, and not bound to provide for the general educational wants of the country. But what makes the school-charge of the Toulouse Lyceum remain moderate, however eminent may be the merits of the Toulouse masters, or the successes of the Toulouse pupils? It is that the Toulouse Lyceum is a public institution, administered in view of the general educational wants of France, and not of its own individual preponderance. And what makes (or made, alas!) the school-charge of the Sorèze College remain moderate, even with a most distinguished and attractive director, like Lacordaire, at its head? It was the organization of a complete system of secondary schools throughout France, the abundant supply of institutions, with at once respectable guarantees and reasonable charges, fixing a general mean of school-cost which even the most successful private school cannot venture much to exceed.

After all, it is the 'educational home', and not Bradfield or Marlborough, which supplies us with the nearest approach to that rate of charges which secondary instruction, if it is ever to be organized on a great scale, and to reach those who are in need of it, must inevitably adopt. People talk of the greater cheapness of foreign countries, and of the dearness of this; everything costs more here, they say, than it does abroad; good education, like everything else. I do not wish to dispute, I am willing to make some allowance for this plea; one must be careful not to make too much, however, or we shall find ourselves to the end of the chapter with a secondary instruction failing just where our present secondary instruction fails – a secondary instruction which, out of the multitude needing it, a few, and only a few, make sacrifices to get; the many, who do not like sacrifices, go without it. If we fix a school-charge varying from £25 to £50 a year, I am sure we have fixed the outside rate which the great body of those needing secondary instruction will ever pay. Sir John Coleridge analyses this body into 'the clergy of moderate or contracted incomes' (and that means the immense majority of the clergy), 'officers of the army and navy, medical men, solicitors, and gentry of large families and small means'. Many more elements might be enumerated. Why are the manufacturers left out? The very rich, among these, are to be counted by ones, the middling sort by hundreds. And when Sir John Coleridge separates 'tenant-farmers, small landholders, and retail tradesmen', into a class by themselves, and proposes to appropriate a separate class of schools for them, he carries the process of distinction and demarcation further than I can think quite desirable. But taking the constituent parts of the class requiring a liberal education as he assigns them, it seems to me certain that a sum ranging from £25 to £50 a year is as much as those whom he enumerates can in general be expected to pay for a son's education, and as much as they need be called upon to pay for a sound and valuable education, if secondary instruction were organized as it might be. It must be remembered, however, that a reduced rate of charge for boarders, at a good boarding-school, is not by any means the only benefit to the class of parents in question – perhaps not even the principal benefit – which the organization of secondary instruction brings with it. It brings with it, also, by establishing its schools in proper numbers, and all over the country, facilities for bringing up many boys as day-scholars who are now brought up as boarders. At present many people send their sons to a boarding-school when they would much rather keep them at home, because they have no suitable school within reach. Opinions differ as to whether it is best for a boy to live at home or to go away to school, but there can be no doubt which of the two modes of bringing him up is the cheapest for his parents; and those (and they are many) who think that the continuation of home-life along with his schooling is far best for the boy himself, would enjoy a double benefit in having suitable schools made accessible to them.

But I must not forget that an institution, or rather a group of institutions, exists, offering to the middle classes, at a charge scarcely higher than that of the £20 'educational home', an education affording considerable guarantees for its sound character. I mean the College of St Nicholas, Lancing, and its affiliated schools. This institution certainly demands a word of notice here, and no word of mine, regarding Mr Woodard and his labours,[3] shall be wanting in unfeigned interest and respect for them. Still, I must confess that, as I read Mr Woodard's programme, and as I listened to an excellent sermon from the Dean of Chichester in recommendation of it, that programme and that sermon seemed to me irresistibly to lead towards conclusions which they did not reach, and the conclusions which they did reach were far from satisfying. Mr Woodard says with great truth: 'It may be asked, why cannot the shop-keeper-class educated their own children without charity? It may be answered, scarcely any class in the country does educate its own children without some aid. Witness the enormous endowments of our universities and public schools, where the sons of our well-to-do people resort. Witness our national schools supported by State grants, and by parochial and national subscriptions. On the other hand, the lower middle class' (Mr Woodard might quite properly have said the middle class in general), 'politically a very important one, is dependent to a great extent for its education on private desultory enterprise. This class, in this land of education, gets *nothing* out of the millions given annually for this purpose to every class except themselves.' In his sermon Dr Hook spoke, in his cordial, manly way, much to the same effect.

This was the grievance; what was the remedy? That this great class should be rescued from the tender mercies of private desultory enterprise? That, in this land of education, it should henceforth get something out of the millions given annually for this purpose to every class except itself? That in an age when 'enormous endowments' – the form which public aid took in earlier ages, and taking which form public aid founded in those ages the universities and the public schools for the benefit, along with the upper class, of this very middle class which is now, by the irresistible course of events, in great measure excluded from them – that in an age, I say, when these great endowments, this medieval form of public aid, have ceased, public aid should be brought to these classes in that simpler and more manageable form which in modern societies it assumes – the form of public grants, with the guarantees of supervision and responsibility? The universities receive public grants – not to speak of the payment of certain professors* by the State – for that the State regards the endowments of the universities as in reality public grants, it proves by assuming to itself the right of interfering in the disposal of them; the elementary schools receive public grants. Why, then, should not our secondary schools receive public grants? But this question Mr Woodard (I do not blame him for it, he had a special function to perform) never touches. He falls back on an Englishman's favourite panacea – a subscription. He has built a school at Lancing, and a school at Shoreham, and he proposes to build a bigger school than either at Balcombe. He asks for a certain number of subscribers to give him contributions for a certain number of years, at certain rates, which he has calculated. I cannot see how, in this way, he will be delivering English secondary instruction from the hands of 'private desultory enterprise'. What English secondary instruction wants is these two things: sufficiency of provision of fit schools, sufficiency of securities for their fitness. Mr Woodard proposes to establish one great school in Sussex, where he has got two already. What sort of a provision is this for that need which is, on his own showing, so urgent? He hopes, indeed, that 'if the public will

*These professors are now nominally paid by the university; but the university pays them in consideration of the remission to her, by the State, of certain duties of greater amount than the salaries which the State used to pay to these professors. They are still, therefore, in fact, paid by the State.

assist in raising this one school, it will lead to a general extension of middle-class education all over England.' But in what number of years? How long are we to wait first? And then we have to consider the second great point – that of *securities*. Suppose Mr Woodard's hopes to be fulfilled – suppose the establishment of the Balcombe school to have led to the establishment of like schools all over England – what securities shall we have for the fitness of these schools? Sussex is not a very large and populous county, but, even if we limit ourselves to the ratio adopted for Sussex, of three of these schools to a county, that gives us 120 of them for England proper only, without taking in Wales. I have said that the eminence of the master may be in itself a sound security for the worth of a school; but, when I look at the number of these schools wanted, when I look at the probable position and emoluments of their teachers, I cannot think it reasonable to expect that all of them, or anything like all, will be provided with masters of an eminence to make all further guarantees unnecessary. But, perhaps, they will all be affiliated to the present institution at Lancing, and, in some degree, under its supervision? Well, then, that gives us, as the main regulative power of English secondary instruction, as our principal security for it, the Provost and Fellows of St Nicholas College, Lancing I have the greatest, the most sincere respect for Mr Woodard and his coadjutors – I should be quite ready to accept Mr Woodard's name as sufficient security for any school which he himself conducts – but I should hesitate, I confess, before accepting Mr Woodard and his colleagues, or any similar body of private persons, as my final security for the right management of a great national concern, as the last court of appeal to which the interests of English secondary instruction were to be carried. Their constitution is too close, their composition too little national. Even if this or that individual were content to take them as his security, the bulk of the public would not. We saw this the other day, when imputations were thrown out against Lancing, and our proposed security had to find security for itself. It had no difficulty in so doing; Mr Woodard has, it cannot be repeated too often, governed Lancing admirably; all I mean is – and Mr Woodard himself would probably be the first to agree with me – that, to command public confidence for a great national system of schools, one needs a security larger, ampler, more national, than any which, by the very nature of things, Mr Woodard and his friends can quite supply.

But another and a very plausible security has been provided for secondary instruction by the zeal and energy of Mr Acland and Dr Temple; I mean, the Oxford and Cambridge Middle Class Examinations.[4] The good intentions and the activity of the promoters of these examinations cannot be acknowledged too gratefully; good has certainly been accomplished by them; yet it is undeniable that this security also is, in its present condition, quite insufficient. I write, not for the professed and practised educationist, but for the general reader; above all, for the reader of that class which is most concerned in the question which I am raising, and which I am most solicitous to carry with me – the middle class. Therefore, I shall use the plainest and most unprofessional language I can, in attempting to show what the promoters of these university examinations try to do, what they have accomplished, wherein they have failed. They try to make *security* do for us all that we want in the improvement of our secondary education. They accept the 'educational homes' at present scattered all over the country; they do not aim at replacing them by other and better institutions; they do not visit or criticize them; but they invite them to send select pupils to certain local centres, and when the pupils are there, they examine them, class them, and give prizes to the best of them. Undoubtedly this action of the universities has given a certain amount of stimulus to these schools, and has done them a certain amount of good. But any one can see how far this action falls, and must fall, short of what is required. Any one can see that the examination of a few select scholars from a school, not at the school itself, not preceded or followed by an inspection of the school itself, affords no solid security for the good condition of their school. Any one can see that it is for the interest of an unscrupulous master to give all his care to his few cleverest pupils, who will serve him as an advertisement, while he neglects the common bulk of his pupils, whose backwardness there will be nobody to expose. I will not, however, insist too strongly on this last mischief, because I really believe that, serious as is its danger, it has not so much prevailed as to counterbalance the benefit which the mere stimulus of these examinations has given. All I say is, that this stimulus is an insufficient security. Plans are now broached for reinforcing university examination by university inspection. There we get a far more solid security. And I agree with Sir John Coleridge, that a body fitter than the Universities to exercise this inspection could not be found. It is indispensable that it should be exercised in the name, and on the responsibility, of a great public body; therefore the Society of Arts, which deserves thanks for its readiness to help in improving secondary instruction, is hardly, perhaps, from its want of weight, authority, and importance, qualified to exercise it: but whether it is exercised by the State, or by great and august corporations like Oxford and Cambridge, the value of the security is equally good; and learned corporations, like the universities, have a certain natural fitness for discharging what is, in many respects, a learned function. It is only as to the power of the universities to organize, equip, and keep working an efficient system of inspection for secondary schools that I am in doubt; organization and regularity are as indispensable to this guarantee as weight and authority. Can the universities organize and pay a body of inspectors to travel all over England, to visit, at least once in every year, the four or five hundred endowed schools of this country, and its unnumbered 'educational homes'; can they supply a machinery for regulating the action of these gentlemen, giving effect to the information received from them, printing their reports, circulating them through the country? The French University could; but the French University was a department of State. If the English universities cannot, the security of their inspection will be precarious; if they can, there can be no better.

No better *security*. But English secondary instruction wants, I said, two things: sufficient provision of good schools, sufficient security for these schools continuing good. Granting that the universities may give us the second, I do not see how they are to give us the first. It is not enough merely to provide a staff of inspectors and examiners, and still to leave the children of our middle class scattered about through the numberless obscure endowed schools and 'educational homes' of this country, some of them good,* many of them middling, most of them bad; but none of them great institutions, none of them invested with much consideration or dignity. What is wanted for the English middle class is *respected* schools, as well as *inspected* ones. I will explain what I mean.

The education of each class in society has, or ought to have, its ideal, determined by the wants of that class, and by its destination. Society may be imagined so uniform that one education shall be suitable for all its members; we have not a society of that kind, nor has any European country. We have to regard the condition of classes, in dealing with education; but it is right to take into account not their immediate condition only, but their wants, their destination – above all, their evident pressing wants, their evident proximate destination. Looking at English society at this moment, one may say that the ideal for the education of each of its classes to follow, the aim which the education of each should particularly endeavour to reach, is different. Mr Hawtrey, whose admirable and fruitful labours at St Mark's School entitle him to be heard with great respect, lays it down as

*A friendly critic in the museum complains that my censure of private schools is too sweeping, that I set them all down, all without exception, as utterly bad; he will allow me to point to these words as my answer. No doubt there are some masters of cheap private schools who are doing honest and excellent work; but no one suffers more than such men themselves do from a state of things in which, from the badness of the majority of these schools, a discredit is cast over them all, bad and good alike; no one would gain more by obtaining a public, trustworthy discrimination of bad from good, an authentic recognition of merit. The teachers of these schools would then have, in their profession, a career; at present they have none.

an absolute proposition that the *family is the type of the school.*[5] I do not think that is true for the schools of all classes alike. I feel sure my father, whose authority Mr Hawtrey claims for this maxim, would not have laid it down in this absolute way. For the wants of the highest class – of the class which frequents Eton, for instance – not *school a family*, but rather *school a little world*, is the right ideal. I cannot concede to Mr Hawtrey that, for the young gentlemen who go to Eton, our grand aim and aspiration should be, in his own words, 'to make their boyhood a joyous one, by gentle usage and friendly confidence on the part of the master'. Let him believe me, the great want for the children of luxury is not this sedulous tenderness, this smoothing of the rose-leaf for them; I am sure that, in fact, it is not by the predominance of the family and parental relation in its school-life that Eton is strongest: and it is well that this is so. It seems to me that, for the class frequenting Eton, the grand aim of education should be to give them those good things which their birth and rearing are least likely to give them; to give them (besides mere book-learning) the notion of a sort of republican fellowship, the practice of a plain life in common, the habit of self-help. To the middle class, the grand aim of education should be to give largeness of soul and personal dignity; to the lower class, feeling, gentleness, humanity. Here, at last, Mr Hawtrey's ideal of the *family* as the type for the school, comes in its due place; for the children of poverty it is right, it is needful to set oneself first to 'make their boyhood a joyous one, by gentle usage and friendly confidence on the part of the master'; for them the great danger is not insolence from over-cherishing, but insensibility from over-neglect. Mr Hawtrey's labours at St Mark's have been excellent and fruitful, just because he has here applied his maxim where it was the right maxim to apply. Yet even in this sphere Mr Hawtrey's maxim must not be used too absolutely or too long. Human dignity needs almost as much care as human sensibility. First, undoubtedly, you must make men feeling; but the moment you have done that, you must lose no time in making them magnanimous. Mr Hawtrey will forgive me for saying that perhaps his danger lies in pressing the spring of gentleness, of confidence, of child-like docility, of 'kindly feeling of the dependent towards the patron who is furthering his well-being', a little too hard. The energy and manliness, which he values as much as any one, run perhaps some little risk of etiolating. At least, I think I can see some indications of this danger in the reports – pleasing as in most respects they are – of his boys' career in the world after they have left school. He does so much for them at St Mark's, that he brings them to the point at which the ideal of education changes, and the prime want for their culture becomes identical with the prime want for the culture of the middle classes. Their fibre has been suppled long enough; now it wants fortifying.

To do Eton justice, she does not follow Mr Hawtrey's ideal; she does not supple the fibre of her pupils too much; and, to do the parents of these pupils justice, they have in general a wholesome sense of what their sons do really most want, and are not by any means anxious that school should over-foster them. But I am afraid our middle classes have not quite to the same degree this just perception of the true wants of their offspring. They wish them to be comfortable at school, to be sufficiently instructed there, and not to cost much. Hence the eager promise of 'home comforts' with school teaching, all on terms 'inclusive and moderate', from the conscientious proprietor of the educational home. To be sure, they do not get what they wish. So long as human nature remains what it is, they never will get it, until they take some better security for it than a prospectus. But suppose they get the security of inspection exercised by the universities, or by any other trustworthy authority. Some good such an inspection would undoubtedly accomplish; certain glaring specimens of charlatanism it might probably expose, certain gross cases of mishandling and neglect it might put a stop to. It might do a good deal for the school teaching. and something for the home comforts. It can never make these last what the prospectuses promise, what the parents who believe the prospectuses hope for, what they might even really have for their money; for only secondary instruction organized on a great and regular scale can give this at such cheap cost, and so to organize secondary instruction the inspection we are supposing has no power. But even if it had the power, if secondary instruction were organized on a great and regular scale, if it were a national concern, it would not be by ensuring to the offspring of the middle classes a more solid teaching at school, and a larger share of home comforts than they at present enjoy there (though certainly it would do this), that such a secondary instruction would confer upon them the greatest boon. Its greatest boon to the offspring of these classes would be its giving them great, honourable, public institutions for their nurture – institutions conveying to the spirit, at the time of life when the spirit is most penetrable, the salutary influences of greatness, honour and nationality – influences which expand the soul, liberalize the mind, dignify the character.

Such institutions are the great public schools of England and the great universities; with these influences, and some others to which I just now pointed, they have formed the upper class of this country – a class with many faults, with many shortcomings, but imbued, on the whole, and mainly through these influences, with a high magnanimous, governing spirit, which has long enabled them to rule, not ignobly, this great country, and which will still enable them to rule it until they are equalled or surpassed. These institutions had their origin in endowments; and the age of endowments is gone. Beautiful and venerable as are many of the aspects under which it presents itself, this form of public establishment of education, with its limitations, its preferences, its ecclesiastical character, its inflexibility, its inevitable want of foresight, proved, as time rolled on, to be subject to many inconveniences, to many abuses. On the Continent of Europe a clean sweep has in general been made of this old form of establishment, and new institutions have arisen upon its ruins. In England we have kept our great school and college foundations, introducing into their system what correctives and palliatives were absolutely necessary. Long may we so keep them! But no such palliatives or correctives will ever make the public establishment of education which sufficed for earlier ages suffice for this, nor persuade the stream of endowment, long since failing and scanty, to flow again for our present needs as it flowed in the middle ages. For public establishments modern societies have to betake themselves to the State; that is, to *themselves in their collective and corporate character*. On the Continent, society has thus betaken itself to the State for the establishment of education. The result has been the formation of institutions like the Lyceum of Toulouse; institutions capable of great improvement, by no means to be extolled absolutely, by no means to be imitated just as they are; but institutions formed by modern society, with modern modes of operation, to meet modern wants; and in some important respects, at any rate, meeting those wants. These institutions give to a whole new class – to the middle class taken at its very widest – not merely an education for whose teaching and boarding there is valid security, but something – not so much I admit, but something – of the same enlarging, liberalizing sense, the sense of belonging to a great and honourable public institution, which Eton and our three or four great public schools give to our upper class only, and to a small fragment broken off from the top of our middle class. That is where England is weak, and France, Holland, and Germany are strong. Education is and must be a matter of public establishment. Other countries have replaced the defective public establishment made by the middle ages for their education with a new one, which provides for the actual condition of things. We in England keep our old public establishment for education. That is very well; but then we must not forget to supplement it where it falls short. We must not neglect to provide for the actual condition of things.

I have no pet scheme to press, no crotchet to gratify, no fanatical zeal for giving this or that particular shape to the public establishment of our secondary instruction. All I say is, that it is most urgent to give to the establishment of it a wider, a truly public character, and that only the State can give this. If the matter is but once fairly taken in hand, and by competent agency, I am satisfied. In this country we do not move fast; we do not organize great wholes all in a day. But if the State only granted for secondary instruction the sum which it originally granted for primary – £20,000 a year – and employed this sum in founding scholarships for secondary schools, with the stipulation that all the schools which sent pupils to compete for these scholarships should admit inspection, a beginning would have been made; a beginning which I truly believe would, at the end of ten years' time, be found to have raised the character of secondary instruction all through England. If more than this can be attempted at first, Sir John Coleridge, in his two excellent letters on this subject to the *Guardian*, perfectly indicates the right course to take: indeed, one could wish nothing better than to commit the settlement of this matter to men of such prudence, moderation, intelligence, and public character as Sir John Coleridge. The four or five hundred endowed schools, whose collective operations now give so little result, should be turned to better account; amalgamation should be used, the most useful of these institutions strengthened, the most useless suppressed, the whole body of them be treated as one whole, destined harmoniously to cooperate towards one end. What should be had in view is to constitute, in every county, at least one great centre of secondary instruction with low charges, with the security of inspection, and with a public character. These institutions should bear some such title as that of Royal Schools, and should derive their support, mainly, of course, from school-fees, but partly also, from endowments – their own, or those appropriated to them – and partly from scholarships supplied by public grants. Wherever it is possible, wherever, that is, their scale of charges is not too high, or their situation not too unsuitable, existing schools of good repute should be adopted as the Royal Schools. Schools such as Mr Woodard's, such as King Edward's School at Birmingham, such as the Collegiate School at Liverpool, at once occur to one as suitable for this adoption; it would confer upon them, besides its other advantages, a public character which they are now without. Probably the very best medicine which could be devised for the defects of Eton, Harrow, and the other schools which the Royal Commissioners have been scrutinizing, would be the juxtaposition, and, to a certain extent, the competition, of establishments of this kind. No wise man will desire to see root-and-branch work made with schools like Eton or Harrow, or to see them diverted from the function which they at present discharge, and, on the whole, usefully. Great subversive changes would here be out of place; it is an addition of new that our secondary instruction wants, not a demolition of old, or, at least, not of this old. But to this old I cannot doubt that the apparition and operation of this desirable new would give a very fruitful stimulus; as this new, on its part, would certainly be very much influenced and benefited by the old.

The repartition of the charge of this new secondary instruction, the mode of its assessment, the constitution of the bodies for regulating the new system, the proportion and character of functions to be assigned to local and to central authority respectively, these are matters of detail and arrangement which it is foreign to my business here to discuss, and, I hope, quite foreign to my disposition to haggle and wrangle about. They are to be settled upon a due consideration of circumstances, after an attentive scrutiny of our existing means of operation, and a discriminating review of the practice of other countries. In general, if it is agreed to give a public and coherent organization to secondary instruction, few will dispute that its particular direction, in different localities, is best committed to local bodies, properly constituted, with a power of supervision by an impartial central authority, and of resort to this authority in the last instance. Of local bodies, bad or good, administering education, we have already plenty of specimens in this country; it would be difficult for the wit of man to devise a better governing body for its purpose than the trustees of Rugby School, or a worse governing body than the trustees of Bedford School. To reject the bad in the examples offering themselves, to use the good, and to use it with just regard to the present purpose, is the thing needful. Undoubtedly these are important matters; but undoubtedly, also, it is not difficult to settle them properly; not difficult, I mean, for ordinary good sense, and ordinary good temper. The intelligence, fairness, and moderation which, in practical matters, our countrymen know so well how to exercise, make one feel quite easy in leaving these common-sense arrangements to them.

I am more anxious about the danger of having the whole question misconceived, of having false issues raised upon it. One of these false issues I have already noticed. People say: 'After all, your Toulouse Lyceum is not so good as Eton.' But the Toulouse Lyceum is for the middle class, Eton for the upper class. I will allow that the upper class, amongst us, is very well taken care of, in the way of schools, already. But is the middle class? The Lyceum loses, perhaps, if compared with Eton; but does it not gain if compared with the 'Classical and Commercial Academy'? And it is with this that the comparison is to be instituted. Again, the French Lyceum is reproached with its barrack life, its want of country air and exercise, its dismalness, its rigidity, its excessive supervision. But these defects do not come to secondary instruction from its connexion with the State; they are not necessary results of that connexion; they come to French secondary instruction from the common French and continental habitudes in the training of children and school-boys – habitudes that do not enough regard physical well-being and play. They may be remedied in France, and men's attention is now strongly drawn to them there; there has even been a talk of moving the lyceums into the country, though this would have its inconveniences. But at any rate, these defects need not attend the public establishment of secondary instruction in England, and assuredly, with our notions of training, they would not attend them. Again, it is said that France is a despotically governed country, and that its lyceums are a part of its despotism. But Switzerland is not a despotically-governed country, and it has its lyceums just as much as France. Again, it is said that in France the lyceums are the only schools allowed to exist, that this is monopoly and tyranny, and that the lyceums themselves suffer by the want of competition. There is some exaggeration in this complaint, as the existence of Sorèze, and other places like Sorèze, testifies; still the restraints put upon private enterprise in founding schools in France, are, no doubt, mischievously strict; the refusal of the requisite authorization for opening a private school is often vexatious; the lyceums would really be benefited by the proximity of other, and sometimes rival, schools. But who supposes that any check would ever be put, in England, upon private enterprise in founding schools? Who supposes that the authorization demanded in France for opening a private school would ever be demanded in England, that it would ever be possible to demand it, that it would ever be desirable? Who supposes that all the benefits of a public establishment of instruction are not to be obtained without it? It is for what it does itself that this establishment is so desirable, not for what it prevents others from doing. Its letting others alone does not prevent it from itself having a most useful work to do, and a work which can be done by no one else. The most zealous friends of free instruction upon the Continent feel this. One of the ablest of them, M. Dollfus, lately published in the *Revue Germanique* some most interesting remarks on the defects of the French school system, as at present regulated. He demands freedom for private persons to open schools without any authorization at all. But does he contest the right of the State to have its own schools, to make a public establishment of instruction? So far from it, he treats this as a right beyond all contestation, as a clear duty. He treats as certain, too, the right of the State to inspect all private schools once opened, though he denies the right, and the good policy, of its putting the present obstacles in the way of opening them.

But there is a catchword which, I know, will be used against me. England is the country of cries and catchwords; a country where public life is so much carried on by means of parties must be. That English public life should be carried on as it is, I believe to be an excellent thing; but it is certain that all modes of life have their special inconveniences, and every sensible man, however much he may hold a particular way of life to be the best, and may be bent on adhering to it, will yet always be sedulous to guard himself against its inconveniences. One of these is, certainly, in English public life, the prevalence of cries and catchwords, which are very apt to receive an application, or to be used with an absoluteness, which do not belong to them; and then they tend to narrow our spirit and to hurt our practice. It is good to make a catchword of this sort come down from its stronghold of commonplace, to force it to move about before us in the open country, and to show us its real strength. Such a catchword as this: *the State had better leave things alone*. One constantly hears that as an absolute maxim; now, as an absolute maxim, it has really no force at all. The absolute maxims are those which carry to man's spirit their own demonstration with them; such propositions as, *duty is the law of human life*, *man is morally free*, and so on. The proposition, *the State had better leave things alone*, carries no such demonstration with it; it has, therefore, no absolute force; it merely conveys a notion which certain people have generalized from certain facts which have come under their observation, and which, by a natural vice of the human mind, they are then prone to apply absolutely. Some things the State had better leave alone, others it had better not. Is this particular thing one of these, or one of those? – that, as to any particular thing, is the right question. Now, I say that education is one of those things which the State ought not to leave alone, which it ought to establish. It is said that in education given, wholly or in part, by the State, there is something eleemosynary, pauperizing, degrading; that the self-respect and manly energy of those receiving it are likely to become impaired, as I have said that the manly energy of those who are too much made to feel their dependence upon a parental benefactor, is apt to become impaired. Well, now, is this so? Is a citizen's relation to the State that of a dependent to a parental benefactor? By no means; it is that of a member in a partnership to the whole firm. The citizens of a State, the members of a society, are really a partnership; 'a partnership', as Burke nobly says, 'in all science, in all art, in every virtue, in all perfection.' Towards this great final design of their connexion, they apply the aids which cooperative association can give them. This applied to education will, undoubtedly, give the middling person a better schooling than his own individual unaided resources could give him; but he is not thereby humiliated, he is not degraded; he is wisely and usefully turning his associated condition to the best account. Considering his end and destination, he is bound so to turn it; certainly he has a right so to turn it. Certainly he has a right – to quote Burke again – 'to a fair portion of all which society, *with all its combinations of skill and force*, can do in his favour.' Men in civil society have the right – to quote Burke yet once more (one cannot quote him too often) – as 'to the acquisitions of their parents and to the fruits of their own industry', '*to the improvement of their offspring, to instruction in life*, and to consolation in death.'

How vain, then, and how meaningless, to tell a man who, for the instruction of his offspring, receives aid from the State, that he is humiliated! by receiving help for himself as an individual from himself in his corporate and associated capacity! help to which his own money, as a tax-payer, contributes, and for which, as a result of the joint energy and intelligence of the whole community in employing its powers, he himself deserves some of the praise! He is more humiliated than one is humiliated by being on the foundation of the Charterhouse or of Winchester, or by holding a scholarship or a fellowship at Oxford or Cambridge. Nay (if there be any humiliation here), not so much. For the amount of benefaction, the amount of obligation, the amount, therefore, I suppose, of humiliation, diminishes as the public character of the aid becomes more undeniable. He is no more humiliated than when he crosses London Bridge, or walks down the King's Road, or visits the British Museum. But it is one of the extraordinary inconsistencies of some English people in this matter, that they keep all their cry of humiliation and degradation for help which the State offers. A man is not pauperized, is not degraded, is not oppressively obliged, by taking aid for his son's schooling from Mr Woodard's subscribers, or from the next squire, or from the next rector, or from the next ironmonger, or from the next druggist; he is only pauperized when he takes it from the State, when he helps to give it himself!

This matter of State intervention in the establishment of public instruction is so beset with misrepresentation and misconception, that I must, before concluding, go into it a little more fully. I want the middle classes (it is for them, above all, I write), the middle classes so deeply concerned in this matter, so numerous, so right-intentioned, so powerful, to look at the thing with impartial regard to its simple reason and to its present policy.

The State mars everything which it touches, say some. It attempts to do things for private people, and private people could do them a great deal better for themselves. 'The State', says *The Times*, 'can hardly aid education without cramping and warping its growth, and mischievously interfering with the laws of its natural development.' 'Why should persons in Downing Street', asks Dr Temple,[6] 'be at all better qualified than the rest of the world for regulating these matters?' Happily, however, this agency, at once so mischievous and so blundering, is in our country little used. 'In this country', says *The Times* again, 'people cannot complain of the State, because the State never promised them anything, *but, on the contrary, always told them it could do them no good.* The result is, none are fed with false hopes.' So it is, and so it will be to the end. 'This is something more than a system with us; *it is usage, it is a necessity.* We shall go on for ages doing as we have done.'

Whether this really is so or not, it seems as if it *ought* not to be so. 'Government', says Burke (to go back to Burke again), 'is a contrivance of human wisdom to provide for human wants. Men have a right that these wants should be provided for by this wisdom.' We are a free people, we have made our own government. Our own wisdom has planned our contrivance for providing for our own wants. And what sort of a contrivance has our wisdom made? According to *The Times*, a contrivance of which the highest merit is, that it candidly avows its own impotency. It does not provide for our wants, but then it 'always told us' it could not provide for them. It does not fulfil its function, but then it 'never fed us with false hopes' that it would. It is perfectly useless, but perfectly candid. And it will always remain what it is now; it will always be a contrivance which contrives nothing: this with us 'is usage, it is a necessity'. Good heavens! what a subject for self-congratulation! What bitterer satire on us and our institutions could our worst enemy invent?

Dr Temple may well ask, 'Why should persons in Downing Street be at all better qualified than the rest of the world for regulating such matters as education?' Why should not a sporting rector in Norfolk, or a fanatical cobbler in Northamptonshire, be just as good a judge of what is wise, equitable, and expedient in public education, as an Education Minister? Why, indeed? The Education Minister is a part of our contrivance for providing for our wants, and we have seen what that contrivance is worth. It might have been expected, perhaps, that in contriving a provision for a special want, we should have sought for some one with a special skill. But we know that our contrivance will do no good, so we may as well let Nimrod manage as Numa.

From whence can have arisen, in this country, such contemptuous disparagement of the efficiency and utility of State action? Whence such studied depreciation of an agency which to Burke, or, indeed, to any reflecting man, appears an agency of the greatest possible power and value? For several reasons. In the first place, the government of this country is, and long has been, in the hands of the aristocratic class. Where the aristocracy is a small oligarchy, able to find employment for all its members in the administration of the State, it is not the enemy, but the friend of State action; for State action is then but its own action under another name, and it is itself directly aggrandized by all that aggrandizes the State. But where, as in this country, the aristocracy is a very large class, by no means coterminous with the executive, but overlapping it and spreading far beyond it, it is the natural enemy rather than the friend of State action; for only a small part of its members can directly administer the State, and it is not for the interest of the remainder to give to this small part an excessive preponderance. Nay, this small part will not be apt to seek it; for its interest in its order is permanent, while its interest in State function is transitory, and it obeys an instinct which attaches it by preference to its order. The more an aristocracy has of that profound political sense by which the English aristocracy is so much distinguished, the more its members obey this instinct; and, by doing so, they signally display their best virtues, moderation, prudence, sagacity; they prevent fruitful occasions of envy, dissension, and strife; they do much to insure the permanence of their order, its harmonious action, and continued predominance. A tradition unfavourable to much State action in home concerns (foreign are another thing) is thus insensibly established in the Government itself. This tradition, this essentially aristocratic sentiment, gains even those members of the Government who are not of the aristocratic class. In the beginning they are overpowered by it; in the end they share it. When the shepherd Daphnis first arrives in heaven, he naturally bows to the august traditions of his new sphere – *candidus insuetum miratur limen Olympi.* By the time the novelty of his situation has worn off, he has come to think just as the immortals do; he is not by conviction the foe of State interference; the worthy Daphnis is all for letting things alone – *amat bonus otia Daphnis.*

Far from trying to encroach upon individual liberty, far from seeking to get everything into its own hands, such a Government has a natural and instinctive tendency to limit its own functions. It turns away from offers of increased responsibility or activity; it deprecates them. To propose increased responsibility and activity to an aristocratic Government is the worst possible way of paying one's court to it. *The Times* is its genuine mouthpiece, when it says that the business of Government, in domestic concerns, is negative – to prevent disorder, jobbery, and extravagance; that it need 'have no notion of securing the future, not even of regulating the present'; that it may and ought to 'leave the course of events to regulate itself, and trust the future to the security of the unknown laws of human nature and the unseen influences of higher powers.' This is the true aristocratic theory of civil government: to have recourse as little as possible to State action, to the collective action of the community; to leave as much as possible to the individual, to local government. And why? Because the members of an artistocratic class are preponderating individuals, with the local government in their hands. No wonder that they do no wish to see the State overshadowing them and ordering them about. Since the feudal epoch, the palmy time of local government, the State has overlaid individual action quite enough. Mr Adderley[7] remembers with a sigh that 'Houses of

Correction were once voluntary institutions.' Go a little further back, and the court of justice was a voluntary institution; the gallows was a voluntary institution; voluntary, I mean, in Mr Adderley's sense of the word voluntary – not depending on the State, but on the local government, on the lord of the soil, on the preponderating individual. The State has overlaid the feudal gallows, it has overlaid the feudal court of justice, it has overlaid the feudal House of Correction, and finally, says Mr Adderley, 'it has overlaid our school-system'. What will it do next?

In the aristocratic class, whose members mainly compose and whose sentiment powerfully pervades the executive of this country, jealousy of State action is, I repeat, an intelligible, a profoundly natural feeling. That, amid the temptations of office, they have remained true to it is a proof of their practical sense, their sure tact, their moderation – the qualities which go to make that *governing spirit* for which the English aristocracy is so remarkable. And perhaps this governing spirit of theirs is destined still to stand them in good stead through all the new and changing development of modern society. Perhaps it will give them the tact to discern the critical moment at which it becomes of urgent national importance that an agency, not in itself very agreeable to them, should be used more freely than heretofore. They have had the virtue to prefer the general interest of their order to personal temptations of aggrandizing themselves through this agency; perhaps they will be capable of the still higher virtue of admitting, in the general interest of their country, this agency, in spite of the natural prejudices and the seeming immediate interest of their own order. Already there are indications that this is not impossible. No thoughtful observer can have read Lord Derby's remarks last session on the regulation of our railway system, can have followed the course of a man like Sir John Pakington on the Education question, can have watched the disposition of the country gentlemen on a measure like Mr Gladstone's Government Annuities Bill, without recognizing that political instinct, that governing spirit, which often in the aristocratic class of this country is wiser both than the unelastic pedantry of theorizing Liberalism, and than their own prejudices.

The working classes have no antipathy to State action. Against this, or against anything else, indeed, presented to them in close connexion with some proceeding which they dislike, it is no doubt quite possible to get them to raise a cry; but to the thing itself they have no objection. Quite the contrary. They often greatly embarrass their Liberal friends and patrons from other classes, one of whose favourite catchwords is *no State interference*, by their resolute refusal to adopt this Shibboleth, to embrace this article of their patrons' creed. They will join with them in their liberalism, not in their crotchets. Left to themselves, they are led, as by their plain interest, so, too, by their natural disposition, to welcome the action of the State in their behalf.

It is the middle class that has been this action's great enemy. And originally it had good reason to be its enemy. In the youth and early manhood of the English middle class, the action of the State was at the service of an ecclesiastical party. This party used the power of the State to secure their own predominance, and to enforce conformity to their own tenets. The stronghold of Nonconformity then, as now, was in the middle class; in its struggle to repel the conformity forced upon it, the middle class underwent great suffering and injustice; and it has never forgotten them. It has never forgotten that the hand which smote it – the hand which did the bidding of its High Church and prelatical enemies – was the hand of the State. It has confronted the State with hostile jealousy ever since. The State tried to do it violence, so it does not love the State; the State failed to subdue it, so it does not respect the State. It regards it with something of aversion and something of contempt. It professes the desire to limit its functions as much as possible, to restrict its action to matters where it is indispensably necessary, to make of it a mere tax-collector and policeman – the hewer of wood and drawer of water to the community.

There is another cause also which indisposes the English middle class to increased action on the part of the State. M. Amédée Thierry, in his 'History of the Gauls', observes, in contrasting the Gaulish and Germanic races, that the first is characterized by the instinct of intelligence and mobility, and by the preponderant action of individuals; the second, by the instinct of discipline and order, and by the preponderant action of bodies of men. This general law of M. Thierry's has to submit to many limitations, but there is a solid basis of truth in it. Applying the law to a people mainly of German blood like ourselves, we shall best perceive its truth by regarding the middle class of the nation. Multitudes, all the world over, have a good deal in common; aristocracies, all the world over, have a good deal in common. The peculiar national form and habit exist in the masses at the bottom of society in a loose, rudimentary, potential state; in the few at the top of society, in a state modified and reduced by various cultures. The man of the multitude has not yet solidified into the typical Englishman; the man of the aristocracy has been etherealized out of him. The typical Englishman is to be looked for in the middle class. And there we shall find him, with a complexion not ill-suiting M. Thierry's law; with a spirit not very open to new ideas, and not easily ravished by them; not, therefore, a great enthusiast for universal progress, but with a strong love of discipline and order – that is, of keeping things settled, and much as they are; and with a disposition, instead of lending himself to the onward-looking statesman and legislator, to act with bodies of men of his own kind, whose aims and efforts reach no further than his own. Poverty and hope make man the friend of ideals, therefore the multitude has a turn for ideals; culture and genius make man the friend of ideals, therefore the gifted or highly trained few have a turn for ideals. The middle class has the whet neither of poverty nor of culture; it is not ill-off in the things of the body, and it is not highly trained in the things of the mind; therefore it has little turn for ideals: it is self-satisfied. This is a chord in the nature of the English middle class which seldom fails, when struck, to give an answer, and which some people are never weary of striking. All the variations which are played on the endless theme of *local self-government* rely on this chord. Hardly any local government is, in truth, in this country, exercised by the middle class; almost the whole of it is exercised by the aristocratic class. Every locality in France – that country which our middle class is taught so much to compassionate – has a genuine municipal government, in which the middle class has its due share; and by this municipal government all matters of local concern (schools among the number) are regulated; not a country parish in England has any effective government of this kind at all. But what is meant by the habit of local self-government, on which our middle class is so incessantly felicitated, is its habit of voluntary combination, in bodies of its own arranging, for purposes of its own choosing – purposes to be carried out within the limits fixed for a private association by its own powers. When the middle class is solemnly warned against State interference, lest it should destroy 'the habit of self-reliance and love of local self-government', it is this habit, and the love of it, that are meant. When we are told that 'nothing can be more dangerous than these constant attempts on the part of the Government to take from the people the management of its own concerns', this is the sort of management of our own concerns that is meant; not the management of them by a regular local government, but the management of them by chance private associations. It is our habit of acting through these associations which, says Mr Roebuck,[8] saves us from being 'a set of helpless imbeciles, totally incapable of attending to our own interests.' It is in the event of this habit being at all altered that, according to the same authority, 'the greatness of this country is gone'.* And the middle class, to whom that habit is familiar and very dear, will never be insensible to language of this sort.

* Mr Roebuck, in his recent excellent speech at Sheffield, has shown that in popular education, at any rate, he does not mean these maxims to apply without restriction. But perhaps it is a little incautious for a public man ever to throw out, without guarding himself, maxims of this kind; for, on the one hand, in this country such maxims are sure never to be lost sight of; on the other, but too many people are sure always to be prone to use them amiss, and to push their application much further than it ought to go.

Finally, the English middle class has a strong practical sense and habit of affairs, and it sees that things managed by the Government are often managed ill. It sees them treated sometimes remissly, sometimes vexatiously, now with a paralysing want of fruitful energy, now with an over-busy fussiness, with rigidity, with formality, without due consideration of special circumstances. Here, too, it finds a motive disinclining it to trust State-action, and leading it to give a willing ear to those who declaim against it.

Now, every one of these motives of distrust is respectable. Every one of them has, or once had, a solid ground. Every one of them points to some virtue in those actuated by it, which is not to be suppressed, but to find true conditions for its exercise. The English middle class was quite right in repelling State action, when the State suffered itself to be made an engine of the High Church party to persecute Nonconformists. It gave an excellent lesson to the State in so doing. It rendered a valuable service to liberty of thought and to all human freedom. If State action now threatened to lend itself to one religious party against another, the middle class could be quite right in again thwarting and confining it. But can it be said that the State now shows the slightest disposition to take such a course? Is such a course the course towards which the modern spirit carries the State? Does not the State show, more and more, the resolution to hold the balance perfectly fair between religious parties? The middle class has it in its own power, more than any other class, to confirm the State in this resolution. This class has the power to make it thoroughly sure – in organizing, for instance, any new system of public instruction – that the State shall treat all religious persuasions with exactly equal fairness. If, instead of holding aloof, it will now but give its aid to make State-action equitable, it can make it so.

Again, as to the 'habits of self-reliance and the love of local self-government.' People talk of Government *interference*, Government *control*, as if State action were necessarily something imposed upon them from without; something despotic and self-originated; something which took no account of their will, and left no freedom to their activity. Can any one really suppose that, in a country like this, State action – in education, for instance – can ever be that, unless we choose to make it so? We can give it what form we will. We can make it our agent, not our master. In modern societies the agency of the State, in certain matters, is so indispensable, that it will manage, with or without our common consent, to come into operation somehow; but when it has introduced itself without the common consent – when a great body, like the middle class, will have nothing to say to it – then its course is indeed likely enough to be not straightforward, its operation not satisfactory. But, by all of us consenting to it, we remove any danger of this kind. By really agreeing to deal in our collective and corporate character with education, we can form ourselves into the best and most efficient of voluntary societies for managing it. We can make State action upon it a genuine local government of it, the faithful but potent expression of our own activity. We can make the central Government that mere court of disinterested review and correction, which every sensible man would always be glad to have for his own activity. We shall have all our self-reliance and individual action still (in this country we shall always have plenty of them, and the parts will always be more likely to tyrannize over the whole than the whole over the parts), but we shall have had the good sense to turn them to account by a powerful, but still voluntary, organization. Our beneficence will be 'beneficence acting *by rule*' (that is Burke's definition of law, as instituted by a free society), and all the more effective for that reason. Must this make us 'a set of helpless imbeciles, totally incapable of attending to our own interests'? Is this 'a grievous blow aimed at the independence of the English character'? Is 'English self-reliance and independence' to be perfectly satisfied with what it produces already without this organization? In middle-class education it produces, without it, the educational home and the classical and commercial academy. Are we to be proud of that? Are we to be satisfied with that? Is 'the greatness of this country' to be seen in that? But it will be said that, awakening to a sense of the badness of our middle-class education, we are beginning to improve it. Undoubtedly we are; and the most certain sign of that awakening, of those beginnings of improvement, is the disposition to resort to a public agency, to 'beneficence working *by rule*', to help us on faster with it. When we really begin to care about a matter of this kind, we cannot help turning to the most efficient agency at our disposal. Clap-trap and commonplace lose their power over us; we begin to see that, if State action has often its inconveniences, our self-reliance and independence are best shown in so arranging our State action as to guard against those inconveniences, not in foregoing State action for fear of them. So it was in elementary education. Mr Baines[9] says that this was already beginning to improve, when Government interfered with it. Why, it was because we were all beginning to take a real interest in it, beginning to improve it, that we turned to Government – to ourselves in our corporate character – to get it improved faster. So long as we did not care much about it, we let it go its own way, and kept singing Mr Roebuck's fine old English stave about 'self-reliance'. We kept crying just as he cries now: 'Nobody has the same interest to do well for a man as he himself has.' That was all very pleasant so long as we cared not a rush whether the people were educated or no. The moment we began to concern ourselves about this, we asked ourselves what our song was worth. We asked ourselves how the bringing up of our labourers and artisans – they 'doing for themselves', and 'nobody having the same interest to do well for a man as he himself has' – was being done. We found it was being done detestably. Then we asked ourselves whether casual, precarious, voluntary beneficence, or 'beneficence acting by rule', was the better agency for doing it better. We asked ourselves if we could not employ our public resources on this concern, if we could not make our beneficence act upon it by rule, without losing our 'habit of self-reliance', without 'aiming a grievous blow at the independence of the English character.' We found that we could; we began to do it; and we left Mr Baines[9] to sing in the wilderness.

Finally, as to the objection that our State action – our 'beneficence working by rule' – often bungles and does its work badly. No wonder it does. The imperious necessities of modern society force it, more or less, even in this country, into play; but it is exercised by a class to whose cherished instincts it is opposed – the aristocratic class; and it is watched by a class to whose cherished prejudices it is opposed – the middle class. It is hesitatingly exercised and jealously watched. It therefore works without courage, cordiality, or belief in itself. Under its present conditions it must work so, and, working so, it must often bungle. But it need not work so; and the moment the middle class abandons its attitude of jealous aversion, the moment they frankly put their hand to it, the moment they adopt it as an instrument to do them service, it will work so no longer. Then it will not bungle; then, if it is applied, say, to education, it will not be fussy, baffling, and barren; it will bring to bear on this concern the energy and strong practical sense of the middle class itself.

But the middle class must make it do this. They must not expect others to do the business for them. It is they whose interest is concerned in its being done, and they must do it for themselves. Why should the upper class – the aristocratic class – do it for them? What motive – except the distant and not very peremptory one of their general political sense, their instinct for taking the course which, for the whole country's sake, ought to be taken – have the aristocratic class to impel them to go counter to all their natural maxims, nay, and to all their seeming interest? They do not want new schools for their children. The great public schools of the country are theirs already. Their numbers are not such as to overflow these few really public schools; their fortunes are such as to make the expensiveness of these schools a matter of indifference to them. The Royal Commissioners, whose report has just appeared, do not, indeed, give a very brilliant picture of the book-learning of these schools. But it is not the book-learning (easy to be improved if there is a will to improve it) that this class make their first care; they make their first care the tone, temper, and habits generated in these schools. So long as they generate a public spirit, a free spirit, a high spirit, a governing spirit, they are not ill-satisfied. Their children are fitted to succeed them in the government of the country. Why should they concern themselves to change this state of things? Why should they create competitors for their own children? Why should they labour to endow another class with those great instruments of power - a public spirit, a free spirit, a high spirit, a governing spirit? Why should they do violence to that distaste for State action, which, in an aristocratic class, is natural and instinctive, for the benefit of the middle class?

No; the middle class must do this work for themselves. From them must come the demand for the satisfaction of a want that is theirs. They must leave off being frightened at shadows. They may keep (I hope they always will keep) the maxim that self-reliance and independence are the most invaluable of blessings, that the great end of society is the perfecting of the individual, the fullest, freest, and worthiest development of the individual's activity. But that the individual may be perfected, that his activity may be worthy, he must often learn to quit old habits, to adopt new, to go out for himself, to transform himself. It was said, and truly said, of one of the most unwearied and successful strivers after human perfection that have ever lived – Wilhelm von Humboldt – that it was a joy to him to feel himself modified by the operation of a foreign influence. And this may well be a joy to a man whose centre of character and whose moral force are once securely established. Through this he makes growth in perfection. Through this he enlarges his being and fills up gaps in it; he unlearns old prejudices and learns new excellences; he makes advance towards inward light and freedom. Societies may use this means of perfection as well as individuals, and it is a characteristic (perhaps the best characteritic) of our age, that they are using it more and more. Let us look at our neighbour, France. What strikes a thoughtful observer most in modern France, is the great, wide breach which is being made in the old French mind; the strong flow with which a foreign thought is pouring in and mixing with it. There is an extraordinary increase in the number of German and English books read there, books the most unlike possible to the native literary growth of France. There is a growing disposition there to pull to pieces old stock French commonplaces, and to put a bridle upon old stock French habitudes. France will not, and should not, like some English liberals, run a-muck against State action altogether; but she shows a tendency to control her excessive State action, to reduce it within just limits where it has overpassed them, to make a larger part for free local activity and for individuals. She will not, and should not, like Sir Archibald Alison, cry down her great Revolution as the work of Satan; but she shows more and more the power to discern the real faults of that Revolution, the real part of delusion, impotence, and transitoriness in the work of 1789 or of 1791, and to profit by that discernment.

Our middle class has secured for itself that centre of character and that moral force which are, I have said, the indispensable basis upon which perfection is to be founded. To securing them, its vigour in resisting the State, when the State tried to tyrannize over it, has contributed not a little. In this sense, it may be said to have made way towards perfection by repelling the State's hand. Now it has to enlarge and to adorn its spirit. I cannot seriously argue with those who deny that the independence and free action of the middle class is now, in this country, immutably secure; I cannot treat the notion of the State now overriding it and doing violence to it, as anything but a vain chimera. Well, then, if the State can (as it can) be of service to the middle class in the work of enlarging its mind and adorning its spirit, it will now make way towards perfection by taking the State's hand. State action is not in itself unfavourable to the individual's perfection, to his attaining his fullest development. So far from it, it is in ancient Greece, where State action was omnipresent, that we see the individual at his very highest pitch of free and fair activity. This is because, in Greece, the individual was strong enough to fashion the State into an instrument of his own perfection, to make it serve, with a thousand times his own power, towards his own ends. He was not enslaved by it, he did not annihilate it, but he used it. Where, in modern nations, the State has maimed and crushed individual activity, it has been by operating as an alien, exterior power in the community, a power not originated by the community to serve the common weal, but entrenched among them as a conqueror with a weal of its own to serve. Just because the vigour and sturdiness of the people of this country have prevented, and will always prevent, the State from being anything of this kind, I believe we, more than any modern people, have the power of renewing, in our national life, the example of Greece. I believe that we, and our American kinsmen, are specially fit to apply State action with advantage, because we are specially sure to apply it voluntarily.

Two things must, I think, strike any one who attentively regards the English middle class at this moment. One is the intellectual ferment which is taking place, or rather, which is beginning to take place, amongst them. It is only in its commencement as yet; but it shows itself at a number of points, and bids fair to become a great power. The importance of a change, placing in the great middle class the centre of the intellectual life of this country, can hardly be over-estimated. I have been reproved for saying that the culture and intellectual life of our highest class seem to me to have somewhat flagged since the last century. That is my opinion, indeed, and all that I see and hear strengthens rather than shakes it. The culture of this class is not what it used to be. Their value for high culture, their belief in its importance, is not what it used to be. One may see it in the public schools, one may see it in the universities. Whence come the deadness, the want of intellectual life, the poverty of acquirement after years of schooling, which the Commissioners, in their remarkable and interesting report, show us so prevalent in our most distinguished public schools? What gives to play and amusement, both there and at the universities, their present overweening importance, so that home critics cry out: 'The real studies of Oxford are its games', and foreign critics cry out: 'At Oxford the student is still the mere schoolboy'? The most experienced and acute of Oxford heads of houses told me himself, that when he spoke to an undergraduate the other day about trying for some distinguished scholarship, the answer he got was: 'Oh, the men from the great schools don't care for those things now; the men who care about them are the men from Marlborough, Cheltenham, and the second-rate schools.' Whence, I say, does this slackness, this sleep of the mind, come, except from a torpor of intellectual life, a dearth of ideas, an indifference to fine culture or disbelief in its necessity, spreading through the bulk of our highest class, and influencing its rising generation? People talk as if the culture of this class had only changed; the Greek and Roman classics, they say, are no longer in vogue as they were in Lord Chesterfield's time. Well, if this class had only gone from one source of high culture to another; if only, instead of reading Homer and Cicero, it now read Goethe and Montesquieu – but it does not; it reads *The Times* and the *Agricultural Journal.* And it devotes itself to practical life. And it amuses itself. It is not its rising generation only which loves play; never in all its history has our whole highest class shown such zeal for enjoying life, for amusing itself. It would be absurd to make this a matter of reproach against it. The triumphs of material progress multiply the means of material enjoyment; they attract all classes, more and more, to taste of this enjoyment; on the highest class, which possesses in the amplest measure these means, they must needs exercise this attraction very powerfully. But every thoughtful observer can perceive that the ardour for amusement and enjoyment, often educative and quickening to a toil-numbed working class or a strait-laced middle class, whose great want is expansion, tends to become enervative and weakening to an aristocratic class – a class which must rule by superiority of all kinds, superiority not to be won without contention of spirit and a certain severity. I think, therefore, both that the culture of our highest class has declined, and that this declension, though natural and venial, impairs its power.

Yet in this vigorous country everything has a wonderful ability for self-restoration, and he would be a bold prophet who should deny that the culture of our highest class may recover itself. But however this may be, there is no doubt that a liberal culture, a fullness of intellectual life, in the middle class, is a far more important matter, a far more efficacious stimulant to national progress, than the same powers in an aristocratic class. Whatever may be its culture, an aristocratic class will always have at bottom, like the young man in Scripture with great possessions, an inaptitude for ideas; but, besides this, high culture or ardent intelligence, pervading a large body of the community, acquire a breath of basis, a sum of force, an energy of central heat for radiating further, which they can never possess when they pervade a small upper class only. It is when such a broad basis is obtained, that individual genius gets its proper nutriment, and is animated to put forth its best powers; this is the secret of rich and beautiful epochs in national life; the epoch of Pericles in Greece, the epoch of Michelangelo in Italy, the epoch of Shakespeare in England. Our actual middle class has not yet, certainly, the fine culture, or the living intelligence, which quickened great bodies of men at these epochs; but it has the forerunner, the preparer, the indispensable initiator; it is traversed by a strong intellectual ferment. It is the middle class which has real mental ardour, real curiosity; it is the middle class which is the great reader; that immense literature of the day which we see surging up all round us – literature the absolute value of which it is almost impossible to rate too humbly, literature hardly a word of which will reach, or deserves to reach, the future – it is the middle class which calls it forth, and its evocation is at least a sign of a widespread mental movement in that class. Will this movement go on and become fruitful: will it conduct the middle class to a high and commanding pitch of culture and intelligence? That depends on the sensibility which the middle class has for *perfection*; that depends on its power to *transform itself.*

And it is not yet manifest how far it possesses this power. For – and here I pass to the second of those two things which particularly, I have said, strike any one who observes the English middle class just now – in its public action this class has hitherto shown only the power and disposition to *affirm itself,* not at all the power and disposition to *transform itself.* That, indeed, is one of the deep-seated instincts of human nature, but of vulgar human nature – of human nature not high-souled and aspiring after perfection – to esteem itself for what it is, to try to establish itself just as it is, to try even to impose itself with its stock of habitudes, pettinesses, narrownesses, shortcomings of every kind, on the rest of the world as a conquering power. But nothing has really a right to be satisfied with itself, to be and remain itself, except that which has reached perfection; and nothing has the right to impose itself on the rest of the world as a conquering force, except that which is of higher perfection than the rest of the world. And such is the fundamental constitution of human affairs, that the measure of right proves also, in the end, the measure of power. Before the English middle class can have the right or the power to assert itself absolutely, it must have greatly perfected itself. It has been jokingly said of this class, that all which the best of it cared for was summed up in this alliterative phrase – *Business and Bethels:* and that all which the rest of it cared for was the *Business* without the *Bethels*. No such jocose and slighting words can convey any true sense of what the religion of the English middle class has really been to it; what a source of vitality, energy, and persistent vigour. 'They who wait on the Lord', says Isaiah, in words not less true than they are noble, '*shall renew their strength*'; and the English middle class owes to its religion not only comfort in the past, but also a vast latent force of unworn life and strength for future progress. But the Puritanism of the English middle class, which has been so great an element of strength to them, has by no means brought them to perfection; nay, by the rigid mould in which it has cast their spirit, it has kept them back from perfection. The most that can be said of it is, that it has supplied a stable basis on which to build perfection; it has given them character, though it has not given them culture. But it is in making endless additions to itself, in the endless expansion of its powers, in endless growth in wisdom and beauty, that the spirit of the human race finds its ideal; to reach this ideal, culture is an indispensable aid, and that is the true value of culture. The life of aristocracies, with its large and free use of the world, its conversance with great affairs, its exemption from sordid cares, its liberation from the humdrum provincial round, its external splendour and refinement, is a kind of outward shadow of this ideal, a prophecy of it; and there lies the secret of the charm of aristocracies, and of their power over men's minds. In a country like England, the middle class, with its industry and its Puritanism, and nothing more, will never be able to make way beyond a certain point, will never be able to divide power with the aristocratic class, much less to win for itself a preponderance of power. While it only tries to affirm its actual self, to impose its actual self, it has no charm for men's minds, and can achieve no great triumphs. And this is all it attempts at present. The Conservative reaction, of which we hear so much just now, is in great part merely a general indisposition to let the middle-class spirit, working by its old methods, and having only its old self to give us, establish itself at all points and become master of the situation. Particularly on Church questions is this true. In this sphere of religion, where feeling and beauty are so all-important, we shrink from giving to the middle-class spirit, limited as we see it, with its sectarianism, its under-culture, its intolerance, its bitterness, its unloveliness, too much its own way. Before we give it quite its own way, we insist on its making itself into something larger, newer, more fruitful. This is what the recent Church-Rate divisions[10] really mean, and the lovers of perfection, therefore, may accept them without displeasure. They are the voice of the nation crying to the *untransformed* middle class (if it will receive it) with a voice of thunder: 'The future is not yours!'

And let me say, in passing, that the indifference, so irritating to some persons, with which European opinion has received the break-up of the old American Union has at bottom a like ground. I put the question of slavery on one side; so far as the resolution of that question depends on the issue of the conflict between the North and the South, every one may wish this party or that to prevail. But Mr Bright and Mr Cobden extol the old American Republic as something interesting and admirable in itself, and are displeased with those who are not afflicted at its disaster, and not jealous for its restoration.[11] Mr Bright is an orator of genius; Mr Cobden is a man of splendid understanding. But why do they refuse to perceive that, apart from all class-jealousy of aristocracies towards a democratic republic, there existed in the most impartial and thoughtful minds a profound dissatisfaction with the spirit and tendencies of the old American Union, a strong aversion to their unchecked triumph, a sincere wish for the disciplining and correcting of them? And what were the old United States but a colossal expression of the English middle-class spirit, somewhat more accessible to ideas there than here, because of the democratic air it breathed, much more arrogant and overweening there than here, because of the absence of all check and counterpoise to it – but there, as here, greatly needing to be liberalized, enlarged, and ennobled, before it could with advantage be suffered to assert itself absolutely? All the energy and success in the world could not have made the United States admirable so long as their spirit had this imperfection. Even if they had overrun the whole earth, their old national style would have still been detestable, and Mr Beecher would have still been a heated barbarian. But they could not thus triumph, they could not make their rule thus universal, so long as their spirit was thus imperfect. They had not power enough over the minds of men. Now they are transforming their spirit in the furnace of civil war; with what success we shall in due time see. But the lovers of perfection in America itself ought to rejoice – some of them, no doubt, do rejoice – that the national spirit should be compelled, even at any cost of suffering, to transform itself, to become something higher, ampler, more gracious. To be glad that it should be compelled thus to transform itself, that it should not be permitted to triumph untransformed, is no insult, no unkindness; it is a homage to perfection. It is a religious devotion to that providential order which forbids the final supremacy of imperfect things. God keeps tossing back to the human race its failures, and commanding it to try again.

In the Crusade of Peter the Hermit, where the hosts that marched were not filled after the usual composition of armies, but contained along with the fighters whole families of people – old men, women, and children, swept by the universal torrent of enthusiasm towards the Holy Land – the marches, as might have been expected, were tedious and painful. Long before Asia was reached, long before even Europe was half traversed, the little childen in that travelling multitude began to fancy, with a natural impatience, that their journey must surely be drawing to an end; and every evening, as they came in sight of some town which was the destination of that day's march, they cried out eagerly to those who were with them, '*Is this Jerusalem?*' No, poor children, not this town, nor the next, nor yet the next, is Jerusalem; Jerusalem is far off, and it needs time, and strength, and much endurance to reach it. Seas and mountains, labour and peril, hunger and thirst, disease and death, are between Jerusalem and you.

So, when one marks the ferment and stir of life in the middle class at this moment, and sees this class impelled to take possession of the world, and to assert itself and its own actual spirit absolutely, one is disposed to exclaim to it, '*Jerusalem is not yet*. Your present spirit is not Jerusalem, is not the goal you have to reach, the place you may be satisfied in.' And when one says this, they sometimes fancy that one has the same object as others who say the same to them; that one means that they are to yield themselves to be moulded by some existing force,their rival; that one wishes Nonconformity to take the law from actual Anglicanism, and the middle class from the present governing class; that one thinks Anglicanism Jerusalem, and the English aristocratic class Jerusalem.

I do not mean, or wish, or think this, though many, no doubt, do. It is not easy for a reflecting man, who has studied its origin, to feel any vehement enthusiasm for Anglicanism; Henry VIII and his parliaments have taken care of that. One may esteem it as a beneficent social and civilizing agent. One may have an affection for it from life-long associations, and for the sake of much that is venerable and interesting which it has inherited from antiquity. One may cherish gratitude to it – and here, I think, Mr Goldwin Smith, who fights against it the battle of the Nonconformists with so much force and so much ability, is a little ungrateful – for the shelter and basis for culture which this, like other great nationally established forms of religion, affords; those who are born in them can get forward on their road, instead of always eyeing the ground on which they stand and disputing about it. But actual Anglicanism is certainly not Jerusalem, and I should be sorry to think it the end which Nonconformity and the middle class are to reach. The actual governing class, again, the English aristocratic class (in the widest sense of the word *aristocratic*) – I cannot wish that the rest of the nation, the new and growing part of the nation, should be transformed in spirit exactly according to the image of that class. The merits and services of that class no one rates higher than I do; no one appreciates higher than I do the value of the relative standard of elevation, refinement and grandeur, which they have exhibited; no one would more strenuously oppose the relinquishing of this for any lower standard. But I cannot hide from myself that while modern societies increasingly tend to find their best life in a free and heightened spiritual and intellectual activity, to this tendency aristocracies offer at least a strong passive resistance, by their eternal prejudices, their incurable dearth of ideas. In modern, rich, and industrial societies, they tend to misplace the ideal for the classes below them; the immaterial chivalrous ideal of high descent and honour is, by the very nature of the case, of force only for aristocracies themselves; the immaterial modern ideal of spiritual and intellectual perfection through culture, they have not to communicate. What they can and do communicate is the material ideal of splendour of wealth, and weight of property. And this ideal is the ideal truly operative upon our middle classes at this moment. To be as rich as they can, that they may reach the splendour of wealth and weight of property, and, with time, the importance, of the actual head of society, is their ambition. I do not blame them, or the class from which they get their ideal; all I say is, that the good ideal for humanity, the true Jerusalem, is an ideal more spiritual than splendid wealth and boundless property, an ideal in which more can participate. The beloved friends of humanity have been those who made it feel its ideal to be in the things of the mind and spirit, to be in an internal condition separable from wealth and accessible to all – men like St Francis, the ardent bridegroom of poverty; men like the great personages of antiquity, almost all of them, as Lacordaire was so fond of saying, poor. Therefore, that the middle class should simple take its ideal from the aristocratic class, I do not wish. That the aristocratic class should be able absolutely to assert itself and its own spirit, is not my desire. No, no; they are not Jerusalem.

The truth is, the English spirit has to accomplish an immense evolution; not, as that spirit at this moment presents itself in any class or description amongst us, can one be perfectly satisfied with it, can one wish it to prevail just as it it.

But in a transformed middle class, in a middle class raised to a higher and more genial culture, we may find, not perhaps Jerusalem, but, I am sure, a notable stage towards it. In that great class, strong by its numbers, its energy, its industry, strong by its freedom from frivolity, not by any law of nature prone to immobility of mind, actually at this moment agitated by a spreading ferment of mind, in that class, liberalized by an ampler culture, admitted to a wider sphere of thought, living by larger ideas, with its provincialism dissipated, its intolerance cured, its pettinesses purged away – what a power there will be, what an element of new life for England! Then let the middle class rule, then let it affirm its own spirit, when it has thus perfected itself.

And I cannot see any means so direct and powerful for developing this great and beneficent power as the public establishment of schools for the middle class. By public establishment they may be made cheap and accessible to all. By public establishment they may give securities for the culture offered in them being really good and sound, and the best that our time knows. By public establishment they may communicate to those reared in them the sense of being brought in contact with their country, with the national life, with the life of the world; and they will expand and dignify their spirits by communicating this sense to them. I can see no other mode of institution which will offer the same advantages in the same degree.

I cannot think that the middle class will be much longer insensible to its own evident interests. I cannot think that, for the pleasure of being complimented on their self-reliance by Lord Fortescue and *The Times*, they will much longer forego a course leading them to their own true dignity instead of away from it. I know that with men who have reached or passed the middle of life, the language and habits of years form a network round the spirit through which it cannot easily break; and among the elder leaders of the middle class there are men whom I would give much to persuade – men of weight and character, like Mr Baines, men of character and culture too, like Mr Miall[12] – whom I must not, I fear, hope to persuade. But among the younger leaders of this class – even of that part of it where resistance is most to be apprehended, among the younger Dissenting ministers, for instance – there exists, I do believe, a disposition not fixedly averse to the public establishment of education for the middle classes – a willingness, at any rate, to consider a project of this kind on its merits. Amongst them particularly is the ferment and expansion of mind, of which I have spoken, perceptible; their sense of the value of culture, and their culture itself, increases every day. Well, the old bug-bear which scares us all away from the great confessed means of best promoting this culture – the religious difficulty, as it is called – is potent only so long as these gentlemen please. It rests solely with themselves to procure the public establishment of secondary instruction upon a perfectly equitable basis as regards religious differences. If its establishment is suffered to fix itself in private hands, those hands will be the clergy's. It is to the honour of the clergy – of their activity, of their corporate spirit, of their sense of a pressing want – that this should be so. But in that case the dominant force in settling the teaching in the schools will be clerical. Their organization will be ecclesiastical. Mr Woodard tells us so himself; and indeed he (very naturally) makes a merit of it. This is not what the Dissenters want, neither is it what the movement of the modern spirit tends to. But when instruction has once been powerfully organized in this manner, it is very difficult for the State afterwards to interfere for the purpose of giving effects to the requirements of the modern spirit. It is met by vested interests – by legitimate vested interests – not to be conciliated without great delay and difficulty. It is not easy for the State to impose a conscience clause on primary schools, when the establishment of those schools has been for the most part made by the clergy. It is not easy to procure the full benefits of the national universities to Nonconformists, when Anglicanism has got a vested interest in the colleges. Neither will it be easy hereafter, in secondary instruction, to settle the religious difficulty equitably, if the establishment of that instruction shall have been effected by private bodies in which clerical influence predominates.

I hope the middle class will not much longer delay to take a step on which its future value and dignity and influence so much depend. By taking this step they will indirectly confer a great boon upon the lower class also. This obscure embryo, only just beginning to move, travailing in labour and darkness, so much left out of account when we celebrate the glories of our Atlantis, now and then, by so mournful a glimpse, showing itself to us in Lambeth, or Spitalfields, or Dorsetshire; this immense working class, now so without a practicable passage to all the joy and beauty of life, for whom in an aristocratic class, which is unattainable by them, there is no possible ideal, for whom in a middle class, narrow, ungenial, and unattractive, there is no adequate ideal, will have, in a cultured, liberalized, ennobled, transformed middle class, a point towards which it may hopefully work, a goal towards which it may with joy direct its aspirations.

Children of the future, whose day has not yet dawned, you, when that day arrives, will hardly believe what obstructions were long suffered to prevent its coming! You who, with all your faults, have neither the aridity of aristocracies, nor the narrow-mindedness of middle classes, you, whose power of simple enthusiasm is your great gift, will not comprehend how progress towards man's best perfection – the adorning and ennobling of his spirit – should have been reluctantly undertaken; how it should have been for years and years retarded by barren commonplaces, by worn-out claptraps. You will wonder at the labour of its friends in proving the self-proving; you will know nothing of the doubts, the fears, the prejudices they had to dispel; nothing of the outcry they had to encounter; of the fierce protestations of life from policies which were dead and did not know it, and the shrill querulous upbraiding from publicists in their dotage. But you, in your turn, with difficulties of your own, will then be mounting some new step in the arduous ladder whereby man climbs towards his perfection; towards that unattainable but irresistible lode-star, gazed after with earnest longing, and invoked with bitter tears; the longing of thousands of hearts, the tears of many generations.

Culture and Anarchy (1868–9)

Estote ergo vos perfecti![1]

Introduction

In one of his speeches a short time ago, that fine speaker and famous Liberal, Mr Bright,[2] took occasion to have a fling at the friends and preachers of culture. 'People who talk about what they call *culture!*' said he, contemptuously; 'by which they mean a smattering of the two dead languages of Greek and Latin.' And he went on to remark, in a strain with which modern speakers and writers have made us very familiar, how poor a thing this culture is, how little good it can do to the world, and how absurd it is for its possessors to set much store by it. And the other day a younger Liberal than Mr Bright, one of a school whose mission it is to bring into order and system that body of truth with which the earlier Liberals merely fumbled, a member of the University of Oxford, and a very clever writer, Mr Frederic Harrison,[3] developed, in the systematic and stringent manner of his school, the thesis which Mr Bright had propounded in only general terms. 'Perhaps the very silliest cant of the day', said Mr Frederic Harrison, 'is the cant about culture. Culture is a desirable quality in a critic of new books, and sits well on a professor of *belles-lettres*; but as applied to politics, it means simply a turn for small fault-finding, love of selfish ease, and indecision in action. The man of culture is in politics one of the poorest mortals alive. For simple pedantry and want of good sense no man is his equal. No assumption is too unreal, no end is too unpractical for him. But the active exercise of politics requires common sense, sympathy, trust, resolution, and enthusiasm, qualities which your man of culture has carefully rooted up, lest they damage the delicacy of his critical olfactories. Perhaps they are the only class of responsible beings in the community who cannot with safety be entrusted with power.'

Now for my part I do not wish to see men of culture asking to be entrusted with power; and, indeed, I have freely said, that in my opinion the speech most proper, at present, for a man of culture to make to a body of his fellow-countrymen who get him into a committee-room, is Socrates's *Know thyself!*, and this is not a speech to be made by men wanting to be entrusted with power. For this very indifference to direct political action I have been taken to task by the *Daily Telegraph*, coupled, by a strange perversity of fate, with just that very one of the Hebrew prophets whose style I admire the least, and called 'an elegant Jeremiah'. It is because I say (to use the words which the *Daily Telegraph* puts in my mouth): 'You mustn't make a fuss because you have no vote – that is vulgarity; you mustn't hold big meetings to agitate for reform bills and to repeal corn laws – that is the very height of vulgarity – it is for this reason that I am called, sometimes an elegant Jeremiah, sometimes a spurious Jeremiah, a Jeremiah about the reality of whose mission the writer in the *Daily Telegraph* has his doubts. It is evident, therefore, that I have so taken my line as not to be exposed to the whole brunt of Mr Frederic Harrison's censure. Still, I have often spoken in praise of culture, I have striven to make all my works and ways serve the interests of culture. I take culture to be something a great deal more than what Mr Frederic Harrison and others call it, 'a desirable quality in a critic of new books'. Nay, even though to a certain extent I am disposed to agree with Mr Frederic Harrison, that men of culture are just the class of responsible beings in this community of ours who cannot properly, at present, be entrusted with power, I am not sure that I do not think this the fault of our community rather than of the men of culture. In short, although, like Mr Bright and Mr Frederic Harrison, and the editor of the *Daily Telegraph*, and a large body of valued friends of mine, I am a Liberal, yet I am a Liberal tempered by experience, reflection, and renouncement, and I am, above all, a believer in culture. Therefore I propose now to try and inquire, in the simple unsystematic way which best suits both my taste and my powers, what culture really is, what good it can do, what is our own special need of it; and I shall seek to find some plain grounds on which a faith in culture – both my own faith in it and the faith of others – may rest securely.

Sweetness and light

The disparagers of culture make its motive curiosity; sometimes, indeed, they make its motive mere exclusiveness and vanity. The culture which is supposed to plume itself on a smattering of Greek and Latin is a culture which is begotten by nothing so intellectual as curiosity; it is valued either out of sheer vanity and ignorance or else as an engine of social and class distinction, separating its holder, like a badge or title, from other people who have not got it. No serious man would call this *culture*, or attach any value to it, as culture, at all. To find the real ground for the very different estimate which serious people will set upon culture, we must find some motive for culture in the terms of which may lie a real ambiguity; and such a motive the word *curiosity* gives us.

I have before now pointed out that we English do not, like the foreigners, use this word in a good sense as well as in a bad sense. With us the word is always used in a somewhat disapproving sense. A liberal and intelligent eagerness about the things of the mind may be meant by a foreigner when he speaks of curiosity, but with us the word always conveys a certain notion of frivolous and unedifying activity. In the *Quarterly Review*, some little time ago, was an estimate of the celebrated French critic, M. Sainte-Beuve, and a very inadequate estimate it in my judgement was. And its inadequacy consisted chiefly in this: that in our English way it left out of sight the double sense really involved in the word *curiosity*, thinking enough was said to stamp M. Sainte-Beuve with blame if it was said that he was impelled in his operations as a critic by curiosity, and omitting either to perceive that M. Sainte-Beuve himself, and many other people with him, would consider that this was praiseworthy and not blameworthy, or to point out why it ought really to be accounted worthy of blame and not of praise. For as there is a curiosity about intellectual matters which is futile, and merely a disease, so there is certainly a curiosity – a desire after the things of the mind simply for their own sakes and for the pleasure of seeing them as they are – which is, in an intelligent being, natural and laudable. Nay, and the very desire to see things as they are implies a balance and regulation of mind which is not often attained without fruitful effort, and which is the very opposite of the blind and diseased impulse of mind which is what we mean to blame when we blame curiosity. Montesquieu says: 'The first motive which ought to impel us to study is the desire to augment the excellence of our nature, and to render an intelligent being yet more intelligent.' This is the true ground to assign for the genuine scientific passion, however manifested, and for culture, viewed simply as a fruit of this passion; and it is a worthy ground, even though we let the term *curiosity* stand to describe it.

But there is of culture another view, in which not solely the scientific passion, the sheer desire to see things as they are, natural and proper in an intelligent being, appears as the ground of it. There is a view in which all the love of our neighbour, the impulses towards action, help, and beneficence, the desire for removing human error, clearing human confusion, and diminishing human misery, the noble aspiration to leave the world better and happier than we found it – motives eminently such as are called social – come in as part of the grounds of culture, and the main and pre-eminent part. Culture is then properly described not as having its origin in curiosity, but as having its origin in the love of perfection; it is *a study of perfection*. It moves by the force, not merely or primarily of the scientific passion for pure knowledge, but also of the moral and social passion for doing good. As, in the first view of it, we took for its worthy motto Montesquieu's words, 'To render an intelligent being yet more intelligent!' so, in the second view of it, there is no better motto which it can have than these words of Bishop Wilson,[4] 'To make reason and the will of God prevail!'

Only, whereas the passion for doing good is apt to be over-hasty in determining what reason and the will of God say, because its turn is for acting rather than thinking and it wants to be beginning to act; and whereas it is apt to take its own conceptions, which proceed from its own state of development and share in all the imperfections and immaturities of this, for a basis of action; what distinguishes culture is, that it is possessed by the scientific passion as well as by the passion of doing good; that it demands worthy notions of reason and the will of God, and does not readily suffer its own crude conceptions to substitute themselves for them. And knowing that no action or institution can be salutary and stable which is not based on reason and the will of God, it is not so bent on acting and instituting, even with the great aim of diminishing human error and misery ever before its thoughts, but that it can remember that acting and instituting are of little use, unless we know how and what we ought to act and to institute.

This culture is more interesting and more far-reaching than that other, which is founded solely on the scientific passion for knowing. But it needs times of faith and ardour, times when the intellectual horizon is opening and widening all round us, to flourish in. And is not the close and bounded intellectual horizon within which we have long lived and moved now lifting up, and are not new lights finding free passage to shine in upon us? For a long time there was no passage for them to make their way in upon us, and then it was of no use to think of adapting the world's action to them. Where was the hope of making reason and the will of God prevail among people who had a routine which they had christened reason and the will of God, in which they were inextricably bound, and beyond which they had no power of looking? But now the iron force of adhesion to the old routine – social, political, religious – has wonderfully yielded; the iron force of exclusion of all which is new has wonderfully yielded. The danger now is, not that people should obstinately refuse to allow anything but their old routine to pass for reason and the will of God, but either that they should allow some novelty or other to pass for these too easily, or else that they should underrate the importance of them altogether, and think it enough to follow action for its own sake, without troubling themselves to make reason and the will of God prevail therein. Now, then, is the moment for culture to be of service, culture which believes in making reason and the will of God prevail, believes in perfection, is the study and pursuit of perfection, and is no longer debarred, by a rigid invincible exclusion of whatever is new, from getting acceptance for its ideas, simply because they are new.

The moment this view of culture is seized, the moment it is regarded not solely as the endeavour to see things as they are, to draw towards a knowledge of the universal order which seems to be intended and aimed at in the world, and which it is a man's happiness to go along with or his misery to go counter to – to learn, in short, the will of God – the moment, I say, culture is considered not merely as the endeavour to *see* and *learn* this, but as the endeavour, also, to make it *prevail*, the moral, social, and beneficent character of culture becomes manifest. The mere endeavour to see and learn the truth for our own personal satisfaction is indeed a commencement for making it prevail, a preparing the way for this, which always serves this, and is wrongly, therefore, stamped with blame absolutely in itself and not only in its caricature and degeneration. But perhaps it has got stamped with blame, and disparaged with the dubious title of curiosity, because in comparison with this wider endeavour of such great and plain utility it looks selfish, petty, and unprofitable.

And religion, the greatest and most important of the efforts by which the human race has manifested its impulse to perfect itself – religion, that voice of the deepest human experience – does not only enjoin and sanction the aim which is the great aim of culture, the aim of setting ourselves to ascertain what perfection is and to make it prevail; but also, in determining generally in what human perfection consists, religion comes to a conclusion identical with that which culture – culture seeking the determination of this question through *all* the voices of human experience which have been heard upon it, of art, science, poetry, philosophy, history, as well as of religion, in order to give a greater fullness and certainty to its solution – likewise reaches. Religion says: *The kingdom of God is within you*; and culture, in like manner, places human perfection in an *internal* condition, in the growth and predominance of our humanity proper, as distinguished from our animality. It places it in the ever-increasing efficacy and in the general harmonious expansion of those gifts of thought and feeling, which make the peculiar dignity, wealth, and happiness of human nature. As I have said on a former occasion: 'It is in making endless additions to itself, in the endless expansion of its powers, in endless growth in wisdom and beauty, that the spirit of the human race finds its ideal. To reach this ideal, culture is an indispensable aid, and that is the true value of culture.' Not a having and a resting, but a growing and a becoming, is the character of perfection as culture conceives it; and here, too, it coincides with religion.

And because men are all members of one great whole, and the sympathy which is in human nature will not allow one member to be indifferent to the rest or to have a perfect welfare independent of the rest, the expansion of our humanity, to suit the idea of perfection which culture forms, must be a *general* expansion. Perfection, as culture conceives it, is not possible while the individual remains isolated. The individual is required, under pain of being stunted and enfeebled in his own development if he disobeys, to carry others along with him in his march towards perfection, to be continually doing all he can to enlarge and increase the volume of the human stream sweeping thitherward. And here, once more, culture lays on us the same obligation as religion, which says, as Bishop Wilson has admirably put it, that 'to promote the kingdom of God is to increase and hasten one's own happiness.'

But, finally, perfection – as culture from a thorough disinterested study of human nature and human experience learns to conceive it – is a harmonious expansion of *all* the powers which make the beauty and worth of human nature, and is not consistent with the over-development of any one power at the expense of the rest. Here culture goes beyond religion, as religion is generally conceived by us.

If culture, then, is a study of perfection, and of harmonious perfection, general perfection, and perfection which consists in becoming something rather than in having something, in an inward condition of the mind and spirit, not in an outward set of circumstances – it is clear that culture, instead of being the frivolous and useless thing which Mr Bright, and Mr Frederic Harrison, and many other Liberals are apt to call it, has a very important function to fulfil for mankind. And this function is particularly important in our modern world, of which the whole civilization is, to a much greater degree than the civilization of Greece and Rome, mechanical and external, and tends constantly to become more so. But above all in our own country has culture a weighty part to perform, because here that mechanical character, which civilization tends to take everywhere, is shown in the most eminent degree. Indeed nearly all the characters of perfection, as culture teaches us to fix them, meet in this country with some powerful tendency which thwarts them and sets them at defiance. The idea of perfection as an *inward* condition of the mind and spirit is at variance with the mechanical and material civilization in esteem with us, and nowhere, as I have said, so much in esteem as with us. The idea of perfection as a *general* expansion of the human family is at variance with our strong individualism, our hatred of all limits to the unrestrained swing of the individual's personality, our maxim of 'every man for himself'. Above all, the idea of perfection as a *harmonious* expansion of human nature is at variance with our want of flexibility, with our inaptitude for seeing more than one side of a thing, with our intense energetic absorption in the particular pursuit we happen to be following. So culture has a rough task to achieve in this country. Its preachers have, and are likely long to have, a hard time of it, and they will much oftener be regarded, for a great while to come, as elegant or spurious Jeremiahs than as friends and benefactors. That, however, will not prevent their doing in the end good service if they persevere. And, meanwhile, the mode of action they have to pursue, and the sort of habits they must fight against, ought to be made quite clear for every one to see, who may be willing to look at the matter attentively and dispassionately.

Faith in machinery is, I said, our besetting danger; often in machinery most absurdly disproportioned to the end which this machinery, if it is to do any good at all, is to serve; but always in machinery, as if it had a value in and for itself. What is freedom but machinery? What is population but machinery? What is coal but machinery? What are railroads but machinery? What is wealth but machinery? What are, even, religious organizations but machinery? Now almost every voice in England is accustomed to speak of these things as if they were precious ends in themselves, and therefore had some of the characters of perfection indisputably joined to them. I have before now noticed Mr Roebuck's[5] stock argument for proving the greatness and happiness of England as she is, and for quite stopping the mouths of all gainsayers. Mr Roebuck is never weary of reiterating this argument of his, so I do not know why I should be weary of noticing it. 'May not every man in England say what he likes?' Mr Roebuck perpetually asks; and that, he thinks, is quite sufficient, and when every man may say what he likes, our aspirations ought to be satisfied. But the aspirations of culture, which is the study of perfection, are not satisfied, unless what men say, when they may say what they like, is worth saying – has good in it, and more good than bad. In the same way *The Times*, replying to some foreign strictures on the dress, looks, and behaviour of the English abroad, urges that the English ideal is that every one should be free to do and to look just as he likes. But culture indefatigably tries, not to make what each raw person may like the rule by which he fashions himself; but to draw ever nearer to a sense of what is indeed beautiful, graceful, and becoming, and to get the raw person to like that.

And in the same way with respect to railroads and coal. Every one must have observed the strange language current during the late discussions as to the possible failure of our supplies of coal. Our coal, thousands of people were saying, is the real basis of our national greatness; if our coal runs short, there is an end of the greatness of England. But what *is* greatness, culture makes us ask. Greatness is a spiritual condition worthy to excite love, interest, and admiration; and the outward proof of possessing greatness is that we excite love, interest, and admiration. If England were swallowed up by the sea tomorrow, which of the two, a hundred years hence, would most excite the love, interest, and admiration of mankind – would most, therefore, show the evidences of having possessed greatness – the England of the last twenty years, or the England of Elizabeth, of a time of splendid spiritual effort, but when our coal, and our industrial operations depending on coal, were very little developed? Well, then, what an unsound habit of mind it must be which makes us talk of things like coal or iron as constituting the greatness of England, and how salutary a friend is culture, bent on seeing things as they are, and thus dissipating delusions of this kind and fixing standards of perfection that are real!

Wealth, again, that end to which our prodigious works for material advantage are directed – the commonest of commonplaces tells us how men are always apt to regard wealth as a precious end in itself; and certainly they have never been so apt thus to regard it as they are in England at the present time. Never did people believe anything more firmly than nine Englishmen out of ten at the present day believe that our greatness and welfare are proved by our being so very rich. Now, the use of culture is that it helps us, by means of its spiritual standard of perfection, to regard wealth as but machinery, and not only to say as a matter of words that we regard wealth as but machinery, but really to perceive and feel that it is so. If it were not for this purging effect wrought upon our minds by culture, the whole world, the future as well as the present, would inevitably belong to the Philistines. The people who believe most that our greatness and welfare are proved by our being very rich, and who most give their lives and thoughts to becoming rich, are just the very people whom we call Philistines. Culture says: 'Consider these people, then, their way of life, their habits, their manners, the very tones of their voice; look at them attentively; observe the literature they read, the things which give them pleasure, the words which come forth out of their mouths, the thoughts which make the furniture of their minds; would any amount of wealth be worth having with the condition that one was to become just like these people by having it?' And thus culture begets a dissatisfaction which is of the highest possible value in stemming the common tide of men's thoughts in a wealthy and industrial community, and which saves the future, as one may hope, from being vulgarized, even if it cannot save the present.

Population, again, and bodily health and vigour, are things which are nowhere treated in such an unintelligent, misleading, exaggerated way as in England. Both are really machinery; yet how many people all around us do we see rest in them and fail to look beyond them! Why, one has heard people, fresh from reading certain articles of *The Times* on the Registrar-General's returns of marriages and births in this country, who would talk of our large English families in quite a solemn strain, as if they had something in itself beautiful, elevating, and meritorious in them; as if the British Philistine would have only to present himself before the Great Judge with his twelve children, in order to be received among the sheep as a matter of right!

But bodily health and vigour, it may be said, are not to be classed with wealth and population as mere machinery; they have a more real and essential value. True; but only as they are more intimately connected with a perfect spiritual condition than wealth or population are. The moment we disjoin them from the idea of a perfect spiritual condition, and pursue them, as we do pursue them, for their own sake and as ends in themselves, our worship of them becomes as mere worship of machinery, as our worship of wealth or population, and as unintelligent and vulgarizing a worship as that is. Every one with anything like an adequate idea of human perfection has distinctly marked this subordination to higher and spiritual ends of the cultivation of bodily vigour and activity. 'Bodily exercise profiteth little; but godliness is profitable unto all things', says the author of the Epistle to Timothy. And the utilitarian Franklin says just as explicitly, 'Eat and drink such an exact quantity as suits the constitution of thy body, *in reference to the services of the mind.*' But the point of view of culture, keeping the mark of human perfection simply and broadly in view, and not assigning to this perfection, as religion or utilitarianism assigns to it, a special and limited character, this point of view, I say, of culture is best given by these words of Epictetus, 'It is a sign of ἀφυΐα,' says he – that is, of a nature not finely tempered – 'to give yourselves up to things which relate to the body; to make, for instance, a great fuss about exercise, a great fuss about eating, a great fuss about drinking, a great fuss about walking, a great fuss about riding. All these things ought to be done merely by the way: the formation of the spirit and character must be our real concern.' This is admirable; and, indeed, the Greek word εὐφυΐα, a finely tempered nature, gives exactly the notion of perfection as culture brings us to conceive it: a harmonious perfection, a perfection in which the characters of beauty and intelligence are both present, which unites 'the two noblest of things', as Swift, who of one of the two, at any rate, had himself all too little, most happily calls them in his *Battle of the Books* – 'the two noblest of things, *sweetness and light*'. The εὐφυής is the man who tends towards sweetness and light; the ἀφυής, on the other hand, is our Philistine. The immense spiritual significance of the Greeks is due to their having been inspired with this central and happy idea of the essential character of human perfection; and Mr Bright's misconception of culture, as a smattering of Greek and Latin, comes itself, after all, from this wonderful significance of the Greeks having affected the very machinery of our education, and is in itself a kind of homage to it.

In thus making sweetness and light to be characters of perfection, culture is of like spirit with poetry, follows one law with poetry. Far more than on our freedom, our population, and our industrialism, many amongst us rely upon our religious organizations to save us. I have called religion a yet more important manifestation of human nature than poetry, because it has worked on a broader scale for perfection, and with greater masses of men. But the idea of beauty and of a human nature perfect on all its sides, which is the dominant idea of poetry, is a true and invaluable idea, though it has not yet had the success that the idea of conquering the obvious faults of our animality, and of a human nature perfect on the moral side – which is the dominant idea of religion – has been enabled to have; and it is destined, adding to itself the religious idea of a devout energy, to transform and govern the other.

The best art and poetry of the Greeks, in which religion and poetry are one, in which the idea of beauty and of a human nature perfect on all sides adds to itself a religious and devout energy, and works in the strength of that, is on this account of such surpassing interest and instructiveness for us, though it was – as, having regard to the human race in general, and, indeed, having regard to the Greeks themselves, we must own – a premature attempt, an attempt which for success needed the moral and religious fibre in humanity to be more braced and developed than it had yet been. But Greece did not err in having the idea of beauty, harmony, and complete human perfection, so present and paramount. It is impossible to have this idea too present and paramount; only, the moral fibre must be braced too. And we, because we have braced the moral fibre, are not on that account in the right way, if at the same time the idea of beauty, harmony, and complete human perfection, is wanting or misapprehended amongst us; and evidently it *is* wanting or misapprehended at present. And when we rely as we do on our religious organizations, which in themselves do not and cannot give us this idea, and think we have done enough if we make them spread and prevail, then, I say, we fall into our common fault of overvaluing machinery.

Nothing is more common than for people to confound the inward peace and satisfaction which follows the subduing of the obvious faults of our animality with what I may call absolute inward peace and satisfaction – the peace and satisfaction which are reached as we draw near to complete spiritual perfection, and not merely to moral perfection, or rather to relative moral perfection. No people in the world have done more and struggled more to attain this relative moral perfection than our English race has. For no people in the world has the command to *resist the devil*, to *overcome the wicked one*, in the nearest and most obvious sense of those words, had such a pressing force and reality. And we have had our reward, not only in the great worldly prosperity which our obedience to this command has brought us, but also, and far more, in great inward peace and satisfaction. But to me few things are more pathetic than to see people, on the strength of the inward peace and satisfaction which their rudimentary efforts towards perfection have brought them, employ, concerning their incomplete perfection and the religious organizations within which they have found it, language which properly applies only to complete perfection, and is a far-off echo of the human soul's prophecy of it. Religion itself, I need hardly say, supplies them in abundance with this grand language. And very freely do they use it; yet it is really the severest possible criticism of such an incomplete perfection as alone we have yet reached through our religious organizations.

The impulse of the English race towards moral development and self-conquest has nowhere so powerfully manifested itself as in Puritanism. Nowhere has Puritanism found so adequate an expression as in the religious organization of the Independents. The modern Independents have a newspaper, the *Nonconformist*, written with great sincerity and ability. The motto, the standard, the profession of faith which this organ of theirs carries aloft, is, 'The Dissidence of Dissent and the Protestantism of the Protestant Religion'. There is sweetness and light, and an ideal of complete harmonious human perfection! One need not go to culture and poetry to find language to judge it. Religion, with its instinct for perfection, supplies language to judge it, language, too, which is in our mouths every day. 'Finally, be of one mind, united in feeling', says St Peter. There is an ideal which judges the Puritan ideal: 'The Dissidence of Dissent and the Protestantism of the Protestant Religion!' And religious organizations like this are what people believe in, rest in, would give their lives for! Such, I say, is the wonderful virtue of even the beginnings of perfection, of having conquered even the plain faults of our animality, that the religious organization which has helped us to do it can seem to us something precious, salutary, and to be propagated, even when it wears such a brand of imperfection on its forehead as this. And men have got such a habit of giving to the language of religion a special application, of making it a mere jargon, that for the condemnation which religion itself passes on the shortcomings of their religious organizations they have no ear; they are sure to cheat themselves and to explain this condemnation away. They can only be reached by the criticism which culture, like poetry, speaking a language not to be sophisticated, and resolutely testing these organizations by the ideal of a human perfection complete on all sides, applies to them.

But men of culture and poetry, it will be said, are again and again failing, and failing conspicuously, in the necessary first stage to a harmonious perfection, in the subduing of the great obvious faults of our animality, which it is the glory of these religious organizations to have helped us to subdue. True, they do often so fail. They have often been without the virtues as well as the faults of the Puritan; it has been one of their dangers that they so felt the Puritan's faults that they too much neglected the practice of his virtues. I will not, however, exculpate them at the Puritan's expense. They have often failed in morality, and morality is indispensable. And they have been punished for their failure, as the Puritan has been rewarded for his performance. They have been punished wherein they erred; but their ideal of beauty, of sweetness and light, and a human nature complete on all its sides, remains the true ideal of perfection still; just as the Puritan's ideal of perfection remains narrow and inadequate, although for what he did well he has been richly rewarded. Notwithstanding the mighty results of the Pilgrim Fathers' voyage, they and their standard of perfection are rightly judged when we figure to ourselves Shakespeare or Virgil – souls in whom sweetness and light, and all that in human nature is most humane, were eminent – accompanying them on their voyage, and think what intolerable company Shakespeare and Virgil would have found them! In the same way let us judge the religious organizations which we see all around us. Do not let us deny the good and the happiness which they have accomplished; but do not let us fail to see clearly that their idea of human perfection is narrow and inadequate, and that the Dissidence of Dissent and the Protestantism of the Protestant Religion will never bring humanity to its true goal. As I said with regard to wealth: let us look at the life of those who live in and for it – so I say with regard to the religious organizations. Look at the life imaged in such a newspaper as the *Nonconformist* – a life of jealousy of the Establishment, disputes, tea-meetings, openings of chapels, sermons; and then think of it as an ideal of a human life completing itself on all sides, and aspiring with all its organs after sweetness, light, and perfection!

Another newspaper, representing, like the *Nonconformist*, one of the religious organizations of this country, was a short time ago giving an account of the crowd at Epsom on the Derby day, and of all the vice and hideousness which was to be seen in that crowd; and then the writer turned suddenly round upon Professor Huxley, and asked him how he proposed to cure all this vice and hideousness without religion. I confess I felt disposed to ask the asker this question: and how do you propose to cure it with such a religion as yours? How is the ideal of a life so unlovely, so unattractive, so incomplete, so narrow, so far removed from a true and satisfying ideal of human perfection, as is the life of your religious organization as you yourself reflect it, to conquer and transform all this vice and hideousness? Indeed, the strongest plea for the study of perfection as pursued by culture, the clearest proof of the actual inadequacy of the idea of perfection held by the religious organizations – expressing, as I have said, the most widespread effort which the human race has yet made after perfection – is to be found in the state of our life and society with these in possession of it, and having been in possession of it I know not how many hundred years. We are all of us included in some religious organization or other; we all call ourselves, in the sublime and aspiring language of religion which I have before noticed, *children of God*. Children of God – it is an immense pretension! And how are we to justify it? By the works which we do, and the words which we speak. And the work which we collective children of God do, our grand centre of life, our *city* which we have builded for us to dwell in, is London! London, with its unutterable external hideousness, and with its internal canker of *publicè egestas, privatim opulentia*[6] – to use the words which Sallust puts into Cato's mouth about Rome – unequalled in the world! The word, again, which we children of God speak, the voice which most hits our collective thought, the newspaper with the largest circulation in England, nay, with the largest circulation in the whole world, is the *Daily Telegraph*! I say that when our religious organizations – which I admit to express the most considerable effort after perfection that our race has yet made – land us in no better result than this, it is high time to examine carefully their idea of perfection, to see whether it does not leave out of account sides and forces of human nature which we might turn to great use; whether it would not be more operative if it were more complete. And I say that the English reliance on our religious organizations and on their ideas of human perfection just as they stand, is like our reliance on freedom, on muscular Christianity, on population, on coal, on wealth – mere belief in machinery, and unfruitful; and that it is wholesomely counteracted by culture, bent on seeing things as they are, and on drawing the human race onwards to a more complete, a harmonious perfection.

Culture, however, shows its single-minded love of perfection, its desire simply to make reason and the will of God prevail, its freedom from fanaticism, by its attitude towards all this machinery, even while it insists that it *is* machinery. Fanatics, seeing the mischief men do themselves by their blind belief in some machinery or other – whether it is wealth and industrialism, or whether it is the cultivation of bodily strength and activity, or whether it is a political organization, or whether it is a religious organization – oppose with might and main the tendency to this or that political and religious organization, or to games and athletic exercises, or to wealth and industrialism, and try violently to stop it. But the flexibility which sweetness and light give, and which is one of the rewards of culture pursued in good faith, enables a man to see that a tendency may be necessary, and even, as a preparation for something in the future, salutary, and yet that the generations or individuals who obey this tendency are sacrificed to it, that they fall short of the hope of perfection by following it; and that its mischiefs are to be criticized, lest it should take too firm a hold and last after it has served its purpose.

Mr Gladstone well pointed out, in a speech at Paris – and others have pointed out the same thing – how necessary is the present great movement towards wealth and industrialism, in order to lay broad foundations of material well-being for the society of the future. The worst of these justifications is, that they are generally addressed to the very people engaged, body and soul, in the movement in question; at all events, that they are always seized with the greatest avidity by these people, and taken by them as quite justifying their life; and that thus they tend to harden them in their sins. Now culture admits the necessity of the movement towards fortune-making and exaggerated industrialism, readily allows that the future may derive benefit from it; but insists, at the same time, that the passing generations of industrialists – forming, for the most part, the stout main body of Philistinism – are sacrificed to it. In the same way, the result of all the games and sports which occupy the passing generation of boys and young men may be the establishment of a better and sounder physical type for the future to work with. Culture does not set itself against the games and sports; it congratulates the future, and hopes it will make a good use of its improved physical basis; but it points out that our passing generation of boys and young men is, meantime, sacrificed. Puritanism was perhaps necessary to develop the moral fibre of the English race, Nonconformity to break the yoke of ecclesiastical domination over men's minds and to prepare the way for freedom of thought in the distant future; still, culture points out that the harmonious perfection of generations of Puritans and Nonconformists have been, in consequence, sacrificed. Freedom of speech may be necessary for the society of the future, but the young lions of the *Daily Telegraph* in the meanwhile are sacrificed. A voice for every man in his country's government may be necessary for the society of the future, but meanwhile Mr Beales and Mr Bradlaugh[7] are sacrificed.

Oxford, the Oxford of the past, has many faults; and she has heavily paid for them in defeat, in isolation, in want of hold upon the modern world. Yet we in Oxford, brought up amidst the beauty and sweetness of that beautiful place, have not failed to seize one truth – the truth that beauty and sweetness are essential characters of a complete human perfection. When I insist on this, I am all in the faith and tradition of Oxford. I say boldly that this our sentiment for beauty and sweetness, our sentiment against hideousness and rawness, has been at the bottom of our attachment to so many beaten causes, of our opposition to so many triumphant movements. And the sentiment is true, and has never been wholly defeated, and has shown its power even in its defeat. We have not won our political battles, we have not carried our main points, we have not stopped our adversaries' advance, we have not marched victoriously with the modern world; but we have told silently upon the mind of the country, we have prepared currents of feeling which sap our adversaries' position when it seems gained, we have kept up our own communications with the future. Look at the course of the great movement which shook Oxford to its centre some thirty years ago! It was directed, as any one who reads Dr Newman's *Apology* may see, against what in one word may be called 'liberalism'. Liberalism prevailed; it was the appointed force to do the work of the hour; it was necessary, it was inevitable that it should prevail. The Oxford movement was broken, it failed; our wrecks are scattered on every shore: *Quae regio in terris nostri non plena laboris?* But what was it, this liberalism, as Dr Newman saw it, and as it really broke the Oxford movement? It was the great middle-class liberalism, which had for the cardinal points of its belief the Reform Bill of 1832, and local self-government, in politics; in the social sphere, free-trade, unrestricted competition, and the making of large industrial fortunes; in the religious sphere, the Dissidence of Dissent and the Protestantism of the Protestant Religion. I do not say that other and more intelligent forces than this were not opposed to the Oxford movement: but this was the force which really beat it; this was the force which Dr Newman felt himself fighting with; this was the force which till only the other day seemed to be the paramount force in this country, and to be in possession of the future; this was the force whose achievements fill Mr Lowe[8] with such inexpressible admiration, and whose rule he was so horror-struck to see threatened. And where is this great force of Philistinism now? It is thrust into the second rank, it is become a power of yesterday, it has lost the future. A new power has suddenly appeared, a power which it is impossible yet to judge fully, but which is certainly a wholly different force from middle-class liberalism; different in its cardinal points of belief, different in its tendencies in every sphere. It loves and admires neither the legislation of middle-class Parliaments, nor the local self-government of middle-class vestries, nor the unrestricted competition of middle-class industrialists, nor the dissidence of middle-class Dissent and the Protestantism of middle-class Protestant religion. I am not now praising this new force, or saying that its own ideals are better; all I say is, that they are wholly different. And who will estimate how much the currents of feeling created by Dr Newman's movement, the keen desire for beauty and sweetness which it nourished, the deep aversion it manifested to the hardness and vulgarity of middle-class liberalism, the strong light it turned on the hideous and grotesque illusions of middle-class Protestantism – who will estimate how much all these contributed to swell the tide of secret dissatisfaction which has mined the ground under the self-confident liberalism of the last thirty years, and has prepared the way for its sudden collapse and supersession? It is in this manner that the sentiment of Oxford for beauty and sweetness conquers, and in this manner long may it continue to conquer!

In this manner it works to the same end as culture, and there is plenty of work for it yet to do. I have said that the new and more democratic force which is now superseding our old middle-class liberalism cannot yet be rightly judged. It has its main tendencies still to form. We hear promises of its giving us administrative reform, law reform, reform of education, and I know not what; but those promises come rather from its advocates, wishing to make a good plea for it and to justify it for superseding middle-class liberalism, than from clear tendencies which it has itself yet developed. But meanwhile it has plenty of well-intentioned friends against whom culture may with advantage continue to uphold steadily its ideal of human perfection; that this is *an inward spiritual activity, having for its characters increased sweetness, increased light, increased life, increased sympathy*. Mr Bright, who has a foot in both worlds, the world of middle-class liberalism and the world of democracy, but who brings most of his ideas from the world of middle-class liberalism in which he was bred, always inclines to inculcate that faith in machinery to which, as we have seen, Englishmen are so prone, and which has been the bane of middle-class liberalism. He complains with a sorrowful indignation of people who 'appear to have no proper estimate of the value of the franchise', he leads his disciples to believe – what the Englishman is always too ready to believe – that having a vote, like having a large family, or a large business, or large muscles, has in itself some edifying and perfecting effect upon human nature. Or else he cries out to the democracy – 'the men', as he calls them, 'upon whose shoulders the greatness of England rests', he cries out to them, 'See what you have done! I look over this country and see the cities you have built, the railroads you have made, the manufactures you have produced, the cargoes which freight the ships of the greatest mercantile navy the world has ever seen! I see that you have converted by your labours what was once a wilderness, these islands, into a fruitful garden; I know that you have created this wealth, and are a nation whose name is a word of power throughout all the world.' Why, this is just the very style of laudation with which Mr Roebuck or Mr Lowe debauches the minds of the middle classes, and makes such Philistines of them. It is the same fashion of teaching a man to value himself not on what he *is*, not on his progress in sweetness and light, but on the number of the railroads he has constructed, or the bigness of the tabernacle he has built. Only the middle classes are told they have done it all with their energy, self-reliance, and capital, and the democracy are told they have done it all with their hands and sinews. But teaching the democracy to put its trust in achievements of this kind is merely training them to be Philistines to take the place of the Philistines whom they are superseding; and they too, like the middle class, will be encouraged to sit down at the banquet of the future without having on a wedding garment, and nothing excellent can then come from them. Those who know their besetting faults, those who have watched them and listened to them, or those who will read the instructive account recently given of them by one of themselves, the *Journeyman Engineer*, will agree that the idea which culture sets before us of perfection – an increased spiritual activity, having for its characters increased sweetness, increased light, increased life, increased sympathy – is an idea which the new democracy needs far more than the idea of the blessedness of the franchise, or the wonderfulness of its own industrial performances.

Other well-meaning friends of this new power are for leading it, not in the old ruts of middle-class Philistinism, but in ways which are naturally alluring to the feet of democracy, though in this country they are novel and untried ways. I may call them the ways of Jacobinism. Violent indignation with the past, abstract systems of renovation applied wholesale, a new doctrine drawn up in black and white for elaborating down to the very smallest details a rational society for the future – these are the ways of Jacobinism. Mr Frederic Harrison and other disciples of Comte – one of them, Mr Congreve, is an old friend of mine, and I am glad to have an opportunity of publicly expressing my respect for his talents and character – are among the friends of democracy who are for leading it in paths of this kind. Mr Frederic Harrison is very hostile to culture, and from a natural enough motive; for culture is the eternal opponent of the two things which are the signal marks of Jacobinism – its fierceness, and its addiction to an abstract system. Culture is always assigning to system-makers and systems a smaller share in the bent of human destiny than their friends like. A current in people's minds sets towards new ideas; people are dissatisfied with their old narrow stock of Philistine ideas, Anglo-Saxon ideas, or any other; and some man, some Bentham or Comte, who has the real merit of having early and strongly felt and helped the new current, but who brings plenty of narrowness and mistakes of his own into his feeling and help of it, is credited with being the author of the whole current, the fit person to be entrusted with its regulation and to guide the human race.

The excellent German historian of the mythology of Rome, Preller, relating the introduction at Rome under the Tarquins of the worship of

Apollo, the god of light, healing, and reconciliation, will have us observe that it was not so much the Tarquins who brought to Rome the new worship of Apollo, as a current in the mind of the Roman people which set powerfully at that time towards a new worship of this kind, and away from the old run of Latin and Sabine religious ideas. In a similar way, culture directs our attention to the natural current there is in human affairs, and to its continual working, and will not let us rivet our faith upon any one man and his doings. It makes us see not only his good side, but also how much in him was of necessity limited and transient; nay, it even feels a pleasure, a sense of an increased freedom and of an ampler future, in so doing.

I remember, when I was under the influence of a mind to which I feel the greatest obligations, the mind of a man who was the very incarnation of sanity and clear sense, a man the most considerable, it seems to me, whom America has yet produced – Benjamin Franklin – I remember the relief with which, after long feeling the sway of Franklin's imperturbable common-sense, I came upon a project of his for a new version of the Book of Job, to replace the old version, the style of which, says Franklin, has become obsolete, and thence less agreeable. 'I give', he continues, 'a few verses, which may serve as a sample of the kind of version I would recommend.' We all recollect the famous verse in our translation: 'Then Satan answered the Lord and said, "Doth Job fear God for nought?"' Franklin makes this: 'Does your Majesty imagine that Job's good conduct is the effect of mere personal attachment and affection?' I well remember how, when first I read that, I drew a deep breath of relief, and said to myself, 'After all, there is a stretch of humanity beyond Franklin's victorious good sense!' So, after hearing Bentham cried loudly up as the renovator of modern society, and Bentham's mind and ideas proposed as the rulers of our future, I open the *Deontology*. There I read, 'While Xenophon was writing his history and Euclid teaching geometry, Socrates and Plato were talking nonsense under pretence of teaching wisdom and morality. This morality of theirs consisted in words; this wisdom of theirs was the denial of matters known to every man's experience.' From the moment of reading that, I am delivered from the bondage of Bentham! the fanaticism of his adherents can touch me no longer. I feel the inadequacy of his mind and ideas for supplying the rule of human society, for perfection.

Culture tends always thus to deal with the men of a system, of disciples, of a school; with men like Comte, or the late Mr Buckle[9], or Mr Mill. However much it may find to admire in these personages, or in some of them, it nevertheless remembers the text, 'Be not ye called Rabbi!' and it soon passes on from any Rabbi. But Jacobinism loves a Rabbi; it does not want to pass on from its Rabbi in pursuit of a future and still unreached perfection; it wants its Rabbi and his ideas to stand for perfection, that they may with the more authority recast the world; and for Jacobinism, therefore, culture – eternally passing onwards and seeking – is an impertinence and an offence. But culture, just because it resists this tendency of Jacobinism to impose on us a man with limitations and errors of his own along with the true ideas of which he is the organ, really does the world and Jacobinism itself a service.

So, too, Jacobinism, in its fierce hatred of the past and of those whom it makes liable for the sins of the past, cannot away with the inexhaustible indulgence proper to culture, the consideration of circumstances, the severe judgement of actions joined to the merciful judgement of persons. 'The man of culture is in politics', cries Mr Frederic Harrison, 'one of the poorest mortals alive!' Mr Frederic Harrison wants to be doing business, and he complains that the man of culture stops him with a 'turn for small fault-finding, love of selfish ease, and indecision in action'. Of what use is culture, he asks, except for 'a critic of new books or a professor of *belles-lettres*?' Why, it is of use because, in presence of the fierce exasperation which breathes, or rather, I may say, hisses through the whole production in which Mr Frederic Harrison asks that question, it reminds us that the perfection of human nature is sweetness and light. It is of use because, like religion – that other effort after perfection – it testifies that, where bitter envying and strife are, there is confusion and every evil work.

The pursuit of perfection, then, is the pursuit of sweetness and light. He who works for sweetness and light, works to make reason and the will of God prevail. He who works for machinery, he who works for hatred, works only for confusion. Culture looks beyond machinery, culture hates hatred; culture has one great passion, the passion for sweetness and light. It has one even yet greater – the passion for making them *prevail*. It is not satisfied till we *all* come to a perfect man; it knows that the sweetness and light of the few must be imperfect until the raw and unkindled masses of humanity are touched with sweetness and light. If I have not shrunk from saying that we must work for sweetness and light, so neither have I shrunk from saying that we must have a broad basis, must have sweetness and light for as many as possible. Again and again I have insisted how those are the happy moments of humanity, how those are the marking epochs of a people's life, how those are the flowering times for literature and art and all the creative power of genius, when there is a *national* glow of life and thought, when the whole of society is in the fullest measure permeated by thought, sensible to beauty, intelligent and alive. Only it must be *real* thought and *real* beauty; *real* sweetness and *real* light. Plenty of people will try to give the masses, as they call them, an intellectual food prepared and adapted in the way they think proper for the actual condition of the masses. The ordinary popular literature is an example of this way of working on the masses. Plenty of people will try to indoctrinate the masses with the set of ideas and judgements constituting the creed of their own profession or party. Our religious and political organizations give an example of this way of working on the masses. I condemn neither way; but culture works differently. It does not try to teach down to the level of inferior classes; it does not try to win them for this or that sect of its own, with ready-made judgements and watchwords. It seeks to do away with classes; to make the best that has been thought and known in the world current everywhere; to make all men live in an atmosphere of sweetness and light, where they may use ideas, as it uses them itself, freely – nourished, and not bound by them.

This is the *social idea*; and the men of culture are the true apostles of equality. The great men of culture are those who have had a passion for diffusing, for making prevail, for carrying from one end of society to the other, the best knowledge, the best ideas of their time; who have laboured to divest knowledge of all that was harsh, uncouth, difficult, abstract, professional, exclusive; to humanize it, to make it efficient outside the clique of the cultivated and learned, yet still remaining the *best* knowledge and thought of the time, and a true source, therefore, of sweetness and light. Such a man was Abelard in the Middle Ages, in spite of all his imperfections; and thence the boundless emotion and enthusiasm which Abelard excited. Such were Lessing and Herder in Germany, at the end of the last century; and their services to Germany were in this way inestimably precious. Generations will pass, and literary monuments will accumulate, and works far more perfect than the works of Lessing and Herder will be produced in Germany; and yet the names of these two men will fill a German with a reverence and enthusiasm such as the names of the most gifted masters will hardly awaken. And why? Because they *humanized* knowledge; because they broadened the basis of life and intelligence; because they worked powerfully to diffuse sweetness and light, to make reason and the will of God prevail. With Saint Augustine they said, 'Let us not leave thee alone to make in the secret of thy knowledge, as thou didst before the creation of the firmament, the division of light from darkness; let the children of thy spirit, placed in their firmament, make their light shine upon the earth, mark the division of night and day, and announce the revolution of the times; for the old order is passed, and the new arises; the night is spent, the day is come forth; and thou shalt crown the year with thy blessing, when thou shalt send forth labourers into thy harvest sown by other hands than theirs; when thou shalt send forth new labourers to new seed-times, whereof the harvest shall be not yet.'

Doing as one likes

I have been trying to show that culture is, or ought to be, the study and pursuit of perfection; and that of perfection as pursued by culture, beauty and intelligence, or, in other words, sweetness and light, are the main characters. But hitherto I have been insisting chiefly on beauty, or sweetness, as a character of perfection. To complete rightly my design, it evidently remains to speak also of intelligence, or light, as a character of perfection.

First, however, I ought perhaps to notice that, both here and on the other side of the Atlantic, all sorts of objections are raised against the 'religion of culture', as the objectors mockingly call it, which I am supposed to be promulgating. It is said to be a religion proposing *parmaceti*, or some scented salve or other, as a cure for human miseries; a religion breathing a spirit of cultivated inaction, making its believer refuse to lend a hand at uprooting the definite evils on all sides of us, and filling him with antipathy against the reforms and reformers which try to extirpate them. In general, it is summed up as being not practical, or – as some critics familiarly put it – all moonshine. That Alcibiades, the editor of the *Morning Star*, taunts me, as its promulgator, with living out of the world and knowing nothing of life and men. That great austere toiler, the editor of the *Daily Telegraph*, upbraids me – but kindly, and more in sorrow than in anger – for trifling with aesthetics and poetical fancies, while he himself, in that arsenal of his in Fleet Street, is bearing the burden and heat of the day. An intelligent American newspaper, the *Nation*, says that it is very easy to sit in one's study and find fault with the course of modern society, but the thing is to propose practical improvements for it. While, finally, Mr Frederic Harrison, in a very good-tempered and witty satire, which makes me quite understand his having apparently achieved such a conquest of my young Prussian friend, Arminius,[10] at last gets moved to an almost stern moral impatience, to behold, as he says, 'Death, sin, cruelty stalk among us, filling their maws with innocence and youth', and me, in the midst of the general tribulation, handing out my pouncet-box.

It is impossible that all these remonstrances and reproofs should not affect me, and I shall try my very best, in completing my design and in speaking of light as one of the characters of perfection, and of culture as giving us light, to profit by the objections I have heard and read, and to drive at practice as much as I can, by showing the communications and passages into practical life from the doctrine which I am inculcating.

It is said that a man with my theories of sweetness and light is full of antipathy against the rougher or coarser movements going on around him, that he will not lend a hand to the humble operation of uprooting evil by their means, and that therefore the believers in action grow impatient with him. But what if rough and coarse action, ill-calculated action, action with insufficient light, is, and has for a long time been, our bane? What if our urgent want now is, not to act at any price, but rather to lay in a stock of light for our difficulties? In that case, to refuse to lend a hand to the rougher and coarser movements going on round us, to make the primary need, both for oneself and others, to consist in enlightening ourselves and qualifying ourselves to act less at random, is surely the best and in real truth the most practical line our endeavours can take. So that if I can show what my opponents call rough or coarse action, but what I would rather call random and ill-regulated action – action with insufficient light, action pursued because we like to be doing something and doing it as we please, and do not like the trouble of thinking and the severe constraint of any kind of rule – if I can show this to be, at the present moment, a practical mischief and dangerous to us, then I have found a practical use for light in correcting this state of things, and have only to exemplify how, in cases which fall under everybody's observation, it may deal with it.

When I began to speak of culture, I insisted on our bondage to machinery, on our proneness to value machinery as an end in itself, without looking beyond it to the end for which alone, in truth, it is valuable. Freedom, I said, was one of those things which we thus worshipped in itself, without enough regarding the ends for which freedom is to be desired. In our common notions and talk about freedom, we eminently show our idolatry of machinery. Our prevalent notion is – and I quoted a number of instances to prove it – that it is a most happy and important thing for a man merely to be able to do as he likes. On what he is to do when he is thus free to do as he likes we do not lay so much stress. Our familiar praise of the British Constitution under which we live, is that it is a system of checks – a system which stops and paralyses any power in interfering with the free action of individuals. To this effect Mr Bright, who loves to walk in the old ways of the Constitution, said forcibly in one of his great speeches, what many other people are every day saying less forcibly, that the central idea of English life and politics is *the assertion of personal liberty*. Evidently this is so; but evidently, also, as feudalism, which with its ideas and habits of subordination was for many centuries silently behind the British Constitution, dies out, and we are left with nothing but our system of checks, and our notion of its being the great right and happiness of an Englishman to do as far as possible what he likes, we are in danger of drifting towards anarchy. We have not the notion, so familiar on the Continent and to antiquity, of *the State* – the nation in its collective and corporate character, entrusted with stringent powers for the general advantage, and controlling individual wills in the name of an interest wider than that of individuals. We say, what is very true, that this notion is often made instrumental to tyranny; we say that a State is in reality made up of the individuals who compose it, and that every individual is the best judge of his own interests. Our leading class is an aristocracy, and no aristocracy likes the notion of a State authority greater than itself, with a stringent administrative machinery superseding the decorative inutilities of lord-lieutenancy, deputy-lieutenancy, and the *posse comitatus*, which are all in its own hands. Our middle class, the great representative of trade and Dissent, with its maxims of every man for himself in business, every man for himself in religion, dreads a powerful administration which might somehow interfere with it; and besides, it has its own decorative inutilities of vestrymanship and guardianship, which are to this class what lord-lieutenancy and the county magistracy are to the aristocratic class, and a stringent administration might either take these functions out of its hands, or prevent its exercising them in its own comfortable, independent manner, as at present.

Then as to our working class. This class, pressed constantly by the hard daily compulsion of material wants, is naturally the very centre and stronghold of our national idea, that it is man's ideal right and felicity to do as he likes. I think I have somewhere related how M. Michelet said to me of the people of France, that it was 'a nation of barbarians civilized by the conscription.' He meant that through their military service the idea of public duty and of discipline was brought to the mind of these masses, in other respects so raw and uncultivated. Our masses are quite as raw and uncultivated as the French; and so far from their having the idea of public duty and of discipline, superior to the individual's self-will, brought to their mind by a universal obligation of military service, such as that of the conscription – so far from their having this, the very idea of a conscription is so at variance with our English notion of the prime right and blessedness of doing as one likes, that I remember the manager of the Clay Cross works in Derbyshire told me during the Crimean war, when our want of soldiers was much felt and some people were talking of a conscription, that sooner than submit to a conscription the population of that district would flee to the mines, and lead a sort of Robin Hood life under ground.

For a long time, as I have said, the strong feudal habits of subordination and deference continued to tell upon the working class. The modern spirit has now almost entirely dissolved those habits, and the anarchical tendency of our worship of freedom in and for itself, of our superstitious faith, as I say, in machinery, is becoming very manifest. More and more, because of this our blind faith in machinery, because of our want of light to enable us to look beyond machinery to the end for which machinery is valuable, this and that man, and this and that body of men, all over the country, are beginning to assert and put into practice an Englishman's right to do what he likes; his right to march where he likes, meet where he likes, enter where he likes, hoot as he likes, threaten as he likes, smash as he likes. All this, I say, tends to anarchy; and though a number of excellent people, and particularly my friends of the Liberal or progressive party, as they call themselves, are kind enough to reassure us by saying that these are trifles, that a few transient outbreaks of rowdyism signify nothing, that our system of liberty is one which itself cures all the evils which it works, that the educated and intelligent classes stand in overwhelming strength and majestic repose, ready, like our military force in riots, to act at a moment's notice – yet one finds that one's Liberal friends generally say this because they have such faith in themselves and their nostrums, when they shall return, as the public welfare requires, to place and power. But this faith of theirs one cannot exactly share, when one has so long had them and their nostrums at work, and sees that they have not prevented our coming to our present embarrassed condition. And one finds, also, that the outbreaks of rowdyism tend to become less and less of trifles, to become more frequent rather than less frequent; and that meanwhile our educated and intelligent classes remain in their majestic repose, and somehow or other, whatever happens, their overwhelming strength, like our military force in riots, never does act.

How, indeed, *should* their overwhelming strength act, when the man who gives an inflammatory lecture, or breaks down the park railings, or invades a Secretary of State's office, is only following an Englishman's impulse to do as he likes; and our own conscience tells us that we ourselves have always regarded this impulse as something primary and sacred? Mr Murphy lectures at Birmingham, and showers on the Catholic population of that town 'words', says the Home Secretary, 'only fit to be addressed to thieves or murderers.'[11] What then? Mr Murphy has his own reasons of several kinds. He suspects the Roman Catholic Church of designs upon Mrs Murphy; and he says if mayors and magistrates do not care for their wives and daughters, he does. But, above all, he is doing as he likes; or, in worthier language, asserting his personal liberty. 'I will carry out my lectures if they walk over my body as a dead corpse; and I say to the Mayor of Birmingham that he is my servant while I am in Birmingham, and as my servant he must do his duty and protect me.' Touching and beautiful words, which find a sympathetic chord in every British bosom! The moment it is plainly put before us that a man is asserting his personal liberty, we are half disarmed; because we are believers in freedom, and not in some dream of a right reason to which the assertion of our freedom is to be subordinated. Accordingly, the Secretary of State had to say that although the lecturer's language was 'only fit to be addressed to thieves or murderers', yet, 'I do not think he is to be deprived, I do not think that anything I have said could justify the inference that he is to be deprived, of the right of protection in a place built by him for the purpose of these lectures; because the language was not language which afforded grounds for a criminal prosecution.' No, nor to be silenced by Mayor, or Home Secretary, or any administrative authority on earth, simply on their notion of what is discreet and reasonable! This is in perfect consonance with our public opinion, and with our national love for the assertion of personal liberty.

In quite another department of affairs, an experienced and distinguished Chancery Judge relates an incident which is just to the same effect as this of Mr Murphy. A testator bequeathed £300 a year, to be for ever applied as a pension to some person who had been unsuccessful in literature, and whose duty should be to support and diffuse, by his writings, the testator's own views, as enforced in the testator's publications. The views were not worth a straw, and the bequest was appealed against in the Court of Chancery on the ground of its absurdity; but, being only absurd, it was upheld, and the so-called charity was established. Having, I say, at the bottom of our English hearts a very strong belief in freedom, and a very weak belief in right reason, we are soon silenced when a man pleads the prime right to do as he likes, because this is the prime right for ourselves too; and even if we attempt now and then to mumble something about reason, yet we have ourselves thought so little about this and so much about liberty, that we are in conscience forced, when our brother Philistine with whom we are meddling turns boldly round upon us and asks: *have you any light?* – to shake our heads ruefully, and to let him go his own way after all.

There are many things to be said on behalf of this exclusive attention of ours to liberty, and of the relaxed habits of government which it has engendered. It is very easy to mistake or to exaggerate the sort of anarchy from which we are in danger through them. We are not in danger from Fenianism,[12] fierce and turbulent as it may show itself; for against this our conscience is free enough to let us act resolutely and put forth our overwhelming strength the moment there is any real need for it. In the first place, it never was any part of our creed that the great right and blessedness of an Irishman, or, indeed, of anybody on earth except an Englishman, is to do as he likes; and we can have no scruple at all about abridging, if necessary, a non-Englishman's assertion of personal liberty. The British Constitution, its checks, and its prime virtues, are for Englishmen. We may extend them to others out of love and kindness; but we find no real divine law written on our hearts constraining us so to extend them. And then the difference between an Irish Fenian and an English rough is so immense, and the case, in dealing with the

Fenian, so much more clear! He is so evidently desperate and dangerous, a man of a conquered race, a Papist, with centuries of ill-usage to inflame him against us, with an alien religion established in his country by us at his expense, with no admiration of our institutions, no love of our virtues, no talents for our business, no turn for our comfort! Show him our symbolical Truss Manufactory on the finest site in Europe, and tell him that British industrialism and individualism can bring a man to that, and he remains cold! Evidently, if we deal tenderly with a sentimentalist like this, it is out of pure philanthropy.

But with the Hyde Park rioter[13] how different! He is our own flesh and blood; he is a Protestant; he is framed by nature to do as we do, hate what we hate, love what we love; he is capable of feeling the symbolical force of the Truss Manufactory; the question of questions, for him, is a wages question. That beautiful sentence of Sir Daniel Gooch quoted to the Swindon workmen,[14] and which I treasure as Mrs Gooch's Golden Rule, or the Divine Injunction 'Be ye Perfect' done into British – the sentence Sir Daniel Gooch's mother repeated to him every morning when he was a boy going to work – '*Ever remember, my dear Dan, that you should look forward to being some day manager of that concern!*' – this truthful maxim is perfectly fitted to shine forth in the heart of the Hyde Park rough also, and to be his guiding-star through life. He has no visionary schemes of revolution and transformation, though of course he would like his class to rule, as the aristocratic class like their class to rule, and the middle class theirs. But meanwhile our social machine is a little out of order; there are a good many people in our paradisiacal centres of industrialism and individualism taking the bread out of one another's mouths. The rough has not yet quite found his groove and settled down to his work, and so he is just asserting his personal liberty a little, going where he likes, assembling where he likes, bawling as he likes, hustling as he likes. Just as the rest of us – as the country squires in the aristocratic class, as the political dissenters in the middle class – he has no idea of a State, of the nation in its collective and corporate character controlling, as government, the free swing of this or that one of its members in the name of the higher reason of all of them, his own as well as that of others. He sees the rich, the aristocratic class, in occupation of the executive government, and so if he is stopped from making Hyde Park a bear-garden or the streets impassable, he says he is being butchered by the aristocracy.

His apparition is somewhat embarrassing, because too many cooks spoil the broth; because, while the aristocratic and middle classes have long been doing as they like with great vigour, he has been too undeveloped and submissive hitherto to join in the game; and now, when he does come, he comes in immense numbers, and is rather raw and rough. But he does not break many laws, or not many at one time; and, as our laws were made for very different circumstances from our present (but always with an eye to Englishmen doing as they like), and as the clear letter of the law must be against our Englishman who does as he likes and not only the spirit of the law and public policy, and as Government must neither have any discretionary power nor act resolutely on its own interpretation of the law if any one disputes it, it is evident our laws give our playful giant, in doing as he likes, considerable advantage. Besides, even if he can be clearly proved to commit an illegality in doing as he likes, there is always the resource of not putting the law in force, or of abolishing it. So he has his way, and if he has his way he is soon satisfied for the time. However, he falls into the habit of taking it oftener and oftener, and at last begins to create by his operations a confusion of which mischievous people can take advantage, and which, at any rate, by troubling the common course of business throughout the country, tends to cause distress, and so to increase the sort of anarchy and social disintegration which had previously commenced. And thus that profound sense of settled order and security, without which a society like ours cannot live and grow at all, sometimes seems to be beginning to threaten us with taking its departure.

Now, if culture, which simply means trying to perfect oneself, and one's mind as part of oneself, brings us light, and if light shows us that there is nothing so very blessed in merely doing as one likes, that the worship of the mere freedom to do as one likes is worship of machinery, that the really blessed thing is to like what right reason ordains, and to follow her authority, then we have got a practical benefit out of culture. We have got a much wanted principle, a principle of authority, to counteract the tendency to anarchy which seems to be threatening us.

But how to organize this authority, or to what hands to entrust the wielding of it? How to get your State, summing up the right reason of the community, and giving effect to it, as circumstances may require, with vigour? And here I think I see my enemies waiting for me with a hungry joy in their eyes. But I shall elude them.

The State, the power most representing the right reason of the nation, and most worthy, therefore, of ruling – of exercising, when circumstances require it, authority over us all – is for Mr Carlyle the aristocracy.[15] For Mr Lowe,[16] it is the middle class with its incomparable Parliament. For the Reform League, it is the working class, the class with 'the brightest powers of sympathy and readiest powers of action.' Now culture, with its disinterested pursuit of perfection, culture, simply trying to see things as they are in order to seize on the best and to make it prevail, is surely well fitted to help us to judge rightly, by all the aids of observing, reading, and thinking, the qualifications and titles to our confidence of these three candidates for authority, and can thus render us a practical service of no mean value.

So when Mr Carlyle, a man of genius to whom we have all at one time or other been indebted for refreshment and stimulus, says we should give rule to the aristocracy, mainly because of its dignity and politeness, surely culture is useful in reminding us, that in our idea of perfection the characters of beauty and intelligence are both of them present, and sweetness and light, the two noblest of things, are united. Allowing, therefore, with Mr Carlyle, the aristocratic class to possess sweetness, culture insists on the necessity of light also, and shows us that aristocracies, being by the very nature of things inaccessible to ideas, unapt to see how the world is going, must be somewhat wanting in light, and must therefore be, at a moment when light is our great requisite, inadequate to our needs. Aristocracies, those children of the established fact, are for epochs of concentration. In epochs of expansion, epochs such as that in which we now live, epochs when always the warning voice is again heard: *Now is the judgement of this world* – in such epochs aristocracies, with their natural clinging to the established fact, their want of sense for the flux of things, for the inevitable transitoriness of all human institutions, are bewildered and helpless. Their serenity, their high spirit, their power of haughty resistance – the great qualities of an aristocracy, and the secret of its distinguished manners and dignity – these very qualities, in an epoch of expansion, turn against their possessors. Again and again I have said how the refinement of an aristocracy may be precious and educative to a raw nation as a kind of shadow of true refinement; how its serenity and dignified freedom from petty cares may serve as a useful foil to set off the vulgarity and hideousness of that type of life which a hard middle class tends to establish, and to help people to see this vulgarity and hideousness in their true colours. But the true grace and serenity is that of which Greece and Greek art suggest the admirable ideals of perfection – a serenity which comes from having made order among ideas and harmonized them; whereas the serenity of aristocracies, at least the peculiar serenity of aristocracies of Teutonic origin, appears to come from their never having had any ideas to trouble them. And so, in a time of expansion like the present, a time for ideas, one gets perhaps, in regarding an aristocracy, even more than the idea of serenity, the idea of futility and sterility.

One has often wondered whether upon the whole earth there is anything so unintelligent, so unapt to perceive how the world is really going, as an ordinary young Englishman of our upper class. Ideas he has not, and neither has he that seriousness of our middle class which is, as I have often said, the great strength of this class, and may become its salvation. Why, a man may hear a young Dives of the aristocratic class, when the whim takes him to sing the praises of wealth and material comfort, sing them with a cynicism from which the conscience of the veriest Philistine of our industrial middle class would recoil in affright. And when, with the natural sympathy of aristocracies for firm dealing with the multitude, and his uneasiness at our feeble dealing with it at home, an unvarnished young Englishman of our aristocratic class applauds the absolute rulers on the Continent, he in general manages completely to miss the grounds of reason and intelligence which alone can give any colour of justification, any possibility of existence, to those rulers, and applauds them on grounds which it would make their own hair stand on end to listen to.

And all this time we are in an epoch of expansion; and the essence of an epoch of expansion is a movement of ideas, and the one salvation of an epoch of expansion is a harmony of ideas. The very principle of the authority which we are seeking as a defence against anarchy is right reason, ideas, light. The more, therefore, an aristocracy calls to its aid its innate forces – its impenetrability, its high spirit, its power of haughty resistance – to deal with an epoch of expansion, the graver is the danger, the greater the certainty of explosion, the surer the aristocracy's defeat; for it is trying to do violence to nature instead of working along with it. The best powers shown by the best men of an aristocracy at such an epoch are, it will be observed, non-aristocratical powers, powers of industry, powers of intelligence; and these powers thus exhibited, tend really not to strengthen the aristocracy, but to take their owners out of it, to expose them to the dissolving agencies of thought and change, to make them men of the modern spirit and of the future. If, as sometimes happens, they add to their non-aristocratical qualities of labour and thought, a strong dose of aristocratical qualities also – of pride, defiance, turn for resistance – this truly aristocratical side of them, so far from adding any strength to them, really neutralizes their force and makes them impracticable and ineffective.

Knowing myself to be indeed sadly to seek, as one of my many critics says, in 'a philosophy and coherent, interdependent, subordinate, and derivative principles', I continually have recourse to a plain man's expedient of trying to make what few simple notions I have clearer and more intelligible to myself by means of example and illustration. And having been brought up at Oxford in the bad old times, when we were stuffed with Greek and Aristotle, and thought nothing of preparing ourselves by the study of modern languages – as after Mr Lowe's great speech at Edinburgh we shall do – to fight the battle of life with the waiters in foreign hotels, my head is still full of a lumber of phrases we learnt at Oxford from Aristotle, about virtue being in a mean, and about excess and defect, and so on. Once when I had had the advantage of listening to the Reform debates in the House of

Commons, having heard a number of interesting speakers, and among them a well-known lord and a well-known baronet, I remember it struck me, applying Aristotle's machinery of the mean to my ideas about our aristocracy, that the lord was exactly the perfection, or happy mean, or virtue, of aristocracy, and the baronet the excess. And I fancied that by observing these two we might see both the inadequacy of aristocracy to supply the principle of authority needful for our present wants, and the danger of its trying to supply it when it was not really competent for the business. On the one hand, in the brilliant lord, showing plenty of high spirit, but remarkable, far above and beyond his gift of high spirit, for the fine tempering of his high spirit, for ease, serenity, politeness – the great virtues, as Mr Carlyle says, of aristocracy – in this beautiful and virtuous mean, there seemed evidently some insufficiency of light; while, on the other hand, the worthy baronet, in whom the high spirit of aristocracy, its impenetrability, defiant courage, and pride of resistance, were developed even in excess was manifestly capable, if he had his way given him, of causing us great danger, and, indeed, of throwing the whole commonwealth into confusion. Then I reverted to that old fundamental notion of mine about the grand merit of our race being really our honesty. And the very helplessness of our aristocratic or governing class in dealing with our perturbed social condition, their jealousy of entrusting too much power to the State as it now actually exists – that is to themselves – gave me a sort of pride and satisfaction; because I saw they were, as a whole, too honest to try and manage a business for which they did not feel themselves capable.

Surely, now, it is no inconsiderable boon which culture confers upon us, if in embarrassed times like the present it enables us to look at the ins and the outs of things in this way, without hatred and without partiality, and with a disposition to see the good in everybody all round. And I try to follow just the same course with our middle class as with our aristocracy. Mr Lowe talks to us of this strong middle part of the nation, of the unrivalled deeds of our Liberal middle-class Parliament, of the noble, the heroic work it has performed in the last thirty years; and I begin to ask myself if we shall not, then, find in our middle class the principle of authority we want, and if we had not better take administration as well as legislation away from the weak extreme which now administers for us, and commit both to the strong middle part. I observe, too, that the heroes of middle-class liberalism, such as we have hitherto known it, speak with a kind of prophetic anticipation of the great destiny which awaits them, and as if the future was clearly theirs. The advanced party, the progressive party, the party in alliance with the future, are the names they like to give themselves. 'The principles which will obtain recognition in the future,' says Mr Miall,[17] a personage of deserved eminence among the political Dissenters, as they are called, who have been the backbone of middle-class liberalism – 'the principles which will obtain recognition in the future are the principles for which I have long and zealously laboured. I qualified myself for joining in the work of harvest by doing to the best of my ability the duties of seedtime.' These duties, if one is to gather them from the works of the great Liberal party in the last thirty years, are, as I have elsewhere summed them up, the advocacy of free trade, of Parliamentary reform, of abolition of church-rates, of voluntaryism in religion and education, of non-interference of the State between employers and employed, and of marriage with one's deceased wife's sister.[18]

Now I know, when I object that all this is machinery, the great Liberal middle class has by this time grown cunning enough to answer that it always meant more by these things than meets the eye; that it has had that within which passes show, and that we are soon going to see, in a Free Church and all manner of good things, what it was. But I have learned from Bishop Wilson (if Mr Frederic Harrison will forgive my again quoting that poor old hierophant of a decayed superstition): 'If we would really know our heart let us impartially view our actions;' and I cannot help thinking that if our Liberals had had so much sweetness and light in their inner minds as they allege, more of it must have come out in their sayings and doings.

An American friend of the English Liberals says, indeed, that their Dissidence of Dissent has been a mere instrument of the political Dissenters for making reason and the will of God prevail (and no doubt he would say the same of marriage with one's deceased wife's sister); and that the abolition of a State Church is merely the Dissenter's means to this end, just as culture is mine. Another American defender of theirs says just the same of their industrialism and free trade; indeed, this gentleman, taking the bull by the horns, proposes that we should for the future call industrialism culture, and the industrialists the men of culture, and then of course there can be no longer any misapprehension about their true character; and besides the pleasure of being wealthy and comfortable, they will have authentic recognition as vessels of sweetness and light.

All this is undoubtedly specious; but I must remark that the culture of which I talked was an endeavour to come at reason and the will of God by means of reading, observing, and thinking; and that whoever calls anything else culture, may, indeed, call it so if he likes, but then he talks of something quite different from what I talked of. And, again, as culture's way of working for reason and the will of God is by directly trying to know more about them, while the Dissidence of Dissent is evidently in itself no effort of this kind, nor is its Free Church, in fact, a church with worthier conceptions of God and the ordering of the world than the State Church professes, but with mainly the same conceptions of these as the State Church has, only that every man is to comport himself as he likes in professing them – this being so, I cannot at once accept the Nonconformity any more than the industrialism and the other great works of our Liberal middle class as proof positive that this class is in possession of light, and that here is the true seat of authority for which we are in search; but I must try a little further, and seek for other indications which may enable me to make up my mind.

Why should we not do with the middle class as we have done with the aristocratic class – find in it some representative men who may stand for the virtuous mean of this class, for the perfection of its present qualities and mode of being, and also for the excess of them. Such men must clearly not be men of genius like Mr Bright; for, as I have formerly said, so far as a man has genius he tends to take himself out of the category of class altogether, and to become simply a man. Some more ordinary man would be more to the purpose – would sum up better in himself, without disturbing influences, the general liberal force of the middle class, the force by which it has done its great works of free trade, Parliamentary reform, voluntaryism, and so on, and the spirit in which it has done them. Now it happens that a typical middle-class man, the member for one of our chief industrial cities, has given us a famous sentence which bears directly on the resolution of our present question: whether there is light enough in our middle class to make it the proper seat of the authority we wish to establish. When there was a talk some little while ago about the state of middle-class education, our friend, as the representative of that class, spoke some memorable words – 'There had been a cry that middle-class education ought to receive more attention. He confessed himself very much surprised by the clamour that was raised. He did not think that class need excite the sympathy either of the legislature or the public.' Now this satisfaction of our middle-class member of Parliament with the mental state of the middle class was truly representative, and makes good his claim to stand as the beautiful and virtuous mean of that class. But it is obviously at variance with our definition of culture, or the pursuit of light and perfection, which made light and perfection consist, not in resting and being, but in growing and becoming, in a perpetual advance in beauty and wisdom. So the middle class is by its essence, as one may say, by its incomparable self-satisfaction decisively expressed through its beautiful and virtuous mean, self-excluded from wielding an authority of which light is to be the very soul.

Clear as this is, it will be made clearer still if we take some representative man as the excess of the middle class, and remember that the middle class, in general, is to be conceived as a body swaying between the qualities of its mean and of its excess, and on the whole, of course, as human nature is constituted, inclining rather towards the excess than the mean. Of its excess no better representative can possibly be imagined than a Dissenting minister from Walsall, who came before the public in connection with the proceedings at Birmingham of Mr Murphy, already mentioned. Speaking in the midst of an irritated population of Catholics, this Walsall gentleman exclaimed, 'I say, then, away with the Mass! It is from the bottomless pit; and in the bottomless pit shall all liars have their part, in the lake that burneth with fire and brimstone.' And again: 'When all the praties were black in Ireland, why didn't the priests say the hocus-pocus over them, and make them all good again?' He shared, too, Mr Murphy's fears of some invasion of his domestic happiness, 'What I wish to say to you as Protestant husbands is, *take care of your wives*!' And finally, in the true vein of an Englishman doing as he likes, a vein of which I have at some length pointed out the present dangers, he recommended for imitation the example of some churchwardens at Dublin, among whom, he said, 'there was a Luther and also a Melanchthon', who had made very short work with some ritualist or other, hauled him down from his pulpit, and kicked him out of church. Now it is manifest, as I said in the case of our aristocratical baronet, that if we let this excess of the sturdy English middle class, this conscientious Protestant Dissenter, so strong, so self-reliant, so fully persuaded in his own mind, have his way, he would be capable, with his want of light – or, to use the language of the religious world, with his zeal without knowledge – of stirring up strife which neither he nor any one else could easily compose.

And then comes in, as it did also with the aristocracy, the honesty of our race, and by the voice of another middle-class man, Alderman of the City of London and Colonel of the City of London Militia,[19] proclaims that it has twinges of conscience, and that it will not attempt to cope with our social disorders, and to deal with a business which it feels to be too high for it. Every one remembers how this virtuous Alderman-Colonel, or Colonel-Alderman, led his militia through the London streets; how the bystanders gathered to see him pass; how the London roughs, asserting an Englishman's best and most blissful right of doing what he likes, robbed and beat the bystanders; and how the blameless warrior-magistrate refused to let his troops interfere. 'The crowd', he touchingly said afterwards, 'was mostly composed of fine healthy strong men, bent on mischief; if he had allowed his soldiers to interfere they might have been overpowered, their rifles taken from them and used against them by the mob; a riot, in fact, might have ensued, and been attended with bloodshed, compared with which the assaults and loss of property that actually occurred would have been as nothing.' Honest and affecting testimony of the English middle class to its own inadequacy for the authoritative part one's admiration would sometimes incline one to assign to it! 'Who are we', they say by the voice of their Alderman-Colonel, 'that we should not be overpowered if we attempt to cope with social anarchy, our rifles taken from us and used against us by the mob, and we, perhaps, robbed and beaten ourselves? Or what light have we, beyond a free-born Englishman's impulse to do as he likes, which could justify us in preventing, at the cost of bloodshed, other free-born Englishmen from doing as they like, and robbing and beating us as much as they please?'

This distrust of themselves as an adequate centre of authority does not mark the working class, as was shown by their readiness the other day in Hyde Park to take upon themselves all the functions of government. But this comes from the working class being, as I have often said, still an embryo, of which no one can yet quite foresee the final development; and from its not having the same experience and self-knowledge as the aristocratic and middle classes. Honesty it no doubt has, just like the other classes of Englishmen, but honesty in an inchoate and untrained state; and meanwhile its powers of action, which are, as Mr Frederic Harrison says, exceedingly ready, easily run away with it. That it cannot at present have a sufficiency of light which comes by culture – that is, by reading, observing, and thinking – is clear from the very nature of its condition; and, indeed, we saw that Mr Frederic Harrison, in seeking to make a free stage for its bright powers of sympathy and ready powers of action, had to begin by throwing overboard culture, and flouting it as only fit for a professor of *belles-lettres*. Still, to make it perfectly manifest that no more in the working class than in the aristocratic and middle classes can one find an adequate centre of authority – that is, as culture teaches us to conceive our required authority, of light – let us again follow, with this class, the method we have followed with the aristocratic and middle classes, and try to bring before our minds representative men, who may figure to us its virtue and its excess.

We must not take, of course, men like the chiefs of the Hyde Park demonstration, Colonel Dickson[20] or Mr Beales; because Colonel Dickson, by his martial profession and dashing exterior, seems to belong properly, like Julius Caesar and Mirabeau and other great popular leaders, to the aristocratic class, and to be carried into the popular ranks only by his ambition or his genius; while Mr Beales belongs to our solid middle class, and, perhaps, if he had not been a great popular leader, would have been a Philistine. But Mr Odger,[21] whose speeches we have all read, and of whom his friends relate, besides, much that is favourable, may very well stand for the beautiful and virtuous mean of our present working class; and I think everybody will admit that in Mr Odger there is manifestly, with all his good points, some insufficiency of light. The excess of the working class, in its present state of development, is perhaps best shown in Mr Bradlaugh, the iconoclast, who seems to be almost for baptizing us all in blood and fire into his new social dispensation, and to whose reflections, now that I have once been set going on Bishop Wilson's track, I cannot forbear commending this maxim of the good old man, 'Intemperance in talk makes a dreadful havoc in the heart.' Mr Bradlaugh, like our types of excess in the aristocratic and middle classes, is evidently capable, if he has his head given him, of running us all into great dangers and confusion. I conclude, therefore – what indeed, few of those who do me the honour to read this disquisition are likely to dispute – that we can as little find in the working class as in the aristocratic or in the middle class our much-wanted source of authority, as culture suggests it to us.

Well, then, what if we tried to rise above the idea of class to the idea of the whole community, the State, and to find our centre of light and authority there? Every one of us has the idea of country, as a sentiment; hardly any one of us has the idea of the State, as a working power. And why? Because we habitually live in our ordinary selves, which do not carry us beyond the ideas and wishes of the class to which we happen to belong. And we are all afraid of giving to the State too much power, because we only conceive of the State as something equivalent to the class in occupation of the executive government, and are afraid of that class abusing power to its own purposes. If we strengthen the State with the aristocratic class in occupation of the executive government, we imagine we are delivering ourselves up captive to the ideas and wishes of our fierce aristocratical baronet; if with the middle class in occupation of the executive government, to those of our truculent middle-class Dissenting minister; if with the working class, to those of its notorious tribune, Mr Bradlaugh. And with much justice; owing to the exaggerated notion which we English, as I have said, entertain of the right and blessedness of the mere doing as one likes, of the affirming oneself, and oneself just as it is. People of the aristocratic class want to affirm their ordinary selves, their likings and dislikings; people of the middle class the same, people of the working class the same. By our everyday selves, however, we are separate, personal, at war; we are only safe from one another's tyranny when no one has any power; and this safety, in its turn, cannot save us from anarchy. And when, therefore, anarchy presents itself as a danger to us, we know not where to turn.

But by our *best self* we are united, impersonal, at harmony. We are in no peril from giving authority to this, because it is the truest friend we all of us can have; and when anarchy is a danger to us, to this authority we may turn with sure trust. Well, and this is the very self which culture, or the study of perfection, seeks to develop in us; at the expense of our old untransformed self, taking pleasure only in doing what it likes or is used to do, and exposing us to the risk of clashing with every one else who is doing the same! So that our poor culture, which is flouted as so unpractical, leads us to the very ideas capable of meeting the great want of our present embarrassed times! We want an authority, and we find nothing but jealous classes, checks, and a dead-lock; culture suggests the idea of the State. We find no basis for a firm State power in our ordinary selves; culture suggests one to us in our *best self.*

It cannot but acutely try a tender conscience to be accused, in a practical country like ours, of keeping aloof from the work and hope of a multitude of earnest-hearted men, and of merely toying with poetry and aesthetics. So it is with no little sense of relief that I find myself thus in the position of one who makes a contribution in aid of the practical necessities of our times. The great thing, it will be observed, is to find our *best* self, and to seek to affirm nothing but that; not – as we English with our over-value for merely being free and busy have been so accustomed to do – resting satisfied with a self which comes uppermost long before our best self, and affirming that with blind energy. In short – to go back yet once more to Bishop Wilson – of these two excellent rules of Bishop Wilson's for a man's guidance: 'Firstly, never go against the best light you have; secondly, take care that your light be not darkness', we English have followed with praiseworthy zeal the first rule, but we have not given so much heed to the second. We have gone manfully according to the best light we have; but we have not taken enough care that this should be really the best light possible for us, that it should not be darkness. And, our honesty being very great, conscience has whispered to us that the light we were following, our ordinary self, was, indeed, perhaps, only an inferior self, only darkness; and that it would not do to impose this seriously on all the world.

But our best self inspires faith, and is capable of affording a serious principle of authority. For example. We are on our way to what the late Duke of Wellington, with his strong sagacity, foresaw and admirably described as 'a revolution by due course of law'. This is undoubtedly – if we are still to live and grow, and this famous nation is not to stagnate and dwindle away on the one hand, or, on the other, to perish miserably in mere anarchy and confusion – what we are on the way to. Great changes there must be, for a revolution cannot accomplish itself without great changes; yet order there must be, for without order a revolution cannot accomplish itself by due course of law. So whatever brings risk of tumult and disorder, multitudinous processions in the streets of our crowded towns, multitudinous meetings in their public places and parks – demonstrations perfectly unnecessary in the present course of our affairs – our best self, or right reason, plainly enjoins us to set our faces against. It enjoins us to encourage and uphold the occupants of the executive power, whoever they may be, in firmly prohibiting them. But it does this clearly and resolutely, and is thus a real principle of authority, because it does it with a free conscience; because in thus provisionally strengthening the executive power, it knows that it is not doing this merely to enable our aristocratical baronet to affirm himself as against our working-men's tribune, or our middle-class Dissenter to affirm himself as against both. It knows that it is establishing the State, or organ of our collective best self, of our national right reason. And it has the testimony of conscience that it is establishing the State on behalf of whatever great changes are needed, just as much as on behalf of order; establishing it to deal just as stringently, when the time comes, with our baronet's aristocratical prejudices, or with the fanaticism of our middle-class Dissenter, as it deals with Mr Bradlaugh's street-processions.

Barbarians, Philistines, Populace

From a man without a philosophy no one can expect philosophical completeness. Therefore I may observe without shame, that in trying to get a distinct notion of our aristocratic, our middle, and our working class, with a view of testing the claims of each of these classes to become a centre of authority, I have omitted, I find, to complete the old-fashioned analysis which I had the fancy of applying, and have not shown in these classes, as well as the virtuous mean and the excess, the defect also. I do not know that the omission very much matters. Still, as clearness is the one merit which a plain, unsystematic writer, without a philosophy, can hope to have, and as our notion of the three great English classes may perhaps be made clearer if we see their distinctive qualities in the defect, as well as in the excess and in the mean, let us try, before proceeding further, to remedy this omission.

It is manifest, if the perfect and virtuous mean of that fine spirit, which is the distinctive quality of aristocracies, is to be found in a high, chivalrous style, and its excess in a fierce turn for resistance, that its defect must lie in a spirit not bold and high enough, and in an excessive and pusillanimous unaptness for resistance. If, again, the perfect and virtuous mean of that force by which our middle class has done its great works, and of that self-reliance with which it contemplates itself and them, is to be seen in the performances and speeches of our commercial member of Pailiament, and the excess of that force and of that self-reliance in the performances and speeches of our fanatical Dissenting minister, then it is manifest that their defect must lie in a helpless inaptitude for the great works of the middle class, and in a poor and despicable lack of its self-satisfaction.

To be chosen to exemplify the happy mean of a good quality, or set of good qualities, is evidently a praise to a man; nay, to be chosen to exemplify even their excess, is a kind of praise. Therefore I could have no hesitation in taking actual personages to exemplify, respectively, the mean and the excess of aristocratic and middle-class qualities. But perhaps there might be a want of urbanity in singling out this or that personage as the representative of defect. Therefore I shall leave the defect of aristocracy unillustrated by any representative man. But with oneself one may always, without impropriety, deal quite freely; and, indeed, this sort of plain-dealing with oneself has in it, as all the moralists tell us, something very wholesome. So I will venture to humbly offer myself as an illustration of defect in those forces and qualities which make our middle class what it is. The too well-founded reproaches of my opponents declare how little I have lent a hand to the great works of the middle class; for it is evidently these works, and my slackness at them, which are meant, when I am said to 'refuse to lend a hand to the humble operation of uprooting certain definite evils' (such as church-rates and others), and that therefore 'the believers in action grow impatient' with me. The line, again, of a still unsatisfied seeker which I have followed, the idea of self-transformation, of growing towards some measure of sweetness and light not yet reached, is evidently at clean variance with the perfect self-satisfaction current in my class, the middle class, and may serve to indicate in me, therefore, the extreme defect of this feeling. But these confessions, though salutary, are bitter and unpleasant.

To pass, then, to the working class. The defect of this class would be the falling short in what Mr Frederic Harrison calls those 'bright powers of sympathy and ready powers of action', of which we saw in Mr Odger the virtuous mean, and in Mr Bradlaugh the excess. The working class is so fast growing and rising at the present time, that instances of this defect cannot well be now very common. Perhaps Canning's 'Needy Knife-Grinder' (who is dead, and therefore cannot be pained at my taking him for an illustration) may serve to give us the notion of defect in the essential quality of a working class; or I might even cite (since, though he is alive in the flesh, he is dead to all heed of criticism) my poor old poaching friend, Zephaniah Diggs, who, between his hare-snaring and his gin-drinking, has got his powers of sympathy quite dulled and his powers of action in any great movement of his class hopelessly impaired. But examples of this defect belong, as I have said, to a bygone age rather than to the present.

The same desire for clearness, which has led me thus to extend a little my first analysis of the three great classes of English society, prompts me also to improve my nomenclature for them a little, with a view to making it thereby more manageable. It is awkward and tiresome to be always saying the aristocratic class, the middle class, the working class. For the middle class, for that great body which, as we know, 'has done all the great things that have been done in all departments', and which is to be conceived as moving between its two cardinal points of our commercial member of Parliament and our fanatical Protestant Dissenter – for this class we have a designation which now has become pretty well known, and which we may as well still keep for them, the designation of Philistines. What this term means I have so often explained that I need not repeat it here. For the aristocratic class, conceived mainly as a body moving between the two cardinal points of our chivalrous lord and our defiant baronet, we have as yet got no special designation. Almost all my attention has naturally been concentrated on my own class, the middle class, with which I am in closest sympathy, and which has been, besides, the great power of our day, and has had its praises sung by all speakers and newspapers.

Still the aristocratic class is so important in itself, and the weighty functions which Mr Carlyle proposes at the present critical time to commit to it, must add so much to its importance, that it seems neglectful, and a strong instance of that want of coherent philosophic method for which Mr Frederic Harrison blames me, to leave the aristocratic class so much without notice and denomination. It may be thought that the characteristic which I have occasionally mentioned as proper to aristocracies – their natural inaccessibility, as children of the established fact, to ideas – points to our extending to this class also the designation of Philistines; the Philistine being, as is well known, the enemy of the children of light or servants of the idea. Nevertheless, there seems to be an inconvenience in thus giving one and the same designation to two very different classes; and besides, if we look into the thing closely, we shall find that the term Philistine conveys a sense which makes it more peculiarly appropriate to our middle class than to our aristocratic. For 'Philistine' gives the notion of something particularly stiff-necked and perverse in the resistance to light and its children; and therein it specially suits our middle class, who not only do not pursue sweetness and light, but who even prefer to them that sort of machinery of business, chapels, tea-meetings, and addresses from Mr Murphy, which makes up the dismal and illiberal life on which I have so often touched. But the aristocratic class has actually, as we have seen, in its well-known politeness, a kind of image or shadow of sweetness; and as for light, if it does not pursue light, it is not that it perversely cherishes some dismal and illiberal existence in preference to light, but it is lured off from following light by those mighty and eternal seducers of our race which weave for this class their most irresistible charms – by worldly splendour, security, power, and pleasure. These seducers are exterior goods, but in a way they are goods; and he who is hindered by them from caring for light and ideas, is not so much doing what is perverse as what is too natural.

Keeping this in view, I have in my own mind often indulged myself with the fancy of employing, in order to designate our aristocratic class, the name of the 'Barbarians'. The Barbarians, to whom we all owe so much, and who reinvigorated and renewed our worn-out Europe, had, as is well known, eminent merits; and in this country, where we are for the most part sprung from the Barbarians, we have never had the prejudice against them which prevails among the races of Latin origin. The Barbarians brought with them that staunch individualism, as the modern phrase is, and that passion for doing as one likes, for the assertion of personal liberty, which appears to Mr Bright the central idea of English life, and of which we have, at any rate, a very rich supply. The stronghold and natural seat of this passion was in the nobles of whom our aristocratic class are the inheritors; and this class, accordingly, have signally manifested it, and have done much by their example to recommend it to the body of the nation, who already, indeed, had it in their blood. The Barbarians, again, had the passion for field-sports; and they have handed it on to our aristocratic class, who of this passion too, as of the passion for asserting one's personal liberty, are the great natural stronghold. The care of the Barbarians for the body, and for all manly exercises; the vigour, good looks, and fine complexion which they acquired and perpetuated in their families by these means – all this may be observed still in our aristocratic class. The chivalry of the Barbarians, with its characteristics of high spirit, choice manners, and distinguished bearing – what is this but the attractive commencement of the politeness of our aristocratic class? In some Barbarian noble, no doubt, one would have admired, if one could have been then alive to see it, the rudiments of our politest peer. Only, all this culture (to call it by that name) of the Barbarians was an exterior culture mainly. It consisted principally in outward gifts and graces, in looks, manners, accomplishments, prowess. The chief inward gifts which had part in it were the most exterior, so to speak, of inward gifts, those which come nearest to outward ones; they were courage, a high spirit, self-confidence. Far within, and unawakened, lay a whole range of powers of thought and feeling, to which these interesting productions of nature had, from the circumstances of their life, no access. Making allowances for the difference of the times, surely we can observe precisely the same thing now in our aristocratic class. In general its culture is exterior chiefly; all the exterior graces and accomplishments, and the more external of the inward virtues, seem to be principally its portion. It now, of course, cannot but be often in contact with those studies by which, from the world of thought and feeling, true culture teaches us to fetch sweetness and light; but its hold upon these very studies appears remarkably external, and unable to exert any deep power upon its spirit. Therefore the one insufficiency which we noted in the perfect mean of this class was an insufficiency of light. And owing to the same causes, does not a subtle criticism lead us to make, even on the good looks and politeness of our aristocratic class, and of even the most fascinating half of that class, the feminine half, the one qualifying remark, that in these charming gifts there should perhaps be, for ideal perfection, a shade more *soul*?

I often, therefore, when I want to distinguish clearly the aristocratic class from the Philistines proper, or middle class, name the former, in my own mind, the Barbarians. And when I go through the country, and see this and that beautiful and imposing seat of theirs crowning the landscape, 'There', I say to myself, 'is a great fortified post of the Barbarians.'

It is obvious that that part of the working class which, working diligently by the light of Mrs Gooch's Golden Rule, looks forward to the happy day when it will sit on thrones with commercial members of Parliament and other middle-class potentates, to survey, as Mr Bright beautifully says, 'the cities it has built, the railroads it has made, the manufactures it has produced, the cargoes which freight the ships of the greatest mercantile navy the world has ever seen' – it is obvious, I say, that this part of the working class is, or is in a fair way to be, one in spirit with the industrial middle class. It is notorious that our middle-class Liberals have long looked forward to this consummation, when the working class shall join forces with them, aid them heartily to carry forward their great works, go in a body to their tea-meetings, and, in short, enable them to bring about their millennium. That part of the working class, therefore, which does really seem to lend itself to these great aims, may, with propriety, be numbered by us among the Philistines. That part of it, again, which so much occupies the attention of philanthropists at present – the part which gives all its energies to organizing itself, through trades' unions and other means, so as to constitute, first, a great working-class power independent of the middle and aristocratic classes, and then, by dint of numbers, give the law to them and itself reign absolutely – this lively and promising part must also, according to our definition, go with the Philistines; because it is its class and its class instinct which it seeks to affirm – its ordinary self, not its best self; and it is a machinery, an industrial machinery, and power and pre-eminence and other external goods, which fill its thoughts, and not an inward perfection. It is wholly occupied, according to Plato's subtle expression, with the things of itself and not its real self, with the things of the State and not the real State. But that vast portion, lastly, of the working class which, raw and half-developed, has long lain half-hidden amidst its poverty and squalor, and is now issuing from its hiding-place to assert an Englishman's heaven-born privilege of doing as he likes, and is beginning to perplex us by marching where it likes, meeting where it likes, bawling what it likes, breaking what it likes – to this vast residuum we may with great propriety give the name of 'Populace'.

Thus we have got three distinct terms, Barbarians, Philistines, Populace, to denote roughly the three great classes into which our society is divided; and though this humble attempt at a scientific nomenclature falls, no doubt, very far short in precision of what might be required from a writer equipped with a complete and coherent philosophy, yet, from a notoriously unsystematic and unpretending writer, it will, I trust, be accepted as sufficient.

But in using this new, and, I hope, convenient division of English society, two things are to be borne in mind. The first is, that since, under all our class divisions, there is a common basis of human nature, therefore, in every one of us, whether we be properly Barbarians, Philistines, or Populace, there exist, sometimes only in germ and potentially, sometimes more or less developed, the same tendencies and passions which have made our fellow-citizens of other classes what they are. This consideration is very important, because it has great influence in begetting that spirit of indulgence which is a necessary part of sweetness, and which, indeed, when our culture is complete, is, as I have said, inexhaustible. Thus, an English Barbarian who examines himself will, in general, find himself to be not so entirely a Barbarian but that he has in him, also, something of the Philistine, and even something of the Populace as well. And the same with Englishmen of the two other classes.

This is an experience which we may all verify every day. For instance, I myself (I again take myself as a sort of *corpus vile* to serve for illustration in a matter where serving for illustration may not by every one be thought agreeable), I myself am properly a Philistine – Mr Swinburne would add, the son of a Philistine. And although, through circumstances which will perhaps one day be known if ever the affecting history of my conversion comes to be written, I have, for the most part, broken with the ideas and the tea-meetings of my own class, yet I have not, on that account, been brought much the nearer to the ideas and works of the Barbarians or of the Populace. Nevertheless, I never take a gun or a fishing-rod in my hands without feeling that I have in the ground of my nature the self-same seeds which, fostered by circumstances, do so much to make the Barbarian; and that, with the Barbarian's advantages, I might have rivalled him. Place me in one of his great fortified posts, with these seeds of a love for field-sports sown in my nature, with all the means of developing them, with all pleasures at my command, with most whom I met deferring to me, every one I met smiling on me, and with every appearance of permanence and security before me and behind me – then I too might have grown, I feel, into a very passable child of the established fact, of commendable spirit and politeness, and, at the same time, a little inaccessible to ideas and light; not, of course, with either the eminent fine spirit of our type of aristocratic perfection, or the eminent turn for resistance of our type of aristocratic excess, but, according to the measure of the common run of mankind, something between the two. And as to the Populace, who, whether he be Barbarian or Philistine, can look at them without sympathy, when he remembers how often – every time that we snatch up a vehement opinion in ignorance and passion, every time that we long to crush an adversary by sheer violence, every time that we are envious, every time that we are brutal, every time that we adore mere power or success, every time that we add our voice to swell a blind clamour against some unpopular personage, every time that we trample savagely on the fallen – he has found in his own bosom the eternal spirit of the Populace, and that there needs only a little help from circumstances to make it triumph in him untamably.

The second thing to be borne in mind I have indicated several times already. It is this. All of us, so far as we are Barbarians, Philistines, or Populace, imagine happiness to consist in doing what one's ordinary self likes. What one's ordinary self likes differs according to the class to which one belongs, and has its severer and its lighter side; always, however, remaining machinery, and nothing more. The graver self of the Barbarian likes honours and consideration; his more relaxed self, field-sports and pleasure. The graver self of one kind of Philistine likes fanaticism, business, and money-making; his more relaxed self, comfort and tea-meetings. Of another kind of Philistine, the graver self likes rattening; the relaxed self, deputations, or hearing Mr Odger speak. The sterner self of the Populace likes bawling, hustling, and smashing; the lighter self, beer. But in each class there are born a certain number of natures with a curiosity about their best self, with a bent for seeing things as they are, for disentangling themselves from machinery, for simply concerning themselves with reason and the will of God, and doing their best to make these prevail – for the pursuit, in a word, of perfection. To certain manifestations of this love for perfection mankind have accustomed themselves to give the name of genius; implying, by this name, something original and heaven-bestowed in the passion. But the passion is to be found far beyond those manifestations of it to which the world usually gives the name of genius, and in which there is, for the most part, a *talent* of some kind or other, a special and striking faculty of execution, informed by the heaven-bestowed ardour, or genius. It is to be found in many manifestations besides these, and may best be called, as we have called it, the love and pursuit of perfection; culture being the true nurse of the pursuing love, and sweetness and light the true character of the pursued perfection. Natures with this bent emerge in all classes – among the Barbarians, among the Philistines, among the Populace. And this bent always tends to take them out of their class, and to make their distinguishing characteristic not their Barbarianism or their Philistinism, but their *humanity*. They have, in general, a rough time of it in their lives; but they are sown more abundantly than one might think, they appear where and when one least expects it, they set up a fire which enfilades, so to speak, the class with which they are ranked; and, in general, by the extrication of their best self as the self to develop, and by the simplicity of the ends fixed by them as paramount, they hinder the unchecked predominance of that class-life which is the affirmation of our ordinary self, and seasonably disconcert mankind in their worship of machinery.

Therefore, when we speak of ourselves as divided into Barbarians, Philistines, and Populace, we must be understood always to imply that within each of these classes there are a certain number of *aliens*, if we may so call them – persons who are mainly led, not by their class spirit, but by a general *humane* spirit, by the love of human perfection; and that this number is capable of being diminished or augmented. I mean, the number of those who will succeed in developing this happy instinct will be greater or smaller, in proportion both to the force of the original instinct within them, and to the hindrance or encouragement which it meets with from without. In almost all who have it, it is mixed with some infusion of the spirit of an ordinary self, some quantity of class-instinct, and even, as has been shown, of more than one class-instinct at the same time; so that, in general, the extrication of the best self, the predominance of the *humane* instinct, will very much depend upon its meeting, or not, with what is fitted to help and elicit it. At a moment, therefore, when it is agreed that we want a source of authority, and when it seems probable that the right source is our best self, it becomes of vast importance to see whether or not the things around us are, in general, such as to help and elicit our best self, and if they are not, to see why they are not, and the most promising way of mending them.

Now, it is clear that the very absence of any powerful authority amongst us, and the prevalent doctrine of the duty and happiness of doing as one likes, and asserting our personal liberty, must tend to prevent the erection of any very strict standard of excellence, the belief in any very paramount authority of right reason, the recognition of our best self as anything very recondite and hard to come at. It may be, as I have said, a proof of our honesty that we do not attempt to give to our ordinary self, as we have it in action, predominant authority, and to impose its rule upon other people. But it is evident, also, that it is not easy, with our style of proceeding, to get beyond the notion of an ordinary self at all, or to get the paramount authority of a commanding best self, or right reason, recognized. The learned Martinus Scriblerus well says, 'The taste of the bathos is implanted by nature itself in the soul of man; till, perverted by custom or example, he is taught, or rather compelled, to relish the sublime.' But with us everything seems directed to prevent any such perversion of us by custom or example as might compel us to relish the sublime; by all means we are encouraged to keep our natural taste for the bathos unimpaired.

I have formerly pointed out how in literature the absence of any authoritative centre, like an Academy, tends to do this. Each section of the public has its own literary organ, and the mass of the public is without any suspicion that the value of these organs is relative to their being nearer a certain ideal centre of correct information, taste, and intelligence, or farther away from it. I have said that within certain limits, which any one who is likely to read this will have no difficulty in drawing for himself, my old adversary, the *Saturday Review*, may, on matters of literature and taste, be fairly enough regarded, relatively to the mass of newspapers which treat these matters, as a kind of organ of reason. But I remember once conversing with a company of Nonconformist admirers of some lecturer who had let off a great firework, which the *Saturday Review* said was all noise and false lights, and feeling my way as tenderly as I could about the effect of this unfavourable judgement upon those with whom I was conversing. 'Oh', said one who was their spokesman, with the most tranquil air of conviction, 'it is true the *Saturday Review* abuses the lecture, but the *British Banner*' (I am not quite sure it was the *British Banner*, but it was some newspaper of that stamp) 'says that the *Saturday Review* is quite wrong.' The speaker had evidently no notion that there was a scale of value for judgements on these topics, and that the judgements of the *Saturday Review* ranked high on this scale, and those of the *British Banner* low; the taste of the bathos implanted by nature in the literary judgements of man had never, in my friend's case, encountered any let or hindrance.

Just the same in religion as in literature. We have most of us little idea of a high standard to choose our guides by, of a great and profound spirit which is an authority while inferior spirits are none. It is enough to give importance to things that this or that person says them decisively, and has a large following of some strong kind when he says them. This habit of ours is very well shown in that able and interesting work of Mr Hepworth Dixon's, which we were all reading lately, *The Mormons, by One of Themselves*. Here, again, I am not quite sure that my memory serves me as to the exact title, but I mean the well-known book in which Mr Hepworth Dixon described the Mormons, and other similar religious bodies in America, with so much detail and such warm sympathy. In this work it seems enough for Mr Dixon that this or that doctrine has its Rabbi, who talks big to him, has a staunch body of disciples, and, above all, has plenty of rifles. That there are any further stricter tests to be applied to a doctrine, before it is pronounced important, never seems to occur to him. 'It is easy to say', he writes of the Mormons, 'that these saints are dupes and fanatics, to laugh at Joe Smith and his church, but what then? *The great facts remain.* Young and his people are at Utah; a church of 200,000 souls; an army of 20,000 rifles.' But if the followers of a doctrine are really dupes, or worse, and its promulgators are really fanatics, or worse, it gives the doctrine no seriousness or authority the more that there should be found 200,000 souls – 200,000 of the innumerable multitude with a natural taste for the bathos – to hold it, and 20,000 rifles to defend it. And again, of another religious organization in America: 'A fair and open field is not to be refused when hosts so mighty throw down wager of battle on behalf of what they hold to be true, however strange their faith may seem.' A fair and open field is not to be refused to any speaker; but this solemn way of heralding him is quite out of place, unless he has, for the best reason and spirit of man, some significance. 'Well, but', says Mr Hepworth Dixon, 'a theory which has been accepted by men like Judge Edmonds, Dr Hare, Elder Frederick, and Professor Bush!' And again, 'Such are, in brief, the bases of what Newman Weeks, Sarah Horton, Deborah Butler, and the associated brethren, proclaimed in Pratt's Hall as the new covenant!' If he was summing up an account of the doctrine of Plato, or of St Paul, and of its followers, Mr Hepworth Dixon could not be more earnestly reverential. But the question is, have personages like Judge Edmonds, and Newman Weeks, and Elderess Polly, and Elderess Antoinette, and the rest of Mr Hepworth Dixon's heroes and heroines, anything of the weight and significance for the best reason and spirit of man that Plato and St Paul have? Evidently they, at present, have not; and a very small taste of them and their doctrines ought to have convinced Mr Hepworth Dixon that they never could have. 'But', says he, 'the magnetic power which Shakerism is exercising on American thought would of itself compel us', and so on. Now, so far as real thought is concerned – thought which affects the best reason and spirit of man, the scientific or the imaginative thought of the world, the only thought which deserves speaking of in this solemn way – America has up to the present time been hardly more than a province of England, and even now would not herself claim to be more than abreast of England; and of this only real human thought, English thought itself is not just now, as we must all admit, the most significant factor. Neither, then, can American thought be; and the magnetic power which Shakerism exercises on American thought is about as important, for the best reason and spirit of man, as the magnetic power which Mr Murphy exercises on Birmingham Protestantism. And as we shall never get rid of our natural taste for the bathos in religion – never get access to a best self and right reason which may stand as a serious authority – by treating Mr Murphy as his own disciples treat him, seriously, and as if he was as much an authority as any one else: so we shall never get rid of it while our able and popular writers treat their Joe Smiths and Deborah Butlers, with their so many thousand souls and so many thousand rifles, in the like exaggerated and misleading manner, and so do their best to confirm us in a bad mental habit to which we are already too prone.

If our habits make it hard for us to come at the idea of a high best self, of a paramount authority, in literature or religion, how much more do they make this hard in the sphere of politics! In other countries the governors, not depending so immediately on the favour of the governed, have everything to urge them, if they know anything of right reason (and it is at least supposed that governors should know more of this than the mass of the governed), to set it authoritatively before the community. But our whole scheme of government being representative, every one of our governors has all possible temptation, instead of setting up before the governed who elect him, and on whose favour he depends, a high standard of right reason, to accommodate himself as much as possible to their natural taste for the bathos; and even if he tries to go counter to it, to proceed in this with so much flattering and coaxing, that they shall not suspect their ignorance and prejudices to be anything very unlike right reason, or their natural taste for the bathos to differ much from a relish for the sublime. Every one is thus in every possible way encouraged to trust in his own heart; but, 'He that trusteth in his own heart', says the Wise Man, 'is a fool', and at any rate this, which Bishop Wilson says, is undeniably true, 'The number of those who need to be awakened is far greater than that of those who need comfort.'

But in our political system everybody is comforted. Our guides and governors who have to be elected by the influence of the Barbarians, and who depend on their favour, sing the praises of the Barbarians, and say all the smooth things that can be said of them. With Mr Tennyson, they celebrate 'the great broad-shouldered genial Englishman', with his 'sense of duty', his 'reverence for the laws', and his 'patient force', who saves us from the 'revolts, republics, revolutions, most no graver than a schoolboy's barring out', which upset other and less broadshouldered nations. Our guides, who are chosen by the Philistines and who have to look to their favour, tell the Philistines how 'all the world knows that the great middle class of this country supplies the mind, the will, and the power requisite for all the great and good things that have to be done', and congratulate them on their 'earnest good sense, which penetrates through sophisms, ignores commonplaces, and gives to conventional illusions their true value'. Our guides who look to the favour of the Populace, tell them that 'theirs are the brightest powers of sympathy, and the readiest powers of action.'

Harsh things are said too, no doubt, against all the great classes of the community; but these things so evidently come from a hostile class, and are so manifestly dictated by the passions and prepossessions of a hostile class, and not by right reason, that they make no serious impression on those at whom they are launched, but slide easily off their minds. For instance, when the Reform League orators inveigh against our cruel and bloated aristocracy these invectives so evidently show the passions and point of view of the Populace, that they do not sink into the minds of those at whom they are addressed, or awaken any thought or self-examination in them. Again, when our aristocratical baronet describes the Philistines and the Populace as influenced with a kind of hideous mania for emasculating the aristocracy, that reproach so clearly comes from the wrath and excited imagination of the Barbarians, that it does not much set the Philistines and the Populace thinking. Or when Mr Lowe calls the Populace drunken and venal, he so evidently calls them this in an agony of apprehension for his Philistine or middle-class Parliament, which has done so many great and heroic works, and is now threatened with mixture and debasement, that the Populace do not lay his words seriously to heart.

So the voice which makes a permanent impression on each of our classes is the voice of its friends, and this is from the nature of things, as I have said, a comforting voice. The Barbarians remain in the belief that the great broad-shouldered genial Englishman may be well satisfied with himself; the Philistines remain in the belief that the great middle class of this country, with its earnest common-sense penetrating through sophisms and ignoring common-places, may be well satisfied with itself; the Populace, that the working man with his bright powers of sympathy and ready powers of action, may be well satisfied with himself. What hope, at this rate, of extinguishing the taste of the bathos implanted by nature itself in the soul of man, or of inculcating the belief that excellence dwells among high and steep rocks, and can only be reached by those who sweat blood to reach her?

But it will be said, perhaps, that candidates for political influence and leadership, who thus caress the self-love of those whose suffrages they desire, know quite well that they are not saying the sheer truth as reason sees it, but that they are using a sort of conventional language, or what we call clap-trap, which is essential to the working of representative institutions. And therefore, I suppose, we ought rather to say with Figaro, *Qui est-ce qu'on trompe ici?*[22] Now, I admit that often, but not always, when our governors say smooth things to the self-love of the class whose political support they want, they know very well that they are overstepping, by a long stride, the bounds of truth and soberness; and while they talk, they in a manner, no doubt, put their tongue in their cheek. Not always; because, when a Barbarian appeals to his own class to make him their representative and give him political power, he, when he pleases their self-love by extolling broad-shouldered genial Englishmen with their sense of duty, reverence for the laws, and patient force, pleases his own self-love and extols himself, and is, therefore, himself ensnared by his own smooth words. And so, too, when a Philistine wants to be sent to Parliament by his brother Philistines, and extols the earnest good sense which characterizes Manchester and supplies the mind, the will, and the power, as the *Daily News* eloquently says, requisite for all the great and good things that have to be done, he intoxicates and deludes himself as well as his brother Philistines who hear him.

But it is true that a Barbarian often wants the political support of the Philistines; and he unquestionably, when he flatters the self-love of Philistinism, and extols, in the approved fashion, its energy, enterprise, and self-reliance, knows that he is talking clap-trap, and so to say, puts his tongue in his cheek. On all matters where Nonconformity and its catchwords are concerned, this insincerity of Barbarians needing Nonconformist support, and, therefore, flattering the self-love of Nonconformity and repeating its catchwords without the least real belief in them, is very noticeable. When the Nonconformists, in a transport of blind zeal, threw out Sir James Graham's useful Education Clauses in 1843, one-half of their Parliamentary advocates, no doubt, who cried aloud against 'trampling on the religious liberty of the Dissenters by taking the money of Dissenters to teach the tenets of the Church of England', put their tongue in their cheek while they so cried out. And perhaps there is even a sort of motion of Mr Frederic Harrison's tongue towards his cheek when he talks of 'the shriek of superstition', and tells the working class that 'theirs are the brightest powers of sympathy and the readiest powers of action.' But the point on which I would insist is, that this involuntary tribute to truth and soberness on the part of certain of our governors and guides never reaches at all the mass of us governed, to serve as a lesson to us, to abate our self-love, and to awaken in us a suspicion that our favourite prejudices may be, to a higher reason, all nonsense. Whatever by-play goes on among the more intelligent of our leaders, we do not see it; and we are left to believe that, not only in our own eyes, but in the eyes of our representative and ruling men, there is nothing more admirable than our ordinary self, whatever our ordinary self happens to be, Barbarian, Philistine, or Populace.

Thus everything in our political life tends to hide from us that there is anything wiser than our ordinary selves, and to prevent our getting the notion of a paramount right reason. Royalty itself, in its idea the expression of the collective nation, and a sort of constituted witness to its best mind, we try to turn into a kind of grand advertising van, meant to give publicity and credit to the inventions, sound or unsound, of the ordinary self of individuals.

I remember, when I was in North Germany, having this very strongly brought to my mind in the matter of schools and their institution. In Prussia, the best schools are Crown patronage schools, as they are called: schools which have been established and endowed (and new ones are to this day being established and endowed) by the Sovereign himself out of his own revenues, to be under the direct control and management of him or of those representing him, and to serve as types of what schools should be. The Sovereign, as his position raises him above many prejudices and littlenesses, and as he can always have at his disposal the best advice, has evident advantages over private founders in well planning and directing a school; while at the same time his great means and his great influence secure, to a well-planned school of his, credit and authority. This is what, in North Germany, the governors do in the matter of education for the governed; and one may say that they thus give the governed a lesson, and draw out in them the idea of a right reason higher than the suggestions of an ordinary man's ordinary self.

But in England how different is the part which in this matter our governors are accustomed to play! The Licensed Victuallers or the Commercial Travellers propose to make a school for their children; and I suppose, in the matter of schools, one may call the Licensed Victuallers or the Commercial Travellers ordinary men, with their natural taste for the bathos still strong; and a Sovereign with the advice of men like Wilhelm von Humboldt or Schleiermacher may, in this matter, be a better judge, and nearer to right reason. And it will be allowed, probably, that right reason would suggest that, to have a sheer school of Licensed Victuallers' children, or a sheer school of Commercial Travellers' children, and to bring them all up, not only at home but at school too, in a kind of odour of licensed victualism or of bagmanism, is not a wise training to give to these children. And in Germany, I have said, the action of the national guides or governors is to suggest and provide a better. But, in England, the action of the national guides or governors is, for a Royal Prince or a great Minister to go down to the opening of the Licensed Victuallers' or of the Commercial Travellers' school, to take the chair, to extol the energy and self-reliance of the Licensed Victuallers or the Commercial Travellers, to be all of their way of thinking, to predict full success to their schools, and never so much as to hint to them that they are probably doing a very foolish thing, and that the right way to go to work with their children's education is quite different. And it is the same in almost every department of affairs. While, on the Continent, the idea prevails that it is the business of the heads and representatives of the nation, by virtue of their superior means, power, and information, to set an example and to provide suggestions of right reason, among us the idea is that the business of the heads and representatives of the nation is to do nothing of the kind, but to applaud the natural taste for the bathos showing itself vigorously in any part of the community, and to encourage its works.

Now I do not say that the political system of foreign countries has not inconveniences which may outweigh the inconveniences of our own political system; nor am I the least proposing to get rid of our own political system and to adopt theirs. But a sound centre of authority being what, in this disquisition, we have been led to seek, and right reason, or our best self, appearing alone to offer such a sound centre of authority, it is necessary to take note of the chief impediments which hinder, in this country, the extrication or recognition of this right reason as a paramount authority, with a view to afterwards trying in what way they can best be removed.

This being borne in mind, I proceed to remark how not only do we get no suggestions of right reason, and no rebukes of our ordinary self, from our governors, but a kind of philosophical theory is widely spread among us to the effect that there is no such thing at all as a best self and a right reason having claim to paramount authority, or, at any rate, no such thing ascertainable and capable of being made use of; and that there is nothing but an infinite number of ideas and works of our ordinary selves, and suggestions of our natural taste for the bathos, pretty nearly equal in value, which are doomed either to an irreconcilable conflict, or else to a perpetual give and take; and that wisdom consists in choosing the give and take rather than the conflict, and in sticking to our choice with patience and good humour.

And, on the other hand, we have another philosophical theory rife among us, to the effect that without the labour of perverting ourselves by custom or example to relish right reason, but by continuing all of us to follow freely our natural taste for the bathos, we shall, by the mercy of Providence, and by a kind of natural tendency of things, come in due time to relish and follow right reason.

The great promoters of these philosophical theories are our newspapers, which, no less than our Parliamentary representatives, may be said to act the part of guides and governors to us; and these favourite doctrines of theirs I call – or should call, if the doctrines were not preached by authorities I so much respect – the first, a peculiarly British form of Atheism, the second, a peculiarly British form of Quietism. The first-named melancholy doctrine is preached in *The Times* with great clearness and force of style; indeed, it is well known, from the example of the poet Lucretius and others, what great masters of style the atheistic doctrine has always counted among its promulgators. 'It is of no use', says *The Times*, 'for us to attempt to force upon our neighbours our several likings and dislikings. We must take things as they are. Everybody has his own little vision of religious or civil perfection. Under the evident impossibility of satisfying everybody, we agree to take our stand on equal laws and on a system as open and liberal as is possible. The result is that everybody has more liberty of action and of speaking here than anywhere else in the Old World.' We come again here upon Mr Roebuck's celebrated definition of happiness, on which I have so often commented: 'I look around me and ask what is the state of England? Is not every man able to say what he likes? I ask you whether the world over, or in past history, there is anything like it? Nothing. I pray that our unrivalled happiness may last.' This is the old story of our system of checks and every Englishman doing as he likes, which we have already seen to have been convenient enough so long as there were only the Barbarians and the Philistines to do what they liked, but to be getting inconvenient, and productive of anarchy, now that the Populace wants to do what it likes too.

But for all that, I will not at once dismiss this famous doctrine, but will first quote another passage from *The Times*, applying the doctrine to a matter of which we have just been speaking – education. 'The difficulty here' (in providing a national system of education), says *The Times*, 'does not reside in any removable arrangements. It is inherent and native in the actual and inveterate state of things in this country. All these powers and personages, all these conflicting influences and varieties of character, exist, and have long existed among us; they are fighting it out, and will long continue to fight it out, without coming to that happy consummation when some one element of the British character is to destroy or to absorb all the rest.' There it is! The various promptings of the natural taste for the bathos in this man and that amongst us are fighting it out; and the day will never come (and, indeed, why should we wish it to come?) when one man's particular sort of taste for the bathos shall tyrannize over another man's; nor when right reason (if that may be called an element of the British character) shall absorb and rule them all. 'The whole system of this country, like the constitution we boast to inherit, and are glad to uphold, is made up of established facts, prescriptive authorities, existing usages, powers that be, persons in possession, and communities or classes that have won dominion for themselves, and will hold it against all comers.' Every force in the world, evidently, except the one reconciling force, right reason! Barbarian here, Philistine there, Mr Bradlaugh and Populace striking in! – pull devil, pull baker! Really, presented with the mastery of style of our leading journal, the sad picture, as one gazes upon it, assumes the iron and inexorable solemnity of tragic Destiny.

After this, the milder doctrine of our other philosophical teacher, the

Daily News, has, at first, something very attractive and assuaging. The *Daily News* begins, indeed, in appearance, to weave the iron web of necessity round us like *The Times*. 'The alternative is between a man's doing what he likes and his doing what some one else, probably not one whit wiser than himself, likes.' This points to the tacit compact, mentioned in my last paper, between the Barbarians and the Philistines, and into which it is hoped that the Populace will one day enter; the compact, so creditable to English honesty, that since each class has only the ideas and aims of its ordinary self to give effect to, none of them shall, if it exercise power, treat its ordinary self too seriously, or attempt to impose it on others; but shall let these others – the fanatical Protestant, for instance, in his papist-baiting, and the popular tribune in his Hyde Park anarchy-mongering – have their fling. But then the *Daily News* suddenly lights up the gloom of necessitarianism with bright beams of hope. 'No doubt', it says, 'the common reason of society ought to check the aberrations of individual eccentricity.' This common reason of society looks very like our best self or right reason, to which we want to give authority, by making the action of the State, or nation in its collective character, the expression of it. But of this project of ours, the *Daily News*, with its subtle dialectics, makes havoc. 'Make the State the organ of the common reason?' it says. 'You may make it the organ of something or other, but how can you be certain that reason will be the quality which will be embodied in it?' You cannot be certain of it, undoubtedly, if you never try to bring the thing about; but the question is, the action of the State being the action of the collective nation, and the action of the collective nation carrying naturally great publicity, weight, and force of example with it, whether we should not try to put into the action of the State as much as possible of right reason or our best self, which may, in this manner, come back to us with new force and authority; may have visibility, form, and influence; and help to confirm us, in the many moments when we are tempted to be our ordinary selves merely, in resisting our natural taste of the bathos rather than in giving way to it?

But no! says our teacher: 'It is better there should be an infinite variety of experiments in human action; the common reason of society will in the main check the aberrations of individual eccentricity well enough, if left to its natural operation.' This is what I call the specially British form of Quietism, or a devout, but excessive, reliance on an over-ruling Providence. Providence, as the moralists are careful to tell us, generally works in human affairs by human means; so, when we want to make right reason act on individual inclination, our best self on our ordinary self, we seek to give it more power of doing so by giving it public recognition and authority, and embodying it, so far as we can, in the State. It seems too much to ask of

Providence, that while we, on our part, leave our congenital taste for the bathos to its natural operation and its infinite variety of experiments, Providence should mysteriously guide it into the true track, and compel it to relish the sublime. At any rate, great men and great institutions have hitherto seemed necessary for producing any considerable effect of this kind. No doubt we have an infinite variety of experiments and an ever-multiplying multitude of explorers. Even in these few chapters I have enumerated many: the *British Banner*, Judge Edmonds, Newman Weeks, Deborah Butler, Elderess Polly, Brother Noyes, Mr Murphy, the Licensed Victuallers, the Commercial Travellers, and I know not how many more; and the numbers of the noble army are swelling every day. But what a depth of Quietism, or rather, what an over-bold call on the direct interposition of Providence, to believe that these interesting explorers will discover the true track, or at any rate, 'will do so in the main well enough' (whatever that may mean) if left to their natural operation; that is, by going on as they are! Philosophers say, indeed, that we learn virtue by performing acts of virtue; but to say that we shall learn virtue by performing any acts to which our natural taste for the bathos carries us, that the fanatical Protestant comes at his best self by Papist-baiting, or Newman Weeks and Deborah Butler at right reason by following their noses, this certainly does appear over-sanguine.

It is true, what we want is to make right reason act on individual reason, the reason of individuals; all our search for authority has that for its end and aim. The *Daily News* says, I observe, that all my argument for authority 'has a non-intellectual root', and from what I know of my own mind and its poverty I think this so probable, that I should be inclined easily to admit it, if it were not that, in the first place, nothing of this kind, perhaps, should be admitted without examination; and, in the second, a way of accounting for the charge being made, in this particular instance, without good grounds, appears to present itself. What seems to me to account here, perhaps, for the charge, is the want of flexibility of our race, on which I have so often remarked. I mean, it being admitted that the conformity of the individual reason of the fanatical Protestant or the popular rioter with right reason is our true object, and not the mere restraining them, by the strong arm of the State, from Papist-baiting, or railing-breaking – admitting this, we English have so little flexibility that we cannot readily perceive that the State's restraining them from these indulgences may yet fix clearly in their minds that, to the collective nation, these indulgences appear irrational and unallowable, may make them pause and reflect, and may contribute to bringing, with time, their individual reason into harmony with right reason. But in no country, owing to the want of intellectual flexibility above mentioned, is the leaning which is our natural one, and, therefore, needs no recommending to us, so sedulously recommended, and the leaning which is not our natural one, and, therefore, does not need dispraising to us, so sedulously dispraised, as in ours. To rely on the individual being, with us, the natural leaning, we will hear of nothing but the good of relying on the individual; to act through the collective nation on the individual being not our natural leaning, we will hear nothing in recommendation of it. But the wise know that we often need to hear most of that to which we are least inclined, and even to learn to employ, in certain circumstances, that which is capable, if employed amiss, of being a danger to us.

Elsewhere this is certainly better understood than here. In a recent number of the *Westminster Review*, an able writer, but with precisely our national want of flexibility of which I have been speaking, has unearthed, I see, for our present needs, an English translation, published some years ago, of Wilhelm von Humboldt's book, *The Sphere and Duties of Government*. Humboldt's object in this book is to show that the operation of government ought to be severely limited to what directly and immediately relates to the security of person and property. Wilhelm von Humboldt, one of the most beautiful souls that have ever existed, used to say that one's business in life was first to perfect one's self by all the means in one's power, and secondly, to try and create in the world around one an aristocracy, the most numerous that one possibly could, of talents and characters. He saw, of course, that, in the end, everything comes to this – that the individual must act for himself, and must be perfect in himself; and he lived in a country, Germany, where people were disposed to act too little for themselves, and to rely too much on the Government. But even thus, such was his flexibility, so little was he in bondage to a mere abstract maxim, that he saw very well that for his purpose itself, of enabling the individual to stand perfect on his own foundations and to do without the State, the action of the State would for long, long years be necessary. And soon after he wrote his book on *The Sphere and Duties of Government*, Wilhelm von Humboldt became Minister of Education in Prussia; and from his ministry all the great reforms which give the control of Prussian education to the State – the transference of the management of public schools from their old boards of trustees to the State, the obligatory State examination for schoolmasters, and the foundation of the great State University of Berlin – take their origin. This his English reviewer says not a word of. But, writing for a people whose dangers lie, as we have seen, on the side of their unchecked and unguided individual action, whose dangers none of them lie on the side of an over-reliance on the State, he quotes just so much of Wilhelm von Humboldt's example as can flatter them in their propensities, and do them no good; and just what might make them think, and be of use to them, he leaves on one side. This precisely recalls the manner, it will be observed, in which we have seen that our royal and noble personages proceed with the Licensed Victuallers.

In France the action of the State on individuals is yet more preponderant than in Germany; and the need which friends of human perfection feel for what may enable the individual to stand perfect on his own foundations is all the stronger. But what one says of the staunchest of these friends, M. Renan, on State action; and even State action in that very sphere where in France it is most excessive, the sphere of education? Here are his words, 'A Liberal believes in liberty, and liberty signifies the non-intervention of the State. *But such an ideal is still a long way off from us, and the very means to remove it to an indefinite distance would be precisely the State's withdrawing its action too soon.*' And this, he adds, is even truer of education than of any other department of public affairs.

We see, then, how indispensable to that human perfection which we seek is, in the opinion of good judges, some public recognition and establishment of our best self, or right reason. We see how our habits and practice oppose themselves to such a recognition, and the many inconveniences which we therefore suffer. But now let us try to go a little deeper, and to find, beneath our actual habits and practice, the very ground and cause out of which they spring.

Hebraism and Hellenism

This fundamental ground is our preference of doing to thinking. Now this preference is a main element in our nature, and as we study it we find ourselves opening up a number of large questions on every side.

Let me go back for a moment to Bishop Wilson, who says, 'First, never go against the best light you have; secondly, take care that your light be not darkness.' We show, as a nation, laudable energy and persistence in walking according to the best light we have, but are not quite careful enough, perhaps, to see that our light be not darkness. This is only another version of the old story that energy is our strong point and favourable characteristic, rather than intelligence. But we may give to this idea a more general form still, in which it will have a yet larger range of application. We may regard this energy driving at practice, this paramount sense of the obligation of duty, self-control, and work, this earnestness in going manfully with the best light we have, as one force. And we may regard the intelligence driving at those ideas which are, after all, the basis of right practice, the ardent sense for all the new and changing combinations of them which man's development brings with it, the indomitable impulse to know and adjust them perfectly, as another force. And these two forces we may regard as in some sense rivals – rivals not by the necessity of their own nature, but as exhibited in man and his history – and rivals dividing the empire of the world between them. And to give these forces names from the two races of men who have supplied the most signal and splendid manifestations of them, we may call them respectively the forces of Hebraism and Hellenism. Hebraism and Hellenism – between these two points of influence moves our world. At one time it feels more powerfully the attraction of one of them, at another time of the other; and it ought to be, though it never is, evenly and happily balanced between them.

The final aim of both Hellenism and Hebraism, as of all great spiritual disciplines, is no doubt the same: man's perfection of salvation. The very language which they both of them use in schooling us to reach this aim is often identical. Even when their language indicates by variation – sometimes a broad variation, often a but slight and subtle variation – the different courses of thought which are uppermost in each discipline, even then the unity of the final end and aim is still apparent. To employ the actual words of that discipline with which we ourselves are all of us most familiar, and the words of which, therefore, come most home to us, that final end and aim is 'that we might be partakers of the divine nature.' These are the words of a Hebrew apostle, but of Hellenism and Hebraism alike this is, I say, the aim. When the two are confronted, as they very often are confronted, it is nearly always with what I may call a rhetorical purpose; the speaker's whole design is to exalt and enthrone one of the two, and he uses the other only as a foil and to enable him the better to give effect to his purpose. Obviously, with us, it is usually Hellenism which is thus reduced to minister to the triumph of Hebraism. There is a sermon on Greece and the Greek spirit by a man never to be mentioned without interest and respect, Frederick Robertson, in which this rhetorical use of Greece and the Greek spirit, and the inadequate exhibition of them necessarily consequent upon this, is almost ludicrous, and would be censurable if it were not to be explained by the exigencies of a sermon. On the other hand, Heinrich Heine, and other writers of his sort, give us the spectacle of the tables completely turned, and of Hebraism brought in just as a foil and contrast to Hellenism, and to make the superiority of Hellenism more manifest. In both these cases there is injustice and misrepresentation. The aim and end of both Hebraism and Hellenism is, as I have said, one and the same, and this aim and end is august and admirable.

Still, they pursue this aim by very different courses. The uppermost idea with Hellenism is to see things as they really are; the uppermost idea with Hebraism is conduct and obedience. Nothing can do away with this ineffaceable difference. The Greek quarrel with the body and its desires is, that they hinder right thinking; the Hebrew quarrel with them is, that they hinder right acting. 'He that keepeth the law, happy is he'; 'Blessed is the man that feareth the Eternal, that delighteth greatly in his commandments'; that is the Hebrew notion of felicity; and, pursued with passion and tenacity, this notion would not let the Hebrew rest till, as is well known, he had at last got out of the law a network of prescriptions to enwrap his whole life, to govern every moment of it, every impulse, every action. The Greek notion of felicity, on the other hand, is perfectly conveyed in these words of a great French moralist, '*C'est le bonheur des hommes.*' When? When they abhor that which is evil? – No. When they exercise themselves in the law of the Lord day and night? – No. When they die daily? – No. When they walk about the New Jerusalem with palms in their hands? – No. But when they think aright, when their thought hits, '*quand ils pensent juste*'. At the bottom of both the Greek and the Hebrew notion is the desire, native in man, for reason and the will of God, the feeling after the universal order – in a word, the love of God. But, while Hebraism seizes upon certain plain, capital intimations of the universal order, and rivets itself, one may say, with unequalled grandeur of earnestness and intensity on the study and observance of them, the bent of Hellenism is to follow, with flexible activity, the whole play of the universal order, to be apprehensive of missing any part of it, of sacrificing one part to another, to slip away from resting in this or that intimation of it, however capital. An unclouded clearness of mind, an unimpeded play of thought, is what this bent drives at. The governing idea of Hellenism is *spontaneity of consciousness*; that of Hebraism, *strictness of conscience*.

Christianity changed nothing in this essential bent of Hebraism to set doing above knowing. Self-conquest, self-devotion, the following not our own individual will, but the will of God, *obedience*, is the fundamental idea of this form, also, of the discipline to which we have attached the general name of Hebraism. Only, as the old law and the network of prescriptions with which it enveloped human life were evidently a motive-power not driving and searching enough to produce the result aimed at – patient continuance in well-doing, self-conquest – Christianity substituted for them boundless devotion to that inspiring and affecting pattern of self-conquest offered by Jesus Christ; and by the new motive-power, of which the essence was this, though the love and admiration of Christian churches have for centuries been employed in varying, amplifying, and adorning the plain description of it, Christianity, as St Paul truly says, 'establishes the law', and in the strength of the ampler power which she has thus supplied to fulfil it, has accomplished the miracles, which we all see, of her history.

So long as we do not forget that both Hellenism and Hebraism are profound and admirable manifestations of man's life, tendencies, and powers, and that both of them aim at a like final result, we can hardly insist too strongly on the divergence of line and of operation with which they proceed. It is a divergence so great that it most truly, as the prophet Zachariah says, 'has raised up thy sons, O Zion, against thy sons, O Greece!' The difference whether it is by doing or by knowing that we set most store, and the practical consequences which follow from this difference, leave their mark on all the history of our race and of its development. Language may be abundantly quoted from both Hellenism and Hebraism to make it seem that one follows the same current as the other towards the same goal. They are, truly, borne towards the same goal; but the currents which bear them are infinitely different. It is true, Solomon will praise knowing: 'Understanding is a well-spring of life unto him that hath it.' And in the New Testament, again, Jesus Christ is a 'light', and 'truth makes us free'. It is true, Aristotle will undervalue knowing: 'In what concerns virtue,' says he, 'three things are necessary – knowledge, deliberate will, and perseverance; but, whereas the two last are all-important, the first is a matter of little importance.' It is true that with the same impatience with which St James enjoins a man to be not a forgetful hearer, but a *doer of the word*, Epictetus exhorts us to *do* what we have demonstrated to ourselves we ought to do; or he taunts us with futility, for being armed at all points to prove that lying is wrong, yet all the time continuing to lie. It is true, Plato, in words which are almost the words of the New Testament or the Imitation, calls life a learning to die. But underneath the superficial agreement the fundamental divergence still subsists. The understanding of Solomon is 'the walking in the way of the commandments'; this is 'the way of peace', and it is of this that blessedness comes. In the New Testament, the truth which gives us the peace of God and makes us free, is the love of Christ constraining us to crucify, as he did, and with a like purpose of moral regeneration, the flesh with its affections and lusts, and thus establishing, as we have seen, the law. The moral virtues, on the other hand, are with Aristotle but the porch and access to the intellectual, and with these last is blessedness. That partaking of the divine life, which both Hellenism and Hebraism, as we have said, fix as their crowning aim, Plato expressly denies to the man of practical virtue merely, of self-conquest with any other motive than that of perfect intellectual vision. He reserves it for the lover of pure knowledge, of seeing things as they really are – the φιλομαθής.

Both Hellenism and Hebraism arise out of the wants of human nature, and address themselves to satisfying those wants. But their methods are so different, they lay stress on such different points, and call into being by their respective disciplines such different activities, that the face which human nature presents when it passes from the hands of one of them to those of the other, is no longer the same. To get rid of one's ignorance, to see things as they are, and by seeing them as they are to see them in their beauty, is the simple and attractive ideal which Hellenism holds out before human nature; and from the simplicity and charm of this ideal, Hellenism, and human life in the hands of Hellenism, is invested with a kind of aerial ease, clearness, and radiancy; they are full of what we call sweetness and light. Difficulties are kept out of view, and the beauty and rationalness of the ideal have all our thoughts. 'The best man is he who most tries to perfect himself, and the happiest man is he who most feels that he *is* perfecting himself' – this account of the matter by Socrates, the true Socrates of the *Memorabilia*, has something so simple, spontaneous, and unsophisticated about it, that it seems to fill us with clearness and hope when we hear it. But there is a saying which I have heard attributed to Mr Carlyle about Socrates – a very happy saying, whether it is really Mr Carlyle's or not – which excellently marks the essential point in which Hebraism differs from Hellenism. 'Socrates', this saying goes, 'is terribly *at ease in Zion*.' Hebraism – and here is the source of its wonderful strength – has always been severely preoccupied with an awful sense of the impossibility of being at ease in Zion; of the difficulties which oppose themselves to man's pursuit or attainment of that perfection of which Socrates talks so hopefully, and, as from this point of view one might almost say, so glibly. It is all very well to talk of getting rid of one's ignorance, of seeing things in their reality, seeing them in their beauty; but how is this to be done when there is something which thwarts and spoils all our efforts?

This something is *sin*; and the space which sin fills in Hebraism, as compared with Hellenism, is indeed prodigious. This obstacle to perfection fills the whole scene, and perfection appears remote and rising away from earth, in the background. Under the name of sin, the difficulties of knowing oneself and conquering oneself which impede man's passage to perfection, become, for Hebraism, a positive, active entity hostile to man, a mysterious power which I heard Dr Pusey the other day, in one of his impressive sermons, compare to a hideous hunchback seated on our shoulders, and which it is the main business of our lives to hate and oppose. The discipline of the Old Testament may be summed up as a discipline teaching us to abhor and flee from sin; the discipline of the New Testament, as a discipline teaching us to die to it. As Hellenism speaks of thinking clearly, seeing things in their essence and beauty, as a grand and precious feat for man to achieve, so Hebraism speaks of becoming conscious of sin, of awakening to a sense of sin, as a feat of this kind. It is obvious to what wide divergence these differing tendencies, actively followed, must lead. As one passes and repasses from Hellenism to Hebraism, from Plato to St Paul, one feels inclined to rub one's eyes and ask oneself whether man is indeed a gentle and simple being, showing the traces of a noble and divine nature; or an unhappy chained captive, labouring with groanings that cannot be uttered to free himself from the body of this death.

Apparently it was the Hellenic conception of human nature which was unsound, for the world could not live by it. Absolutely to call it unsound, however, is to fall into the common error of its Hebraizing enemies; but it was unsound at that particular moment of man's development, it was premature. The indispensable basis of conduct and self-control, the platform upon which alone the perfection aimed at by Greece can come into bloom, was not to be reached by our race so easily; centuries of probation and discipline were needed to bring us to it. Therefore the bright promise of Hellenism faded, and Hebraism ruled the world. Then was seen that astonishing spectacle, so well marked by the often-quoted words of the prophet Zachariah, when men of all languages of the nations took hold of the skirt of him that was a Jew, saying, '*We will go with you, for we have heard that God is with you.*' And the Hebraism which thus received and ruled a world all gone out of the way and altogether become unprofitable, was, and could not but be, the later, the more spiritual, the more attractive development of Hebraism. It was Christianity; that is to say, Hebraism aiming at self-conquest and rescue from the thrall of vile affections, not by obedience to the letter of a law, but by conformity to the image of a self-sacrificing example. To a world stricken with moral enervation Christianity offered its spectacle of an inspired self-sacrifice; to men who refused themselves nothing, it showed one who refused himself everything; '*my Saviour banished joy!*' says George Herbert. When the *alma Venus*, the life-giving and joy-giving power of nature, so fondly cherished by the Pagan world, could not save her followers from self-dissatisfaction and ennui, the severe words of the apostle came bracingly and refreshingly, 'Let no man deceive you with vain words, for because of these things cometh the wrath of God upon the children of disobedience.' Through age after age and generation after generation, our race, or all that part of our race which was most living and progressive, was *baptized into a death*; and endeavoured, by suffering in the flesh, to cease from sin. Of this endeavour, the animating labours and afflictions of early Christianity, the touching asceticism of medieval Christianity, are the great historical manifestations. Literary monuments of it, each in its own way incomparable, remain in the Epistles of St Paul, in St Augustine's Confessions, and in the two original and simplest books of the Imitation.*

Of two disciplines laying their main stress, the one, on clear intelligence, the other, on firm obedience; the one, on comprehensively knowing the grounds of one's duty, the other, on diligently practising it; the one, on taking all possible care (to use Bishop Wilson's words again) that the light

*The two first books.

we have be not darkness, the other, that according to the best light we have we diligently walk – the priority naturally belongs to that discipline which braces all man's moral powers, and founds for him an indispensable basis of character. And, therefore, it is justly said of the Jewish people, who were charged with setting powerfully forth that side of the divine order to which the words *conscience* and *self-conquest* point, that they were 'entrusted with the oracles of God'; as it is justly said of Christianity, which followed Judaism and which set forth this side with a much deeper effectiveness and a much wider influence, that the wisdom of the old Pagan world was foolishness compared to it. No words of devotion and admiration can be too strong to render thanks to these beneficent forces which have so borne forward humanity in its appointed work of coming to the knowledge and possession of itself; above all, in those great moments when their action was the wholesomest and the most necessary.

But the evolution of these forces, separately and in themselves, is not the whole evolution of humanity – their single history is not the whole history of man; whereas their admirers are always apt to make it stand for the whole history. Hebraism and Hellenism are, neither of them, the *law* of human development, as their admirers are prone to make them; they are, each of them, *contributions* to human development – august contributions, invaluable contributions; and each showing itself to us more august, more invaluable, more preponderant over the other, according to the moment in which we take them, and the relation in which we stand to them. The nations of our modern world, children of that immense and salutary movement which broke up the Pagan world, inevitably stand to Hellenism in a relation which dwarfs it, and to Hebraism in a relation which magnifies it. They are inevitably prone to take Hebraism as the law of human development, and not as simply a contribution to it, however precious. And yet the lesson must perforce be learned, that the human spirit is wider than the most priceless of the forces which bear it onward, and that to the whole development of man Hebraism itself is, like Hellenism, but a contribution.

Perhaps we may help ourselves to see this clearer by an illustration drawn from the treatment of a single great idea which has profoundly engaged the human spirit, and has given it eminent opportunities for showing its nobleness and energy. It surely must be perceived that the idea of immortality, as this idea rises in its generality before the human spirit, is something grander, truer, and more satisfying, than it is in the particular forms by which St Paul, in the famous fifteenth chapter of the Epistle to the Corinthians, and Plato, in the *Phaedo*, endeavour to develop and establish it. Surely we cannot but feel, that the argumentation with which the Hebrew apostle goes about to expound this great idea is, after all, confused and inconclusive; and that the reasoning, drawn from analogies of likeness and equality, which is employed upon it by the Greek philosopher, is over-subtle and sterile. Above and beyond the inadequate solutions which Hebraism and Hellenism here attempt, extends the immense and august problem itself, and the human spirit which gave birth to it. And this single illustration may suggest to us how the same thing happens in other cases also.

But meanwhile, by alternations of Hebraism and Hellenism, of a man's intellectual and moral impulses, of the effort to see things as they really are, and the effort to win peace by self-conquest, the human spirit proceeds; and each of these two forces has its appointed hours of culmination and seasons of rule. As the great movement of Christianity was a triumph of Hebraism and man's moral impulses, so the great movement which goes by the name of the Renascence* was an uprising and reinstatement of man's intellectual impulses and of Hellenism. We in England, the devoted children of Protestantism, chiefly know the Renascence by its subordinate and secondary side of the Reformation. The Reformation has been often called a Hebraizing revival, a return to the ardour and sincereness of primitive Christianity. No one, however, can study the development of Protestantism and of Protestant churches without feeling that into the Reformation too – Hebraizing child of the Renascence and offspring of its fervour, rather than its intelligence, as it undoubtedly was – the subtle Hellenic leaven of the Renascence found its way, and that the exact respective parts, in the Reformation, of Hebraism and of Hellenism, are not easy to separate. But what we may with truth say is, that all which Protestantism was to itself clearly conscious of, all which it succeeded in clearly setting forth in words, had the characters of Hebraism rather than of Hellenism. The Reformation was strong, in that it was an earnest return to the Bible and to doing from the heart the will of God as there written. It was weak, in that it never consciously grasped or applied the central idea of the Renascence – the Hellenic idea of pursuing, in all lines of activity, the law and science, to use Plato's words, of things as they really are. Whatever direct superiority, therefore, Protestantism had over Catholicism was a moral superiority, a superiority arising out of its greater sincerity and earnestness – at the moment of its apparition at any rate – in dealing with the heart and conscience. Its pretensions to an intellectual superiority are in general quite illusory. For Hellenism, for the thinking side in man as distinguished from the acting side, the attitude of mind of Protestantism towards the Bible in no respect differs from the attitude of mind of Catholicism towards the Church. The mental habit of him who imagines that

*I have ventured to give to the foreign word *Renaissance* – destined to become of more common use amongst us as the movement which it denotes comes, as it will come, increasingly to interest us – an English form.

Balaam's ass spoke, in no respect differs from the mental habit of him who imagines that a Madonna of wood or stone winked; and the one, who says that God's Church makes him believe what he believes, and the other, who says that God's Word makes him believe what he believes, are for the philosopher perfectly alike in not really and truly knowing, when they say *God's Church* and *God's Word*, what it is they say, or whereof they affirm.

In the sixteenth century, therefore, Hellenism re-entered the world, and again stood in presence of Hebraism – a Hebraism renewed and purged. Now, it has not been enough observed, how, in the seventeenth century, a fate befell Hellenism in some respects analogous to that which befell it at the commencement of our era. The Renascence, that great re-awakening of Hellenism, that irresistible return of humanity to nature and to seeing things as they are, which in art, in literature, and in physics, produced such splendid fruits, had, like the anterior Hellenism of the Pagan world, a side of moral weakness and of relaxation or insensibility of the moral fibre, which in Italy showed itself with the most startling plainness, but which in France, England, and other countries was very apparent too. Again this loss of spiritual balance, this exclusive preponderance given to man's perceiving and knowing side, this unnatural defect of his feeling and acting side, provoked a reaction. Let us trace that reaction where it most nearly concerns us.

Science has now made visible to everybody the great and pregnant elements of difference which lie in race, and in how signal a manner they make the genius and history of an Indo-European people vary from those of a Semitic people. Hellenism is of Indo-European growth, Hebraism is of Semitic growth; and we English, a nation of Indo-European stock, seem to belong naturally to the movement of Hellenism. But nothing more strongly marks the essential unity of man, than the affinities we can perceive, in this point or that, between members of one family of peoples and members of another. And no affinity of this kind is more strongly marked than that likeness in the strength and prominence of the moral fibre, which, notwithstanding immense elements of difference, knits in some special sort the genius and history of us English, and our American descendants across the Atlantic, to the genius and history of the Hebrew people. Puritanism, which has been so great a power in the English nation, and in the strongest part of the English nation, was originally the reaction in the seventeenth century of the conscience and moral sense of our race, against the moral indifference and lax rule of conduct which in the sixteenth century came in with the Renascence. It was a reaction of Hebraism against Hellenism; and it powerfully manifested itself, as was natural, in a people with much of what we call a Hebraizing turn, with a signal affinity for the bent which was the master-bent of Hebrew life. Eminently Indo-European by its *humour*, by the power it shows, through this gift, of imaginatively acknowledging the multiform aspects of the problem of life, and of thus getting itself unfixed from its own over-certainty, of smiling at its own over-tenacity, our race has yet (and a great part of its strength lies here), in matters of practical life and moral conduct, a strong share of the assuredness, the tenacity, the intensity of the Hebrews. This turn manifested itself in Puritanism, and has had a great part in shaping our history for the last two hundred years. Undoubtedly it checked and changed amongst us that movement of the Renascence which we see producing in the reign of Elizabeth such wonderful fruits. Undoubtedly it stopped the prominent rule and direct development of that order of ideas which we call by the name of Hellenism, and gave the first rank to a different order of ideas. Apparently, too, as we said of the former defeat of Hellenism, if Hellenism was defeated, this shows that Hellenism was imperfect, and that its ascendency at that moment would not have been for the world's good.

Yet there is a very important difference between the defeat inflicted on Hellenism by Christianity eighteen hundred years ago, and the check given to the Renascence by Puritanism. The greatness of the difference is well measured by the difference in force, beauty, significance, and usefulness, between primitive Christianity and Protestantism. Eighteen hundred years ago it was altogether the hour of Hebraism. Primitive Christianity was legitimately and truly the ascendant force in the world at that time, and the way of mankind's progress lay through its full development. Another hour in man's development began in the fifteenth century, and the main road of his progress then lay for a time through Hellenism. Puritanism was no longer the central current of the world's progress, it was a side stream crossing the central current and checking it. The cross and the check may have been necessary and salutary, but that does not do away with the essential difference between the main stream of man's advance and a cross or side stream. For more than two hundred years the main stream of man's advance has moved towards knowing himself and the world, seeing things as they are, spontaneity of consciousness; the main impulse of a great part, and that the strongest part, of our nation has been towards strictness of conscience. They have made the secondary the principal at the wrong moment, and the principal they have at the wrong moment treated as secondary. This contravention of the natural order has produced, as such contravention always must produce, a certain confusion and false movement, of which we are now beginning to feel, in almost every direction, the inconvenience. In all directions our habitual courses of action seem to be losing efficaciousness, credit, and control, both with others and even with ourselves. Everywhere we see the beginnings of confusion, and we want a clue to some sound order and authority. This we can only get by going back upon the actual instincts and forces which rule our life, seeing them as they really are, connecting them with other instincts and forces, and enlarging our whole view and rule of life.

Porro Unum Est Necessarium[23]

The matter here opened is so large, and the trains of thought to which it gives rise are so manifold, that we must be careful to limit ourselves scrupulously to what has a direct bearing upon our actual discussion. We have found that at the bottom of our present unsettled state, so full of the seeds of trouble, lies the notion of its being the prime right and happiness, for each of us, to affirm himself, and his ordinary self; to be doing, and to be doing freely and as he likes. We have found at the bottom of it the disbelief in right reason as a lawful authority. It was easy to show from our practice and current history that this is so; but it was impossible to show why it is so without taking a somewhat wider sweep and going into things a little more deeply. Why, in fact, should good, well-meaning, energetic, sensible people, like the bulk of our countrymen, come to have such light belief in right reason, and such an exaggerated value for their own independent doing, however crude? The answer is: because of an exclusive and excessive development in them, without due allowance for time, place, and circumstance, of that side of human nature, and that group of human forces, to which we have given the general name of Hebraism. Because they have thought their real and only important homage was owed to a power concerned with their obedience rather than with their intelligence, a power interested in the moral side of their nature almost exclusively. Thus they have been led to regard in themselves, as the one thing needful, *strictness of conscience*, the staunch adherence to some fixed law of doing we have got already, instead of *spontaneity of consciousness*, which tends continually to enlarge our whole law of doing. They have fancied themselves to have in their religion a sufficient basis for the whole of their life fixed and certain for ever, a full law of conduct and a full law of thought, so far as thought is needed, as well; whereas what they really have is a law of conduct, a law of unexampled power for enabling them to war against the law of sin in their members and not to serve it in the lusts thereof. The book which contains this invaluable law they call the Word of God, and attribute to it, as I have said, and as, indeed, is perfectly well known, a reach and sufficiency coextensive with all the wants of human nature.

This might, no doubt, be so, if humanity were not the composite thing it is, if it had only, or in quite overpowering eminence, a moral side, and the group of instincts and powers which we call moral. But it has besides, and in notable eminence, an intellectual side, and the group of instincts and powers which we call intellectual. No doubt, mankind makes in general its progress in a fashion which gives at one time full swing to one of these groups of instincts, at another time to the other; and man's faculties are so intertwined, that when his moral side, and the current of force which we call Hebraism, is uppermost, this side will manage somehow to provide, or appear to provide, satisfaction for his intellectual needs; and when his intellectual side, and the current of force which we call Hellenism, is uppermost, this again will provide, or appear to provide, satisfaction for men's moral needs. But sooner or later it becomes manifest that when the two sides of humanity proceed in this fashion of alternate preponderance, and not of mutual understanding and balance, the side which is uppermost does not really provide in a satisfactory manner for the needs of the side which is undermost, and a state of confusion is, sooner or later, the result. The Hellenic half of our nature, bearing rule, makes a sort of provision for the Hebrew half, but it turns out to be an inadequate provision; and again the Hebrew half of our nature, bearing rule, makes a sort of provision for the Hellenic half, but this, too, turns out to be an inadequate provision. The true and smooth order of humanity's development is not reached in either way. And therefore, while we willingly admit with the Christian apostle that the world by wisdom – that is, by the isolated preponderance of its intellectual impulses – knew not God, or the true order of things, it is yet necessary, also, to set up a sort of converse to this proposition, and to say likewise (what is equally true) that the world by Puritanism knew not God. And it is on this converse of the apostle's proposition that it is particularly needful to insist in our own country just at present.

Here, indeed, is the answer to many criticisms which have been addressed to all that we have said in praise of sweetness and light. Sweetness and light evidently have to do with the bent or side in humanity which we call Hellenic. Greek intelligence has obviously for its essence the instinct for what Plato calls the true, firm, intelligible law of things; the law of light, of seeing things as they are. Even in the natural sciences, where the Greeks had not time and means adequately to apply this instinct, and where we have gone a great deal further than they did, it is this instinct which is the root of the whole matter and the ground of all our success; and this instinct the world has mainly learnt of the Greeks, inasmuch as they are humanity's most signal manifestation of it. Greek art, again, Greek beauty, have their root in the same impulse to see things as they really are, inasmuch as Greek art and beauty rest on fidelity to nature – the *best* nature – and on a delicate discrimination of what this best nature is. To say we work for sweetness and light, then, is only another way of saying that we work for Hellenism. But, oh! cry many people, sweetness and light are not enough; you must put strength or energy along with them, and make a kind of trinity of strength, sweetness and light, and then, perhaps, you may do some good. That is to say, we are to join Hebraism, strictness of the moral conscience, and manful walking by the best light we have, together with Hellenism, inculcate both, and rehearse the praises of both.

Or, rather, we may praise both in conjunction, but we must be careful to praise Hebraism most. 'Culture', says an acute, though somewhat rigid critic, Mr Sidgwick,[24] 'diffuses sweetness and light. I do not undervalue these blessings, but religion gives fire and strength, and the world wants fire and strength even more than sweetness and light.' By religion, let me explain, Mr Sidgwick here means particularly that Puritanism on the insufficiency of which I have been commenting and to which he says I am unfair. Now, no doubt, it is possible to be a fanatical partisan of light and the instincts which push us to it, a fanatical enemy of strictness of moral conscience and the instincts which push us to it. A fanaticism of this sort deforms and vulgarizes the well-known work, in some respects so remarkable, of the late Mr Buckle. Such a fanaticism carries its own mark with it, in lacking sweetness; and its own penalty, in that, lacking sweetness, it comes in the end to lack light too. And the Greeks – the great exponents of humanity's bent for sweetness and light united, of its perception that the truth of things must be at the same time beauty – singularly escaped the fanaticism which we moderns, whether we Hellenize or whether we Hebraize, are so apt to show. They arrived – though failing, as has been said, to give adequate practical satisfaction to the claims of man's moral side – at the idea of a comprehensive adjustment of the claims of both the sides in man, the moral as well as the intellectual, of a full estimate of both, and of a reconciliation of both; an idea which is philosophically of the greatest value, and the best of lessons for us moderns. So we ought to have no difficulty in conceding to Mr Sidgwick that manful walking by the best light one has – fire and strength as he calls it – has its high value as well as culture, the endeavour to see things in their truth and beauty, the pursuit of sweetness and light. But whether at this or that time, and to this or that set of persons, one ought to insist most on the praises of fire and strength, or on the praises of sweetness and light, must depend, one would think, on the circumstances and needs of that particular time and those particular persons. And all that we have been saying, and indeed any glance at the world around us shows that with us, with the most respectable and strongest part of us, the ruling force is now, and long has been, a

Puritan force – the care for fire and strength, strictness of conscience, Hebraism, rather than the care for sweetness and light, spontaneity of consciousness, Hellenism.

Well, then, what is the good of our now rehearsing the praises of fire and strength to ourselves, who dwell too exclusively on them already? When Mr Sidgwick says so broadly, that the world wants fire and strength even more than sweetness and light, is he not carried away by a turn for broad generalization? Does he not forget that the world is not all of one piece, and every piece with the same needs at the same time? It may be true that the Roman world at the beginning of our era, or Leo X's Court at the time of the Reformation, or French society in the eighteenth century, needed fire and strength even more than sweetness and light. But can it be said that the Barbarians who overran the empire needed fire and strength even more than sweetness and light; or that the Puritans needed them more; or that Mr Murphy, the Birmingham lecturer, and his friends, need them more?

The Puritan's great danger is that he imagines himself in possession of a rule telling him the *unum necessarium*, or one thing needful, and that he then remains satisfied with a very crude conception of what this rule really is and what it tells him, thinks he has now knowledge and henceforth needs only to act, and, in this dangerous state of assurance and self-satisfaction, proceeds to give full swing to a number of the instincts of his ordinary self. Some of the instincts of his ordinary self he has, by the help of his rule of life, conquered; but others which he has not conquered by this help he is so far from perceiving to need subjugation, and to be instincts of an inferior self, that he even fancies it to be his right and duty, in virtue of having conquered a limited part of himself, to give unchecked swing to the remainder. He is, I say, a victim of Hebraism, of the tendency to cultivate strictness of conscience rather than spontaneity of consciousness. And what he wants is a larger conception of human nature, showing him the number of other points at which his nature must come to its best, besides the points which he himself knows and thinks of. There is no *unum necessarium*, or one thing needful, which can free human nature from the obligation of trying to come to its best at all these points. The real *unum necessarium* for us is to come to our best at all points. Instead of our 'one thing needful', justifying in us vulgarity, hideousness, ignorance, violence – our vulgarity, hideousness, ignorance, violence, are really so many touchstones which try our one thing needful, and which prove that in the state, at any rate, in which we ourselves have it, it is not all we want. And as the force which encourages us to stand staunch and fast by the rule and ground we have is Hebraism, so the force which encourages us to go back upon this rule, and to try the very ground on which we appear to stand, is Hellenism – a turn for giving our consciousness free play and enlarging its range. And what I say is, not that Hellenism is always for everybody more wanted than Hebraism, but that for Mr Murphy at this particular moment, and for the great majority of us his fellow-countrymen, it is more wanted.

Nothing is more striking than to observe in how many ways a limited conception of human nature, the notion of a one thing needful, a one side in us to be made uppermost, the disregard of a full and harmonious development of ourselves, tells injuriously on our thinking and acting. In the first place, our hold upon the rule or standard, to which we look for our one thing needful, tends to become less and less near and vital, our conception of it more and more mechanical, and more and more unlike the thing itself as it was conceived in the mind where it originated. The dealings of Puritanism with the writings of St Paul afford a noteworthy illustration of this. Nowhere so much as in the writings of St Paul, and in that great apostle's greatest work, the Epistle to the Romans, has Puritanism found what seemed to furnish it with the one thing needful, and to give it canons of truth absolute and final. Now all writings, as has been already said, even the most precious writings and the most fruitful, must inevitably, from the very nature of things, be but contributions to human thought and human development, which extend wider than they do. Indeed, St Paul, in the very Epistle of which we are speaking, shows, when he asks, 'Who hath known the mind of the Lord?' – who hath known, that is, the true and divine order of things in its entirety – that he himself acknowledges this fully. And we have already pointed out in another Epistle of St Paul a great and vital idea of the human spirit – the idea of immortality – transcending and overlapping, so to speak, the expositor's power to give it adequate definition and expression.

But quite distinct from the question whether St Paul's expression, or any man's expression, can be a perfect and final expression of truth, comes the question whether we rightly seize and understand his expression as it exists. Now, perfectly to seize another man's meaning, as it stood in his own mind, is not easy; especially when the man is separated from us by such differences of race, training, time, and circumstances as St Paul. But there are degrees of nearness in getting at a man's meaning; and though we cannot arrive quite at what St Paul had in his mind, yet we may come near it. And who, that comes thus near it, must not feel how terms which St Paul employs, in trying to follow with his analysis of such profound power and originality some of the most delicate, intricate, obscure, and contradictory workings and states of the human spirit, are detached and employed by Puritanism, not in the connected and fluid way in which St Paul employs them, and for which alone words are really meant, but in an isolated, fixed, mechanical way, as if they were talismans; and how all trace and sense of St Paul's true movement of ideas, and sustained masterly analysis, is thus lost? Who, I say, that has watched Puritanism – the force which so strongly Hebraizes, which so takes St Paul's writings as something absolute and final, containing the one thing needful – handle such terms as *grace*, *faith*, *election*, *righteousness*, but must feel, not only that these terms have for the mind of Puritanism a sense false and misleading, but also that this sense is the most monstrous and grotesque caricature of the sense of St Paul, and that his true meaning is by these worshippers of his words altogether lost?

Or to take another eminent example, in which not Puritanism only, but, one may say, the whole religious world, by their mechanical use of St Paul's writings, can be shown to miss or change his real meaning. The whole religious world, one may say, use now the word *resurrection* – a word which is so often in their thoughts and on their lips, and which they find so often in St Paul's writings – in one sense only. They use it to mean a rising again after the physical death of the body. Now it is quite true that St Paul speaks of resurrection in this sense, that he tries to describe and explain it, and that he condemns those who doubt and deny it. But it is true, also, that in nine cases out of ten where St Paul thinks and speaks of resurrection, he thinks and speaks of it in a sense different from this – in the sense of a rising to a new life before the physical death of the body, and not after it. The idea on which we have already touched, the profound idea of being baptized into the death of the great exemplar of self-devotion and self-annulment, of repeating in our own person, by virtue of identification with our exemplar, his course of self-devotion and self-annulment, and of thus coming, within the limits of our present life, to a new life, in which, as in the death going before it, we are identified with our exemplar – this is the fruitful and original conception of being *risen with Christ* which possesses the mind of St Paul, and this is the central point round which, with such incomparable emotion and eloquence, all his teaching moves. For him, the life after our physical death is really in the main but a consequence and continuation of the inexhaustible energy of the new life thus originated on this side of the grave. This grand Pauline idea of Christian resurrection is worthily rehearsed in one of the noblest collects of the prayer-Book, and is destined, no doubt, to fill a more and more important place in the Christianity of the future. But meanwhile, almost as signal as the essentialness of this characteristic idea in St Paul's teaching, is the completeness with which the worshippers of St Paul's words as an absolute final expression of saving truth have lost it, and have substituted for the apostle's living and near conception of a resurrection now, their mechanical and remote conception of a resurrection hereafter.

In short, so fatal is the notion of possessing, even in the most precious words or standards, the one thing needful, of having in them, once for all, a full and sufficient measure of light to guide us, and of there being no duty left for us except to make our practice square exactly with them – so fatal, I say, is this notion to the right knowledge and comprehension of the very words or standards we thus adopt, and to such strange distortions and perversions of them does it inevitably lead, that whenever we hear that commonplace which Hebraism, if we venture to inquire what a man knows, is so apt to bring out against us, in disparagement of what we call culture, and in praise of a man's sticking to the one thing needful – *he knows*, says Hebraism, *his Bible!* – whenever we hear this said, we may, without any elaborate defence of culture, content ourselves with answering simply, 'No man, who knows nothing else, knows even his Bible.'

Now the force which we have so much neglected, Hellenism, may be liable to fail in moral strength and earnestness, but by the law of its nature – the very same law which makes it sometimes deficient in intensity when intensity is required – it opposes itself to the notion of cutting our being in two, of attributing to one part the dignity of dealing with the one thing needful, and leaving the other part to take its chance, which is the bane of Hebraism. Essential in Hellenism is the impulse to the development of the whole man, to connecting and harmonizing all parts of him, perfecting all, leaving none to take their chance.

The characteristic bent of Hellenism, as has been said, is to find the intelligible law of things, to see them in their true nature and as they really are. But many things are not seen in their true nature and as they really are, unless they are seen as beautiful. Behaviour is not intelligible, does not account for itself to the mind and show the reason for its existing, unless it is beautiful. The same with discourse, the same with song, the same with worship, all of them modes in which man proves his activity and expresses himself. To think that when one produces in these what is mean, or vulgar, or hideous, one can be permitted to plead that one has that within which passes show; to suppose that the possession of what benefits and satisfies one part of our being can make allowable either discourse like Mr Murphy's, or poetry like the hymns we all hear, or places of worship like the chapels we all see – this it is abhorrent to the nature of Hellenism to concede. And to be, like our honoured and justly honoured Faraday, a great natural philosopher with one side of his being and a Sandemanian with the other,[25] would to Archimedes have been impossible.

It is evident to what a many-sided perfecting of man's powers and activities this demand of Hellenism for satisfaction to be given to the mind by everything which we do, is calculated to impel our race. It has its dangers, as has been fully granted. The notion of this sort of equipollency in man's modes of activity may lead to moral relaxation; what we do not make our one thing needful, we may come to treat not enough as if it were needful, though it is indeed very needful and at the same time very hard. Still, what side in us has not its dangers, and which of our impulses can be a talisman to give us perfection outright, and not merely a help to bring us towards it? Has not Hebraism, as we have shown, its dangers as well as Hellenism? Or have we used so excessively the tendencies in ourselves to which Hellenism makes appeal, that we are now suffering from it? Are we not, on the contrary, now suffering because we have not enough used these tendencies as a help towards perfection?

For we see whither it has brought us, the long exclusive predominance of Hebraism – the insisting on perfection in one part of our nature and not in all; the singling out the moral side, the side of obedience and action, for such intent regard; making strictness of the moral conscience so far the principal thing, and putting off for hereafter and for another world the care for being complete at all points, the full and harmonious development of our humanity. Instead of watching and following on its ways the desire which, as Plato says, 'for ever through all the universe tends towards that which is lovely', we think that the world has settled its accounts with this desire, knows what this desire wants of it, and that all the impulses of our ordinary self which do not conflict with the terms of this settlement, in our narrow view of it, we may follow unrestrainedly, under the sanction of some such text as 'Not slothful in business', or, 'Whatsoever thy hand findeth to do, do it with all thy might', or something else of the same kind. And to any of these impulses we soon come to give that same character of a mechanical, absolute law, which we give to our religion; we regard it, as we do our religion, as an object for strictness of conscience, not for spontaneity of consciousness; for unremitting adherence on its own account, not for going back upon, viewing in its connection with other things, and adjusting to a number of changing circumstances. We treat it, in short, just as we treat our religion – as machinery. It is in this way that the Barbarians treat their bodily exercises, the Philistines their business, Mr Spurgeon his voluntaryism,[26] Mr Bright the assertion of personal liberty, Mr Beales the right of meeting in Hyde Park. In all those cases what is needed is a freer play of consciousness upon the object or pursuit; and in all of them Hebraism, the valuing staunchness and earnestness more than this free play, the entire subordination of thinking to doing, has led to a mistaken and misleading treatment of things.

The newspapers a short time ago contained an account of the suicide of a Mr Smith, secretary to some insurance company, who, it was said, 'laboured under the apprehension that he would come to poverty, and that he was eternally lost.' And when I read these words, it occurred to me that the poor man who came to such a mournful end was, in truth, a kind of type – by the selection of his two grand objects of concern, by their isolation from everything else, and their juxtaposition to one another – of all the strongest, most respectable, and most representative part of our nation. 'He laboured under the apprehension that he would come to poverty, and that he was eternally lost.' The whole middle class have a conception of things – a conception which makes us call them Philistines – just like that of this poor man; though we are seldom, of course, shocked by seeing it take the distressing, violently morbid, and fatal turn, which it took with him. But how generally, with how many of us, are the main concerns of life limited to these two: the concern for making money, and the concern for saving our souls! And how entirely does the narrow and mechanical conception of our secular business proceed from a narrow and mechanical conception of our religious business! What havoc do the united conceptions make of our lives! It is because the second-named of these two master-concerns presents to us the one thing needful in so fixed, narrow, and mechanical a way, that so ignoble a fellow master-concern to it as the first-named becomes possible; and, having been once admitted, takes the same rigid and absolute character as the other.

Poor Mr Smith had sincerely the nobler master-concern as well as the meaner – the concern for saving his soul (according to the narrow and mechanical conception which Puritanism has of what the salvation of the soul is), as well as the concern for making money. But let us remark how many people there are, especially outside the limits of the serious and conscientious middle class to which Mr Smith belonged, who take up with a meaner master-concern – whether it be pleasure, or field-sports, or bodily exercises, or business, or popular agitation – who take up with one of these exclusively, and neglect Mr Smith's nobler master-concern, because of the mechanical form which Hebraism has given to this noble master-concern. Hebraism makes it stand, as we have said, as something talismanic, isolated, and all-sufficient, justifying our giving our ordinary selves free play in bodily exercises, or business, or popular agitation, if we have made our accounts square with this master-concern; and, if we have not, rendering other things indifferent, and our ordinary self all we have to follow, and to follow with all the energy that is in us, till we do. Whereas the idea of perfection at all points, the encouraging in ourselves spontaneity of consciousness, and letting a free play of thought live and flow around all our activity, the indisposition to allow one side of our activity to stand as so all-important and all-sufficing that it makes other sides indifferent – this bent of mind in us may not only check us in following unreservedly a mean master-concern of any kind, but may even, also, bring new life and movement into that side of us with which alone Hebraism concerns itself, and awaken a healthier and less mechanical activity there. Hellenism may thus actually serve to further the designs of Hebraism.

Undoubtedly it thus served in the first days of Christianity. Christianity, as has been said, occupied itself, like Hebraism, with the moral side of man exclusively, with his moral affections and moral conduct; and so far it was but a continuation of Hebraism. But it transformed and renewed Hebraism by criticizing a fixed rule, which had become mechanical, and had thus lost its vital motive power; by letting the thought play freely around this old rule, and perceive its inadequacy; by developing a new motive power, which men's moral consciousness could take living hold of, and could move in sympathy with. What was this but an importation of Hellenism, as we have defined it, into Hebraism? St Paul used the contradiction between the Jew's profession and practice, his shortcomings on that very side of moral affection and moral conduct which the Jew and St Paul, both of them, regarded as all in all ('Thou that sayest a man should not steal, dost thou steal? Thou that sayest a man should not commit adultery, dost thou commit adultery?') for a proof of the inadequacy of the old rule of life in the Jew's mechanical conception of it; and tried to rescue him by making his consciousness play freely around this rule – that is, by a so far Hellenic treatment of it. Even so we, too, when we hear so much said of the growth of commercial immorality in our serious middle class, of the melting away of habits of strict probity before the temptation to get quickly rich and to cut a figure in the world; when we see, at any rate, so much confusion of thought and of practice in this great representative class of our nation – may we not be disposed to say, that this confusion shows that his new motive-power of grace and imputed righteousness has become to the Puritan as mechanical, and with as ineffective a hold upon his practice, as the old motive-power of the law was to the Jew and that the remedy is the same as that which St Paul employed – an importation of what we have called Hellenism into his Hebraism, a making his consciousness flow freely round his petrified rule of life and renew it? Only with this difference: that whereas St Paul imported Hellenism within the limits of our moral part only, this part being still treated by him as all in all; and whereas he well-nigh exhausted, one may say, and used to the very uttermost, the possibilities of fruitfully importing it on that side exclusively; we ought to try and import it – guiding ourselves by the ideal of a human nature harmoniously perfect in all points – into all the lines of our activity. Only by so doing can we rightly quicken, refresh, and renew those very instincts, now so much baffled, to which Hebraism makes appeal.

But if we will not be warned by the confusion visible enough at present in our thinking and acting, that we are in a false line in having developed our Hebrew side so exclusively, and our Hellenic side so feebly and at random, in loving fixed rules of action so much more than the intelligible law of things, let us listen to a remarkable testimony which the opinion of the world around us offers. All the world now sets great and increasing value on three objects which have long been very dear to us, and pursues them in its own way, or tries to pursue them. These three objects are industrial enterprise, bodily exercises, and freedom. Certainly we have, before and beyond our neighbours, given ourselves to these three things with ardent passion and with high success. And this our neighbours cannot but acknowledge; and they must needs, when they themselves turn to these things, have an eye to our example, and take something of our practice.

Now, generally, when people are interested in an object of pursuit, they cannot help feeling an enthusiasm for those who have already laboured successfully at it, and for their success. Not only do they study them, they also love and admire them. In this way a man who is interested in the art of war not only acquaints himself with the performance of great generals, but he has an admiration and enthusiasm for them. So, too, one who wants to be a painter or a poet cannot help loving and admiring the great painters or poets who have gone before him and shown him the way.

But it is strange with how little of love, admiration, or enthusiasm, the world regards us and our freedom, our bodily exercises, and our industrial prowess, much as these things themselves are beginning to interest it. And is not the reason because we follow each of these things in a mechanical manner, as an end in and for itself, and not in reference to a general end of human perfection; and this makes oui pursuit of them uninteresting to humanity, and not what the world truly wants? It seems to them mere machinery that we can, knowingly, teach them to worship – a mere fetish. British freedom, British industry, British muscularity, we work for each of these three things blindly, with no notion of giving each its due proportion and prominence, because we have no ideal of harmonious human perfection before our minds, to set our work in motion, and to guide it. So the rest of the world, desiring industry, or freedom, or bodily strength, yet desiring these not, as we do, absolutely, but as means to something else, imitate, indeed, of our practice what seems useful for them, but us, whose practice they imitate, they seem to entertain neither love nor admiration for.

Let us observe, on the other hand, the love and enthusiasm excited by others who have laboured for these very things. Perhaps of what we call industrial enterprise it is not easy to find examples in former times; but let us consider how Greek freedom and Greek gymnastics have attracted the love and praise of mankind, who give so little love and praise to ours. And what can be the reason of this difference? Surely because the Greeks pursued freedom and pursued gymnastics not mechanically, but with constant reference to some ideal of complete human perfection and happiness. And therefore, in spite of faults and failures, they interest and delight by their pursuit of them all the rest of mankind, who instinctively feel that only as things are pursued with reference to this ideal are they valuable.

Here again, therefore, as in the confusion into which the thought and action of even the steadiest class amongst us is beginning to fall, we seem to have an admonition that we have fostered our Hebraizing instincts, our preference of earnestness of doing to delicacy and flexibility of thinking, too exclusively, and have been landed by them in a mechanical and unfruitful routine. And again we seem taught that the development of our Hellenizing instincts, seeking ardently the intelligible law of things, and making a stream of fresh thought play freely about our stock notions and habits, is what is most wanted by us at present.

Well, then, from all sides, the more we go into the matter, the currents seem to converge, and together to bear us along towards culture. If we look at the world outside us we find a disquieting absence of sure authority. We discover that only in right reason can we get a source of sure authority; and culture brings us towards right reason. If we look at our own inner world, we find all manner of confusion arising out of the habits of unintelligent routine and one-sided growth, to which a too exclusive worship of fire, strength, earnestness, and action, has brought us. What we want is a fuller harmonious development of our humanity, a free play of thought upon our routine notions, spontaneity of consciousness, sweetness and light; and these are just what culture generates and fosters. We will not stickle for a name, and the name of culture one might easily give up, if only those who decry the frivolous and pedantic sort of culture, but wish at bottom for the same things as we do, would be careful on their part, not, in disparaging and discrediting the false culture, to unwittingly disparage and discredit, among a people with little natural reverence for it, the true also. But what we are concerned for is the thing, not the name; and the thing, call it by what name we will, is simply the enabling ourselves, by getting to know, whether through reading, observing, or thinking, the best that can at present be known in the world, to come as near as we can to the firm intelligible law of things, and thus to get a basis for a less confused action and a more complete perfection than we have at present.

And now, therefore, when we are accused of preaching up a spirit of cultivated inaction, of provoking the earnest lovers of action, of refusing to lend a hand at uprooting certain definite evils, of despairing to find any lasting truth to minister to the diseased spirit of our time, we shall not be so much confounded and embarrassed what to answer for ourselves. We shall say boldly that we do not at all despair of finding some lasting truth to minister to the diseased spirit of our time; but that we have discovered the best way of finding this to be not so much by lending a hand to our friends and countrymen in their actual operations for the removal of certain definite evils, but rather in getting our friends and countrymen to seek culture, to let their consciousness play freely round their present operations and the stock notions on which they are founded, show what these are like, and how related to the intelligible law of things, and auxiliary to true human perfection.

Our liberal practitioners

But an unpretending writer, without a philosophy based on interdependent, subordinate, and coherent principles, must not presume to indulge himself too much in generalities. He must keep close to the level ground of common fact, the only safe ground foı understandings without a scientific equipment. Therefore, since I have spoken so slightingly of the practical operations in which my friends and countrymen are at this moment engaged for the removal of certain definite evils, I am bound to take, before concluding, some of those operations, and to make them, if I can, show the truth of what I have advanced.

Probably I could hardly give a greater proof of my confessed inexpertness in reasoning and arguing, than by taking, for my first example of an operation of this kind, the proceedings for the disestablishment of the Irish Church, which we are now witnessing.* It seems so clear that this is surely one of those operations for the uprooting of a certain definite evil in which one's Liberal friends engage, and have a right to complain, and to get impatient, and to reproach one with delicate Conservative scepticism and cultivated inaction, if one does not lend a hand to help them. This does, indeed, seem evident; and yet this operation comes so prominently before us at this moment, it so challenges everybody's regard, that one seems cowardly in blinking it. So let us venture to try and see whether this conspicuous operation is one of those round which we need to let our consciousness play freely and reveal what manner of spirit we are of in doing it; or whether it is one which by no means admits the application of this doctrine of ours, and one to which we ought to lend a hand immediately.

Now it seems plain that the present Church establishment in Ireland is contrary to reason and justice, in so far as the Church of a very small minority of the people there takes for itself all the Church property of the Irish people. And one would think, that property, assigned for the purpose of providing for a people's religious worship when that worship was one, the State should, when that worship is split into several forms, apportion

*Written in 1868.[27]

between those several forms. But the apportionment should be made with due regard to circumstances, taking account only of great differences, which are likely to be lasting, and of considerable communions, which are likely to represent profound and widespread religious characteristics. It should overlook petty differences, which have no serious reason for lasting, and inconsiderable communions, which can hardly be taken to express any broad and necessary religious lineaments of our common nature. This is just in accordance with that maxim about the State which we have more than once used: *The State is of the religion of all its citizens, without the fanaticism of any of them.* Those who deny this, either think so poorly of the State that they do not like to see religion condescend to touch the State, or they think so poorly of religion that they do not like to see the State condescend to touch religion. But no good statesman will easily think thus unworthily either of the State or of religion.

Our statesmen of both parties were inclined, one may say, to follow the natural line of the State's duty, and to make in Ireland some fair apportionment of Church property between large and radically divided religious communions in that country. But then it was discovered that in Great Britain the national mind, as it is called, is grown averse to endowments for religion and will make no new ones; and though this in itself looks general and solemn enough, yet there were found political philosophers to give it a look of more generality and more solemnity still, and to elevate, by their dexterous command of powerful and beautiful language, this supposed edict of the British national mind into a sort of formula for expressing a great law of religious transition and progress for all the world.

But we, who, having no coherent philosophy, must not let ourselves philosophize, only see that the English and Scotch Nonconformists have a great horror of establishments and endowments for religion, which, they assert, were forbidden by Jesus Christ when he said: 'My kingdom is not of this world'; and that the Nonconformists will be delighted to aid statesmen in disestablishing any church, but will suffer none to be established or endowed if they can help it. Then we see that the Nonconformists make the strength of the Liberal Majority in the House of Commons; and that, therefore, the leading Liberal statesmen, to get the support of the Nonconformists, forsake the notion of fairly apportioning Church property in Ireland among the chief religious communions, declare that the national mind has decided against new endowments, and propose simply to disestablish and disendow the present establishment in Ireland without establishing or endowing any other. The actual power, in short, by virtue of which the Liberal party in the House of Commons is now trying to disestablish the Irish Church, is not the power of reason and justice, it is the power of the Nonconformists' antipathy to Church establishments.

Clearly it is this; because Liberal statesmen, relying on the power of reason and justice to help them, proposed something quite different from what they now propose; and they proposed what they now propose, and talked of the decision of the national mind, because they had to rely on the English and Scotch Nonconformists. And clearly the Nonconformists are actuated by antipathy to establishments, not by antipathy to the injustice and irrationality of the present appropriation of Church property in Ireland; because Mr Spurgeon, in his eloquent and memorable letter, expressly avowed that he would sooner leave things as they are in Ireland, that is, he would sooner let the injustice and irrationality of the present appropriation continue, than do anything to set up the Roman image – that is, than give the Catholics their fair and reasonable share of Church property. Most indisputably, therefore, we may affirm that the real moving power by which the Liberal party are now operating the overthrow of the Irish establishment is the antipathy of the Nonconformists to Church establishments, and not the sense of reason or justice, except so far as reason and justice may be contained in this antipathy. And thus the matter stands at present.

Now surely we must all see many inconveniences in performing the operation of uprooting this evil, the Irish Church establishment, in this particular way. As was said about industry and freedom and gymnastics, we shall never awaken love and gratitude by this mode of operation; for it is pursued, not in view of reason and justice and human perfection and all that enkindles the enthusiasm of men, but it is pursued in view of a certain stock notion, or fetish, of the Nonconformists, which proscribes Church establishments. And yet, evidently, one of the main benefits to be got by operating on the Irish Church is to win the affections of the Irish people. Besides this, an operation performed in virtue of a mechanical rule, or fetish, like the supposed decision of the English national mind against new endowments, does not easily inspire respect in its adversaries, and make their opposition feeble and hardly to be persisted in, as an operation evidently done in virtue of reason and justice might. For reason and justice have in them something persuasive and irresistible; but a fetish or mechanical maxim, like this of the Nonconformists, has in it nothing at all to conciliate either the affections or the understanding. Nay, it provokes the counter-employment of other fetishes or mechanical maxims on the opposite side, by which the confusion and hostility already prevalent are heightened. Only in this way can be explained the apparition of such fetishes as are beginning to be set up on the Conservative side against the fetish of the Nonconformists: *The Constitution in danger! The bulwark of British freedom menaced! The lamp of the Reformation put out! No Popery!* and so on. To elevate these against an operation relying on reason and justice to back it, is not so easy, or so tempting to human infirmity, as to elevate them against an operation relying on the Nonconformists' antipathy to Church establishments to back it. For after all, *No Popery!* is a rallying cry which touches the human spirit quite as vitally as *No Church establishments!* – that is to say, neither the one nor the other, in themselves, touch the human spirit vitally at all.

Ought the believers in action, then, to be so impatient with us, if we say, that even for the sake of this operation of theirs itself and its satisfactory accomplishment, it is more important to make our consciousness play freely round the stock notion or habit on which their operation relies for aid, than to lend a hand to it straight away? Clearly they ought not; because nothing is so effectual for operating as reason and justice, and a free play of thought will either disengage the reason and justice lying hid in the Nonconformist fetish, and make them effectual, or else it will help to get this fetish out of the way, and to let statesmen go freely where reason and justice take them.

So, suppose we take this absolute rule, this mechanical maxim of Mr Spurgeon and the Nonconformists, that Church establishments are bad things because Jesus Christ said, 'My kingdom is not of this world.' Suppose we try and make our consciousness bathe and float this piece of petrifaction – for such it now is – and bring it within the stream of the vital movement of our thought, and into relation with the whole intelligible law of things. An enemy and a disputant might probably say that much of the machinery which Nonconformists themselves employ – the Liberation Society which exists already,[28] and the Nonconformist Union which Mr Spurgeon desires to see existing – come within the scope of Christ's words as well as Church establishments. This, however, is merely a negative and contentious way of dealing with the Nonconformist maxim; whereas what we desire is to bring this maxim within the positive and vital movement of our thought. We say, therefore, that Jesus Christ's words mean that his religion is a force of inward persuasion acting on the soul, and not a force of outward constraint acting on the body; and if the Nonconformist maxim against Church establishments and Church-endowments has warrant given to it from what Christ thus meant, then their maxim is good, even though their own practice in the matter of the Liberation Society may be at variance with it.

And here we cannot but remember what we have formerly said about religion, Miss Cobbe, and the British College of Health in the New Road.[29] In religion there are two parts, the part of thought and speculation, and the part of worship and devotion. Jesus Christ certainly meant his religion, as a force of inward persuasion acting on the soul, to employ both parts as perfectly as possible. Now thought and speculation is eminently an individual matter, and worship and devotion is eminently a collective matter. It does not help me to think a thing more clearly that thousands of other people are thinking the same; but it does help me to worship with more emotion that thousands of other people are worshipping with me. The consecration of common consent, antiquity, public establishment, long-used rites, national edifices, is everything for religious worship. 'Just what makes worship impressive', says Joubert, 'is its publicity, its external manifestation, its sound, its splendour, its observance universally and visibly holding its sway through all the details both of our outward and of our inward life.' Worship, therefore, should have in it as little as possible of what divides us, and should be as much as possible a common and public act; as Joubert says again: 'The best prayers are those which have nothing distinct about them, and which are thus of the nature of simple adoration.' For, 'the same devotion', as he says in another place, 'unites men far more than the same thought and knowledge.' Thought and knowledge, as we have said before, is eminently something individual, and of our own; the more we possess it as strictly of our own, the more power it has on us. Man worships best, therefore, with the community; he philosophizes best alone.

So it seems that whoever would truly give effect to Jesus Christ's declaration that his religion is a force of inward persuasion acting on the soul, would leave our thought on the intellectual aspects of Christianity as individual as possible, but would make Christian worship as collective as possible. Worship, then, appears to be eminently a matter for public and national establishment; for even Mr Bright, who, when he stands in Mr Spurgeon's great Tabernacle, is so ravished with admiration, will hardly say that the great Tabernacle and its worship are in themselves, as a temple and service of religion, so impressive and affecting as the public and national Westminster Abbey, or Notre Dame, with their worship. And when, immediately after the great Tabernacle, one comes plump down to the mass of private and individual establishments of religious worship, establishments falling, like the British College of Health in the New Road, conspicuously short of what a public and national establishment might be, then one cannot but feel that Jesus Christ's command to make his religion a force of persuasion to the soul, is, so far as one main source of persuasion is concerned, altogether set at nought.

But perhaps the Nonconformists worship so unimpressively because they philosophize so keenly; and one part of religion, the part of public national worship, they have subordinated to the other part, the part of individual thought and knowledge? This, however, their organization in congregations forbids us to admit. They are members of congregations, not isolated thinkers; and a free play of individual thought is at least as much impeded by membership of a small congregation as by membership of a great Church. Thinking by batches of fifties is to the full as fatal to free thought as thinking by batches of thousands. Accordingly, we have had occasion already to notice that Nonconformity does not at all differ from the Established Church by having worthier or more philosophical ideas about God, and the ordering of the world, than the Established Church has. It has very much the same ideas about these as the Established Church has, but it differs from the Established Church in that its worship is a much less collective and national affair.

So Mr Spurgeon and the Nonconformists seem to have misapprehended the true meaning of Christ's words, *My kingdom is not of this world.* Because, by these words, Christ meant that his religion was to work on the soul. And of the two parts of the soul on which religion works – the thinking and speculative part, and the feeling and imaginative part – Nonconformity satisfies the first no better than the Established Churches, which Christ by these words is supposed to have condemned, satisfy it; and the second part it satisfies even worse than the Established Churches. And thus the balance of advantage seems to rest with the Established Churches; and they seem to have apprehended and applied Christ's words, if not with perfect adequacy, at least less inadequately than the Nonconformists.

Might it not, then, be urged with great force that the way to do good, in presence of this operation for uprooting the Church establishment in Ireland by the power of the Nonconformists' antipathy to publicly establishing or endowing religious worship, is not by lending a hand straight away to the operation, and Hebraizing – that is, in this case, taking an uncritical interpretation of certain Bible words as our absolute rule of conduct – with the Nonconformists? It may be very well for born Hebraizers, like Mr Spurgeon, to Hebraize; but for Liberal statesmen to Hebraize is surely unsafe, and to see poor old Liberal hacks Hebraizing, whose real self belongs to a kind of negative Hellenism – a state of moral indifferency without intellectual ardour – is even painful. And when, by our Hebraizing, we neither do what the better mind of statesmen prompted them to do, nor win the affections of the people we want to conciliate, nor yet reduce the opposition of our adversaries but rather heighten it, surely it may not be unreasonable to Hellenize a little, to let our thought and consciousness play freely about our proposed operation and its motives, dissolve these motives if they are unsound – which certainly they have some appearance, at any rate, of being – and create in their stead, if they are, a set of sounder and more persuasive motives conducting to a more solid operation. May not the man who promotes this be giving the best help towards finding some lasting truth to minister to the diseased spirit of his time, and does he really deserve that the believers in action should grow impatient with him?

But now to take another operation which does not at this moment so excite people's feelings as the disestablishment of the Irish Church, but which, I suppose, would also be called exactly one of those operations of simple, practical, common-sense reform, aiming at the removal of some particular abuse, and rigidly restricted to that object, to which a Liberal ought to lend a hand, and deserves that other Liberals should grow impatient with him if he does not. This operation I had the great advantage of with my own ears hearing discussed in the House of Commons, and recommended by a powerful speech from that famous speaker, Mr Bright. So that the effeminate horror which, it is alleged, I have of practical reforms of this kind, was put to a searching test; and if it survived, it must have, one would think, some reason or other to support it, and can hardly quite merit the stigma of its present name.

The operation I mean was that which the Real Estate Intestacy Bill aimed at accomplishing, and the discussion on this bill I heard in the House of Commons.[30] The bill proposed, as every one knows, to prevent the land of a man who dies intestate from going, as it goes now, to his eldest son, and was thought, by its friends and by its enemies, to be a step towards abating the now almost exclusive possession of the land of this country by the people whom we call the Barbarians. Mr Bright, and other speakers on his side, seemed to hold that there is a kind of natural law or fitness of things which assigns to all a man's children a right to equal shares in the enjoyment of his property after his death; and that if, without depriving a man of an Englishman's prime privilege of doing what he likes by making what will he chooses, you provide that when he makes none his land shall be divided among his family, then you give the sanction of the law to the natural fitness of things, and inflict a sort of check on the present violation of this by the Barbarians.

It occurred to me, when I saw Mr Bright and his friends proceeding in this way, to ask myself a question. If the almost exclusive possession of the land of this country by the Barbarians is a bad thing, is this practical operation of the Liberals, and the stock notion, on which it seems to rest, about the natural right of children to share equally in the enjoyment of their father's property after his death, the best and most effective means of dealing with it? Or is it best dealt with by letting one's thought and consciousness play freely and naturally upon the Barbarians, this Liberal operation, and the stock notion at the bottom of it, and trying to get as near as we can to the intelligible law of things as to each of them?

Now does any one, if he simply and naturally reads his consciousness, discover that he has any rights at all? For my part, the deeper I go in my own consciousness, and the more simply I abandon myself to it, the more it seems to tell me that I have no rights at all, only duties; and that men get this notion of rights from a process of abstract reasoning, inferring that the obligations they are conscious of towards others, others must be conscious of towards them, and not from any direct witness of consciousness at all. But it is obvious that the notion of a right, arrived at in this way, is likely to stand as a formal and petrified thing, deceiving and misleading us; and that the notions got directly from our consciousness ought to be brought to bear upon it, and to control it. So it is unsafe and misleading to say that our children have rights against us; what is true and safe to say is, that we have duties towards our children. But who will find among these natural duties, set forth to us by our consciousness, the obligation to leave to all our children an equal share in the enjoyment of our property? Or, though consciousness tells us we ought to provide for our children's welfare, whose consciousness tells him that the enjoyment of property is in itself welfare? Whether our children's welfare is best served by their all sharing equally in our property, depends on circumstances and on the state of the community in which we live. With this equal sharing, society could not, for example, have organized itself afresh out of the chaos left by the fall of the Roman Empire; and to have an organized society to live in is more for a child's welfare than to have an equal share of his father's property.

So we see how little convincing force the stock notion on which the Real Estate Intestacy Bill was based – the notion that in the nature and fitness of things all a man's children have a right to an equal share in the enjoyment of what he leaves – really has; and how powerless, therefore, it must of necessity be to persuade and win any one who has habits and interests which disincline him to it. On the other hand, the practical operation proposed relies entirely, if it is to be effectual in altering the present practice of the Barbarians, on the power of truth and persuasiveness in the notion which it seeks to consecrate; for it leaves to the Barbarians full liberty to continue their present practice, to which all their habits and interests incline them, unless the promulgation of a notion, which we have seen to have no vital efficacy and hold upon our consciousness, shall hinder them.

Are we really to adorn an operation of this kind, merely because it proposes to *do* something, with all the favourable epithets of simple, practical common-sense, definite; to enlist on its side all the zeal of the believers in action, and to call indifference to it an effeminate horror of useful reforms? It seems to me quite easy to show that a free disinterested play of thought on the Barbarians and their land-holding is a thousand times more really practical, a thousand times more likely to lead to some effective result, than an operation such as that of which we have been now speaking. For if, casting aside the impediments of stock notions and mechanical action, we try to find the intelligible law of things respecting a great land-owning class such as we have in this country, does not our consciousness readily tell us that whether the perpetuation of such a class is for its own real good and for the real good of the community, depends on the actual circumstances of this class and of the community? Does it not readily tell us that wealth, power, and consideration are – and above all when inherited and not earned – in themselves trying and dangerous things? As Bishop Wilson excellently says, 'Riches are almost always abused without a very extraordinary grace.' But this extraordinary grace was in great measure supplied by the circumstances of the feudal epoch, out of which our land-holding class, with its rules of inheritance, sprang. The labour and contentions of a rude, nascent, and struggling society supplied it. These perpetually were trying, chastising, and forming the class whose predominance was then needed by society to give it points of cohesion, and was not so harmful to themselves because they were thus sharply tried and exercised. But in a luxurious, settled and easy society, where wealth offers the means of enjoyment a thousand times more, and the temptation to abuse them is thus made a thousand times greater, the exercising discipline is at the same time taken away, and the feudal class is left exposed to the full operation of the natural law well put by the French moralist: *Pouvoir sans savoir est fort dangereux.*[31] And, for my part, when I regard the young people of this class, it is above all by the trial and shipwreck made of their own welfare by the circumstances in which they live that I am struck. How far better it would have been for nine out of every ten among them, if they had had their own way to make in the world, and not been tried by a condition for which they had not the extraordinary grace requisite!

This, I say, seems to be what a man's consciousness, simply consulted, would tell him about the actual welfare of our Barbarians themselves. Then, as to the effect upon the welfare of the community, how can that be salutary, if a class which, by the very possession of wealth, power and consideration, becomes a kind of ideal or standard for the rest of the community, is tried by ease and pleasure more than it can well bear, and almost irresistibly carried away from excellence and strenuous virtue? This must certainly be what Solomon meant when he said, 'As he who putteth a stone in a sling, so is he that giveth honour to a fool.'

For any one can perceive how this honouring of a false ideal, not of intelligence and strenuous virtue, but of wealth and station, pleasure and ease, is as a stone from a sling to kill in our great middle class, in us who are called Philistines, the desire before spoken of, which by nature for ever carries all men towards that which is lovely; and to leave instead of it only a blind deteriorating pursuit, for ourselves also, of the false ideal. And in those among us Philistines whom the desire does not wholly abandon, yet, having no excellent ideal set forth to nourish and to steady it, it meets with that natural bent for the bathos which together with this desire itself is implanted at birth in the breast of man, and is by that force twisted awry, and borne at random hither and thither, and at last flung upon those grotesque and hideous forms of popular religion which the more respectable part among us Philistines mistake for the true goal of man's desire after all that is lovely. And for the Populace this false idea is a stone which kills the desire before it can even arise; so impossible and unattainable for them do the conditions of that which is lovely appear according to this ideal to be made, so necessary to the reaching of them by the few seems the falling short of them by the many. So that, perhaps, of the actual vulgarity of our Philistines and brutality of our Populace, the Barbarians and their feudal habits of succession, enduring out of their due time and place, are involuntarily the cause in a great degree; and they hurt the welfare of the rest of the community at the same time that, as we have seen, they hurt their own.

But must not, now, the working in our minds of considerations like these, to which culture, that is, the disinterested and active use of reading, reflection, and observation, in the endeavour to know the best that can be known, carries us, be really much more effectual to the dissolution of feudal habits and rules of succession in land than an operation like the Real Estate Intestacy Bill, and a stock notion like that of the natural right of all a man's children to an equal share in the enjoyment of his property; since we have seen that this mechanical maxim is unsound, and that, if it is unsound, the operation relying upon it cannot possibly be effective? If truth and reason have, as we believe, any natural, irresistible effect on the mind of man, it must. These considerations, when culture has called them forth and given them free course in our minds, will live and work. They will work gradually, no doubt, and will not bring us ourselves to the front to sit in high place and put them into effect; but so they will be all the more beneficial. Everything teaches us how gradually nature would have all profound changes brought about; and we can even see, too, where the absolute abrupt stoppage of feudal habits has worked harm. And appealing to the sense of truth and reason, these considerations will, without doubt, touch and move all those of even the Barbarians themselves, who are (as are some of us Philistines also, and some of the Populace) beyond their fellows quick of feeling for truth and reason. For indeed this is just one of the advantages of sweetness and light over fire and strength, that sweetness and light make a feudal class quietly and gradually drop its feudal habits because it sees them at variance with truth and reason, while fire and strength are for tearing them passionately off, because this class applauded Mr Lowe when he called, or was supposed to call, the working class drunken and venal.

But when once we have begun to recount the practical operations by which our Liberal friends work for the removal of definite evils, and in which if we do not join them they are apt to grow impatient with us, how can we pass over that very interesting operation – the attempt to enable a man to marry his deceased wife's sister? This operation, too, like that for abating the feudal customs of succession in land, I have had the advantage of myself seeing and hearing my Liberal friends labour at.

I was lucky enough to be present when Mr Chambers brought forward in the House of Commons his bill for enabling a man to marry his deceased wife's sister, and I heard the speech which Mr Chambers then made in support of his bill. His first point was that God's law – the name he always gave to the Book of Leviticus – did not really forbid a man to marry his deceased wife's sister. God's law not forbidding it, the Liberal maxim, that a man's prime right and happiness is to do as he likes, ought at once to come into force, and to annul any such check upon the assertion of personal liberty as the prohibition to marry one's deceased wife's sister. A distinguished Liberal supporter of Mr Chambers, in the debate which followed the introduction of the bill, produced a formula of much beauty and neatness for conveying in brief the Liberal notions on this head: 'Liberty,' said he, 'is the law of human life.' And, therefore, the moment it is ascertained that God's law, the Book of Leviticus, does not stop the way, man's law, the law of liberty, asserts its right, and makes us free to marry our deceased wife's sister.

And this exactly falls in with what Mr Hepworth Dixon, who may almost be called the Colenso[32] of love and marriage – such a revolution does he make in our ideas on these matters, just as Dr Colenso does in our ideas on religion – tells us of the notions and proceedings of our kinsmen in America. With that affinity of genius to the Hebrew genius which we have already noticed, and with the strong belief of our race that liberty is the law of human life, so far as that fixed, perfect, and paramount rule of conscience, the Bible, does not expressly control it, our American kinsmen go again, Mr Hepworth Dixon tells us, to their Bible, the Mormons to the patriarchs and the Old Testament, Brother Noyes to St Paul and the New, and having never before read anything else but their Bible, they now read their Bible over again, and make all manner of great discoveries there. All these discoveries are favourable to liberty, and in this way is satisfied that double craving so characteristic of our Philistine, and so eminently exemplified in that crowned Philistine,

Henry the Eighth – the craving for forbidden fruit and the craving for legality.

Mr Hepworth Dixon's eloquent writings give currency, over here, to these important discoveries; so that now, as regards love and marriage, we seem to be entering, with all our sails spread, upon what Mr Hepworth Dixon, its apostle and evangelist, calls a Gothic Revival, but what one of the many newspapers that so greatly admire Mr Hepworth Dixon's lithe and sinewy style and form their own style upon it, calls, by a yet bolder and more striking figure, 'a great sexual insurrection of our Anglo-Teutonic race'. For this end we have to avert our eyes from everything Hellenic and fanciful, and to keep them steadily fixed upon the two cardinal points of the Bible and liberty. And one of those practical operations in which the Liberal party engage, and in which we are summoned to join them, directs itself entirely, as we have seen, to these cardinal points, and may almost be regarded, perhaps, as a kind of first instalment, or public and parliamentary pledge, of the great sexual insurrection of our Anglo-Teutonic race.

But here, as elsewhere, what we seek is the Philistine's perfection, the development of his best self, not mere liberty for his ordinary self. And we no more allow absolute validity to his stock maxim, *Liberty is the law of human life*, than we allow it to the opposite maxim, which is just as true, *Renouncement is the law of human life*. For we know that the only perfect freedom is, as our religion says, a service; not a service to any stock maxim, but an elevation of our best self, and a harmonizing in subordination to this, and to the idea of a perfected humanity, all the multitudinous, turbulent, and blind impulses of our ordinary selves. Now, the Philistine's great defect being a defect in delicacy of perception, to cultivate in him this delicacy, to render it independent of external and mechanical rule, and a law to itself, is what seems to make most for his perfection, his true humanity. And his true humanity, and therefore his happiness, appears to lie much more, so far as the relations of love and marriage are concerned, in becoming alive to the finer shades of feeling which arise within these relations, in being able to enter with tact and sympathy into the subtle instinctive propensions and repugnances of the person with whose life his own life is bound up, to make them his own, to direct and govern in harmony with them the arbitrary range of his personal action, and thus to enlarge his spiritual and intellectual life and liberty, than in remaining insensible to these finer shades of feeling and this delicate sympathy, in giving unchecked range, so far as he can, to his mere personal action, in allowing no limits or government to this except such a mechanical external law imposes, and in thus really narrowing, for the satisfaction of his ordinary self, his spiritual and intellectual life and liberty.

Still more must this be so when his fixed eternal rule, his God's law, is supplied to him from a source which is less fit, perhaps, to supply final and absolute instructions on this particular topic of love and marriage than on any other relation of human life. Bishop Wilson, who is full of examples of that fruitful Hellenizing within the limits of Hebraism itself, of that renewing of the stiff and stark notions of Hebraism by turning upon them a stream of fresh thought and consciousness, which we have already noticed in St Paul – Bishop Wilson gives an admirable lesson to rigid Hebraizers, like Mr Chambers, asking themselves, Does God's law (that is, the Book of Leviticus) forbid us to marry our wife's sister? Does God's law (that is, again, the Book of Leviticus) allow us to marry our wife's sister? – when he says, 'Christian duties are founded on reason, not on the sovereign authority of God commanding what He pleases; God cannot command us what is not fit to be believed or done, all his commands being founded in the necessities of our nature.' And, immense as is our debt to the Hebrew race and its genius, incomparable as is its authority on certain profoundly important sides of our human nature, worthy as it is to be described as having uttered, for those sides, the voice of the deepest necessities of our nature, the statutes of the divine and eternal order of things, the law of God – who, that is not manacled and hoodwinked by his Hebraism, can believe that, as to love and marriage, our reason and the necessities of our humanity have their true, sufficient, and divine law expressed for them by the voice of any Oriental and polygamous nation like the Hebrews? Who, I say, will believe, when he really considers the matter, that where the feminine nature, the feminine ideal, and our relations to them, are brought into question, the delicate and apprehensive genius of the Indo-European race, the race which invented the Muses, and chivalry, and the Madonna, is to find its last word on this question in the institutions of a Semitic people, whose wisest kind had seven hundred wives and three hundred concubines?

If here again, therefore, we minister better to the diseased spirit of our time by leading it to think about the operation our Liberal friends have in hand, than by lending a hand to this operation ourselves, let us see, before we dismiss from our view the practical operations of our Liberal friends, whether the same thing does not hold good as to their celebrated industrial and economical labours also. Their great work of this kind is, of course, their free-trade policy. This policy, as having enabled the poor man to eat untaxed bread, and as having wonderfully augmented trade, we are accustomed to speak of with a kind of thankful solemnity. It is chiefly on their having been our leaders in this policy that Mr Bright founds for himself and his friends the claim, so often asserted by him, to be considered guides of the blind, teachers of the ignorant, benefactors slowly and laboriously developing in the Conservative party and in the country that which Mr Bright is fond of calling *the growth of intelligence* – the object, as is well known, of all the friends of culture also, and the great end and aim of the culture that we preach.

Now, having first saluted free-trade and its doctors with all respect, let us see whether even here, too, our Liberal friends do not pursue their operations in a mechanical way, without reference to any firm intelligible law of things, to human life as a whole, and human happiness; and whether it is not more for our good, at this particular moment at any rate, if, instead of worshipping free-trade with them Hebraistically, as a kind of fetish, and helping them to pursue it as an end in and for itself, we turn the free stream of our thought upon their treatment of it, and see how this is related to the intelligible law of human life, and to national well-being and happiness. In short, suppose we Hellenize a little with free-trade, as we Hellenized with the Real Estate Intestacy Bill, and with the disestablishment of the Irish Church by the power of the Nonconformists' antipathy to religious establishments, and see whether what our reprovers beautifully call ministering to the diseased spirit of our time is best done by the Hellenizing method of proceeding, or by the other.

But first let us understand how the policy of free-trade really shapes itself for our Liberal friends, and how they practically employ it as an instrument of national happiness and salvation. For as we said that it seemed clearly right to prevent the Church property of Ireland from being all taken for the benefit of the Church of a small minority, so it seems clearly right that the poor man should eat untaxed bread, and, generally, that restrictions and regulations which, for the supposed benefit of some particular person or class of persons, make the price of things artificially high here, or artificially low there, and interfere with the natural flow of trade and commerce, should be done away with. But in the policy of our Liberal friends free-trade means more than this, and is specially valued as a stimulant to the production of wealth, as they call it, and to the increase of the trade, business, and population of the country. We have already seen how these things – trade, business, and population – are mechanically pursued by us as ends precious in themselves, and are worshipped as what we call fetishes; and Mr Bright, I have already said, when he wishes to give the working class a true sense of what makes glory and greatness, tells it to look at the cities it has built, the railroads it has made, the manufactures it has produced. So to this idea of glory and greatness the free-trade which our Liberal friends extol so solemnly and devoutly, has served – to the increase of trade, business, and population; and for this it is prized. Therefore, the untaxing of the poor man's bread has, with this view of national happiness, been used not so much to make the existing poor man's bread cheaper or more abundant, but rather to create more poor men to eat it; so that we cannot precisely say that we have fewer poor men than we had before free-trade, but we can say with truth that we have many more centres of industry, as they are called, and much more business, population, and manufactures. And if we are sometimes a little troubled by our multitude of poor men, yet we know the increase of manufactures and population to be such a salutary thing in itself, and our free-trade policy begets such an admirable movement, creating fresh centres of industry and fresh poor men here, while we were thinking about our poor men there, that we are quite dazzled and borne away, and more and more industrial movement is called for, and our social progress seems to become one triumphant and enjoyable course of what is sometimes called, vulgarly, outrunning the constable.

If, however, taking some other criterion of man's well-being than the cities he has built and the manufactures he has produced, we persist in thinking that our social progress would be happier if there were not so many of us so very poor, and in busying ourselves with notions of in some way or other adjusting the poor man and business one to the other, and not multiplying the one and the other mechanically and blindly, then our Liberal friends, the appointed doctors of free-trade, take us up very sharply. 'Art is long', says *The Times*, 'and life is short; for the most part we settle things first and understand them afterwards. Let us have as few theories as possible; what is wanted is not the light of speculation. If nothing worked well of which the theory was not perfectly understood, we should be in sad confusion. The relations of labour and capital, we are told, are not understood, yet trade and commerce, on the whole, work satisfactorily.' I quote from *The Times* of only the other day. But thoughts like these, as I have often pointed out, are thoroughly British thoughts, and we have been familiar with them for years.

Or, if we want more of a philosophy of the matter than this, our free-trade friends have two axioms for us, axioms laid down by their justly esteemed doctors, which they think ought to satisfy us entirely. One is, that, other things being equal, the more population increases, the more does production increase to keep pace with it; because men by their numbers and contact call forth all manner of activities and resources in one another and in nature, which, when men are few and sparse, are never developed. The other is, that, although population always tends to equal the means of subsistence, yet people's notions of what subsistence is enlarge as civilization advances, and take in a number of things beyond the bare necessaries of life; and thus, therefore, is supplied whatever check on population is needed. But the error of our friends is precisely, perhaps, that they apply axioms of this sort as if they were self-acting laws which will put themselves into operation without trouble or planning on our part, if we will only pursue free-trade, business, and population zealously and staunchly. Whereas the real truth is, that, however the case might be under other circumstances, yet in fact, as we now manage the matter, the enlarged conception of what is included in *subsistence* does not operate to prevent the bringing into the world of numbers of people who but just attain to the barest necessaries of life or who even fail to attain to them; while, again, though production may increase as population increases, yet it seems that the production may be of such a kind, and so related, or rather non-related, to population, that the population may be little the better for it.

For instance, with the increase of population since Queen Elizabeth's time the production of silk-stockings has wonderfully increased, and silk-stockings have become much cheaper, and procurable in greater abundance by many more people, and tend perhaps, as population and manufactures increase, to get cheaper and cheaper, and at last to become, according to Bastiat's favourite image, a common free property of the human race, like light and air. But bread and bacon have not become much cheaper with the increase of population since Queen Elizabeth's time, nor procurable in much greater abundance by many more people; neither do they seem at all to promise to become, like light and air, a common free property of the human race. And if bread and bacon have not kept pace with our population, and we have many more people in want of them now than in Queen Elizabeth's time, it seems vain to tell us that silk-stockings have kept pace with our population, or even more than kept pace with it, and that we are to get our comfort out of that.

In short, it turns out that our pursuit of free-trade, as of so many other things, has been too mechanical. We fix upon some object, which in this case is the production of wealth, and the increase of manufactures, population, and commerce through free-trade, as a kind of one thing needful, or end in itself; and then wc pursue it staunchly and mechanically, and say that it is our duty to pursue it staunchly and mechanically, not to see how it is related to the whole intelligible law of things and to full human perfection, or to treat it as the piece of machinery, of varying value as its relations to the intelligible law of things vary, which it really is.

So it is of no use to say to *The Times*, and to our Liberal friends rejoicing in the possession of their talisman of free-trade, that about one in nineteen of our population is a pauper, and that, this being so, trade and commerce can hardly be said to prove by their satisfactory working that it matters nothing whether the relations between labour and capital are understood or not; nay, that we can hardly be said not to be in sad confusion. For here our faith in the staunch mechanical pursuit of a fixed object comes in, and covers itself with that imposing and colossal necessitarianism of *The Times* which we have before noticed. And this necessitarianism, taking for granted that an increase in trade and population is a good in itself, one of the chiefest of goods, tells us that disturbances of human happiness caused by ebbs and flows in the tide of trade and business, which, on the whole, steadily mounts, are inevitable and not to be quarrelled with. This firm philosophy I seek to call to mind when I am in the East of London, whither my avocations often lead me; and, indeed, to fortify myself against the depressing sights which on these occasions assail us, I have transcribed from *The Times* one strain of this kind, full of the finest economical doctrine, and always carry it about with me. The passage is this:

> The East End is the most commercial, the most industrial, the most fluctuating region of the metropolis. It is always the first to suffer; for it is the creature of prosperity, and falls to the ground the instant there is no wind to bear it up. The whole of that region is covered with huge docks, shipyards, manufactories, and a wilderness of small houses, all full of life and happiness in brisk times, but in dull times withered and lifeless, like the deserts we read of in the east. Now their brief spring is over. There is no one to blame for this; it is the result of Nature's simplest laws!

We must all agree that it is impossible that anything can be firmer than this, or show a surer faith in the working of free-trade, as our Liberal friends understand and employ it.

But, if we still at all doubt whether the indefinite multiplication of manufactories and small houses can be such an absolute good in itself as to counterbalance the indefinite multiplication of poor people, we shall learn that this multiplication of poor people, too, is an absolute good in itself, and the result of divine and beautiful laws. This is indeed a favourite thesis with our Philistine friends, and I have already noticed the pride and gratitude with which they receive certain articles in *The Times*, dilating in thankful and solemn language on the majestic growth of our population. But I prefer to quote now, on this topic, the words of an ingenious young Scotch writer, Mr Robert Buchanan, because he invests with so much imagination and poetry this current idea of the blessed and even divine character which the multiplying of population is supposed in itself to have. 'We move to multiplicity', says Mr Robert Buchanan. 'If there is one quality which seems God's, and his exclusively, it seems that divine philoprogenitiveness, that passionate love of distribution and expansion into living forms. Every animal added seems a new ecstasy to the Maker; every life added, a new embodiment of his love. He would *swarm* the earth with beings. There are never enough. Life, life, life – faces gleaming, hearts beating – must fill every cranny. Not a corner is suffered to remain empty. The whole earth breeds, and God glories.'

It is a little unjust, perhaps, to attribute to the Divinity exclusively this philoprogenitiveness, which the British Philistine, and the poorer class of Irish, may certainly claim to share with him; yet how inspiriting is here the whole strain of thought! and these beautiful words, too, I carry about with me in the East of London, and often read them there. They are quite in agreement with the popular language one is accustomed to hear about children and large families, which describes children as *sent*. And a line of poetry, which Mr Robert Buchanan throws in presently after the poetical prose I have quoted,

'Tis the old story of the fig-leaf time

this fine line, too, naturally connects itself, when one is in the East of London, with the idea of God's desire to *swarm* the earth with beings; because the swarming of the earth with beings does indeed, in the East of London, so seem to revive *the old story of the fig-leaf time*, such a number of the people one meets there having hardly a rag to cover them; and the more the swarming goes on, the more it promises to revive this old story. And when the story is perfectly revived, the swarming quite completed, and every cranny choke-full, then, too, no doubt, faces in the East of London will be gleaming faces, which Mr Robert Buchanan says it is God's desire they should be, and which every one must perceive they are not at present, but, on the contrary, very miserable.

But to prevent all this philosophy and poetry from quite running away with us, and making us think with *The Times*, and our practical Liberal free-traders, and the British Philistines generally, that the increase of houses and manufactories, or the increase of population, are absolute goods in themselves, to be mechanically pursued, and to be worshipped like fetishes, to prevent this, we have got that notion of ours immovably fixed, of which I have long ago spoken, the notion that culture, or the study of perfection, leads us to conceive of no perfection as being real which is not a *general* perfection, embracing all our fellow-men with whom we have to do. Such is the sympathy which binds humanity together, that we are indeed, as our religion says, members of one body, and if one member suffer, all the members suffer with it. Individual perfection is impossible so long as the rest of mankind are not perfected along with us. 'The *multitude* of the wise is the welfare of the world', says the wise man. And to this effect that excellent and often-quoted guide of ours, Bishop Wilson, has some striking words, 'It is not', says he, 'so much our neighbour's interest as our own that we love him.' And again he says, 'Our salvation does in some measure depend upon that of others.' And the author of the *Imitation* puts the same thing admirably when he says, '*Obscurior etiam via ad coelum videbatur quando tam pauci regnum coelorum qaerere curabant*; the fewer there are who follow the way to perfection, the harder that way is to find.' So all our fellow-men, in the East of London and elsewhere, we must take along with us in the progress towards perfection, if we ourselves really, as we profess, want to be perfect; and we must not let the worship of any fetish, any machinery, such as manufactures or population – which are not, like perfection, absolute goods in themselves, though we think them so – create for us such a multitude of miserable, sunken, and ignorant human beings, that to carry them all along with us is impossible, and perforce they must for the most part be left by us in their degradation and wretchedness. But evidently the conception of free-trade, on which our Liberal friends vaunt themselves, and in which they think they have found the secret of national prosperity – evidently, I say, the mere unfettered pursuit of the production of wealth, and the mere mechanical multiplying, for this end, of manufactures and population, threatens to create for us, if it has not created already, those vast, miserable, unmanageable masses of sunken people, to the existence of which we are, as we have seen, absolutely forbidden to reconcile ourselves, in spite of all that the philosophy of *The Times* and the poetry of Mr Robert Buchanan may say to persuade us.

Hebraism in general seems powerless, almost as powerless as our free-trading Liberal friends, to deal efficaciously with our ever-accumulating masses of pauperism, and to prevent their accumulating still more. Hebraism builds churches, indeed, for these masses, and sends missionaries among them; above all, it sets itself against the social necessitarianism of *The Times*, and refuses to accept their degradation as inevitable. But with regard to their ever-increasing accumulation, it seems to be led to the very same conclusions, though from a point of view of its own, as our free-trading Liberal friends. Hebraism, with that mechanical and misleading use of the letter of Scripture on which we have already commented, is governed by such texts as: *Be fruitful and multiply*, the edict of God's law, as Mr Chambers would say; or by the declaration of what he would call God's word in the Psalms, that the man who has a great number of children is thereby made happy. And in conjunction with such texts as these, Hebraism is apt to place another text: *The poor shall never cease out of the land.* Thus Hebraism is conducted to nearly the same notion as the popular mind and as Mr Robert Buchanan, that children are *sent*, and that the divine nature takes a delight in swarming the East End of London with paupers. Only, when they are perishing in their helplessness and wretchedness, it asserts the Christian duty of succouring them, instead of saying, like *The Times*, 'Now their brief spring is over; there is nobody to blame for this; it is the result of Nature's simplest laws!' But, like *The Times*, Hebraism despairs of any help from knowledge and says that 'what is wanted is not the light of speculation.'

I remember, only the other day, a good man looking with me upon a multitude of children who were gathered before us in one of the most miserable regions of London – children eaten up with disease, half-sized, half-fed, half-clothed, neglected by their parents, without health, without home, without hope – said to me, 'The one thing really needful is to teach these little ones to succour one another, if only with a cup of cold water; but now, from one end of the country to the other, one hears nothing but the cry for knowledge, knowledge, knowledge!' And yet surely, so long as these children are there in these festering masses, without health, without home, without hope, and so long as their multitude is perpetually swelling, charged with misery they must still be for themselves, charged with misery they must still be for us, whether they help one another with a cup of cold water or no; and the knowledge how to prevent their accumulating is necessary, even to give their moral life and growth a fair chance!

May we not, therefore, say, that neither the true Hebraism of this good man, willing to spend and be spent for these sunken multitudes, nor what I may call the spurious Hebraism of our free-trading Liberal friends – mechanically worshipping their fetish of the production of wealth and of the increase of manufactures and population, and looking neither to the right nor left so long as this increase goes on – avail us much here; and that here, again, what we want is Hellenism, the letting our consciousness play freely and simply upon the facts before us,and listening to what it tells us of the intelligible law of things as concerns them? And surely what it tells us is, that a man's children are not really *sent*, any more than the pictures upon his wall, or the horses in his stable, are *sent*; and that to bring people into the world, when one cannot afford to keep them and oneself decently and not too precariously, or to bring more of them into the world than one can afford to keep thus, is, whatever *The Times* and Mr Robert Buchanan may say, by no means an accomplishment of the divine will or a fulfilment of Nature's simplest laws, but is just as wrong, just as contrary to reason and the will of God, as for a man to have horses, or carriages, or pictures, when he cannot afford them, or to have more of them than he can afford; and that, in the one case as in the other, the larger the scale on which the violation of reason's law is practised, and the longer it is persisted in, the greater must be the confusion and final trouble. Surely no laudations of free-trade, no meetings of bishops and clergy in the East End of London, no reading of papers and reports, can tell us anything about our social condition which it more concerns us to know than that! and not only to know, but habitually to have the knowledge present, and to act upon it as one acts upon the knowledge that water wets and fire burns! And not only the sunken populace of our great cities are concerned to know it, and the pauper twentieth of our population; we Philistines of the middle class, too, are concerned to know it, and all who have to set themselves to make progress in perfection.

But we all know it already! someone will say; it is the simplest law of prudence. But how little reality must there be in our knowledge of it; how little can we be putting it in practice; how little is it likely to penetrate among the poor and struggling masses of our population, and to better our condition, so long as an unintelligent Hebraism of one sort keeps repeating as an absolute eternal word of God and psalm-verse which says that the man who has a great many children is happy; or an unintelligent Hebraism of another sort – that is to say, a blind following of certain stock notions as infallible – keeps assigning as an absolute proof of national prosperity the multiplying of manufactures and population! Surely, the one set of Hebraizers have to learn that their psalm-verse was composed at the resettlement of Jerusalem after the Captivity, when the Jews of Jerusalem were a handful, an undermanned garrison, and every child was a blessing; and that the word of God, or the voice of the divine order of things, declares the possession of a great many children to be a blessing only when it really is so! And the other set of Hebraizers, have they not to learn that if they call their private acquaintances imprudent or unlucky, when, with no means of support for them or with precarious means, they have a large family of children, then they ought not to call the State well managed and prosperous merely because its manufactures and its citizens multiply, if the manufactures, which bring new citizens into existence just as much as if they had actually begotten them, bring more of them into existence than they can maintain, or are too precarious to go on maintaining those whom for a while they maintained?

Hellenism, surely, or the habit of fixing our mind upon the intelligible law of things, is most salutary if it makes us see that the only absolute good, the only absolute and eternal object prescribed to us by God's law, or the divine order of things, is the progress towards perfection – our own progress towards it and the progress of humanity. And therefore, for every individual man, and for every society of men, the possession and multiplication of children, like the possession and multiplication of horses and pictures, is to be accounted good or bad, not in itself, but with reference to this object and the progress towards it. And as no man is to be excused in having horses or pictures, if his having them hinders his own or other's progress towards perfection and makes them lead a servile and ignoble life, so is no man to be excused for having children if his having them makes him or others lead this.

Plain thoughts of this kind are surely the spontaneous product of our consciousness, when it is allowed to play freely and disinterestedly upon the actual facts of our social condition, and upon our stock notions and stock habits in respect to it. Firmly grasped and simply uttered, they are more likely, one cannot but think, to better that condition, than is the mechanical pursuit of free-trade by our Liberal friends.

So that, here as elsewhere, the practical operations of our Liberal friends, by which they set so much store, and in which they invite us to join them and to show what Mr Bright calls a commendable interest, do not seem to us so practical for real good as they think; and our Liberal friends seem to us themselves to need to Hellenize, as we say, a little – that is, to examine into the nature of real good, and to listen to what their consciousness tells them about it – rather than to pursue with such heat and confidence their present practical operations. And it is clear that they have no just cause, so far as regards several operations of theirs which we have canvassed, to reproach us with delicate Conservative scepticism. For often by Hellenizing we seem to subvert stock Conservative notions and usages more effectually than they subvert them by Hebraizing. But, in truth, the free spontaneous play of consciousness with which culture tries to float our stock habits of thinking and acting, is by its very nature, as has been said, disinterested. Sometimes the result of floating them may be agreeable to this party, sometimes to that; now it may be unwelcome to our so called Liberals, now to our so-called Conservatives; but what culture seeks is, above all, to *float* them, to prevent their being stiff and stark pieces of petrifaction any longer. It is mere Hebraizing, if we stop short, and refuse to let our consciousness play freely, whenever we or our friends do not happen to like what it discovers to us. This is to make the Liberal party, or the Conservative party, our one thing needful, instead of human perfection; and we have seen what mischief arises from making an even greater thing than the Liberal or the Conservative party – the predominance of the moral side in man – our one thing needful. But wherever the free play of our consciousness leads us, we shall follow; believing that in this way we shall tend to make good at all points what is wanting to us, and so shall be brought nearer to our complete human perfection.

Everything, in short, confirms us in the doctrine, so unpalatable to the believers in action, that our main business at the present moment is not so much to work away at certain crude reforms of which we have already the scheme in our own mind, as to create, through the help of that culture which at the very outset we began by praising and recommending, a frame of mind out of which the schemes of really fruitful reforms may with time grow. At any rate, we ourselves must put up with our friends' impatience, and with their reproaches against cultivated inaction, and must still decline to lend a hand to their practical operations, until we, for our own part at least, have grown a little clearer about the nature of real good, and have arrived nearer to a condition of mind out of which really fruitful and solid operations may spring.

In the meanwhile, since our Liberal friends keep loudly and resolutely assuring us that their actual operations at present are fruitful and solid, let us in each case keep testing these operations in the simple way we have indicated, by letting the natural stream of our consciousness flow over them freely; and if they stand this test successfully, then let us give them our interest, but not else.

Conclusion

And so we bring to an end what we had to say in praise of culture, and in evidence of its special utility for the circumstances in which we find ourselves, and the confusion which environs us. Through culture seems to lie our way, not only to perfection, but even to safety. Resolutely refusing to lend a hand to the imperfect operations of our Liberal friends, disregarding their impatience, taunts, and reproaches, firmly bent on trying to find in the intelligible laws of things a firmer and sounder basis for future practice than any which we have at present, and believing this search and discovery to be, for our generation and circumstances, of yet more vital and pressing importance than practice itself, we nevertheless may do more, perhaps, we poor disparaged followers of culture, to make the actual present, and the frame of society in which we live, solid and seaworthy, than all which our bustling politicians can do.

For we have seen how much of our disorders and perplexities is due to the disbelief, among the classes and combinations of men, Barbarian or Philistine, which have hitherto governed our society, in right reason, in a paramount best self; to the inevitable decay and break-up of the organizations by which, asserting and expressing in these organizations their ordinary self only, they have so long ruled us; and to their irresolution, when the society, which their conscience tells them they have made and still manage not with right reason but with their ordinary self is rudely shaken, in offering resistance to its subverters. But for us – who believe in right reason, in the duty and possibility of extricating and elevating our best self, in the progress of humanity towards perfection – for us the framework of society, that theatre on which this august drama has to unroll itself, is sacred; and whoever administers it, and however we may seek to remove them from their tenure of administration, yet, while they administer, we steadily and with undivided heart support them in repressing anarchy and disorder; because without order there can be no society, and without society there can be no human perfection.

And this opinion of the intolerableness of anarchy we can never forsake, however our Liberal friends may think a little rioting, and what they call popular demonstrations, useful sometimes to their own interests and to the interests of the valuable practical operations they have in hand, and however they may preach the right of an Englishman to be left to do as far as possible what he likes, and the duty of his government to indulge him and connive as much as possible and abstain from all harshness of repression. And even when they artfully show us operations which are undoubtedly precious, such as the abolition of the slave-trade, and ask us if, for their sake, foolish and obstinate governments may not wholesomely be frightened by a little disturbance, the good design in view and the difficulty of overcoming opposition to it being considered – still we say no, and that monster-processions in the streets and forcible irruptions into the parks, even in professed support of this good design, ought to be unflinchingly forbidden and repressed; and that far more is lost than is gained by permitting them. Because a State in which law is authoritative and sovereign, a firm and settled course of public order, is requisite if man is to bring to maturity anything precious and lasting now, or to found anything precious and lasting for the future.

Thus, in our eyes, the very framework and exterior order of the State, whoever may administer the State, is sacred; and culture is the most resolute enemy of anarchy, because of the great hopes and designs for the State which culture teaches us to nourish. But as, believing in right reason, and having faith in the progress of humanity towards perfection, and ever labouring for this end, we grow to have clearer sight of the ideas of right reason, and of the elements and helps of perfection, and come gradually to fill the framework of the State with them, to fashion its internal composition and all its laws and institutions conformably to them, and to make the State more and more the expression, as we say, of our best self, which is not manifold, and vulgar, and unstable, and contentious, and ever-varying, but one, and noble, and secure, and peaceful, and the same for all mankind – with what aversion shall we not *then* regard anarchy, with what firmness shall we not check it, when there is so much that is so precious which it will endanger!

So that, for the sake of the present, but far more for the sake of the future, the lovers of culture are unswervingly and with a good conscience the opposers of anarchy. And not as the Barbarians and Philistines, whose honesty and whose sense of humour make them shrink, as we have seen, from treating the State as too serious a thing, and from giving it too much power – for indeed the only State they know of, and think they administer, is the expression of their ordinary self. And though the headstrong and violent extreme among them might gladly arm this with full authority, yet their virtuous mean is, as we have said, pricked in conscience at doing this; and so our Barbarian Secretaries of State let the Park railings be broken down, and our Philistine Alderman-Colonels let the London roughs rob and beat the bystanders. But we, beholding in the State no expression of our ordinary self, but even already, as it were, the appointed frame and prepared vessel of our best self, and, for the future, our best self's powerful, beneficent, and sacred expression and organ – we are willing and resolved, even now, to strengthen against anarchy the trembling hands of our Barbarian Home Secretaries, and the feeble knees of our Philistine Alderman-Colonels; and to tell them, that it is not really on behalf of their own ordinary self that they are called to protect the Park railings, and to suppress the London roughs, but on behalf of the best self both of themselves and of all of us in the future.

Nevertheless, though for resisting anarchy the lovers of culture may prize and employ fire and strength, yet they must, at the same time, bear constantly in mind that it is not at this moment true, what the majority of people tell us, that the world wants fire and strength more than sweetness and light, and that things are for the most part to be settled first and understood afterwards. We have seen how much of our present perplexities and confusion this untrue notion of the majority of people amongst us has caused, and tends to perpetuate. Therefore the true business of the friends of culture now is, to dissipate this false notion, to spread the belief in right reason and in a firm intelligible law of things, and to get men to try, in preference to staunchly acting with imperfect knowledge, to obtain some sounder basis of knowledge on which to act. This is what the friends and lovers of culture have to do, however the believers in action may grow impatient with us for saying so, and may insist on our lending a hand to their practical operations and showing a commendable interest in them.

To this insistence we must indeed turn a deaf ear. But neither, on the other hand, must the friends of culture expect to take the believers in action by storm, or to be visibly and speedily important, and to rule and cut a figure in the world. Aristotle says that those for whom alone ideas and the pursuit of the intelligible law of things can, in general, have much attraction, are principally the young, filled with generous spirit and with a passion for perfection; but the mass of mankind, he says, follow seeming goods for real, bestowing hardly a thought upon true sweetness and light; 'and to *their* lives', he adds mournfully, 'who can give another and a better rhythm?' But, although those chiefly attracted by sweetness and light will probably always be the young and enthusiastic, and culture must not hope to take the mass of mankind by storm, yet we will not therefore, for our own day and for our own people, admit and rest in the desponding sentence of Aristotle. For is not this the right crown of the long discipline of Hebraism, and the due fruit of mankind's centuries of painful schooling in self-conquest, and the just reward, above all, of the strenuous energy of our own nation and kindred in dealing honestly with itself and walking steadfastly according to the best light it knows – that when in the fullness of time it has reason and beauty offered to it, and the law of things as they really are, it should at last walk by this true light with the same staunchness and zeal with which it formerly walked by its imperfect light? And thus man's two great natural forces, Hebraism and Hellenism, will no longer be dissociated and rival, but will be a joint force of right thinking and strong doing to carry him on towards perfection. This is what the lovers of culture may perhaps dare to augur for such a nation as ours.

Therefore, however great the changes to be accomplished, and however dense the array of Barbarians, Philistines, and Populace, we will neither despair on the one hand, nor, on the other, threaten violent revolution and change. But we will look forward cheerfully and hopefully to 'a revolution', as the Duke of Wellington said, 'by due course of law'; though not exactly such laws as our Liberal friends are now, with their actual lights, fond of offering to us.

But if despondency and violence are both of them forbidden to the believer in culture, yet neither, on the other hand, is public life and direct political action much permitted to him. For it is his business, as we have seen, to get the present believers in action, and lovers of political talking and doing, to make a return upon their own minds, scrutinize their stock notions and habits much more, value their present talking and doing much less; in order that, by learning to think more clearly, they may come at last to act less confusedly. But how shall we persuade our Barbarian to hold lightly to his feudal usages; how shall we persuade our Nonconformist that his time spent in agitating for the abolition of church establishments would have been better spent in getting worthier ideas of God and the ordering of the world, or his time spent in battling for voluntaryism in education better spent in learning to value and found a public and national culture; how shall we persuade, finally, our Alderman-Colonel not to be content with sitting in the hall of judgement or marching at the head of his men of war, without some knowledge how to perform judgement and how to direct men of war – how, I say, shall we persuade all these of this, if our Alderman-Colonel sees that we want to get his leading-staff and his scales of justice for our own hands; or the Nonconformist, that we want for ourselves his platform; or the Barbarian, that we want for ourselves his pre-eminency and function?

Certainly they will be less slow to believe, as we want them to believe, that the intelligible law of things has in itself something desirable and precious, and that all place, function, and bustle are hollow goods without it, if they see that we ourselves can content ourselves with this law, and find in it our satisfaction, without making it an instrument to give us for ourselves place, function, and bustle.

And although Mr Sidgwick says that social usefulness really means 'losing oneself in a mass of disagreeable, hard, mechanical details', and though all the believers in action are fond of asserting the same thing, yet, as to lose ourselves is not what we want, but to find ourselves through finding the intelligible law of things, this assertion too we shall not blindly accept, but shall sift and try it a little first. And if we see that because the believers in action, forgetting Goethe's maxim, 'to act is easy, to think is hard', imagine there is some wonderful virtue in losing oneself in a mass of mechanical details, therefore they excuse themselves from much thought about the clear ideas which ought to govern these details, then we shall give our chief care and pains to seeking out those ideas and to setting them forth; being persuaded that if we have the ideas firm and clear, the mechanical details for their execution will come a great deal more simply and easily than we now suppose.

At this exciting juncture, then, while so many of the lovers of new ideas, somewhat weary, as we too are, of the stock performances of our Liberal friends upon the political stage, are disposed to rush valiantly upon this public stage themselves, we cannot at all think that for a wise lover of new ideas this stage is the right one. Plenty of people there will be without us – country gentlemen in search of a club, demagogues in search of a tub, lawyers in search of a place, industrialists in search of gentility – who will come from the east and from the west, and will sit down at that Thyesteän banquet of claptrap which English public life for these many years past has been. And, so long as those old organizations, of which we have seen the insufficiency – those expressions of our ordinary self, Barbarian or Philistine – have force anywhere, they will have force in Parliament. There, the man whom the Barbarians send, cannot but be impelled to please the Barbarians' ordinary self, and their natural taste for the bathos; and the man whom the Philistines send, cannot but be impelled to please those of the Philistines. Parliamentary Conservatism will and must long mean this, that the Barbarians should keep their heritage; and Parliamentary Liberalism, that the Barbarians should pass away, as they will pass away, and that into their heritage the Philistines should enter. This seems, indeed, to be the true and authentic promise of which our Liberal friends and Mr Bright believe themselves the heirs, and the goal of that great man's labours. Presently, perhaps, Mr Odger and Mr Bradlaugh will be there with their mission to oust both Barbarians and Philistines, and to get the heritage of the Populace.

We, on the other hand, are for giving the heritage neither to the Barbarians nor to the Philistines, nor yet to the Populace; but we are for the transformation of each and all of these according to the law of perfection. Through the length and breadth of our nation a sense – vague and obscure as yet – of weariness with the old organizations, of desire for this transformation, works and grows. In the House of Commons the old organizations must inevitably be most enduring and strongest, the transformation must inevitably be longest in showing itself; and it may truly be averred, therefore, that at the present juncture the centre of movement is not in the House of Commons. It is in the fermenting mind of the nation; and his is for the next twenty years the real influence who can address himself to this.

Pericles was perhaps the most perfect public speaker who ever lived, for he was the man who most perfectly combined thought and wisdom with feeling and eloquence. Yet Plato brings in Alcibiades, declaring that men went away from the oratory of Pericles, saying it was very fine, it was very good, and afterwards thinking no more about it; but they went away from hearing Socrates talk, he says, with the point of what he had said sticking fast in their minds, and they could not get rid of it. Socrates has drunk his hemlock and is dead; but in his own breast does not every man carry about with him a possible Socrates, in that power of a disinterested play of consciousness upon his stock notions and habits, of which this wise and admirable man gave all through his lifetime and great example, and which was the secret of his incomparable influence? And he who leads men to call forth and exercise in themselves this power, and who busily calls it forth and exercises it in himself, is at the present moment, perhaps, as Socrates was in his time, more in concert with the vital working of men's minds, and more effectually significant than any House of Commons' orator, or practical operator in politics.

Every one is now boasting of what he has done to educate men's minds and to give things the course they are taking. Mr Disraeli educates, Mr Bright educates, Mr Beales educates. We, indeed, pretend to educate no one, for we are still engaged in trying to clear and educate ourselves. But we are sure that the endeavour to reach, through culture, the firm intelligible law of things, we are sure that the detaching ourselves from our stock notions and habits, that a more free play of consciousness, an increased desire for sweetness and light, and all the bent which we call Hellenizing, is the master-impulse even now of the life of our nation and of humanity – somewhat obscurely perhaps for this actual moment, but decisively and certainly for the immediate future; and that those who work for this are the sovereign educators.

Docile echoes of the eternal voice, pliant organs of the infinite will, such workers are going along with the essential movement of the world; and this is their strength, and their happy and divine fortune. For if the believers in action, who are so impatient with us and call us effeminate, had had the same good fortune, they would, no doubt, have surpassed us in this sphere of vital influence by all the superiority of their genius and energy over ours. But now we go the way the human race is going, while they abolish the Irish Church by the power of the Nonconformists' antipathy to establishments, or they enable a man to marry his deceased wife's sister.

Notes

Introduction

1. e.g. Raymond Williams, *Culture and Society 1780–1950* (1961, Penguin, p. 128); J. Dover Wilson (ed.), *Culture and Anarchy* (1960, Cambridge University Press, pp. xiv–xv).

2. For a fuller account, see Gillian Sutherland, *Elementary Education in the Nineteenth Century* (1971, Historical Association).

3. For a fuller account see R. L. Archer, *Secondary Education in the Nineteenth Century* (1921, Cambridge University Press) and T. W. Bamford, *The Rise of the Public Schools* (1967, Nelson).

4. This is an area of some controversy; see Peter Mathias, *The First Industrial Nation* (1969, Methuen, pp. 137–8) and Michael Sanderson, 'Literacy and social mobility in the Industrial Revolution in England', *Past and Present* (1972, August, no. 56).

5. To his mother, 31 January 1871, *The Letters of Matthew Arnold*, G. W. E. Russell (ed.). These are available in so many editions that it seems simplest to cite them by date and correspondent.

6. *Letters*, to his wife, 15 October 1851.

7. *The Times* (13 November 1886, p. 5), reprinted in *Essays, Letters and Reviews by Matthew Arnold*, Fraser Neiman (ed.) (1960, Harvard University Press, pp. 306–11).

8. Robert Lowe was extremely able, although disliked by many of his fellow Liberals for his intellectual arrogance and biting sarcasm. He led the revolt against the parliamentary reform bill which brought down the Gladstone–Russell government in 1866; but was nevertheless made Chancellor of the Exchequer in Gladstone's government 1868–74; see A. Patchett Martin, *Life and Letters of the Rt Hon. Robert Lowe, Viscount Sherbrooke* (1889, Longman, 2 vols). Lowe was again to be a target of Arnold's in *Culture and Anarchy* (see below).

9. Parliamentary Papers (1886, xxv, qq. 5833–6080). Cf. also T. H. Ward (ed.), *The Reign of Queen Victoria* (1887, Smith, Elder & Co., vol. 2, p. 260).

10. *Letters*, to his wife, 28 March 1862.

11. W. F. Connell, *The Educational Thought and Influence of Matthew Arnold* (1961, Routledge & Kegan Paul, p. 17).

12. Sir G. W. Kekewich, *The Education Department and After* (1920, Constable, p. 10). See also Richard Johnson, 'Administrators in education before 1870: patronage, social position and role' and Gillian Sutherland, 'Administrators

in education after 1870: patronage, professionalism and expertise', in Gillian Sutherland (ed.), *Studies in the Growth of Nineteenth-Century Government* (1972, Routledge & Kegan Paul).

13. Cf. also Williams, *Culture and Society* (see above, note 1), pp. 126–34.

14. *Letters*, to his mother, 16 February 1859.

15. See Lionel Trilling, *Matthew Arnold* (1949, Allen & Unwin, 2nd edn, chapter 12); H. F. Lowry (ed.), *The Letters of Matthew Arnold to Arthur Hugh Clough* (1932, Oxford University Press), 'Introductory – I'; for surveys of Dr Arnold's work and influence, see David Newsome, *Godliness and Good Learning* (1961, Murray) and T. W. Bamford, *Thomas Arnold* (1960, Cresset).

16. *Letters to Clough* (see note 15 above) Appendix I.

17. Thomas Arnold, *Lectures on Modern History* (1842, Longman, pp. 10–11).

18. A. P. Stanley, *The Life and Correspondence of Thomas Arnold, D.D.* (1845, 2 vols, Fellowes & Co., vol. 1, p. 111).

19. Stanley (vol. 1, pp. 123–4) (see above note 18).

20. The relationship of *Culture and Anarchy* to Arnold's literary work can best be pursued through a study of the texts themselves in vols. 2–5 of R. H. Super's edition of *The Complete Prose Works of Matthew Arnold* (University of Michigan Press).

Report for 1852

1. At this date one pupil-teacher was allowed for every forty or fifty children regularly attending. Pupil-teachers were apprentice-teachers. A series of Privy Council Minutes issued in the autumn of 1846 had provided for the apprenticeship of children of thirteen and over to a teacher in schools of which HMI approved. During a period of five years they were to do some of the teaching, guided by the teacher, and also receive additional instructions from him. HMI was to inspect their work at the end of each year and, if satisfactory, the school received grants both for the maintenance of the pupil-teacher and for the augmentation of the teacher's salary.

2. Matthew Arnold's predecessor as HMI in the district.

3. A system of giving collective lessons to children of mixed ages grouped in a series of galleries, much favoured in the Glasgow Normal School for the training of teachers.

4. The 'monitorial' system, much used by Joseph Lancaster, the founder of the British and Foreign School Society, whereby the master taught the older boys, who then passed on all they knew to the younger children.

The Twice-Revised Code (1862)

1. The Code was 'twice-revised' because after the first introduction of a 'Revised Code' at the end of June 1861, further minor modifications were announced in February 1862. Arnold refers to these at the end of the essay. For the background see above, pp. 11–12.

2. Dr C. J. Vaughan, a pupil of Dr Arnold's at Rugby, and until 1859 headmaster of Harrow, had published a pamphlet *The Revised Code of the Committee of Council on Education Dispassionately Considered in 1861* approving of the scheme.

3. The 'Voluntaries' were those Dissenters who opposed all State aid to education – see W. F. Connell, *Educational Thought and Influence of Matthew Arnold* (1961, pp. 37–45). Prominent among them were Francis Crossley, a Liberal MP from 1852–72, Edward Baines, editor of the *Leeds Mercury* and MP for Leeds 1859–74, and Edward Miall, a Congregational minister, editor of the *Nonconformist*, MP for Rochdale 1852–7 and Bradford 1869–74. Miall was a a member of the Newcastle Commission and was subsequently to lead the campaign for the disestablishment of the Anglican Church. See also Arnold's comments about him in *Culture and Anarchy*.

4. 'Face boldly up to the problems of the future in the society in which you find yourself; enter with sympathy and intelligence into its feelings and thoughts, establishing those common bonds of morality without which the advantages of education and fortune arouse envy rather than respect.'

Report for 1869

1. Under this Minute of the Committee of the Privy Council schools were entitled to an additional grant of 1s. 4d. per child, to a maximum of £8, if at least one-fifth of the children over six, who regularly attended, passed an examination not only in the '3Rs' but also in 'one or more specific subjects of secular instruction'. During the 1870s more grants were tacked on in this fashion and a category of 'class' subjects was added to that of 'specific' subjects. For a full account of this, see Gillian Sutherland, *Policy-Making in Elementary Education 1870–1895* (Oxford University Press, 1973, ch. 7).

Report for 1880

1. Sir John Lubbock was a scientist and anthropologist of some distinction and throughout the 1870s he campaigned in the Commons for more science teaching in elementary schools. For the Codes of the 1870s, see the preceding note; also Arnold's own discussion in this report.

Ecce, Convertimur ad Gentes (1879)

1. The title is a quotation from the Vulgate Bible, Acts of the Apostles Chapter 13, verse 46. The Authorized Version translates the phrase, 'Lo, we turn to the Gentiles'. Paul and Barnabas, preaching in Antioch, were given an enthusiastic reception by the Gentiles but a hostile one by the Jews. They told the Jewish community therefore, 'It was necessary that the Word of God should first have been spoken to you: but seeing ye put it from you and judge yourselves unworthy of everlasting life, lo, we turn to the Gentiles.'

2. Henry Fawcett was Professor of Political Economy at Cambridge 1863–84 and Postmaster-General in Gladstone's government 1880–84.

3. For John Bright, see below, *A French Eton*, note 11.

The Popular Education of France, chapter 14: The Popular Education of France and England Compared. Results on the People (1861)

1. 'Guizot's education law' was the legislation of 1833 which required every French commune to establish a primary school. Sir John Pakington was a somewhat eccentric Tory radical MP who introduced unsuccessful bills for national elementary education in 1855 and again in 1857.

2. 'The head of the household shall decide whether his children take part in religious intruction.'

3. 'The greatness of our country lies in the combination of a search for mental and spiritual nourishment with the satisfaction of our material needs', *Memoires*, vol. 2.

4. 'A nation of Barbarians civilized by compulsory military service.'

The Popular Education of France, Introduction: Democracy (1861)

1. 'They are able because they are seen to be able.'

2. Lycées. For a useful short account of the French educational system in the nineteenth century, see John E. Talbott, *The Politics of Educational Reform in France 1918–1940* (1969, Princeton University Press, chapter 1).

A French Eton or Middle-Class Education and the State (1863–4)

1. R. H. Super suggests that the 'Grand Detective' was Sir John Taylor Coleridge, a contemporary and great friend of Dr Arnold, who published in 1860 *Public School Education: A Lecture Delivered at the Athanaeum Tiverton.* This seems plausible. Certainly, later in the essay, Arnold quotes directly from letters written to the *Guardian* in November 1863 on the same subject by Coleridge.

The Royal Commission sat from 1861 to 1864 and was known by the name of its chairman, Lord Clarendon.

2. 'It is your own affair.'

3. On Woodard and his schools, see Brian Heeney, *Mission to the Middle Classes. The Woodard Schools 1848–1891* (1969, SPCK).

4. These were ultimately to become the Oxford and Cambridge Local Examinations; see John Roach, *Public Examinations in England 1850–1900* (1971, Cambridge University Press, parts 1 and 2).

5. The Rev. Stephen Hawtrey, who had formerly taught mathematics at Eton, founded a small school in his parish at Windsor to educate his choirboys and wrote a number of pamphlets about his work and ideas.

6. Frederick Temple, another of Dr Arnold's pupils, served as HMI 1853–7, was headmaster of Rugby 1858–69, then Bishop of Exeter and subsequently Archbishop of Canterbury.

7. C. B. Adderley was Vice-President of the Committee of Council on Education in the Conservative government of 1858–9. He was created Lord Norton in 1878.

8. J. A. Roebuck (1801–79) was a vociferous radical MP who took an extreme anti-interventionist stance.

9. For Edward Baines, see above, note 3 to *The Twice-Revised Code* (p. 273).

10. Church Rates were levied by the vestry on the whole parish, including Dissenters, for the upkeep of the parish church. Bills to abolish Church Rates passed the Commons in 1858, 1860 and 1867, but only succeeded in passing the Lords in 1868.

11. Richard Cobden and John Bright were first elected to the Commons, in 1841 and 1843 respectively, as representatives of the Anti-Corn Law League and thus of the manufacturing interest. After the repeal of the Corn Laws in 1846 they were associated with the Liberals. Both supported the North during the American Civil War and thus attacked the South for breaking up the Union. Cobden died in 1865, but Bright lived on until 1889 and accepted Cabinet office in Gladstone's first two governments: see John Morley, *Life of Richard Cobden* (1879, T. Fisher Unwin, 2 vols.) and G. M. Trevelyan, *Life of John Bright* (Constable, 1913). For their role and significance and the importance of Dissenting and manufacturing interests generally in the Liberal party, see John Vincent, *The Formation of the Liberal Party 1857–1868* (Constable, 1966).

12. For Edward Miall, see above, *The Twice-Revised Code*, note 3 (p. 273).

Culture and Anarchy (1868–9)

1. 'Be ye therefore perfect!' The Gospel according to St Matthew, chapter 5, verse 48. The Latin is that of the Vulgate Bible.

2. For John Bright, see above, note 11 to *A French Eton* (this page).

3. Frederic Harrison, formerly Fellow of Wadham College, Oxford, was one of the leading English followers of Auguste Comte, or Positivists, and a regular contributor to the *Fortnightly Review*. Arnold goes on to quote from an article of 1867 called 'Our Venetian Constitution'. For the English Positivists, see W. M. Simon, *European Positivism in the Nineteenth Century* (Cornell University Press, 1963).

4. Thomas Wilson (1663–1775) was Bishop of Sodor and Matthew Arnold much enjoyed his *Maxims*.

5. For J. A. Roebuck, see above, note 8 to *A French Eton* (this page).

6. 'Public squalor and private wealth.'

7. Edmond Beales (1803–81) and Charles Bradlaugh (1833–91) were leading members of the Reform League, which campaigned for parliamentary reform during the 1860s (see below, note 13, this page). Bradlaugh was also a leading Secularist; see Hypatia Bradlaugh Bonner, *Charles Bradlaugh: A Record of His Life and Work* (1894, T. Fisher Unwin).

8. For Robert Lowe, see above, Introduction, note 8 (p. 271).

9. H. T. Buckle wrote the *History of Civilization in England* (1857, J. W. Parkin & Son).

10. Frederic Harrison's article in the *Fortnightly Review* in 1867, called 'Culture: a dialogue', took the form of an exchange between himself and Arminius von Thunder-ten-dronck, the Prussian whom Arnold had invented in his dialogues *Friendship's Garland* to voice some of his fiercest criticisms of English society.

11. In 1867 William Murphy, an 'agent of the London Protestant Electoral Union', delivered a series of anti-Catholic lectures in the centre of Birmingham. He provoked rioting, but continued to insist upon his right of free speech in the words Arnold goes on to quote.

12. The Fenians were an Irish-American revolutionary and terrorist organization.

13. In 1866 the Reform League organized a monster demonstration in Hyde Park, despite a prohibition from the Commissioner of Police acting on instruction from the Home Secretary, Spencer Walpole. The railings of the Park were torn up. Troops were called out but did not actually come into contact with the rioters. For a full account of the Reform League's activities, see Royden Harrison, *Before the Socialists: Studies in Labour and Politics' 1861–1881* (1965, Routledge & Kegan Paul, chapter 3).

14. Sir Daniel Gooch was chairman of the directors of the Great Western Railway from 1865 to 1889. The GWR's locomotive and carriage works were at Swindon.

15. For Thomas Carlyle's views on aristocracy, see 'Shooting Niagara: and After?' in *Macmillan's Magazine* (1867).

16. For Robert Lowe, see above, Introduction, note 8 (p. 271).

17. For Edward Miall, see above, *The Twice-Revised Code*, note 3 (p. 273).

18. Thomas Chambers, MP for Marylebone, brought in two bills to legalize marriage with a deceased wife's sister during the 1860s. Both were defeated.

19. In 1867 the City of London Militia paraded from their barracks into the centre of London, led by their Colonel, Alderman Samuel Wilson. The parade attracted a large crowd, a number of whom were robbed and pushed around by gangs of toughs. Colonel Wilson declined to intervene – it was a matter for the police – and afterwards defended himself in the words Arnold goes on to quote.

20. Lieutenant Colonel Lothian Sheffield Dickson was another prominent member of the Reform League.

21. George Odger was Secretary of the London Trades Council 1862–72, besides being an active member of the Reform League.

22. 'Who is being cheated here?'

23. 'But one thing is needful', The Gospel according to St Luke, chapter 10, verse 42. The Latin is that of the Vulgate Bible.

24. Henry Sidgwick, 'The prophet of culture', *Macmillan's Magazine* (1867). Sidgwick was Knightbridge Professor of Moral Philosophy at Cambridge and one of the founders of Newnham College.

25. Michael Faraday (1791–1867), the English physicist, was a follower of John Sandeman, who led a secession from the Scottish Presbyterians and practised a rigid and primitive Calvinism.

26. Charles Haddon Spurgeon (1834–92) was a leading Particular Baptist minister and evangelical preacher; from 1861 he was the minister at the Metropolitan Tabernacle.

27. In March 1868 Gladstone, from the Opposition front bench, carried a series of resolutions through the Commons for the disestablishment of the Episcopalian Church in Ireland. The issue bulked large during the General Election in the autumn of 1868 and legislation to implement the resolutions was the first major measure carried by Gladstone's ministry in 1869.

28. The Society for the Liberation of Religion from State Patronage and Control, founded in 1853 by Edward Miall.

29. In his essay, 'The function of criticism at the present time', Arnold had criticized the inadequacies of Frances Power Cobbe's contributions to the debate on the state of religion in Europe and compared them with the building called the British College of Health in the New Road 'the grand name without the grand thing'.

30. The Real Estate Intestacy Bill was debated and defeated in the Commons in 1866.

31. 'Power without knowledge is very dangerous'.

32. J. W. Colenso, Bishop of Natal, had written at length on the arithmetical inconsistencies of the Pentateuch, and Arnold had already attacked the naïveté of such an approach in 'The Bishop and the Philosopher'.

Lawrence on Education

Edited by Joy and Raymond Williams

D. H. Lawrence was the first major English novelist to have direct experience of our modern system of organized schooling for everyone: the son of a miner, he got his education on scholarships and went on to teach in a state school. As a result, his writing on the subject represents, in the words of Raymond Williams, 'a changing record of a life's experience of education – its environment, its procedures and its consequences – which is in its way unique'.

The best of this writing has now been brought together by Joy and Raymond Williams so that it is possible to study the tensions, and sometimes even the contradictions, in Lawrence's ideas on education. In the essays, poems, letters and excerpts from the novels which make up this collection, one has an intriguing picture of a great writer dealing with a variety of questions which are bound to face any serious educationalist: the problems of self-expression and discipline, of sex education and human relationships, of a segregated educational system and a hierarchical society, and so on. Raymond Williams argues in his long introduction that what finally emerges is not a settled position, and certainly not a doctrine, but an emphasis which 'has lived and living experience in it'. That, above all, is why we should listen to Lawrence on education.